EXPLAINING CHRISTIAN ORIGINS AND EARLY JUDAISM

BIBLICAL INTERPRETATION SERIES

Editors
R. Alan Culpepper and Ellen van Wolde

Associate Editors
David E. Orton and Rolf Rendtorff

Editorial Board
Janice Capel Anderson – Mieke Bal – Phyllis A. Bird
Erhard Blum – Werner H. Kelber
Ekkehard W. Stegemann – Vincent L. Wimbush
Jean Zumstein

Number 89

EXPLAINING CHRISTIAN ORIGINS AND EARLY JUDAISM

Contributions from Cognitive and Social Science

Edited by
Petri Luomanen, Ilkka Pyysiäinen, and Risto Uro

SBL PRESS

Atlanta

Copyright © 2007 by Koninklijke Brill NV, Leiden, The Netherlands

This edition is published under license from Koninklijke Brill NV, Leiden, The Netherlands, by SBL Press.

All rights reserved. No part of this work may be reproduced or transmitted in any form or by any means, electronic or mechanical, including photocopying and recording, or by means of any information storage or retrieval system, except as may be expressly permitted by the 1976 Copyright Act or in writing from the publisher. Requests for permission should be addressed in writing to the Rights and Permissions Office, SBL Press, 825 Houston Mill Road, Atlanta, GA 30329 USA.

Library of Congress Control Number: 2016930615

Printed on acid-free paper.

CONTENTS

Preface vii

Introduction: Social and Cognitive Perspectives in the
   Study of Christian Origins and Early Judaism 1
   Petri Luomanen, Ilkka Pyysiäinen, and Risto Uro

PART ONE
THE PROMISE OF THE COGNITIVE SCIENCE OF RELIGION

The Promise of Cognitive Science for the Study of
   Early Christianity 37
   Luther H. Martin

The Mystery of the Stolen Body: Exploring Christian
   Origins 57
   Ilkka Pyysiäinen

The Emergence of Early Christian Religion: A Naturalistic
   Approach 73
   István Czachesz

A Cognitive Approach to Ritual Systems in First-Century
   Judaism 95
   Kimmo Ketola

Gnostic Rituals from a Cognitive Perspective 115
   Risto Uro

PART TWO
CONCEPTUAL BLENDING IN EARLY CHRISTIANITY

Conceptual Blending in the *Exegesis on the Soul* 141
  Hugo Lundhaug

Conceptual Blending and Early Christian Imagination 161
  Vernon K. Robbins

PART THREE
SOCIO-COGNITIVE APPROACHES TO CHRISTIAN ORIGINS AND EARLY JUDAISM

The Sociology of Knowledge, the Social Identity Approach
  and the Cognitive Science of Religion 199
  Petri Luomanen

"Remember My Fetters": Memorialisation of Paul's
  Imprisonment 231
  Philip F. Esler

Social Identities and Group Phenomena in Second Temple
  Judaism
  Raimo Hakola 259

Social Identity in the Qumran Movement: The Case of the
  Penal Code 277
  Jutta Jokiranta

Epilogue 299
  Troels Engberg-Pedersen

Index 313

PREFACE

This collection of essays is rooted in an ongoing exchange of ideas between historians and cognitive scientists of religion. In Finland, this dialogue has been going on especially between scholars of comparative religion and biblical scholars—a phenomenon that is probably unique compared to discussions elsewhere. An important impetus has been Ilkka Pyysiäinen's book *How Religion Works* (2001) as well as his research project on "Mind and Society in the Transmission of Religion," funded by the Academy of Finland. These captured the attention of a few Finnish biblical scholars, the other two editors of this volume, Petri Luomanen and Risto Uro, in particular. It is, however, doubtful whether this dialogue would have ever gone beyond occasional musings over a beer without the editors of this book having temporarily become colleagues at the then newly founded *Helsinki Collegium for Advanced Studies* in 2003. The daily life at the *Collegium* provided ample opportunities for discussions and also the facilities and infrastructure for more systematic cooperation. Encouraged by the fruitful exchange of opinions and new ideas, gained from a Finnish-language seminar, an international symposium on "Body, Mind, and Society in Early Christianity" was organized in August–September 2005 at the *Collegium*.

The symposium was arranged with the idea of a publication in mind. The organizers extended the invitation to multidisciplinarily-oriented biblical scholars and representatives of the cognitive science of religion. The aim was to elicit contributions where the authors took the risk of writing on subjects not within their specific areas of expertise: cognitively-oriented scholars of comparative religion were invited to write on biblical and related themes and biblical scholars to engage themselves with the application and discussion of the new cognitive approaches. The editors owe warm thanks to the contributors for the keen interest—and often enthusiasm—with which everyone accepted the challenge and devoted their time to this endeavor. Special thanks go to Luther Martin who graciously gave his time and energy in helping to find the best channel for the publication of this volume.

A number of networks and institutions supported the organizing of the international symposium that set the stage for the scholarly exchange of ideas published in this book. The *Helsinki Collegium for Advanced Studies* hosted the symposium with the help of its skillful and always friendly administrative staff. In addition to the Director of the *Collegium*, Juha Sihvola, the editors owe gratitude to Jenni Laitinen, Taina Seiro, Iiris Sinervuo and Maria Soukkio. The *Academy of Finland* provided direct funding for the symposium and also supported it through one of its Centres of Excellence, the *Research Unit for the Formation of Early Jewish and Christian Ideology*, directed by Heikki Räisänen. The financial support of the *Nordic Network for the Study of Early Christianity in its Greco-Roman Context*—flexibly arranged with the help of Halvor Moxnes—was also indispensable for the symposium.

In addition to the contributors to this volume, several other Finnish and international scholars and students participated in the symposium giving papers and responses. The editors are grateful to all participants whose questions and critical comments gave important feedback and ideas for the preparation of the essays of this volume. During the symposium, one participant stood out from the audience with perceptive questions and constructive criticism. His responses were so illuminating that it was deemed appropriate to also offer them to the readers of this volume in the form of an Epilogue—many thanks to Troels Engberg-Pedersen for his contribution!

The editors want to express their gratitude to the staff at Brill and to members of the editorial board of the *Biblical Interpretation Series* for their prompt acceptance of the volume in the series. As usual, Loes Schouten and Ivo Romein have been most kind and helpful during the various stages of the publication process. Many warm thanks also to Margot Stout Whiting for revising the English of the several non-native speakers in this volume.

In Helsinki and Oxford, May 28, 2007
Petri Luomanen, Ilkka Pyysiäinen, Risto Uro

INTRODUCTION: SOCIAL AND COGNITIVE PERSPECTIVES IN THE STUDY OF CHRISTIAN ORIGINS AND EARLY JUDAISM

Petri Luomanen, Ilkka Pyysiäinen and Risto Uro

At first sight, it seems that the cognitive science of religion and biblical studies or the study of early Judaism and early Christianity have very little in common. The cognitive science of religion is a new multidisciplinary field that emerged in the 1990s, drawing on cognitive science, cognitive and developmental psychology, neuroscience, evolutionary biology and anthropology (Lawson 2000; Pyysiäinen and Anttonen 2002; Tremlin 2006). It focuses on cross-culturally recurrent patterns in religious thought, experience, and practice, explaining these regularities in terms of the architecture of the human mind. A basic presupposition is that there are no specifically religious cognitive mechanisms or processes; what is known as "religion" is based on ordinary cognitive processes that also support non-religious behavior (Lawson and McCauley 1990; McCauley and Lawson 2002; Boyer 1994, 2001, 2003a; Pyysiäinen 2001, 2004b; Atran 2002; Atran and Norenzayan 2004; Tremlin 2006).

Biblical studies and related fields, on the other hand, mostly operate on a quite different level of explanation and interpretation. The majority of scholars engaged in the study of biblical—as well as other Jewish and early Christian—texts are historically and culturally oriented. They are interested in particular historical events, traditions or trajectories that influenced the texts under study, emphasizing the cultural construction of the phenomena studied. In fact, an appeal to universals or cross-cultural regularities may sound rather unfashionable in the postmodern situation in which all kinds of "totalities" have fallen into disrepute (Adam 1995: 11).

We are, however, convinced that recent developments in the cognitive science of religion can contribute to the historical study of religions in general and early Judaism and early Christianity in particular. We believe so basically for three reasons. First, the cognitive science of religion has introduced concepts, perspectives, and theories which may be fruitfully applied to the study of early Judaism and early Christianity and which may open up new perspectives in research. These include the idea of ontological intuitions, the "epidemiology" of beliefs, and new theories of rituals which are, of course, classic themes in comparative religion (but notably not in biblical studies). In addition, the theory of conceptual blending provides a helpful cognitive tool for analyzing religion as crystallized in textual traditions. These perspectives and theories are used in several essays of this book.

Second, although an undisputable success story, the emergence of social-scientific approaches in biblical studies during recent decades has left us with some unanswered and nagging questions. These concern, for example, the applicability of models originally developed for the study of quite different societies than those in which the biblical texts were written. We are convinced that the theories and results in the cognitive science of religion can shed new light on some points of controversy in this ongoing discussion.

Third, in recent years, social-scientific exegesis has utilized theories that have obvious connections to cognitive psychology and to questions that the pioneers of the cognitive science of religion have also touched upon. The so-called *social identity approach* applied in several essays of this volume draws on Henri Tajfel's experiments on human perception and categorization which are clearly cognitive phenomena (see Tajfel 1981; Abrams and Hogg 1990a). Furthermore, the study of social/cultural memory, which has begun to attract biblical scholars as a possible new means of casting light on the transmission of Jewish and Christian traditions (cf. Kirk and Thatcher 2005; Esler in this volume), also brings to the fore the question of how people cognitively construct their histories. Because this construction is constrained by basic memory functions and mechanisms of on-line social cognition, we believe that bringing these theories into closer interaction with the present cognitive science of religion will add to their explanatory potential.

In the following, we briefly elaborate on these three points, hoping to promote interdisciplinary discussion among scholars in early Jewish and early Christian studies and the cognitive science of religion. We will start with a short introduction to the cognitive science of religion, providing examples of how theories and models developed thus far have been utilized or might be utilized in the historical study of religions, such as early Judaism and early Christianity.

1. *Applying the Cognitive Science of Religion to History of Religions*

1.1. *The Pioneers*

The cognitive science of religion truly emerged in the 1990s, although its first landmark is Dan Sperber's short but important book *Rethinking Symbolism* published in 1975. In that book, Sperber argued that so-called "symbolism" is best understood as a cognitive mechanism that participates in the construction of knowledge as well as in the functioning of memory. It is not a special instrument of social communication or a property of phenomena that could be considered apart from this mechanism (Sperber 1995: xi–xii, 146–47). When a piece of information is difficult to understand but yet is felt to be important, the symbolic mechanism is triggered. It consists of a set of searches in memory, trying to find information that would somehow fit with the target information. It is striking how little influence Sperber's groundbreaking study has had on biblical studies which, nonetheless, have long been influenced by various insights from symbolist anthropology

Later, Sperber developed the "relevance theory" of communication based on the idea that the contents of messages must always be reconstructed by the receiver by making inferences from some material tokens (e.g., phonemes, letters) (Sperber and Wilson 1988). It is not possible to "copy and paste" ideas from one mind to another, as it were. The related "epidemiological" model of the differential spread of representations in and across cultures thus must take into account the fact that it is the structures of the mind that make some ideas more appealing and easier to spread than others (Sperber 1996b; see below).

An important general impetus for the cognitive science of religion has been Thomas Lawson and Robert McCauley's *Rethinking Religion* (1990), which was partly inspired by Sperber's book. Relying on Chomsky's *Syntactic Structures*, the authors tried to show that humans have intuitive knowledge of ritual structures (see also McCauley and Lawson 2002). In the same year as *Rethinking Religion* appeared, the young philosopher-turned-anthropologist, Pascal Boyer, published a small book with the title *Tradition as Truth and Communication*, putting forward a psychological explanation for the construction of traditional knowledge. This idea then grew into a scientific program for explaining the nature and formation of religious concepts and beliefs (Boyer 1994, 2001). In its latest version, this program includes an evolutionary account of the development of the basic cognitive categories and mechanisms that also make religious thought possible (Boyer 2001, 2003a). The theoretical foundations and practical implications of this view for scholars of religion have been evaluated and elaborated by Ilkka Pyysiäinen in a number of publications (Pyysiäinen 2001, 2004a,b).

Boyer, like Justin Barrett (2004), emphasizes that religious traditions are typified by "counterintuitive" representations. Counterintuitiveness means that a represented entity is intuitively assigned to an ontological category but is also understood to contain one element that contradicts the intuitive expectations we have about objects belonging to that category. A panhuman intuitive ontology consists of intuitions concerning such ontological domains as *person, animal, plant,* and *artifact* (Boyer 1994: 101, 1998: 878). Intuitive expectations are tacit and spontaneous; we are usually not conscious of having them. Should someone point out that someone else has the belief "Cats do not talk," that person's spontaneous reaction would be one of astonishment: everyone knows *that*.

Everything that contradicts our category-specific intuitive expectations about objects in basic ontological categories is counterintuitive. Counterintuitiveness does not mean it is false, funny, or deluded. As our everyday intuitions do not necessarily describe reality correctly, counterintuitive concepts need not necessarily be erroneous (Boyer 1994: 100–119, 2001: 51–122). In minimally counterintuitive representations, one minor "tweak" either adds one counterintuitive feature or deletes an intuitive feature in the representation in question. The idea of a cat that talks, for example, is counterintuitive in the sense that we do not normally expect animals to talk.

Counterintuitive representations are cognitively optimal when minimal counterintuitiveness makes them attention-grabbing while their intuitive features make them easy to process (Boyer 2001; Atran 2002; Atran and Norenzayan; Norenzayan and Atran 2004; Barrett 2004). An otherwise ordinary statue which yet hears prayers is an example of a cognitively optimal representation. Having the agentive capacity to hear and to understand is a violation of expectations in the artifact category. The idea of a statue that hears prayers *from afar* would involve two violations (an artifact hearing and hearing from afar) and thus be a maximally counterintuitive representation (Boyer 2001: 86; Atran 2002: 95–107; Atran and Norenzayan 2004: 722).

Boyer and Ramble (2001) as well as Barrett and Nyhof (2001) found, in their psychological experiments, that when subjects had to recall lists of items and events they had read about in the context of a short story, their recall was better for minimally counterintuitive representations than for intuitive ones. Minimally counterintuitive representations also survived the best in artificial transmission to others in three "generations" of subjects. The experiments carried out in the USA were replicated in Nepal (Buddhist monks) and in Gabon (lay-people) with very much the same results.

Atran (2002: 105), however, observes that, in laboratory experiments, the nature of the task may make subjects pay special attention to nonnatural representations and that intuitive representations thus lose their privileged status. When counterintuitive representations are not presented in the context of an exciting, sciencefiction-like narrative, intuitive representations are recalled the best (Atran and Norenzayan 2004: 721–23; Norenzayan and Atran 2004: 159). Studies conducted by Lauren Gonce, Afzal Upal and colleagues seem to confirm this. Upal and colleagues argue that minimally counterintuitive representations are better recalled when the narrative context creates an expectation for counterintuitive concepts which people may thus experience as intuitive. As different types of discourse activate different kinds of background knowledge, people can, for example, expect the attack of aliens when watching a science fiction movie but not when listening to radio news (Upal 2005; Gonce et al. 2006; Upal et al. 2007; Tweney et al. 2006).

Context thus seems to play a crucial role in item recall. In real life, concepts are usually embedded in a context and it is in this context that their counterintuitiveness is evaluated (Tweney et al. 2006; Gonce et al. 2006). Think of the following embedding of the counterintuitive concept of a "flying cow:"

> Looking through the kitchen window, I saw the flying cow. The twister had lifted the animal 50 feet above the ground (Tweney et al. 2006: 486).

One who reads only the first sentence, is led to interpret the flying cow as a minimally counterintuitive concept whereas the second sentence provides a context in which the flying cow becomes an intuitive concept. Thus, context can make apparently counterintuitive concepts intuitive. But even when counterintuitiveness is retained, a relevant context can make it something to be expected. This has actually been recognized by Boyer all along. People can simply become so routinized in using some counterintuitive concepts that their counterintuitiveness is no longer recognized (Boyer 1994: 120; Sperber 1994: 62). Although, for example, a person without a body is a counterintuitive concept, one may regard it as perfectly natural that God is a bodiless spirit. God is the one exception to the general rule "No person without a body." After becoming routinized in using a counterintuitive concept, one is no longer aware of its counterintuitiveness; the concept is then actually changed into an intuitive concept. This serves here as an example of how mental structures channel the evolution of traditions (Pyysiäinen 2005).

The pioneers of the cognitive science of religion share the conviction that experimental cognitive psychology can yield the kind of knowledge needed for truly scientific explanations of religious thought and practice. Laboratory experiments are one important means of testing hypotheses about human cognitive mechanisms; it is these mechanisms that we also use in religious thought (see Barrett 2004). Although we do not wish to restrict the word "science" only to experimental research, we indeed believe that experimental psychology, also, has much to offer to the history of religions.

1.2. *Epidemiology and Counterintuitiveness*

The study of the transmission of religious traditions has always been important for biblical scholars; they could thus benefit from cognitive theories of the recall and spread of ideas and beliefs. However, biblical scholars have often sought to trace the "authentic" or "original" cores of biblical traditions, whether relying on the form-critical "evolutionary" model of oral traditions and the concept of *Sitz im Leben* (Bultmann 1968) or on the idea of a more solid and fixed tradition (Gerhardsson 1961). More recent contributions have emphasized the fluidity of oral traditions in contrast to written modes of transmission (Kelber 1983; Silberman 1987; Wansbrough 1991; Dewey 1994; Dunn 2000), highlighting the difficulties involved in the attempts to reconstruct the original forms or *ipsissima verba* of the biblical traditions that originate in oral transmission. The cognitive science of religion provides models and theories that help explain the role of literacy and other external memory stores in human cognition. The role of writing in the development of hierarchical institutions, for example, has recently been debated (Whitehouse 2000: 172–80; Boyer 2001: 77–81; Pyysiäinen 2004b: 147–71).

A still more recent approach in biblical studies has taken the concept of "social memory" as a tool for analyzing the transmission of biblical traditions (Kirk and Thatcher 2005; cf. also Esler in this volume). This approach emphasizes that what is recalled is always constrained by social factors. There is no doubt that memory is conditioned by various social factors (this view was already anticipated by the form critics in biblical studies) and various kinds of external memory aids, most notably writing. However, it is equally true that memory is constrained by the cognitive mechanisms of the mind that the cognitive science of religion seeks to explicate.

In the cognitive analysis of cultural transmission, it is possible to focus either on how specific ideas relate to cognitive structures (Bering 2002, 2006) or on the differential spread of ideas in and across cultures (see Barrett 2003). In this latter line of thinking, cultures are understood as precipitations of cognition and communication in populations (Sperber 1996b: 97); there is always overlap between cultures as well as differences within cultures. Cultures and traditions are not closed systems and they do not determine individual thinking and behavior in such a way as postulated in extreme constructionism (e.g., Geertz 1973; see Pyysiäinen 2005). We should not simply put cultural concepts in opposition to individual or "innate" concepts as though they were two mutually exclusive classes of concepts. "Being cultural" only means that some individual concepts have become widespread (Boyer 2003b). Everyone grows up in a community, and whatever genetically specified, innate cognitive mechanisms there are, they always operate in a context, processing shared information. Likewise, whatever we learn from the cultural environment is always constrained by the structures of the mind. Cultural transmission thus always involves inferential processes (Sperber and Wilson 1988).

We already briefly referred to Sperber's "epidemiological" model (this label is perhaps not the most fortunate one since it easily evokes negative associations). In the standard epidemiological model, the transmission of religious concepts and beliefs is regarded as being channeled by ordinary cognitive structures in the sense that those religious concepts that trigger intuitive mechanisms of mind are naturally selected for cultural transmission (see Boyer in press; Pyysiäinen 2004a). Cultural transmission works analogously to natural selection in the sense that some items are more "fit" for selection because the human mind is better prepared for processing some ideas than others. Whatever corresponds to human intuitions is easy to process in an almost automatic fashion while abstract, reflective thinking requires much effort and the use of such external memory stores as paper and pen, books, computers, and so forth (see Pyysiäinen 2004a).

According to Sperber (1996b), three facts about the human mind make certain ideas naturally appealing. (1) Ideas that resonate with intuitive ways of thinking are easy to process; (2) ideas that are relevant in the sense that processing them yields new information tend to persist; and (3) ideas that are easy to recall because they are somehow attention-grabbing have a selective advantage.

Sperber's model has been presented as a contribution to anthropology but it can also be applied in historical studies. Because the epidemiology of beliefs or representations focuses on explaining why some ideas are more "contagious" than others, the perspective is different from the study of origins which has traditionally dominated biblical studies (as well as the early phase of religious studies). Thus, it introduces an alternative point of view to the development for Jewish and Christian traditions.

Sperber's and Boyer's selective models focus on generalities of religion, trying to explain its cognitive basis. The models have not been extensively applied to explain the development of any single belief, set of beliefs, or a tradition. In this volume, Pyysiäinen's essay is this kind of an attempt to explain the spread of Christian beliefs, however.

1.3. Intuitions and Theology

Recent interest in the social world of the Bible and in various microhistorical issues such as family, kinship, economy, sickness and healing, and purity and impurity as an alternative to the study of theological ideas, finds an interesting theoretical and empirical confirmation in the distinction between intuitions and theology as it has been made in the cognitive science of religion. A written theology is not an exhaustive catalog of the beliefs of the members of a group. Theological doctrines are rather artifacts that serve as cues directing people's inferences; being exposed to some official theological formulations triggers mental representations that are more salient than others to start with. Although we can often predict more or less accurately what kinds of ideas people will end up entertaining after being exposed to certain teachings, there are no necessary links between these ideas and the theological stimuli. The actually represented ideas do not mechanically follow from the perceived stimuli; they are brought about by an active inferential or associative process in the mind (see Sperber and Wilson 1988). The actual religious thought and behavior of individuals is thus not based on making applied deductions from theological systems. There is now some experimental evidence to support this view (Barrett and Keil 1996; Barrett 1998).

In experimental studies, Barrett and Keil (1996) found that American college students had two kinds of representations of God: the theological concept was based on such rehearsed cultural knowledge as, for example, that God is omniscient, omnipotent, and so forth. In fast online reasoning tasks, the subjects unconsciously used a more human-like ("anthropomorphic") representation of God, however. Barrett (1998) replicated the study in India, substituting Brahman, Shiva, Vishnu, and Krishna for God with essentially the same result. The theologically correct concept of God did not have the required inferential potential. The subjects had to rely on an unorthodox, intuitive concept of God that allowed for the needed inferences. The distinction between intuitions and reflective thinking thus seems to be partly paralleled by the distinction between "real-time" religion, on the one hand, and theology based on "off-line" cognition and the book-mind interaction, on the other hand (see Pyysiäinen 2004b: 147–71).

Barrett's and Boyer's distinction between off-line theology and on-line intuitions springs from research in social psychology, neuropsychology, and cognitive science focusing on two distinct reasoning systems in humans, often referred to as automatic and controlled processes (see Pyysiäinen 2004a; Tremlin 2006: 172–82). Automatic processes are fast, work without conscious effort, and cannot be initiated or terminated at will. Controlled processes are the opposite of this and support reflective thinking (see Sun 2002; Wyer and Srull 1994; Chaiken and Trope 1999). Automatic processes thus more or less correspond to what Boyer (1994) and Barrett (2004) call "intuitions." Intuitions here mean presuppositions that intrude on explicit reasoning, although they are not voluntarily or even consciously brought into the chain of inferences and their validity cannot be assessed. They thus tend to override more reflective beliefs.

It is, therefore, one thing to write the history of religious ideas as they are found in texts and another thing to try to go beyond the texts and write the history of what was really going on in real-time religion (see Pyysiäinen 2005). Luther Martin's essay in this volume is an attempt to show how cognitive theories can be applied in the history of religions to supplement and provide correctives to the traditional approaches (also Pyysiäinen in this volume). The so-called "history of mentalities" that emerged from the *Annales* School in French historical writing in the 1920s is one such approach that could be further elaborated from a cognitive perspective (see Revel and Hunt 1995). Czachesz' essay is an attempt to develop completely new cognitive tools that could help us understand and explain the development of early Christianity.

1.4. *Rituals*

As Claude Lévi-Strauss once quipped, gods are not only good to think about but also good to eat. Eating here refers to ritual meals that help generate and maintain common knowledge in a group (see Chwe 2001; Pyysiäinen 2004b: 135–46). The category of rituals is a vague one, however; rituals manifest a particular mode of action, while there is not necessarily any common feature shared by all the situations in which this mode of action is used. There is no unified set of phenomena that a theory of religious ritual could explain (Boyer and Liénard 2006: Liénard and Boyer 2006).

For analytical purposes, rituals have been divided into calendrical rites, crisis rites, and rites of passage in which a person or persons are moved to a new social position (Honko 1979). In reference to rites of passage, Boyer (2001: 229–63) argues that (1) there are panhuman evolved mechanisms of the mind, specialized in handling information about social relationships; (2) that these mechanisms are tacit and intuitive and we are normally not conscious of them and cannot perceive how they function; and (3) that therefore the ways in which changes in social position are brought about have an aura of magic around them. Boyer also points out that, beginning from infancy, we repeatedly see our cultural elders associate a given ritual with given social effects. This, then, explains why we are conditioned to think that rituals causally produce the desired social effects as well as why we are motivated to stick to these ritual behaviors and to transmit them to future generations.

According to Lawson and McCauley (1990), religious rituals can be differentiated from other kinds of rituals by the fact that, in them, the causal powers of the ritual are ascribed to some counterintuitive agent (also McCauley and Lawson 2002; cf. Boyer 2001: 236, 256). Lawson and McCauley argue at length that people have intuitive knowledge about ritual structures because rituals follow the general pattern of *action* (vs. something just happening): someone does something for someone by means of something. Only religious rituals include a "culturally postulated superhuman agent" (a CPS agent) either as the actor, patient, or instrument of the ritual action. Barrett and Lawson (2001) have experimentally shown that, in judging whether a hypothetical ritual is effective, people regard having an appropriate intentional agent as relatively more important than the particular action.

Just as any performance of action presupposes certain earlier performances of actions, so also rituals presuppose other rituals. Normally, such chains of actions can be traced back to earlier enabling actions endlessly; this is not so with religious ritual actions. Although they presuppose previous enabling actions, there are unequivocal limits to their number. A minister, for example, is capable of ritually pronouncing a couple man and wife *because* (s)he himself/herself has undergone the ritual of ordination. The bishop who ordained the minister was able to do so *because* he himself had received a proper ordination. The chain of ordinations can, in principle, be traced back to St. Peter who was ordained by Jesus. But it is with Jesus as God that the chain stops. God does not need any enabling rituals to be able to establish "super-permanent" effects. This supposed fact about Christian rituals is one instance of the more general principle that counterintuitive agents terminate an otherwise endless regression of enabling rituals (Lawson and McCauley 1990; McCauley and Lawson 2002). Underlying this argument is a similar view of God as foundation, as in the medieval proofs for the existence of God, relying on the Aristotelian idea of an unmoved mover and first cause, albeit Lawson and McCauley are not attempting to prove anything about the existence of God.

Some rituals, like baptisms and funerals, are performed only once for any one patient; others can be performed on a regular basis. Lawson and McCauley think that some rituals are not repeated for one and the same patient because a counterintuitive agent is the active agent (directly or indirectly) in those rituals. These are called special agent rituals in the sense that the active agent is a counterintuitive agent. And, "when the gods act...the effects are super-permanent" and the ritual in question need not be repeated for the same patient (McCauley 2001: 132; see McCauley and Lawson 2002: 122). This is so because some religious arrangements are regarded as super-permanent: as it is thought that mere humans cannot establish any such arrangements, they are ascribed to counterintuitive agents. In other types of rituals, a counterintuitive agent is involved in the role of a patient or an instrument. These special patient/instrument rituals can be repeated for the same patient time and again (McCauley 2001: 130–33; McCauley and Lawson 2002: 120–22). Influenced by Chomsky's linguistic theory, Lawson and McCauley see the placement of agency as a simple yes or no question, although it might be argued that in religious rituals agency can also be reciprocal (cf. Ketola and Jokiranta in this volume).

The fact that some rituals provoke a great deal of emotion while some do not is of importance. It could easily be argued that the amount of emotional arousal depends on the frequency of performance: routinized rituals apparently cannot provoke emotions (Whitehouse 1995, 2002, 2004; but cf. Boyer and Liénard 2006). Lawson and McCauley, however, argue that the amount of emotion depends on whether the ritual is a special agent or a special patient/instrument ritual (that is, on the *form* of the ritual). Only special agent rituals involve sensory pageantry and provoke intense emotions (as compared to other rituals in the same tradition). This is so because, if a ritual is to have a super-permanent effect, the participants must be convinced that the effect really is permanent. Therefore, the rituals are arranged to be as emotionally provocative as possible, with emotions signaling to people that something very significant is going on. (McCauley 2001: 130–33; McCauley and Lawson 2002: 120–22.) However, the differences and interconnections between ritual frequency and ritual form may eventually turn out to be manifestations of some more general factors (Atran 2002: 290–91). Ritual form and ritual frequency may be two alternative—but not exclusive—means of creating a feeling that an intimate presence of counterintuitive agents is involved (Pyysiäinen 2001: 91–95).

Harvey Whitehouse has put forward the modes theory of religiosity based on the division between the imagistic and doctrinal modes of cultural transmission. McCauley and Lawson (2002) call this the "ritual frequency theory" (Whitehouse 1995, 2000, 2002, 2004; cf. Pyysiäinen 2006; Whitehouse 1996). Whitehouse argues that all religious traditions tend to develop either towards large-scale organizations characterized by orthodoxy and dry ritual routine (doctrinal mode), or towards small-scale communities placing emphasis on emotionally arousing rituals without any sanctioned interpretation of their meaning (imagistic mode). The idea of the two modes is based on the view that rituals are a means of maintaining and transmitting religious traditions and that memory plays a crucial role here. The modes are characterized by 12 variables (Table 1.1.) none of which is considered to be more fundamental than the others.

A "mode" means an abstract "attractor position" that emerges from the interaction of the 12 variables. This entails that there are certain special causal mechanisms that produce attraction between the various imagistic variable contents as well as between doctrinal variable con-

Table 1.1. The two modes of religiosity (Whitehouse 2004: 74).

	Doctrinal	Imagistic
Psychological Features		
1. Transmissive frequency	High	Low
2. Level of arousal	Low	High
3. Principal memory system	Semantic schemas and implicit scripts	Episodic/flashbulb memory
4. Ritual meaning	Learned/acquired	Internally generated
5. Techniques of revelation	Rhetoric/logical integration, narrative	Iconicity, multivocality multivalence
Sociopolitical Features		
6. Social cohesion	Diffuse	Intense
7. Leadership	Dynamic	Passive/absent
8. Inclusivity/exclusivity	Inclusive	Exclusive
9. Spread	Rapid/efficient	Slow/inefficient
10. Scale	Large scale	Small scale
11. Degree of uniformity	High	Low
12. Structure	Centralized	Noncentralized

tents. Likewise, these mechanisms also prevent imagistic and doctrinal contents from attracting each other (see Boyer 2005). Thus, imagism and doctrinality are not types of religiosity but rather abstract ideal types. We cannot simply divide religious traditions into imagistic and doctrinal ones; most traditions contain elements from both. Although most living religiosity seems to consist of a mixture of imagistic and doctrinal elements, Whitehouse believes that this is somewhat anomalous and that, in the long run, religions will develop towards either the imagistic or the doctrinal attractor position. This view is not without its problems.

For one thing, the crucial factor seems not to be the time scales. Whitehouse seems rather to be after some kind of distinction between what happens in empirical reality versus what are the ideal relationships between variable contents (see Pyysiäinen 2006). The two attractor positions are not real phenomena but rather abstractions expressing ideal constellations. It is, however, rather difficult to see what it is that determines these ideal positions. One might try to explain this by an analogy to Chomsky's distinction between linguistic competence and performance which inspired Lawson and McCauley. At the level of ideal competence, religions fall neatly either to the imagistic or the doctrinal slot. The reason why this does not happen in real religious traditions is that the human performance is constrained by factors external to the modal variables. This, however, makes the theory a purely formal theory with the consequence that its empirical testing is as difficult as that of Chomsky's theory, which has kept on assuming ever new forms, apparently without any obvious reason (e.g., Pinker and Jackendoff 2005).

These problems are reflected in Ketola's and Uro's essays. Ketola also attempts to create a pragmatic synthesis of the two ritual theories. As both theories seem to include important insights about ritual behavior and the transmission of religion, it is necessary to find a way of using them to construct a theory—or at least a set of hypotheses—that could be applied in the historical study of Judaism and early Christianity. This is not only a cognitive problem but also intimately tied to other problems that have been explored in biblical studies using, for example, social identity theories.

1.5. *Conceptual Blending*

The idea of counterintuitive representations and their memory effects puts a heavy emphasis on the formal properties of mental representations: it is the structure, not the content of the representations that makes them easily spread. This structure, then, is explained with reference to human cognitive architecture. However, a historian of religion cannot neglect questions of content. We must ask how the specific contents of various types of religious concepts and beliefs are constructed. As they obviously result from a kind of "reshuffling"[1] of components of perceptual experience, it becomes necessary to find tools to explain how this reshuffling happens. Some scholars of religion have therefore turned to the literature on metaphors (Lakoff and Johnson 1980; Lakoff 1987) and the so-called mental spaces and conceptual integration and blending (Fauconnier 1994, 1997; Fauconnier and Turner 1996, 1998, 2002).

While Lakoff and Johnson have studied linguistic metaphors in English and especially the human body as a source of metaphors, the theory of conceptual blending approaches meaning on the basis of the idea

---

[1] The concept of "reshuffling" is taken from Peter Munz (1959: 55, 1973: 56) who argues that in folktales, legends, myths, dreams, and so forth, events appear in non-normal relations, being "re-shuffled like a pack of cards."

of the so-called "mental spaces." These are locally constructed abstract domains within which concepts acquire their meaning. They are "small conceptual packets constructed as we think and talk, for purposes of local understanding and action" (Fauconnier and Turner 1996: 113, 1998: 137, 2002: 40). There are then mappings between various spaces based on such linguistic devices as pronouns and anaphora. The basic idea is very similar to the one explaining how counterintuitive representations are constructed; here the focus, however, is not on individual concepts or representations but on larger units, the mental spaces within which concepts acquire meaning.

Conceptual blending requires: (1) the so-called generic space containing the abstract structure common to the (2) two or more input spaces; and (3) a blended space that contains the elements of the input spaces and the elements of the blend (Fauconnier and Turner 2002: 46). Thus, conceptual blends differ from mere metaphors in which one domain is simply conceptualized on the basis of another (Lakoff and Johnson 1980; Lakoff 1987). Representations of magical rituals, for example, can be understood as mental spaces in which the profane and the sacred spaces have been blended (Sørensen 2007).

In this volume, Lundhaug uses *blending theory* to explain the metaphor of the "womb of the soul" in the Nag Hammadi tractate the *Exegesis on the Soul* (NHC II,6), trying to show its rhetorical function and its relation to other conceptual metaphors in the tractate. Robbins borrows the concept of "rhetorical dialects" from the Emory University sociolinguist Benjamin Hardy, arguing that the first century Christian discourse consisted of six "rhetorolects" that were dynamically blended. Robbins thus first breaks the Christian discourse into its constitutive units and then shows how the creativity of this discourse is based on a blending of these units in various ways. Conceptual blending thus offers a mediating approach between the standard model of the cognitive science of religion (Boyer 2005: 4–7) and more content-oriented approaches.

2. *Open Questions in Social-Scientific Biblical Interpretation*

The social-scientific study of the Bible emerged in the1970s as a reaction against the "biblical theology" movement that was influential before and after the World War II (Garrett 1992). Scholars began to criticize the one-sided concentration on the history of ideas (Meeks 1972) and the "methodological docetism" (Scroggs 1980) of the established methods. To put body and soul back together again, as it were, and to avoid limiting early Christian reality to mere theological or dogmatic systems, they sought help from the methods used and insights achieved in the social sciences. Many of the pioneering works had a clear functionalist orientation (Theissen 1977; Meeks 1972, 1983). In contrast to the focus on the original forms or genetic relationships, scholars inspired by social-scientific approaches sought to discover the social function of the biblical traditions and beliefs in their cultural and historical settings.

Social-scientific biblical criticism has grown into a major movement in the field and has produced a huge number of studies using various theoretical traditions of the social sciences, such as Berger and Luckmann's sociology of knowledge (Meeks 1972; Esler 1987; Horrell 1993, 2001), Weber's typology of charisma (Theissen 1977; Holmberg 1978), the grid and group model by Mary Douglas (Malina 1986; Neyrey 1986), sectarian studies (Gager 1975; Elliott 1981), Mediterranean anthropology (Rohrbaugh 1996), medical anthropology (Pilch 2000), Anthony Giddens' structuration theory (Horrell 1996), and the social identity approach (Esler 1998a, 2003), to mention a few examples (see also Esler 1995b; Blasi, Duhaime, and Turcotte 2002; Stegemann, Malina, and Theissen 2002). It has become more and more difficult to give a summary of the main questions and developments within this field (for descriptions at different stages of the movement, see, e.g., Elliott 1986; Holmberg 1990; Osiek 1992; Martin 1999; Horrell 2002; Esler 2004). It seems, however, that two issues especially often come up when the development and status of social-scientific exegesis is reviewed, namely cultural distance and the role of models.

2.1. *Bridging the Cultural Gap*

One important current in the social-scientific study of the Bible emphasizes the cultural distance between the ancient biblical world and the situation of the modern interpreter who usually lives in a Western society. The agenda of this approach was laid out by Bruce Malina in his groundbreaking *The New Testament World* (1981, 3rd ed. 2001), and was later elaborated by the members of the so-called Context Group (see, e.g., Malina and Neyrey 1988; Rohrbough 1996; Pilch 2001). Malina and his co-workers focus on the pivotal cultural values and norms of the ancient (to some degree also present) Mediterranean world: honor and shame, the non-individualist view of person ("dyadic personality"), the perception of limited good, kinship values, and purity rules. The main objective of the Context Group is to promote an approach which would avoid the perils of ethnocentric and anachronistic readings and to pay heed to the strikingly different social dynamics at work in the biblical texts. Malina's models, borrowed from cultural anthropology, are illuminating and didactic; they have helped students and scholars to become sensitive to the social distance between the biblical texts and modern Western cultural values and to familiarize themselves with the "strange" world of the biblical authors.

However, as indispensable as it is for biblical scholars (or for anthropologists as well), the emphasis on social distance or cultural difference is only one side of the coin. As Malina himself notes, his cultural reading of the Bible assumes that "all human beings are somewhat the same and somewhat different" and he focuses "on *the interplay of similarities and differences* within human communities" (1981: 8–9; italics added). Thus, in his chapter on purity and impurity, Malina writes that "every culture has...purity rules, since every culture has a classification system," although he quickly adds that the Western individualistic horizon of limitless good generates a totally different set of rules than was dominate in first-century Palestine (p. 129).

The cognitive science of religion, however, focuses on the cross-cultural cognitive basis of categorization and its manifestation in various kinds of recurrent ideas and patterns. The widespread phenomenon of fear of pollution and contagion and the related avoidance behavior is but one example (see Sperber 1996a; Nemeroff and Rozin 2000; Boyer 2001; Fessler and Navarrete 2003). Although the cognitive explanations of contagion are often general and do not give direct answers to questions in the analysis of particular issues within a specific cultural context—a problem we also have with sociological explanations (Horrell 1996: 13, 22–26)—they can contribute to understanding the obvious overlap in categorization in various cultures (e.g., Atran 1998). Thus the cognitive perspective can help counterbalance the one-sided emphasis on social distance.

Malina and the Context Group's polarized models of differences between the Western and Mediterranean values (see, e.g., Malina and Neyrey 1988) are one way of conceptualizing the cultural situation of early Judaism and early Christianity. The cognitive approach, envisioned in this book, offers another alternative which would focus on what Malina calls the "interplay of similarities and differences within human communities." If "similarities" are sought in the cognitive basis of human cultures and behavior and "differences" in the cultural concepts and rationalizations, the analysis of the "interplay" between these two could turn out to be beneficial. For example, one could focus on analyzing how the idea of corpse impurity developed in early Judaism and early Christianity and how Christianity gradually changed people's behavioral reactions towards corpses. The avoidance of impure corpses may well have an evolutionary basis (Boyer 2001: 243–48) and thus it is very difficult to change a person's emotional reactions to corpses. Cultural education and practices such as burying the deceased beneath churches and in churchyards (Samellas 2002; Sellew 2006), however, might mold people's reflective ideas of and behavioral reactions to corpses.

2.2. *Models*

The use of models has been an important cause of debate among sociologically and socio-historically-oriented scholars of early Judaism and early Christianity (Malina 1982; Elliott 1986, 1993; Garrett 1992; Esler 1995a, 2000; Horrell 1996, 2000; Martin 1999; Luomanen 2002). At first, the central role of the term "model" in this methodological discussion may appear somewhat strange to a social or cognitive scientist not versed in the jargon of biblical scholars since critical discussion on the validity and usefulness of models has by and large not been of much importance in the social sciences (cf. Horrell 1996: 10).

One reason for the centrality of the topic of models is that the pioneers of social-scientific exegesis have drawn on the distinction between theories and models made by Thomas Carney (1975). Carney distinguishes between theories that are based on "axiomatic laws" and present "general principles," and models that "act as a link between theories and observations," providing a simplified "framework which can be brought to bear on some pertinent data" (cf. Elliot 1986: 4–5, 1993: 8; Holmberg 1990: 12–15; Esler 1987: 9–16). Occasionally, social scientifically oriented scholars have also used the term "model" to characterize large-scale research frameworks, such as structural-functionalism (Malina 1982: 233; Esler 1987: 9, 1998b: 254; cf. Elliott 1986: 7; Horrell 1996: 10–11). Some critics have found this confusing (Horrell 1996: 9–12; Martin 1999: 129–30), but in this regard, biblical scholars do not fare worse than social scientists in general (cf. Marshall 1998: 427).

Whether abstract or concrete, models have become a practical means of introducing new perspectives and questions to the study of biblical texts. In particular, scholars affiliated with the Context Group have advocated models as practical heuristics to overcome the cultural distance between the modern Western individualistic culture and the ancient Mediterranean culture; this has made models a central topic in the discussion.

Although the discussion of models among biblical scholars has some characteristic (terminological) features of its own, the basic methodological and theoretical problems are typical of the social sciences in general: should models be taken as mere heuristic tools or as a means of explaining, testing and predicting? Is it possible to employ models developed in quite distant (either modern industrialized or contemporary non-industrialized) societies to ancient biblical societies? Do models presume a deterministic view of life and social order as opposed to a view which grants more freedom to individual actors? The debate includes several issues and it would be impossible to deal with all the aspects of the discussion within the limits of this introduction. Thus, we will focus only on some aspects where we believe that allying the social-scientific study of early Judaism and early Christianity more closely with the cognitive science of religion would offer new perspectives on the debate (see also Martin in this volume).

Those who advocate the use of models often follow Carney in stating that there is no choice as to whether to use models or not since model construction is an inevitable part of the basic human processes of perception and categorization (Carney 1975: 5; Elliott 1986: 5–6, 1993: 44–45; Esler 1994: 12; 1995a: 4, 1998b: 255). Presumably, a closer interaction with recent cognitive research might help explicate the character of these processes that have not only constrained the thinking of the ancients under investigation but also their modern interpreters.

The advocates of the use of models have responded to the critics who claim that models presume "positivism" or "determinism" or "filling-in gaps" (Stowers 1985; Garrett 1992; Horrell 1996: 18–22; Martin 1999: 130) by emphasizing that models are only heuristic tools that have no ontological reality. They only help find new questions and frameworks which may—or may not—prove to be helpful in understanding the texts (Elliott 1993: 43–45; Esler 1995a:7; 1998b: 256). However, this rather pragmatic approach to the usefulness of models leaves open the question of *why* a certain model or framework finds "responsive data" in the text (cf. Esler 1998b: 256). This makes the use of models vulnerable to the criticism that predetermined models direct the interpreters towards finding what they seek (Horrell 1996: 15–16). By bringing the cognitive scientific point of view into this discussion, it should be possible to give more nuanced answers to the question of why a model fits the data. Are there only coincidental correspondences between cultural variables of two temporally distinct cultures or does the model embody cross-culturally valid generalities in human cognition?

Our discussion of the social identity approach in the following section—as well as several essays of this book that apply this approach—serve as but a few examples of how a model that has been used in the social-scientific study of early Judaism and early Christianity can be brought to closer interaction with cognitive science. In the case of the social identity approach, it seems clear that its usability is at least partly based on the fact that modern observations about basic human processes of social categorization find responsive data in the text because the writers of the texts were subject to same constraints of perception as we are.

The cognitive science of religion is a self-consciously science-based approach. In this sense, it aligns with the social-*scientific* camp of biblical scholars who stress the use of testable models and theories against those who advocate less model-based, yet social or social-historical approaches. As noted above, the criticism of determinism has often been leveled against those who favor model-based approaches in biblical studies. We, however, think that an important question to ask is whether models are supported by evidence, not whether they are deterministic. Furthermore, explaining human behavior does not necessarily in itself mean determinism because explaining consists not only of forming general laws, but also unique events can be explained with reference to the underlying causal factors. The cognitive science of religion which focuses on why there are cross-culturally recurrent patterns in human thought and behavior can also be used to explain the various unique manifestations of more general principles. It thus can shed new light on the general question of the use of deductive models and theories in historical research.

3. Toward a New Synthesis: The Social Identity Approach, Social Memory and Cognitive Science

3.1. The Social Identity Approach: Beyond Laboratory Experiments?

The expression *social-identity approach* is an umbrella term which nowadays refers to Henri Tajfel and John Turner's *social identity theory* that was mainly developed in the 1970s, to Turner's *self-categorization theory* developed in the middle of the 1980s, and to later adaptations of these theories. Social identity theory and self-categorization theory are closely related; self-categorization theory, however, focuses more on the cognitive processes through which persons come to see and feel themselves as members of a group, as well as on the question of how membership in the group influences an individual's behavior (Abrams and McGarty 1990: 11). Although self-categorization theory today is usually connected with the name of John Turner, the theory itself draws on the research on perception and cognition that Tajfel conducted in the beginning of his scientific career in the 1950s and 1960s.

Social psychologists showed growing interest in the social identity approach during the 1990s (Hogg and Abrams 1999), and Philip Esler introduced it to New Testament research in his books on Galatians (1998a) and Romans (2003). It is no coincidence that several essays in this volume deal with the approach (Esler, Hakola, Jokiranta, and Luomanen); the "built-in" cognitive interface of the social identity approach was one of the things that convinced us of the benefits of bringing together scholars of the cognitive science of religion and social-scientifically oriented scholars of early Judaism and early Christianity. Since the basic concepts and theories of the social identity approach are presented in various essays in this volume (see especially Luomanen), we here only try to illuminate the cognitive background of the approach and its present status in social psychological research.

Tajfel was one of the key scholars in developing a distinctively European social psychology. Tajfel's (1981) collection of essays from different phases of his career clearly shows how the author's attitude towards social psychological research was shaped by his own experiences during the World War II. Tajfel emphasizes that although many features of group behavior have their roots in the cognition of individuals, there are also significant aspects of group behavior that cannot be reduced to individual psychology. In Tajfel's view, social psychological research should be able to transcend the limits of analyzing individual and presocial motives by illuminating the factors that make people behave the way they do in groups and in actual historical situations (Tajfel 1981: 38–41). The social identity approach was consciously developed as a corrective to the reductionism and individualism that characterized social psychological research in the 1950s and 1960s (Abrams and Hogg 1990a: 1–9). In contrast to laboratory experiments, it focused on studying real-life intergroup relations. According to Hogg and Abrams, this was "an assault on the hollowness of explanations of international conflict, genocide and so on, purely in terms of individuality without any consideration of sociohistorical factors" (Hogg and Abrams 1988: 13).

Tajfel has undoubtedly inspired scholars who favor phenomenological and interpretative approaches rather than "sterile" laboratory experiments which they think cannot reach what is truly social in human behavior. Against this background, it might appear futile to search for a common ground for a fruitful exchange between the cognitive science of religion and the social identity approach. We, however, do not regard laboratory experiments and the study of real-life social psychological phenomena as two mutually exclusive options. Instead, we think that recent developments in cognitive science can also contribute to social theorizing on intragroup, intergroup and cultural phenomena (see Cohen 2007). In fact, for Tajfel, "social psychology is not a catalogue of individual, or even group, idiosyncrasies of social behavior" (Tajfel 1981: 23). Laboratory experiments also characterized the early stages of his own career and he continued to prefer theories "which can be tested experimentally" (Tajfel 1981: 18). However, he kept emphasizing that in the case of the study of *social* behavior, the experimental conditions always tend to become socially "contaminated" by the research arrangements more than, for instance, in a case when a general psychologist studies perceptual constancies or short-term memory (Tajfel 1981: 22–23). Recent developments in social psychology again seek to integrate laboratory studies of social cognition with other approaches in social psychology (see below).

3.2. *What is Cognitive in Social Identity Theory?*

Although Tajfel's lifelong pursuit was to develop a properly *social* psychological understanding of prejudice and intergroup conflict, his earliest work focused on perception and the cognitive basis of categorization.

In this regard, he can also be regarded as a pioneer of a cognitive approach to categorization; this then became one of the dominant topics in American research on social cognition (Hogg and Abrams 1999).

There are two basic features of cognitive processing that are fundamental to the social identity approach (including both social identity theory and self-categorization theory): *categorization* and *accentuation*. The cognitive processes of categorization are fundamental to our adaptation to the world in which we live. Categorization simplifies perception. When, for instance, we look at a rainbow, we see it as consisting of different colors. Yet we know from science classes that in reality there is only a continuous distribution of different wavelengths with no borders indicating where one color ends and the next one begins. Categorization helps us to structure the potentially infinite number of different stimuli into a more manageable number of categories (Hogg and Abrams 1988: 19–20).

Categorization is accompanied by accentuation which significantly boosts the process of categorization. In the beginning of the 1960s, Tajfel and Wilkes found that when subjects were judging the length of individual lines on a continuum where the "short" end of the continuum was labeled "A" and the long end "B," they significantly exaggerated the difference between the A-type and B-type of lines. Furthermore, they tended to overestimate the similarity of the lines within the categories of A and B. Thus, all the A-lines were perceived to be more similar than they actually were; their difference in relation to the B-type of lines was also exaggerated (see Hogg and Abrams 1988: 19–20). Further experiments have shown that the same processes of categorization and accentuation also effect the estimation of social stimuli, that is, other people and other groups. It is easy to see the relation of these basic cognitive processes to phenomena that play a central role in intergroup relations: prejudice, ingroup biases, and social stereotypes.

The experiments have shown that there are two important catalysts in the process of categorization. First, accentuation accompanies categorization only in the dimensions people *themselves believe to be somehow connected* to the categorization. Second, the accentuation effect is more pronounced if the *categorization is of high personal value* to the individual observer (Hogg and Abrams 1988: 20). The latter aspect, in particular, is of importance in social categorization because categorization of other people usually has some relevance to our own self-image (Hogg and Abrams 1988: 20–21). In a study where the subjects were asked to classify people with different skin colors, for example, it was noticed that prejudiced subjects accentuated the differences between the skin colors more than non-prejudiced subjects (Tajfel 1981: 77–78). In studies, already conducted in the 1950s, it was also noticed that when anti-Semites and non-anti-Semites were asked to recognize Jews in the pictures showed to them, the anti-Semites found more Jews in the pictures than the non-anti-Semites. One might call this a "better safe than sorry"—principle. In Tajfel's view, the same cognitive phenomenon can be seen in the witch hunts of the past, for example (Tajfel 1981: 154).

Interestingly, recent cognitive experiments on perceptions of race cohere with Tajfel's results, casting new light on the cognitive machinery involved in racial categorization. Cosmides, Tooby and Kurzban (2003) discuss the cognitive systems that might explain the automatic and obviously mandatory racial coding that has been attested in several experiments. Since evolutionary considerations rule out the possibility that there could be a computational system in the human mind specifically designed for this purpose—our hunter-gatherer ancestors were less likely to encounter other races—racial coding must be a by-product of some other systems. Experiments seem to rule out the possibility that racial categorization would be a direct by-product of perceptual/correlational systems (i.e., that observations of similar skin color would form the basis of a racial category). For instance, colors of clothing are not automatically registered if they have no social significance.

According to Cosmides, Tooby and Kurzban (2003), there remain two possible candidates for the relevant systems involved:

(1) Racial categorizations are by-products of the essentialist inference system involved in categorizing natural kinds. This system presumes that objects belonging to the same category all have similar underlying essences that make them for what they are. Notably, this essentialist categorization does not require perceptual similarity; it can be supported by mere labeling (Cosmides, Tooby, and Kurzban 2003: 176; see Ahn et al. 2001).

(2) Another possibility is that there is cognitive machinery designed for tracking coalitional alliances. Of the two alternatives, it is the latter one that seems to be mainly responsible for racial categorization, although it is possible that the essentialist system also contributes to the categorization under some circumstances. The central role of the coalitional systems is inferred from experiments by Kurzban et al. (2001). They showed that subjects who had a lifelong experi-

ence of race as a coalition-predicting cue, revised their categorizations to reflect the new coalitions when they were exposed for four minutes to an alternative situation where coalitional alliances were not predicted by race.

In social psychology, there is an established tradition in the study of intergroup relations going back to M. Sherif's research on boys' summer camps and Tajfel's minimal group experiments (for a summary, see Hakola in this volume). Cosmides, Tooby and Kurzban's recent findings are in agreement with the results of these experiments. The authors correctly note that "the coalitional byproduct hypothesis fits neatly with the literature on ingroup favoritism and outgroup derogation, readily explaining why stereotypes of racial outgroups often include derogatory elements" (Cosmides, Tooby, and Kurzban 2003: 177).

From the point of view of the social identity approach, it is interesting that Cosmides, Tooby and Kurzban trace the racial categorizations back to a cognitive system that is activated in the presence of other humans. In this regard, it coheres with the basic assumptions of social identity research according to which humans are ready to adjust their perceived identities according to available social groups that offer opportunities for the building of positive (self or group) identities. On the other hand, this kind of cognitive research is a useful reminder of the fact that there is no need to contrast cognitive science with more socially-oriented research since carefully planned experiments on individual cognition can also help explain fundamental group processes.

3.3. *Toward a New Synthesis*

In the field of social psychology in the 1970s and 1980s, there was still a split between the cognitively-oriented American research tradition on social cognition and the more socially-oriented European social psychology focusing on social identity. The split had its roots in the growth of a distinctively European social psychology in the late 1960s and the beginning of the 1970s. During the 1970s and 1980s, European social psychology became more and more interested in studying social processes in wider social contexts while the American tradition focused more on the individual cognitive processes. Since the beginning of the 1990s, the gap has lessened; now a growing number of Americans are doing research on social identity while Europeans are also involved in research on social cognition (cf. Leyens, Yzerbyt and Schadron 1994:

103–27; Hogg and Abrams 1999; Nye and Brower 1996a, 1996b; Fiske and Goodwin 1996).

We find the present volume to be in harmony with these recent developments in social psychology. Several of the essays provide examples of how the social identity approach can be connected to more cognitively-oriented theorizing in the study of early Judaism and early Christianity.

Although the pioneers of the social identity approach tended to neglect the historical dimension in the analysis of identities, more recently the situation has changed, with some social identity theorists starting to ask how identities relate to the past and the future (for instance, Cinnirella 1998). In this volume, Esler seeks to integrate the social identity approach with the study of the past by drawing on Maurice Halbwach's idea of collective memory (Halbwachs 1980). Halbwachs, however, tends to ascribe to groups a mental life of their own in a Durkheimian manner, thereby neglecting the question of how memories are transmitted by individuals. Esler tries to solve the problem with the help of cognitive psychological studies on memory. Here he not only develops the social identity approach but also makes an important contribution to the study of collective or social memory which scholars of early Judaism and early Christianity have recently found to be a new and promising area of research (see Kirk and Thatcher 2005). Because the theories of social or collective memory have been applied mainly to questions of the transmission of religious ideas, cognitive scientific theories of cultural transmission can be of much help here.

Luomanen's essay provides examples of concepts and themes (i.e., prototypes, exemplars and ingroup favoritism) that are central to the social identity approach but have also been dealt with in the cognitive science of religion (Sperber and Boyer, in particular). The social identity approach is also applied in Hakola's and Jokiranta's case studies. Hakola's discussion of group phenomena in the Second Temple period approaches the topic from a classic social identity perspective which is closely connected to the cognitive basis of the theory: (re-)categorizations that accentuate ingroup distinctiveness and positive ingroup identity. Jokiranta's analysis of the Qumran community and its penal code provides a historical example of the type of religious fundamentalism Boyer has discussed (2001: 292–96).

4. Conclusion

The multi- and interdisciplinary research envisioned in this introduction is exemplified in many of the essays in this volume. The book has been divided into three sections. Essays in the first section explore the general prospects of the cognitive approaches in the study Christian origins and early Judaism, focusing on such issues as the spread of the resurrection traditions, the emergence of early Christian religion and early Jewish and Christian rituals. The second section contains two applications of conceptual blending theory to early Christian materials. The essays in the third part venture to combine traditional historical and social-scientific approaches with various cognitive perspectives and theories, seeking to conjoin social and cognitive aspects of identity and memory. This volume may still leave many crucial issues open and, perhaps, raise more questions than it can answer. We hope, however, that it will mark the beginning of a fruitful exchange of ideas between scholars interested in the social-scientific study of early Judaism/Christianity and in the cognitive science of religion.

REFERENCES

Abrams, Dominic, and Craig McGarty. 1990. "Self-categorization and Social Identity." In *Social Identity Approach: Constructive and Critical Advances*, edited by Dominic Abrams and Michael A. Hogg, 10–27. New York: Harverster Wheatsheaf.

Abrams, Dominic, and Michael A. Hogg. 1990a. "An Introduction to the Social Identity Approach." In *Social Identity Approach: Constructive and Critical Advances*, edited by Dominic Abrams and Michael A. Hogg, 1–9. New York: Harverster Wheatsheaf.

———, eds. 1990b. *Social Identity Approach: Constructive and Critical Advances*. New York: Harverster Wheatsheaf.

———, eds. 1999. *Social Identity and Social Cognition*. Malden, Mass.: Blackwell.

Adam, Andrew Keith Malcolm 1995. *What is Postmodern Biblical Criticism?* Biblical Studies. Minneapolis, Minn.: Fortress.

Ahn, Woo-Kyong, Charles Kalish, Susan A. Gelman, Douglas L. Medin, Christian Luhmann, Scott Atran, John D. Coley, and Patrick Shafto. 2001. "Why Essences Are Essential in the Psychology of Concepts." *Cognition* 82: 59–69.

Atran, Scott. 1998. "Folk Biology and the Anthropology of Science: Cognitive Universals and Cultural Particulars." *Behavioral and Brain Sciences* 21: 547–609.

———. 2002. *In Gods We Trust: The Evolutionary Landscape of Religion*. New York: Oxford University Press.

Atran, Scott, and Ara Norenzayan. 2004. "Religion's Evolutionary Landscape: Counterintuition, Commitment, Compassion, Communion." *Behavioral and Brain Sciences* 27: 713–30.

Barrett, Justin L. 1998. "Cognitive Constraints on Hindu Concepts of the Divine." *Journal for the Scientific Study of Religion* 37: 608–19.

———. 2003. "Epidemiological and Nativist Accounts in the Cognitive Study of Culture: A Commentary on Pyysiäinen's Innate Fear of Bering's Ghosts." *Journal of Cognition and Culture* 3(3): 226—32.

———. 2004. *Why Would Anyone Believe in God?* Walnut Creek, Calif.: AltaMira.

Barrett, Justin L., and Frank Keil. 1996. "Conceptualizing a Nonnatural Entity: Anthropomorphism in God Concepts." *Cognitive Psychology* 31: 219–47.

Barrett, Justin L., and E. Thomas Lawson. 2001. "Ritual Intuitions: Cognitive Contributions to Judgments of Ritual Efficacy." *Journal of Cognition and Culture* 1(2): 183–201.

Barrett, Justin L., & Melanie A. Nyhof. 2001. "Spreading Non-Natural Concepts: The Role of Intuitive Conceptual Structures in Memory and Transmission of Cultural Materials." *Journal of Cognition and Culture* 1(1): 69–100.

Bering, Jesse M. 2002. "Intuitive Conceptions of Dead Agents' Minds: The Natural Foundations of Afterlife Beliefs as Phenomenological Boundary." *Journal of Cognition and Culture* 2(4): 263–308.

———. 2006. "The Folk Psychology of Souls." *Behavioral and Brain Sciences* 29(5): 453–93.

Blasi, Anthony J., Jean Duhaime, and Paul-André Turcotte, eds. 2002. *Handbook of Early Christianity: Social Science Approaches*. Walnut Creek, Calif.: AltaMira.

Boyer, Pascal. 1990. *Tradition as Truth and Communication*. Cambridge: Cambridge University Press.

———. 1994. *The Naturalness of Religious Ideas: A Cognitive Theory of Religion*. Berkeley: University of California Press.

———. 1998. "Cognitive Tracks of Cultural Inheritance: How Evolved Intuitive Ontology Governs Cultural Transmission." *American Anthropologist* 100(4): 876–89.

———. 2001. *Religion Explained: The Evolutionary Origins of Religious Thought*. New York: Basic Books.

———. 2003a. "Religious Thought and Behaviour as By-products of Brain Function." *Trends in Cognitive Sciences* 7(3): 119–24.

———. 2003b. "Are Ghost Concepts 'Intuitive,' 'Endemic' and 'Innate'?" *Journal of Cognition and Culture* 3(3): 233–43.

———. 2005. "A Reductionistic Model of Distinct Modes of Religious Transmission." In *Mind and Religion: Psychological and Cognitive Foundations of Religiosity*, edited by Harvey Whitehouse and Robert N. McCauley, 3–29. Walnut Creek, Calif.: AltaMira.

———. In press. Specialised Inference Engines as Precursors of Creative Imagination? In *Imaginative Minds*, edited by Ilona Roth. London: British Academy.

Boyer, Pascal, and Pierre Liénard. 2006. "Why Ritualized Behavior? Precaution Systems and Action Parsing in Developmental, Pathological and Cultural Rituals." *Behavioral and Brain Sciences* 29(6), 595–613.

Boyer, Pascal, & Charles Ramble. 2001. "Cognitive Templates for Religious Concepts: Cross-Cultural Evidence for Recall of Counterintuitive Representations." *Cognitive Science* 25, 535–64.

Bultmann, Rudolf. 1968. *The History of the Synoptic Tradition*. Translated by John Marsh. Rev. ed. New York: Harper & Row.

Carney, Thomas. 1975. *The Shape of the Past: Models and Antiquity*. Lawrence, Kans.: Coronado Press.

Chaiken, Shelly, and Yacoov Trope, eds. 1999. *Dual-Process Theories in Social Psychology*. New York: Guilford Press.

Chwe, Michael Suk-Young. 2001. *Rational Ritual: Culture, Coordination, and Common Knowledge*. Princeton: Princeton University Press.

Cinnirella, Marco. 1998. "Exploring Temporal Aspects of Social Identity: The Concept of Possible Social Identities." *European Journal of Social Psychology* 28: 227–48.

Cohen, Emma. 2007. *The Mind Possessed: The Cognition of Spirit Possession in an Afro-Brazilian Religious Tradition*. Oxford: Oxford University Press.

Cosmides, Leda, John Tooby, and Robert Kurzban. 2003. "Perceptions of Race." *Trends in Cognitive Sciences* 7(4): 173–79.
Dewey, Joanna, ed. 1994. *Orality and Textuality in Early Christian Literature*. Semeia 65. Atlanta, Ga.: Scholars Press.
Dunn, James D. G. 2000. "Jesus in Oral Memory: The Initial Stages of the Jesus Tradition." *Society of Biblical Literature Seminar Papers* 39: 287–326.
Elliott, John H. 1981. *A Home for the Homeless: A Social-Scientific Criticism of 1 Peter, Its Situation, and Strategy*. Minneapolis, Minn.: Fortress.
———. 1986. "Social-Scientific Criticism of the New Testament: More on Methods and Models." *Semeia* 35: 1–33.
———. 1993. *What is Social-Scientific Criticism?* Minneapolis, Minn.: Fortress.
Esler, Philip F. 1987. *Community and Gospel in Luke-Acts: Social and Political Motivations in Lucan Theology*. Society for New Testament Studies Monograph Series, 57. Cambridge: Cambridge University Press.
———. 1994. *The First Christians in Their Social Words: Social-Scientific Approaches to New Testament Interpretation*. London: Routledge.
———. 1995a. "Introduction." In *Modelling Early Christianity: Social-Scientific Studies of the New Testament in its Context*, edited by Philip F. Esler, 1–22. London: Routledge.
———, ed. 1995b. *Modelling Early Christianity: Social Scientific Studies of the New Testament in Its Context*. London: Routledge.
———. 1998a. *Galatians*. New Testament Readings. London: Routledge.
———. 1998b. Review of David G. Horrell, *The Social Ethos of Corinthian Correspondence: Interests and Ideology from I Corinthians to I Clement*. *The Journal of Theological Studies* 49: 253–60.
———. 2000. "Models in New Testament Interpretation: A Reply to David Horrell." *Journal for the Study of the New Testament* 78: 107–13.
———. 2003. *Conflict and Identity in Romans: The Social Setting of Paul's Letter*. Minneapolis, Minn.: Fortress.
———. 2004. "The Context Group Project." In *Anthropology and Biblical Studies: Avenues of Approach*, edited by Louise J. Lawrence and Mario I. Aguilar, 46–63. Leiden: Deo Publishing.
Fauconnier, Gilles. [1985] 1994. *Mental Spaces: Aspects of Meaning Construction in Natural Language*. Cambridge: Cambridge University Press.
———. 1997. *Mappings in Thought and Language*. Cambridge: Cambridge University Press.
Fauconnier, Gilles, and Mark Turner. 1996. "Blending as a Central Process of Grammar." In *Conceptual Structure, Discourse, and Language*, edited by Adele E. Goldborg, Stanford, Calif.: University of Stanford Press.
———. 1998. "Conceptual Integration Networks." *Cognitive Science* 22(2): 133–87.
———. 2002. *The Way We Think: Conceptual Blending and the Mind's Hidden Complexities*. New York: Basic Books.
Fessler, Daniel M. T., and Carlos David Navarrete. 2003. "Meat is Good to Taboo: Dietary Proscriptions as a Product of the Interaction of Psychological Mechanisms and Social Processes." *Journal of Cognition and Culture* 3: 1–40.
Fiske, Susan T., and Stephanie A. Goodwin. 1996. "Introduction: Social Cognition Research and Small Group Research, a West Side Story or...?" In *What's Social About Social Cognition?: Research on Socially Shared Cognition in Small Groups*, edited by Judith L. Nye and Aaron M. Brower, xiii–xxxiii. Thousand Oaks, Calif.: Sage Publications.
Gager, John G. 1975. *Kingdom and Community: The Social World of Early Christianity*. Englewood Cliffs, N.J.: Prentice-Hall.
Garrett, Susan R. 1992. "Sociology (Early Christianity)." *Anchor Bible Dictionary* 6: 89–99.
Geertz, Clifford. 1973. *The Interpretation of Cultures*. New York: Basic Books.

Gerhardsson, Birger. 1961. *Memory and Manuscript: Oral Tradition and Written Transmission in Rabbinic Judaism and Early Christianity*. Acta Seminarii Neotestamentici Upsaliensis, XXII. Lund: CWK Gleerup.
Gonce, Lauren O., Afzal Upal, D. Jason Slone, & Ryan D. Tweney. 2006. "Role of Context in Recall of Counterintuitive Concepts." *Journal of Cognition and Culture* 6(3–4): 521–47.
Halbwachs, Maurice. 1980. *The Collective Memory*. Translated by Francis J. Ditter Jr. and Vida Yazdi Ditter, with an introduction by Mary Douglas (French original 1950). New York: Harper.
Hogg, Michael A., and Dominic Abrams. 1988. *Social Identifications: A Social Psychology of Intergroup Relations and Group Processes*. London: Routledge.
———. 1999. "Social Identity and Social Cognition: Historical Background and Current Trends." In *Social Identity and Social Cognition*, edited by Dominic Abrams and Michael A. Hogg, 1–25. Malden, Mass.: Blackwell.
Holmberg, Bengt. 1978. *Paul and Power: The Structure of Authority in the Primitive Church as Reflected in the Pauline Letters*. Coniectanae biblica: New Testament Series, 11. Lund: CWK Gleerup.
———. 1990. *Sociology and the New Testament: An Appraisal*. Minneapolis, Minn.: Fortress.
Honko, Lauri. 1979. "Theories Concerning the Ritual Process." In *Science of Religion: Studies in Methodology*, edited by Lauri Honko, 369–90. Religion and Reason, 13. The Hague: Mouton.
Horrell, David G. 1993. "Converging Ideologies: Berger and Luckmann and the Pastoral Epistles." *Journal for the Study of the New Testament* 50: 85–103.
———. 1996. *The Social Ethos of the Corinthian Correspondence: Interests and Ideology from 1 Corinthians to 1 Clement*. Studies of the New Testament and Its World. Edinburgh T&T Clark.
———. 2000. "Models and Methods in Social-Scientific Interpretation: A Response to Philip Esler." *Journal for the Study of the New Testament* 78: 83–105.
———. 2001. "Berger and New Testament Studies." In *Peter Berger and the Study of Religion*, edited by Linda Woodhead with Paul Heelas and David Martin. London: Routledge.
———. 2002. "Social Sciences Studying Formative Christian Phenomena: A Creative Movement." In *Handbook of Early Christianity: Social Science Approaches*, edited by Anthony J. Blasi, Jean Duhaime, and Paul-André Turcotte, 3–28. Walnut Greek, Calif.: AltaMira.
Kelber, Werner H. 1983. *The Oral and the Written Gospel: The Hermeneutics of Speaking and Writing in the Synoptic Tradition, Mark, Paul, and Q*. Philadelphia, Pa.: Fortress.
Kirk, Alan, and Tom Thatcher, eds. 2005. *Memory, Tradition, and Text: Uses of the Past in Early Christianity*. Semeia Studies, 52. Atlanta, Ga.: Society of Biblical Literature.
Kurzban, Robert, John Tooby, and Leda Cosmides. 2001. "Can Race Be Erased? Coalitional Computation and Social Categorization." *Proceedings of the National Academy of Sciences of the United States of America* 98(26): 15387–92.
Lakoff, George. 1987. *Women, Fire, and Dangerous Things: What Categories Reveal about the Mind*. London: University of Chicago Press.
Lakoff, George, and Mark Johnson. 1980. *Metaphors We Live By*. London: University of Chicago Press.
Lawson, E. Thomas. 2000. "Towards a Cognitive Science of Religion." *Numen* 47: 338–49.
Lawson, E. Thomas, and Robert N. McCauley. 1990. *Rethinking Religion: Connecting Cognition and Culture*. Cambridge: Cambridge University Press.
Leyens, Jaques-Philippe, Vincent Yzerbyt, and Georges Schadron, eds. 1994. *Stereotypes and Social Cognition*. London: Sage Publications.
Liénard, Pierre, and Pascal Boyer. 2006. "Whence Collective Rituals? A Cultural Selection Model of Ritualized Behavior." *American Anthropologist* 108(4): 814–27.

Luomanen, Petri. 2002. "The 'Sociology of Sectarianism' in Matthew: Modeling the Genesis of Early Jewish and Christian Communities." In *Fair Play: Diversity and Conflicts in Early Christianity: Essays in Honour of Heikki Räisänen*, edited by Ismo Dunderberg, Christopher Tuckett, and Kari Syreeni, 107–30. Leiden: Brill.
Malina, Bruce J. [1981] 2001. *The New Testament World: Insights from Cultural Anthropology*. London: SCM Press.
———. 1982. "The Social Sciences and Biblical Interpretation." *Interpretation* 36: 229–42.
———. 1986. *Christian Origins and Cultural Anthropology: Practical Models for Biblical Interpretation*. Atlanta: John Knox.
Malina, Bruce J., and Jerome H. Neyrey. 1988. *Calling Jesus Names: The Social Value of Labels in Matthew*. Sonoma, Calif.: Polebridge Press.
Marshall, Gordon, ed. 1998. *A Dictionary of Sociology*. Oxford: Oxford University Press.
Martin, Dale B. 1999. "Social-Scientific Criticism." In *To Each Its Own Meaning: An Introduction to Biblical Criticisms and Their Application*, edited by Steven L. McKenzie and Stephen R. Haynes, 125–41. Louisville, Ky.: Westminster John Knox.
McCauley, Robert N. 2001. "Ritual, Memory, and Emotion: Comparing Two Cognitive Hypotheses." In *Religion in Mind: Cognitive Perspectives on Religious Belief, Ritual and Experience*, edited by Jensine Andresen, 115–40. Cambridge: Cambridge University Press.
McCauley, Robert N., and E. Thomas Lawson. 2002. *Bringing Ritual to Mind*. Cambridge: Cambridge University Press.
Meeks, Wayne. 1972. "The Man from Heaven in Johannine Sectarianism." *Journal of Biblical Literature* 91: 44–72.
———. 1983. *The First Urban Christians: The Social World of the Apostle Paul*. New Haven, Conn.: Yale University Press.
Munz, Peter. 1959. *Problems of Religious Knowledge*. London: SCM Press.
———. 1973. *When the Golden Bough Breaks: Structuralism of Typology*. London: Routledge.
Nemeroff, Carol, and Paul Rozin. 2000. "The Making of the Magical Mind: The Nature and Function of Sympathetic Magical Thinking." In *Imagining the Impossible: Magical, Scientific, and Religious Thinking in Children*, edited by Karl S. Rosengren, Carl N. Johnson, and Paul L. Harris, 1–34. Cambridge: Cambridge University Press.
Neyrey, Jerome H. 1986. "Body Language in 1 Corinthians: The Use of Anthropological Models for Understanding Paul and His Opponents." *Semeia* 35: 129–70.
Norenzayan, Ara, and Scott Atran. 2004. "Cognitive and Emotional Processes in the Cultural Transmission of Natural and Nonnatural Beliefs." In *The Psychological Foundations of Culture*, edited by Mark Schaller and Christian Crandall, 149–69. Mahwah, N.J.: Lawrence Erlbaum Associates.
Nye, Judith L., and Aaron M. Brower, 1996a. "What Is Social About Social Cognition Research?" In *What's Social About Social Cognition? Research on Socially Shared Cognition in Small Groups*, edited by Judith L. Nye and Aaron M. Brower, 311–23. Thousand Oaks, Calif.: Sage Publications.
———, eds. 1996b. *What's Social About Social Cognition? Research on Socially Shared Cognition in Small Groups*. Thousand Oaks, Calif.: Sage Publications.
Osiek, Carolyn. 1992. "The Social Sciences and the Second Testament: Problems and Challenges." *Biblical Theological Bulletin* 22: 88–95.
Pilch, John J. 2000. *Healing in the New Testament: Insights from Medical and Mediterranean Anthropology*. Minneapolis, Minn.: Fortress
———, ed. 2001. *Social-Scientific Models for Interpreting the Bible: Essays by the Context Group in Honor of Bruce Malina*. Biblical Interpretation Series, 53. Leiden: Brill.
Pinker, Steven, and Ray Jackendoff. 2005. "The Faculty of Language: What's Special about It? *Cognition* 95: 201–36.

Pyysiäinen, Ilkka. 2001. *How Religion Works: Towards a New Cognitive Science of Religion.* Leiden: Brill.
———. 2004a. "Intuitive and Explicit in Religious Thought." *Journal of Cognition and Culture* 4(1): 123–50.
———. 2004b. *Magic, Miracles, and Religion: A Scientist's Perspective.* Walnut Creek, Calif.: AltaMira.
———. 2005. "Intuition, Reflection, and the Evolution of Traditions." In *Moving Beyond New Testament Theology? Essays in Conversation with Heikki Räisänen,* edited by Todd C. Penner and Caroline Vander Stichele, 282–307. Publications of the Finnish Exegetical Society, 88. Helsinki: The Finnish Exegetical Society; Göttingen: Vandenhoeck & Ruprecht.
———. 2006. "Memories: Religion and Cultural Transmission. A book review essay based on Peter Richerson and Robert Boyd, *Not by Genes Alone: How Culture Transformed Human Evolution,* and Harvey Whitehouse, *Modes of Religiosity: A Cognitive Theory of Religious Transmission.*" *Anthropological Quarterly* 79(2): 341–53.
Pyysiäinen, Ilkka, and Veikko Anttonen, eds. 2002. *Current Approaches in the Cognitive Science of Religion.* London: Continuum.
Revel, Jacques, and Lynn Hunt (Eds.). 1995. *Histories: French Construction of the Past.* Tr. by Arthur Goldhammer et al. New York: New Press.
Rohrbaugh, Richard, ed. 1996. *The Social Sciences and New Testament Interpretation.* Peabody, Mass.: Hendrickson.
Samellas, Antigone. 2002. *Death in the Eastern Mediterranean (50–600 A.D.).* Studien und Texte zu Antike und Christentum, 12. Tübingen: Mohr Siebeck.
Scroggs, Robin. 1980. "The Sociological Interpretation of the New Testament: The Present State of Research." *New Testament Studies* 26: 164–79.
Sellew, Philip H. 2006. "Jesus and the Voice from beyond the Grave: *Gospel of Thomas* 42 in the Context of Funerary Epigraphy." In *Thomasine Traditions in Antiquity: The Social and the Cultural World of the Gospel of Thomas,* edited by Jon Ma. Asgeirsson, April D. DeConick and Risto Uro, 39–73. Nag Hammadi and Manichaean Studies, 59. Leiden: Brill.
Silberman, Lou H., ed. 1987. *Orality, Aurality and Biblical Narrative.* Semeia, 39. Decatur, Ga.: Scholars Press.
Sørensen, Jesper. 2007. *A cognitive theory of magic.* Walnut Creek, Calif.: AltaMira Press.
Sperber, Dan. [1975] 1995. *Rethinking Symbolism.* Cambridge: Cambridge University Press.
———. 1994. "The Modularity of Thought and the Epidemiology of Representations." In *Mapping the Mind,* edited by Lawrence A. Hirschfeld, and Susan A. Gelman, 39–67. Cambridge: Cambridge University Press.
———. 1996a. "Why Are Perfect Animals, Hybrids, and Monsters Food for Symbolic Thought?" *Method & Theory in the Study of Religion* 8: 143–69.
———. 1996b. *Explaining Culture: A Naturalistic Approach.* Oxford: Blackwell.
Sperber, Dan, and Deirdre Wilson. [1986] 1988. *Relevance: Communication and Cognition.* Cambridge, Mass.: Harvard University Press.
Stegemann, Wolfgang, Bruce J. Malina, and Gerd Theissen, eds. 2002. *The Social Setting of Jesus and the Gospels.* Minneapolis, Minn.: Fortress.
Stowers, Stanley K. 1985. "The Social Sciences and the Study of Early Christianity." In *Approaches to Ancient Judaism.* Vol. 5 of *Studies in Judaism in Its Greco-Roma Context,* edited by W. S. Green, 149–81. Atlanta, Ga.: Scholars Press.
Sun, Ron. 2002. *Duality of Mind: A Bottom up Approach toward Cognition.* Mahwah, N.J.: Erlbaum.
Tajfel, Henri. 1981. *Human Groups and Social Categories: Studies in Social Psychology.* Cambridge: Cambridge University Press.

Theissen, Gerd. 1977. *Soziologie der Jesusbewegung: Ein Beitrag zur Entstehungsgeschichte des Urchristentums.* Theologische Existenz heute, 194. Munich: Kaiser.

Tremlin, Todd. 2006. *Minds and Gods: The Cognitive Foundations of Religion.* New York: Oxford University Press.

Tweney, Ryan et. al. "The Creative Structuring of Counterintuitive Worlds." *Journal of Cognition and Culture* 6(3–4): 483–98.

Upal, Afzal. 2005. "Role of Context in Memorability of Intuitive and Counterintuitive Concepts." In *Proceedings of 27th Annual Meeting of the Cognitive Science Society*, 2224–29. Mahwah; N.J.: Erlbaum.

Upal, Afzal, et. al. 2007. "Contextualizing Counterintuitiveness: How Context Affects Comprehension and Memorability of Counterintuitive Concepts." *Cognitive Science* 31, 1–25.

Wansbrough, Henry, ed. 1991. *Jesus and the Oral Gospel Tradition.* Journal for the Study of the New Testament: Supplement Series, 64. Sheffield: Sheffield Academy Press.

Whitehouse, Harvey. 1995. *Inside the Cult: Religious Innovation and Transmission in Papua New Guinea.* Oxford: Clarendon Press.

———. 1996. "Jungles and Computers: Neuronal Group Selection and the Epidemiology of Representations." *Journal of the Royal Anthropological Institute* (NS) 1: 99–116.

———. 2000. *Arguments and Icons: Divergent Modes of Religiosity.* Oxford: Oxford University Press.

———. 2002. "Modes of Religiosity: Towards a Cognitive Explanation of the Sociopolitical Dynamics of Religion." *Method & Theory in the Study of Religion* 14(3–4): 293–315.

———. 2004. Whitehouse, Harvey. 2004. *Modes of Religiosity: A Cognitive Theory of Religious Transmission.* Walnut Creek, CA: AltaMira.

Wyer, Robert S., and Srull, Thomas K., eds. [1984] 1994. *Handbook of Social Cognition.* Hillsdale, N.J.: Erlbaum.

PART ONE

THE PROMISE OF THE COGNITIVE SCIENCE OF RELIGION

THE PROMISE OF COGNITIVE SCIENCE FOR THE STUDY OF EARLY CHRISTIANITY

Luther H. Martin

> *Mind is the material of history.... If history is not a mere puppet show, then it must be the history of mental processes.... [T]hose matters which come first in the rational order of things—the cognitive functions of the mind—come last from the standpoint of our awareness and our observation.*
> —Georg Simmel (1905: vii, 39, 43)

If, as the German sociologist and philosopher of history Georg Simmel suggested at the beginning of the last century, "the material of history" is—in the phrasing of his English translator—"the cognitive functions of the mind" (*"die Erkenntnisfunktion des Geistes"*; in the fifth edition of his work, he speaks also of *"die psychologische Tatsächlichkeit[en]"* [1923: 4]), then history can be defined as the history of mental representations. The history of religions, then, would be the history of representations of superhuman agents—those legions of deities and devils, angels and demons, spirits and saints that inhabit all religious traditions—and of those ideas and practices that have been legitimated by claims to their authority. And since cognitive scientists have now shown that the superhuman inflections of such claims are the products of quite ordinary cognitive functions (Boyer 2001), the history of religions requires no special *heilsgeschichtliche* method (see Simmel 1905: 59; Collingwood 1956: 9; Lease 2003). The methodological problems that confront the historian of religions are, in other words, no different from those that arise in any historical study.

Whereas historians have traditionally been concerned with mapping the influences of historical antecedents and contexts on their evidence, cognitivists are concerned with mapping the influences and constraints of human cognition upon these same data. By understanding mental representations as the products of neurophysiological functions, they join the array of possible material explanations for historical formations alongside, for example, those of geopolitical or economic forces (Boyer 2003; on the materiality of the mental, see also Godelier 1986). The historical record is constrained, in other words, not only by antecedents and exigencies explicit in the environment of brains but also by implicit capacities and innate constraints characteristic of mind itself. Because historical remains are mental representations, externally inscribed and preserved, historians must be able to discriminate between and to organize their fragmentary and incomplete remains in ways consonant with the ubiquitous processes and dynamics of the "mental processes" ("*psychischer Vorgänger*") that produced them. An understanding of these data in both their explicit and implicit totality can contribute to historians pursuing their reconstructive work with greater confidence than might be the case when they work from the influence of explicit factors alone.

In this presentation, I should like to reflect on the work of the historian and on the appropriateness and utility of cognitive theorizing for historical method. I shall attempt to illustrate that utility with reference to the historical study of early Christianity.

1. *Cognition and History*

1.1. *Historical Thinking is a Natural Form of Cognition*

Historians and cognitivists alike have argued that historical thinking is a natural form of human cognition. The American historian Carl Becker, for example, writing in 1932, already argued that "everyman [is] his own historian" (Becker 1969). By analogy to the mathematical operation of reducing a fraction to its lowest terms, Becker reduced the conventional view of history, the "knowledge of events that have occurred in the past," to a view of history as "the memory" of what historians since Hegel have termed "*res gestae*"—"things said and done" (Becker 1969: 7; Hegel 1861: 60). Becker considered such memories to be "essential to the performance of the simplest acts of daily life" (Becker 1969: 10). We create the fiction of our quotidian present, he argued, "by robbing the past," that is, "by holding on to the most recent events and pretending they all belong to our immediate perceptions" (Becker 1969: 11). By tacitly "reënforcing and enriching" "immediate perceptions," we are able, thereby, to "live in a world of semblance more spacious and satisfying than is to be found within the narrow confines of the fleeting present moment." It is these memories of what we have said and done, Becker concluded, that is the "fundamental thing which enables... [each and all of us] to have... a history" (Becker 1969: 10–11). Researchers ranging from phenomenologists to neuroscientists have arrived at similar conclusions (Lloyd 2004: 249–332). Our ordinary mnemonic proclivity for producing a historical consciousness is, in other words, simply "our psychological condition at rest, a way of thinking that requires little effort and [that] comes quite naturally" (Wineburg 2001: 19). This natural cognitive process underlies our human proclivity for and familiarity with such narrative representations as histories, dramatic presentations and religious myths.

1.2. *Historiographical Thinking Is a Historicized Form of Natural Cognition*

If historical thinking reflects an ordinary process of human cognition, *historiographical* thinking represents a specialized and professionalized version of this ordinary process (Becker 1969: 16–23; Collingwood 1956: 268; see also Sutton 1998: 207). Such professionalization represents a particularized configuration of mental representations that results from an interaction of historians' cognitive systems with their own environment and that, consequently, become imposed upon the ambiguities of their data. The historicized cognition of professional historians retains from natural cognition, in other words, an inevitable tendency towards representing the past in terms of contemporary sensibilities, a species of ethnocentrism known to historians as "presentism" (see Simmel 1905: 47; Donald 1991: 1). This "presentism" is characteristic not only of modern historiography but, of course, of the production of the historical evidence itself—as biblical scholars are well aware.

2. *The Presentism of Historicized Cognition*

2.1. *The Narrative Bias of Historians*

A prominent example of historiographical presentism is the bias of professional historians for narrative accounts (after the Latin sense of *historia* rather than its Greek sense of 'inquiry'), complete with a beginning, a middle, and an end (Aristotle, *Poetica* 7.3). This narrative bias is so great that historians have often sought stories where none may have existed. For example, historians of Graeco-Roman religions have sought for decades to discover the mythological narrative(s) of Mithraism by decoding the rich remains of its material culture. Mithraism seems, however, to have maintained no widely adhered to myth or story since it never developed—as did Christianity—any centralized institutional structure capable of sustaining a shared narrative (Martin 2005a). Nevertheless, some cognitively inspired researchers have concluded that the predominance of narrative behavior and evidence documented from the past five thousand years simply represents "the way we think" (e.g., Turner 1996; Fauconnier-Turner 2002). Such researchers omit, however, consideration of how mental representations become blended into enduring narrative structures—if they are. Nor do they offer any cognitive basis for the broad appeal of some but not all of these narratives to audiences beyond the social contexts of their production (Stiller et al. 2003: 398).

In a preliminary study of Shakespeare's plays, for example, Stiller, Nettle and Dunbar have suggested that successful stories—those that are often told and that have become widely disseminated—reflect thematic representations of life as they have been shaped by behavioral ecology. These themes include mate choice, for example, or those of survival, group cohesion, or the triumph of heroes in the face of diversity (Stiller et al. 2003; see now Gottschall and Wilson 2005).

In addition to such representational thematics, Stiller et al. concluded that successful stories seem also to be structured by cognitive constraints, whereby the cognitive load of such stories challenges, without exceeding limits upon, the social cognition of intended readers. While the total number of characters in a given story may approach thirty or forty, for example, the possibilities of social interactions our cognitive machinery is able to handle is limited to fifteen or fewer main characters, the size of actual groups of close friends. And the number of speaking characters whose mental states a reader is readily able to follow at any one time is limited to three or four in any particular episode. If, for dramatic reasons or for those of historical content, more characters are deemed necessary to the narrative structure, the cognitive burden of the reader is eased by the construction of serial episodes, of plots within plots, or by the insertion of helpful mnemonic references (Stiller et al. 2003; Dunbar et al. 2005: 140–41, 144–45). It would be telling to analyze such narrative constructions as the New Testament gospels in light of these constraints.

The Analogical Evidence of Material Culture

A number of anthropologists and evolutionary psychologists have argued that not all historically fixed cognition is organized syntactically as narrative; some may be organized paratactically as *analogia rerum gestarum* (e.g., Bateson 1972: 372–74; 411–25; Barth 1975: 207–14;

1987: 69–70, 75; Donald 1991: 337; Whitehouse 2000: 64–65, 88–91; 2004: 44–45, 100–104, 114–18). In contrast to the logical (or linear) organization of narrative thinking, the neuroscientist Gerald Edelman has associated such analogical thinking with selectionism and pattern recognition (Edelman 2004: 147). While the products of such analogical abilities "can be richly creative," they are necessarily ambiguous (Edelman 2004: 147; on cognitive analyses of analogy, see, Gentner et al. 2001). The ambiguity of material culture, which may be encoded either narratively or analogically, is a case in point.

The uncertainty concerning the encoding of Christian material culture, for example, arises from the fact that this evidence contradicts the gospel narratives on virtually all of its central themes. The cross, for example, and sacrificial representations surrounding the cross such as the "eucharistic" meal of bread and wine, are not documented from Christian material culture until the fourth century (Snyder 2003: 58–64). Some of this imagery is clearly organized typologically, a technique for establishing analogies—in the case of some Christian material culture, between the Old and New Testaments (Malbon 1990: 42–43). But what of the rest? As the biblical scholar Nils Peter Lemche has rightly concluded, the question of exactly how the remains of material culture should be read is itself a historical conclusion "to be demonstrated and not accepted in advance of the historical analysis" (Lemche 1998: 30). Nevertheless, neither biblical scholars nor historians of religion have yet even attempted to integrate the evidence of Christian material culture into their histories of early Christianity, even though a comprehensive survey of this evidence was published a quarter of a century ago (Snyder 1985, rev. 2003).

The Textual Evidence for Analogies
Yet another identifiable mode of human thinking may be termed an *enumeratio rerum gestarum*, that is, a cataloging of things said and done. Claude Lévi-Strauss has argued, for example, that the proliferation of concepts throughout human cultures is the consequence of differential processes of classification that are based upon a natural human concern to enumerate properties of the observers' environment (Lévi-Strauss 1966: 1–10). Such enumerated representations of knowledge are encoded as clusters of information that are organized visually, independent of any grammar or phonography (Donald 1991: 285–92), such as lists (Gordon 1999) and taxonomies (Foucault 1970: 218). Richard Gordon has concluded that such "spatial organization[s] of

material[s]," independent of any "authorial presence," claims authority for the autonomy of paratactic or analogical representations (Gordon 1999: 199). And Lera Boroditsky has argued that we develop a temporal sense of sequentiality, requisite for narrative, by analogy to our prior visual and tactile experiences of space (Boroditsky 2000).

Whereas analogies, and even narratives, may drift over time in order to maintain maximum memorability (Sperber 1996: 95), extensive lists or complex taxonomies are difficult to encode in working memory (Miller 1956). Rather they increasingly require external memory devices in order more accurately to fix and to preserve information, as surviving invoices, genealogies and astronomical tables in early Mesopotamian cuneiform writing instantiate.

As biblical scholars well know, the earliest evidence for the early Christianities are enumerations of the sayings of Jesus, Q and the *Gospel of Thomas*, for which the underlying principles of association—if any—remain contested but which certainly are not organized according to any discernible narrative structure. In addition to these Christian materials, we might also mention listing in the Graeco-Roman magical texts (Gordon 1999), the numerous anthologies of poetic and philosophical *florilegia* common to the Hellenistic period (Chadwick 1969) and the *Florilegium* or eschatological *Midrash* from Qumran (4QFlor) (Allegro 1956: 176; 1958). Such enumerated representations of knowledge are so significant a part of the historical record of Western antiquity that some biblical scholars, following historians of Mesopotamian antiquity, have even proposed establishing a field of *Listenwissenschaft* (von Soden 1936; Alt 1951; see the discussion by Smith 1982: 44–48). Might such lists of sayings be organized on analogical rather than serial principles?

While analogies can, of course, be presented in story form, narrative does not, to repeat, represent the *only* way *Homo sapiens* think; it represents rather but *one* way we think. And how knowledge is thought will, in the conclusion of the anthropologist Fredrik Barth, "entail a definition of the nature of the object of knowledge" (Barth 1987: 75).

2.2. *Historicized Cognition and the Problem of Periodization*

In addition to the narrative bias of historians, a further example of "presentism" is exemplified by the way in which professional historians have shaped and prejudged their evidence—however evaluated—by framing it in cultural contexts and historical periods. Situating historical data in their cultural context, of course, explains nothing; rather, it is the culture context that requires explanation (Lawson and McCauley 1993; Atran 2002: 10; Tooby and Cosmides 1992).

Anticipating by almost fifty years arguments about culture as an abstraction requiring explanation, Karl Popper argued that "history" too is such an abstraction (Popper [1945] 1950: 463). While historical generalizations, such as periodizations, have heuristic warrant if explicitly and carefully stipulated, they often represent distortions of the historical evidence born of the interests of professional historians. Is, for example, a Hellenistic period of religious history, to be described *politically* as the period between the conquests of Alexander and those of Augustus, as this age was originally delineated by J. G. Droysen (Droysen Vol. I, 1836: 3)? Is a new Christian period of religious history also to be described politically from the birth of Jesus in the time of this same Caesar Augustus, as New Testament theologians so eagerly accepted on the basis of the Lukan testament (Luke 2:1–7)? Or might a Hellenistic period of *religious* history better be periodized as culminating with the legitimization of Christianity by Constantine at the beginning of the fourth century—or more decisively, with the official establishment of Christianity over non-Christian religions that was decreed by Theodosius at the end of that century (Martin 1983: 132–37)? And is the so-called Great Man theory of history, itself a revision of eighteenth-century political criteria for periodization in light of the values of nineteenth-century romanticism (e.g., Thomas Carlyle 1840), the best way in which to organize the ideas and events originated from and transmitted by ordinary human minds at all—whether that great man is Alexander or Augustus, Constantine or Theodosius, Jesus or Paul? Might not twentieth-century histories of *mentalités*, influenced by anthropological methods, provide more adequate criteria for historiographical periodization (Martin 2004b)? From a cognitive perspective, of course, *mentalités* would not be understood as the product of social construction but as a consequence of distributed mental representations, transmitted on the basis, perhaps, of the epidemiological model suggested by Dan Sperber (Sperber 1996), or perhaps more intentionally, as proposed by the cognitive anthropologist Harvey Whitehouse (2004).

2.3. *Cognition, Transmission and History*

Historians are concerned with matters of transmission, perhaps preeminently so. Not every mental representation that is possible, however, is successfully transmitted and not all mental representations that are transmitted become public. As this important insight is expressed by Whitehouse,

> religion [for example] is not the sum of all mental events, actions, and artifacts created by religious people. Rather, it consists of all those private and public representations that have become widely distributed as recognizably similar tokens of the same thing.... And so, the challenge of... [a history of religions] is, first and foremost, one of identifying particular mechanisms that drive the selection of culturally widespread representations in preference to all the other representations that fleeting occur in [or, we might add, that are imported into] any population. (Whitehouse 2004: 7; see Lawson 1994.)

To identify these mechanisms of selection, Whitehouse has proposed a theory of divergent modes of religious transmission, which he terms "doctrinal" and "imagistic." According to Whitehouse's theory, these divergent modes of religiosity are the consequence of an interrelationship between and interdependency among multiple variables, an epistemological premise that is familiar to historians and evolutionary theorists alike (Gaddis 2002: 53; Donald 1991: 139). These variables include the alternative ways by which religious knowledge is processed and encoded, the ways by which this knowledge relies on and is constrained by different systems of memory, and the ways by which the scale and structure of religious traditions and their patterns of distribution and transformation are determined over time.

The doctrinal modality is characterized by a set of beliefs, which must remain stable, and/or by practices, the performance of which must be precise, and which become encoded in semantic memory through repetition as a set of scripts or schemas. Such scripted doctrines and practices are themselves readily repeatable and are, consequently, readily able to be distributed by missionaries and teachers beyond the core group. If a hierarchical leadership and centralized structure is developed to control and to maintain these doctrines and practices, they can become the basis for widespread community.

By contrast, the mode of transmission characteristic of the imagistic modality is infrequently performed rituals that exhibit high sensory pageantry, epitomized by dramatic, even traumatic, initiatory rites. The emotional salience generally associated with such dramatic events ensures that they will be encoded in the episodic or autobiographical memory system from which recall is relatively precise. Although any initially shared meaning for these enigmatic events may well remain occluded with personal constructions of analogical significance resulting, a strong sense of group solidarity will be produced among fellow participants since their recall will focus upon the details of those who have together experienced such terrifying ordeals. This sense of "kinship," forged under common conditions of stress, results in a perseverance of small face-to-face communities. And although the analogical meanings attributed such ordeals by individual participants may become shaped over time by the initiating authorities, the resulting corpus of knowledge will remain local, a characteristic of the initiatory group.

By the first century C.E., religious traditions in the Roman world had indeed diverged into the modalities predicted by Whitehouse.

3. *Towards a Cognitive History of Roman Religions (Including the Early Christianities)*

3.1. *Divergent Modes of Religious Transmission in the Roman World*

The official state religion of the Roman Empire conformed to the variables predicted by Whitehouse for the doctrinal mode of religiosity. Roman religion was concerned with "the meaning of Roman life and history" (Beard et al. 1998, I: 75, 113), and the values of this "Romanness" (Turcan 1996: 195) were transmitted and codified through countless iterations and reiterations of sacrificial practices that resulted in a set of officially sanctioned ritual scripts. By the time of the Empire, these scripts were maintained and transmitted by a hierarchy of religio-political authorities: domestically by the *paterfamilias*, by the *magister* of the *collegia*, and at the state level by the public priests or, upon occasion, by action of the Roman Senate itself (Scheid 2003: 79–80). From 12 B.C.E., all of the "fixed and formal" practices of Roman religion became subject to prescribed and precise regulations (Pliny, *Naturalis Historia* 28.11; Beard et al. 1996, II: 129) that were controlled, according to the first century C.E. Roman historian Valerius Maximus, by "the knowledge of the *pontifices*" (Val. Max., 1.1.1a–b; Beard et al. 1998, I: 192).

In contrast to the doctrinal modality of the official Roman religion, an imagistic mode of religiosity became widely and popularly instantiated throughout the Roman Empire by the Hellenistic mystery cults, especially those of Dionysus, Cybele, Isis, and Mithras, from the first and second centuries C.E. The dramatic initiatory practices of these cults, aptly termed "rites of terror," began with preparations that included somatic and psychological deprivations such as fasting, meditation and, perhaps, psychotropic medication. The rites themselves were held in darkness and involved exposure to life-threatening ordeals—or at least threat of such—and employed such dramatic effects as light shows, displays of bizarre imagery, the use of masks and costumes, and sounds of evocative rhythms produced by exotic instruments and chanting. Finally, the initiates emerged from the psychological disorientation of their nocturnal ordeals into an anticipated light of cognitive reorientation that was termed in the Graeco-Roman world "rebirth" (Thomassen 2003: 221). In contrast to the repetitive routines that were characteristic of ritual practice in the doctrinal modality, such ritually induced "experiences" of enlightenment could only be encoded into the episodic memory system of initiates as unique events to be recalled as the focus for what Whitehouse terms "spontaneous exegetical reflections." Such personal revelations, over time, could be consolidated into the local knowledge characteristic of such initiatory groups or, at best, of regionally proximate cells (Martin 2005b).

Although scholars generally identify the sundry mystery traditions on the basis of their claims upon a common patron deity, none of these cults, to our knowledge, ever developed even the idea of centralized organization. In the absence of such bureaucratic structure, any religious ideas or practices attributed by historians to these associations in common remain incidental inferences from a shared culture (Smith 1990: 116–42) or historiographical confabulations.

The proliferation of small-scale groups in the face of Roman imperialism is unsurprising given the evolutionary history of *Homo sapiens*. As Pascal Boyer has observed:

> our systems for social interaction did not evolve in the context of vast groups and abstract institutions.... We evolved as small bands of foragers and that kind of existence is the context in which we developed the special features of our social mind. Sedentary settlements, large tribes, kingdoms and other such modern institutions are [a very recent development]. (Boyer 2001: 250.)

When large-scale political societies did develop, Boyer notes, people nevertheless still tended to cluster in face-to-face "solidarity-based groups" (Boyer 2001: 249). As I have noted elsewhere, the United States, for example, is rife with what the nineteenth-century French observer Alexis de Tocqueville described as "secondary associations" (Tocqueville 1900: II.2.5). As a more recent observer has noted, again with reference to the United States, such subcultures arise and flourish most notably "in places that lack rootedness" (Sides 1992: 17–18). It was such a decline in traditional locative definitions of sociality that was characteristic of the Hellenistic world and that occasioned the rise of secondary associations throughout the Roman Empire (Martin 2004a).

Boyer reports further that such "solidarity-based groups" always tend to be of "the same size and involve similar emotions, regardless of the country, language, size of the institution or town, and other differences" (Boyer 2001: 249). The ubiquity of such predictable social characteristics suggests the operation of panhuman constraints. Arguments have been made, for example, that the extent of group size—like the number of characters in a successful story—is structured by constraints upon the information processing capacities of human brains (Dunbar 1993) and by those of short-term memory (D'Andrade 1995: 42–44). The emergence and perseverance of small-scale societies represents, it would seem, an evolutionary and cognitive optimum for sociopolitical organization by *H. sapiens* (Tiger and Fox 1971: 238–39; Willhoite 1981: 251). The early Christianities offer no exception.

3.2. *Divergent Modes of Religious Transmission among the Early Christianities*

Since publication in 1934 of Walter Bauer's influential *Rechtgläubigkeit und Ketzerei im ältesten Christentum*, historians and biblical scholars have increasingly recognized that the evidence for early Christianity documents a plurality of small, autonomous groups, similar to those familiar from the Hellenistic mysteries. The historiographical task has been, first of all, to discriminate among these various early Christian groups, which biblical scholars have accomplished on the basis of their *form-, traditions-, and redaktionsgeschichtliche* inquiries into the textual productions of these groups. More recently, some biblical scholars have sought to discern from these texts, as from any social manufacture, what might be deduced about the various interests and intents of the differing groups that produced and transmitted them. Although these researchers have neglected the evidence of Christian material culture and attended solely to textual evidence, a commitment to the narrative record that continues to establish the agenda for their research, they have nevertheless proposed a tentative inventory of various early "Christian" groups (Cameron and Miller 2004). Once differentiated, the evidence suggests that at least some of the early Christian groups conformed to the imagistic modality of religion described by Whitehouse and documented from Graeco-Roman religiosity generally.

Imagistic Modalites among the Early Christianities
Admission into the early Christian groups was by an initiatory rite of baptism (Thomassen 2003). Although it might be somewhat venturesome to characterize this initiatory practice as a "rite of terror," it was modeled, it would seem, on the still undomesticated desert practices of John the Baptist, especially as these are portrayed in Q (Matt 3:7–10// Luke 3:7–9) and in the synoptic gospels (Matt 3:1–17; Mark 1:2–11; Luke 3:1–22). The widespread influence of this enigmatic figure is further documented among the early Christianities from the gospels of John (John 1:15–34), Thomas (*Gos. Thom.* 46) and the Jewish-Christian Gospel of the Ebionites (Epiphanius, *Panarion* 30.13.7–8), in the epistles of Paul (1 Cor 12:13) and from early Church practices (Acts 2:38–41), as well as from Christian material culture (Snyder 2003: 77, 111–22). Although the dramatic rites seemingly associated with early Christian baptism soon became replaced, among some groups at least, with *catacheses* (e.g., the *Didache*), second- and third-century sources still speak of preparations for this Christian rite that required the nakedness of initiates (Hippolytus, *Traditio apostolica* 21.3), nocturnal fasts and vigils, confessions of sin (Tertullian, *De baptismo* 20; Justin Martyr, *1 Apol.* 61), renunciations of the devil, and daily exorcisms (Tertullian, *De corona militis* 3; Hippolytus, *Trad. ap.* 20.3). At the end of the second century, Tertullian could still compare Christian baptism with Mithraic initiatory rites (Tertullian, *Bapt.* 5; *De praescriptione haereticorum* 40).

In addition to the cognitive shocks that may have been induced by early Christian rites of baptism, the parables of Jesus, which most certainly circulated independently of and prior to their subsequent narrative catchments, have been characterized as ambiguous stories drawn from everyday life whose analogical "vividness or strangeness" seem designed to deliver an "imaginative shock" to their hearers (Gragg 2004, following Dodd 1936: 5; Jeremias 1955; Funk 1966: 138–39). Similarly, the collected sayings of Jesus in Q and in the *Gospel of Thomas* have been described as being largely local, enigmatic and evocative (Mack 1993: 105; on the "local" character of these sayings, see Arnal 2001). In addition to the initiatory baptismal rites, in other words, the imaginative surprises that were conveyed by the parable and sayings traditions may well have induced among Christian converts the "spontaneous exegetical reflections" that are characteristic of the personal "revelations" predicted for the imagistic modality of transmission. The opening challenge of the *Gospel of Thomas* to find "meaning" in the "obscure (or hidden)" sayings of Jesus exemplifies this technique as verbal expression (*Gos. Thom.* 1) and recalls Richard Reitzenstein's suggestion at the beginning of the last century for the existence of *Lese-Mysterien* or "literary mysteries" in which "revelations" might be evoked through the written word (Reitzenstein 1927: 52, 64). The cognitive anthropologist Brian Malley has recently shown how one contemporary group of evangelical Christians is still able to find such personal meanings even from the canonical narratives of the Bible (Malley 2004).

Doctrinal Modalities of Religion among Early Christians
Initially, it seems as if Paul's revelatory experience of conversion might also conform to the variables predicted for the imagistic mode of religiosity. What Paul took to be "revelation," however, was apparently based upon his considered interpretation of some form of spontaneously excited neural activity rather than upon any such activity that had been ritually induced as a technique for the transmission of knowledge (Boyer 2003: 121). And indeed, Paul specifically emphasizes that his revelation was not the result of any mode of transmission (Gal 1: 11–12). Rather, Paul insisted that salvific knowledge was not to be obtained through ritual practices such as baptism but by faith (Rom 1:16, 17; 3:26, 28, 30, etc.). And although Paul acknowledged that he had, in fact, baptized a few people in Corinth, he nevertheless asserted that Christ had not sent him "to baptize but to preach" (1 Cor 1:14–17). Although Pauline communities continued to practice baptism, this rite wasn't the initiatory ritual associated with revelation that it seemed to be for the Jesus groups but, rather, indicated membership in an anonymous (spiritual) community of correctly held faith (1 Cor 12: 13).

Paul's view of right faith is nowhere more clearly expressed than in his opposition to the charismatic practices of the Christian community in Corinth (1 Cor 12)—yet another example of a Christian group operating on the basis of personal revelation. Paul insisted that such spiritual practices, and especially glossolalia, be regulated by instruction (*oikodomē, katēchēsis*) and by reasoned interpretation (*nous, diermēnia*) (1 Cor 14:5, 13–15). And he leaves little doubt that it is his own authority that is to be the criterion for the correctly reasoned interpretation to which the local revelations associated with spiritual practices must yield. For *his* teachings, he asserts, are themselves "a command of the Lord" (1 Cor 14:37). "If any one does not recognize this," Paul concludes, "he is not recognized" (1 Cor 14:38) and can, as Paul so bluntly put it, simply "go to hell" (*anathema estō*) (Gal 1:6–9).

Paul continued his didactic relationship with the communities he had founded through his subsequent correspondence with them, in which he persisted in attempting to formulate the tenants of his faith as an authoritative script to be learned and disseminated. Paul did not realize his vision of a centralized form of Christianity with himself as the arbiter of orthodoxy, even within his own "Pauline" communities, as ongoing disputes within them illustrates (e.g., Gal 1:6–9; 1 Cor 1:10–17). Nevertheless he articulated a principle of authority and transmission that later developed into the doctrinal modality of Christian orthodoxy (Meade 1987: 116–18), a development clearly evident in deutero-Pauline traditions (Meade 1987: 122–30).

3.3. *The Emergence of "the" Christian Story*

If enumerated or analogical forms of knowledge are permanently to survive and be transmitted, they must be inscribed in some form of material culture, as was the case with Mesopotamian lists, or they must be blended into the more memorable and transmissible framework of narrative. It is unsurprising, therefore, that the sayings and parables attributed to Jesus, all of which initially circulated independently of any narrative structure, would, for mnemonic and transmissive reasons drift towards narratives that might be readily rehearsed and widely comprehended (Sperber 1996: 95). But why, in the case of the early Christianities, was the drift that proved successful towards *biographical* narrative? Although the Greeks had long shown interest in the lives of their heroes, especially in their funerary orations, the biographical form *per se* seems only to have emerged late in the first century C.E. or early in the second with Plutarch's *Lives* and Arrian's *Life of Alexander*. While some of these tended towards apotheosis, none of them recounted the life of an incarnate deity.

Cognitive scientists of religion have shown that tacit apprehensions of gods seem always to ensure that they are represented as intentional agents capable of social interactions (e.g., Barrett 1998, 1999; Barrett and Keil 1996). These anthropomorphic representations of gods are cognitive constructions based upon our "theory of mind," our ability to attribute to others beliefs and desires like our own (Baron-Cohen 1995) and with whom, consequently, we can relate. Unlike accounts of great deeds by the august deities of Rome or of the salvific accomplishments of the cosmic gods of the Mysteries, the biographical narratives of Jesus constructed the Christian Son of God as a socially accessible and abiding friend. It is interesting to note that Mithras, the Roman *Sol Invictus*, has recently been re-represented by contemporary neo-paganists precisely as the beloved friend of initiates (Nabarz 2005: ix, 5), as, indeed, is his earliest association in the *Rig-Veda* (Bivar 1994: 61). The biographical narratives into which the early Christian aphorisms and analogies were consolidated provided, in other words, a mnemonic framework for a story about a divine actor which was in greater accord with tacit cognitive templates than were those offered by alternative Roman religions. The cognitive appeal of these biographically framed consolidations was rendered even more attractive—and memorable—by the inclusion of miracle stories which grabbed the attention not only of the fictional characters of the narratives but that of the readers of these narratives as well.

The conventional privileging of self-interested narratives by historians has not resulted in any convincing historical explanations for the perseverance and dominance of one modality of Christianity in the face of its alternatives—Christian or non-Christian. Nor have efforts to discover the social interests of those traditions, since these descriptions tend to describe commonalities shared by the various contemporaneous social formations. It would seem, rather, that any historical explanation for the successful consolidation, perseverance, and eventual religious dominance of a particular form of Christian knowledge would benefit from a consideration of the ways by which mental processes have shaped these contents and the cognitive dynamics of their transmission.

4. *Conclusion*

Historiography sometimes seems fraught with insurmountable problems. Because of its generally incomplete character, a consequence both of accident and of intent, and its frequently ambiguous quality, historical evidence often appears to be incommensurable if not incomprehensible. Historians must always presume, therefore, some theoretical framework, whether acknowledged or not, if their historiographical accounts are to make any coherent sense (Simmel 1905: 47–51). As Simmel already proposed, historians may well benefit from acknowledging and beginning with mental reality, which comes "first in the rational order of things" and which might well invest historical remains with significance and pattern.

I do not intend to suggest that approaches to the past based on cognitive theorizing can or should replace the specialized methods of professional historians. I do propose, however, that the conclusions of cognitive scientists can offer well-founded theories that can supplement and provide correctives to these traditional tools. And it can do so by identifying and explaining data that have been produced by ordinary processes of human cognition but that have otherwise been neglected in favor of more explicit forms of data or evidence which historians have, for one reason or another, come to privilege. These theories can contribute insights into how and why some representations of historical occurrences emerged, were selected for, and remembered but not others that may have been culturally, historically, or cognitively possible. They also promise explanations for how and why religious representations have been exploited as efficient ways by which elaborated and complex information such as codes of behavior or morality, social knowledge, or political ideology have been legitimated and successfully transmitted over time.

Proposals for applying cognitive theorizing to historiographical methods raises questions concerning the employment of *any* theorizing for connecting the dots of surviving data. When, in other words, historians are confronted with insufficient evidence from which to piece together a plausible scenario for their historiographical reconstructions, how many data are required to justify completing that scenario on the basis of theoretical modeling? If, for example, a theory predicts the presence of a specific number of stipulated variables for organizing a particular historical scenario and some but not all of these variables are documented from the surviving evidence, are historians, in the absence of explicit evidence to the contrary, justified in filling out their target scenario on the basis of that theoretical model? What constitutes a sufficient number of the predicted variables responsibly to do so? And what, exactly, is the explanatory basis for the range of variables deployed in the first place? Such questions invoke, of course, the judgement of the historian, and instantiate why historiography, despite advances in scientifically based modeling, will never be an exact science—though it might become much more exact than when left solely to the subjective inferences of individual historians.

REFERENCES

Allegro, John M. 1956. "Further Messianic References in Qumrân Literature." *Journal of Biblical Literature* 75: 174–87.
———. 1958. "Fragments of a Qumrân Scroll of Eschatological Midrashim." *Journal of Biblical Literature* 77: 350–54.

Alt, Albrecht, 1951. "Die Weisheit Salamos." *Theologische Literaturzeitung* 76: 139–44.
Arnal, William E. 2001. *Jesus and the Village Scribes.* Minneapolis, Minn.: Fortress.
Atran, Scott. 2002. *In Gods We Trust: The Evolutionary Landscape of Religion.* New York: Oxford University Press.
Baron-Cohen, Simon. 1995. *Mindblindness: An Essay on Autism and Theory of Mind.* Cambridge, Mass.: MIT Press.
Barrett, Justin L. 1998. "Cognitive Constraints of Hindu Concepts of the Divine." *Journal for the Scientific Study of Religion* 37: 608–19.
———. 1999. "Theological Correctness: Cognitive Constraints and the Study of Religion." *Method & Theory in the Study of Religion* 11: 325–39.
Barrett, Justin L, and Frank C. Keil. 1996. "Anthropomorphism and God Concepts: Conceptualizing a Non-Natural Entity." *Cognitive Psychology* 31: 219–47.
Barth, Fredrik. 1975. *Ritual Knowledge among the Baktaman of New Guinea.* New Haven, Conn.: Yale University Press.
———. 1987. *Cosmologies in the Making: A Generative Approach to Cultural Variation in Inner New Guinea.* Cambridge: Cambridge University Press.
Bateson, Gregory. 1972. *Steps to an Ecology of Mind.* New York: Ballantine.
Bauer, Walter. 1934. *Rechtgläubigkeit und Ketzerei im ältesten Christentum.* Tübingen: Mohr/Siebeck. English translation, edited by R. Kraft and G. Krodel. Philadelphia: Fortress, 1971.
Beard, Mary, John North, and Simon Price. 1998. *Religions of Rome*, Vol. 1: *A History*; Vol. II: *A Sourcebook.* Cambridge: Cambridge University Press.
Becker, Carl L. [1932.] 1969. "Everyman His Own Historian." *American Historical Review* 37: 221–36. Reprinted and cited here from *The Historian as Detective: Essays on Evidence*, edited by R. W. Winks, 5–23. New York: Harper & Row.
Bivar, A. D. H. 1994. "Towards an Integrated Picture of Ancient Mithraism." In *Studies in Mithraism*, edited by J. R. Hinnells, 61–73. Rome: "L'Erma" di Bretschneider.
Boroditsky, Lera. 2000. "Metaphoric Structuring: Understanding Time through Spatial Metaphors." *Cognition* 75: 1–28.
Boyer, Pascal. 2001. *Religion Explained: The Evolutionary Origins of Religious Thought.* New York: Basic Books.
———. 2003. "Religious Thought and Behaviour as By-products of Brain Function." *Trends in Cognitive Sciences* 7, 3: 119–24.
Cameron, Ron, and Merrill Miller, eds. 2004. *Redescribing Christian Origins.* Atlanta, Ga.: Scholar's Press/Leiden: E. J. Brill.
Carlyle, Thomas. 1840. *On Heroes, Hero-Worship, and the Heroic in History.* London: Chapman and Hull.
Chadwick, Henry. 1969. "Florilegium." In *Reallexikon für Antike und Christentum*, edited by Th.Klauser, Vol. VII:. 1131–60. Stuttgart: Anton Hiersemann.
Collingwood, Robin G. [1946.] 1956. *The Idea of History.* New York: Oxford University Press.
D'Andrade, Roy. 1995. *The Development of Cognitive Anthropology.* Cambridge: Cambridge University Press.
Dodd, C. H. 1936. *The Parables of the Kingdom.* New York: Charles Scribner's Sons.
Donald, Merlin. 1991. *Origins of the Modern Mind: Three Stages in the Evolution of Culture and Cognition.* Cambridge, Mass.: Harvard University Press.
Droysen, Johan G. 1836. *Geschichte des Hellenismus*, 3 vols. (1836–1843; 2nd ed., 1877; new ed. by Erich Bayer, 1952–1953). Reprint, München: Deutscher Taschenbuch, 1980.
Dunbar, Robin. I. M. 1993. "Coevolution of Neocortical Size, Groups Size and Language in Humans." *Behavioral and Brain Sciences* 16: 681–735.
Dunbar, Robin, Louise Barrett, and John Lycett. 2005. *Evolutionary Psychology: A Beginner's Guide: Human Behaviour, Evolution and the Mind.* Oxford: Oneworld.
Edelman, Gerald M. 2004. *Wider Than the Sky: The Phenomenal Gift of Consciousness.* New Haven: Yale University Press.

Fauconnier, Gilles, and Mark Turner. 2002. *The Way We Think: Conceptual Blending and the Mind's Hidden Complexities*. New York: Basic Books.

Foucault, Michel. 1970. *The Order of Things: An Archaeology of the Human Sciences*. New York: Random House.

Funk, Robert W. 1966. *Language, Hermeneutic and Word of God*. New York: Harper & Row.

Gaddis, John Lewis. 2002. *The Landscape of History: How Historians Map the Past*. Oxford: Oxford University Press.

Gentner, Dedre, Keith J. Holyoak, and Boicho N. Kokinov. 2001. *The Analogical Mind: Perspectives from Cognitive Science*. Cambridge, Mass.: MIT Press.

Godelier, Maurice. 1986. *The Mental and the Material: Thought, Economy and Society*. Translated by M. Thom. London: Verso.

Gordon, Richard. 1999. "'What's in a List?' Listing in Greek and Graeco-Roman Malign Magical Texts." In *The World of Ancient Magic: Papers from the First International Samson Eitrem Seminar at the Norwegian Institute at Athens, 4–8 May 1997*, edited by David R. Jordan, Hugo Montgomery and Einar Thomassen, 239–77. Bergen: Norwegian Institute at Athens.

Gottschall, Jonathan, and David Slone Wilson, eds. 2005. *The Literary Animal: Evolution and the Nature of Narrative*. Evanston, Ill.: Northwestern University Press.

Gragg, Douglas L. 2004. "Parables, Cognitive Shock, and Spontaneous Exegetical Reflection: An Application of Harvey Whitehouse's Concept of Imagistic Modality." Unpublished manuscript.

Hegel, G. W. F. 1861. *The Philosophy of History*. Translated by J. Sibree. New York: Dover, 1956.

Jeremias, Joachim. 1955. *The Parables of Jesus*. Translated by S. H. Hooke. New York: Charles Scribner's Sons.

Lawson, E. Thomas. 1994. "Counterintuitive Notions and the Problem of Transmission: The Relevance of Cognitive science for the Study of History." In *History, Historiography and the History of Religions*, edited by Luther H. Martin, special issue of *Historical Reflections/ Réflexions Historiques* 20 (3): 481–95.

Lawson, E. Thomas, and Robert N. McCauley. 1993. "Crisis of Conscience, Riddle of Identity: Making Space for a Cognitive Approach to Religious Phenomena." *Journal of the American Academy of Religion* 61: 201–23.

Lease, Gary. 2003. "Rationality and Evidence: The Study of Religion as a Taxonomy of Human Natural History." In *Rationality and the Study of Religion*, edited by Jeppe S. Jensen and Luther H. Martin. London: Routledge.

Lemche, Niels Peter. 1998. *The Israelites in History and Tradition*. Louisville, Ky.: Westminster John Knox Press.

Lévi-Strauss, Claude. 1966. *The Savage Mind*. Chicago, Ill.: The University of Chicago Press.

Lloyd, Dan. 2004. *Radiant Cool: A Novel Theory of Consciousness*. Cambridge, Mass.: MIT Press.

Mack, Burton L. 1993. *The Lost Gospel: The Book of Q and Christian Origins*. New York: HarperCollins.

Malbon, Elizabeth Struthers. 1990. *The Iconography of the Sarcophagus of Junius Bassus*. Princeton, N.J.: Princeton University Press.

Malley, Brian. 2004. *How the Bible Works: An Anthropological Study of Evangelical Biblicism*. Walnut Creek, Calif.: AltaMira.

Martin, Luther H. 1983. "Why Cecropian Minerva? Hellenistic Religious Syncretism as System." *Numen* 30(2): 131–45.

———. 2004a. "The Very Idea of Globalization: The Case of Hellenistic Empire." In *Hellenisation, Empire and Globalisation: Lessons from Antiquity*, edited by L. H. Martin and P. Pachis, 123–39. Thessaloniki: Vanias.

———. 2004b. "Towards a Scientific History of Religions." In *Theorizing Religions Past: Archaeology, History, and Cognition*, edited by Harvey Whitehouse and Luther H. Martin, 7–14. Walnut Creek, Calif.: AltaMira.

———. 2005a. "Performativity, Discourse and Cognition: 'Demythologizing' the Roman Cult of Mithras." In *Rhetoric and Reality in Early Christianity*, edited by Willi Braun, 187–217. Waterloo: Wilfrid Laurier University Press.

———. 2005b. "Aspects of 'Religious Experience' among the Hellenistic Mystery Religions." *Religion & Theology* 12(3–4): 349–69.

Meade, David G. 1987. *Pseudonymity and Canon: An Investigation into the Relationship of Authorship and Authority in Jewish and Earliest Christian Tradition*. Grand Rapids, Mich.: Eerdmans.

Miller, George A. 1956. "The Magical Number Seven, Plus or Minus Two: Some Limits on Our Capacity for Processing Information." *Psychological Review* 63: 81–97.

Nabarz, Payam. 2005. *The Mysteries of Mithras: The Pagan Belief that Shaped the Christian World*. Rochester, Vt.: Inner Traditions.

Popper, Karl. [1945.] 1950. *The Open Society and Its Enemies*. Princeton, N.J.: Princeton University Press.

Reitzenstein, Richard. 1927 [1956]. *Die hellenistischen Mysterienreligionen: Nach Ihren Grundgedanken und Wirkungen*. Darmstadt: Wissenschaftliche Buchgesellschaft. English translation by John E. Steely. Pittsburgh, Pa.: The Pickwick Press, 1978.

Scheid, John. 2003. *An Introduction to Roman Religion*. Translated by J. Lloyd. Bloomington: Indiana University Press.

Sides, Hampton. 1992. *Stomping Grounds: A Pilgrim's Progress through Eight American Subcultures*. New York: Morrow.

Simmel, Georg. 1905. *The Problems of the Philosophy of History: An Epistemological Essay*. Translation of 2nd ed. by Guy Oakes. New York: Free Press, 1977.

———. 1923. *Die Probleme der Geschichtsphilosophie: Eine erkenntnistheoretische Studie*. Fünfte Aufgabe. Munich: Duncker & Humbolt.

Smith, Jonathan Z. 1982. *Imagining Religion: From Babylon to Jonestown*. Chicago, Ill.: The University of Chicago Press.

———. 1990. *Drudgery Divine: On the Comparison of Early Christianities and the Religions of Late Antiquity*. Chicago, Ill.: The University of Chicago Press.

Snyder, Graydon F. 2003. *Ante-Pacem: Archaeological Evidence of Church Life before Constantine*. 2nd ed. Macon, Ga.: Mercer University Press.

Soden, Wolfram von. 1936. "Leistung und Grenze sumerischer und babylonischer Wissenschaft." *Die Welt als Geschichte* 2: 411–64; 509–57.

Sperber, Dan. 1996. *Explaining Culture: A Naturalistic Approach*. Oxford: Blackwell.

Stiller, James, Daniel Nettle, and Robin I. M. Dunbar. 2003. "The Small World of Shakespeare's Plays." *Human Nature* 14: 397–408.

Sutton, David E. 1998. *Memories Cast in Stone: The Relevance of the Past in Everyday Life*. New York: Berg.

Thomassen, Einar. 2003. "Becoming a Different Person: Baptism as an Initiation Ritual." In *Theoretical Frameworks for the Study of Graeco-Roman Religion*, edited by Luther H. Martin and P. Pachis, 209–22. Thessaloniki: University Studio Press.

Tiger, Lionel, and Robin Fox. 1971. *The Imperial Animal*. New York: Holt, Rinehart and Winston.

Tocqueville, Alexis de. 1900. *Democracy in America*. Rev. ed. translated by H. Reeve. London: The Colonial Press.

Tooby, John, and Leda Cosmides. 1992. "The Psychological Foundations of Culture." In *The Adapted Mind: Evolutionary Psychology and the Generation of Culture*, edited by Jerome H. Barkow, Leda Cosmides, and John Tooby, 3–136. New York: Oxford University Press.

Turcan, Robert. 1996. *The Cults of the Roman Empire*. Translated by A. Nevil. Oxford: Blackwell.

Turner, Mark. 1996. *The Literary Mind: The Origins of Thought and Language*. New York: Oxford University Press.

Whitehouse, Harvey. 2000. *Arguments and Icons: Divergent Modes of Religiosity*. Oxford University Press.

———. 2004. *Modes of Religiosity: A Cognitive Theory of Religious Transmission*. Walnut Creek, Calif.: AltaMira.

Willhoite, Jr., Fred H. 1981. "Rank and Reciprocity: Speculations on Human Emotions and Political Life." In *Sociobiology and Human Politics*, edited by Elliott White. Lexington, Mass.: Lexington Books.

Wineburg, Sam. 2001. *Historical Thinking and Other Unnatural Acts: Charting the Future of Teaching the Past*. Philadelphia, Pa.: Temple University Press.

THE MYSTERY OF THE STOLEN BODY: EXPLORING CHRISTIAN ORIGINS

Ilkka Pyysiäinen

In what follows, I provide one example of how the cognitive science of religion can be profitably applied in the study of early Christianity (see also Martin 2004, 2005, this volume). I focus on the question of what the disciples believed to have happened to Jesus after his death and how their reflections on this affected the early spread of what later came to be known as Christianity.

1. *The Mystery of the Empty Tomb*

Pascal Boyer (2001: 228) bluntly observes that religion may be more about dead bodies than it is about death (as a metaphysical problem). This tentative suggestion is based on anecdotal anthropological evidence and cognitive theorizing on how persons react to the sight of a dead body. What we know for certain is that when a person dies, the corpse poses a very practical problem for the community of the living. As it is only a dead object, it must be disposed of in one way or another; yet the sight of the corpse still triggers the idea of personhood. Our ideas of the agentive properties of the deceased continue although we see biological bodies die (see Bering 2002, 2006). We cannot *see* the agentive properties die just as we do not see thoughts popping up from the brain. Because we do not see how thoughts and emotions emerge from the nervous system, we find it difficult to think that they cease with the death of the body (see Bering 2006).

Because of this cognitive tension, corpses are ritually buried while the ideas about the agentive properties of the deceased continue in our minds more or less as if nothing had happened. Dead agents are represented as absent but existing persons, quite unlike agents prior to their birth (Boyer 2001: 203–28; Bering 2006; cf. Pyysiäinen 2006). Given the importance of the death, burial and resurrection of Jesus for the Christian religion, it is important to ask what the facts about mentally representing dead agents might have to offer for explaining the early origins of Christianity. I start with the legend of the empty tomb and then proceed to analyze the resurrection narratives.

If Jesus was not simply left hanging on the cross, the Romans may have thrown the body in a lime pit (Sawicki 1994: 257), or the Jews might have buried it in a mass grave of executed criminals (Myllykoski 1991–1994: 2.105–6, 2002: 45–46, 81–82; see *m. Sanh.* 6:5–6). Many of the poor urban citizens of Rome in the late Republic (first century B.C.E.) had their corpses thrown into collective pits (*puticuli*) outside the city; especially during epidemics, mass death necessitated mass burials (Hopkins 1983: 207–11). The Romans also habitually left the bodies of crucified criminals unburied (Crossan 1995: 160–63; see Myllykoski 2002: 78–81).

However, the Romans also respected politically harmless Jewish customs. Therefore, if the Jews had asked for the body of Jesus in order to bury it, the Romans would quite likely have agreed. As Jewish customs did not favor the leaving of dead bodies lying around unburied during the Passover festival, it is quite likely that the high priests and other members of the Sanhedrin took care of the burial of the body of Jesus in a mass grave (Myllykoski 2002: 80–81). The rather enigmatic figure of Joseph of Arimathea, "a respected member of the council," may have had something to do with this although the details of the gospel accounts are problematic (Myllykoski 2002: 71–76). However, it suggests that the disciples did not know the exact location of the grave of Jesus. It is, then, at least a plausible hypothesis that the legend of the empty tomb originated when the disciples tried in vain to find the place where Jesus was buried.

Although our mental representations of the agentive properties of dead agents are decoupled from the physical body, we often try to preserve them by connecting them with something concrete, such as a tomb or some kind of memento, a small item that used to belong to the deceased, and so forth (see Fustel de Coulanges 1866: Book I, Ch. 2; Cumont 1922: 3–4, 44–69). Even the collective tombs in the Roman world had individual pigeon-holes marked by inscriptions, testifying to a concern for preserving individuality after death (Hopkins 1983: 216–17).

However, the earliest Christian community in Jerusalem seems not to have known the location of the tomb of Jesus; the place that is presently known as such was first identified by Constantine's mother Helena in 325 (see Myllykoski 2002: 47; cf. Walker 1990: 235–81). There is no evidence of the grave having been venerated as a holy place by the disciples; this lack of a cult of veneration cannot be explained by the supposed fact that the tomb was empty. It is precisely this emptiness that would have made it worthy of veneration, if only the location of the tomb had been known (see also Kirby 2005; Parsons 2005). The human imagination does not operate in a "theologically correct" manner but intuitively, focusing on salient but simple information (Barrett and Keil 1996; Barrett 1999). Therefore, the "theologically correct" belief in resurrection is not likely to have had the power to prevent persons from venerating an empty tomb had they known its location. But if there was no specific physical location to which the disciples could have attached their memories of Jesus, these memories may have become de-individuated, leading to experiences of apparitions of the risen Christ (see Myllykoski 1991–1994: 2.78–121).

It seems that the legends of the burial of Jesus and of the empty tomb did not originally belong together. Some scholars argue that the legend of the empty tomb in Mark 16:1–8 is Mark's own construction (Mack 1988: 308–9; Crossan 1995: 172–77; Carrier 2005). Richard Carrier (2005: 155–57), for example, thinks that Mark only meant it as a symbolic representation of the resurrection, not as a literal description of an empty tomb. Bousset and Bultmann have argued that Mark's description of how the women "said nothing to anyone, because they were afraid" might be based on the fact that the whole incident was Mark's creation (see Myllykoski 2002: 64–65). Others think that Mark utilized a piece of older tradition in his account of the empty tomb (e.g., Myllykoski 1991–1994: 2.106–21).

Paul, however, does not seem to know anything about the women and the empty tomb when he explains that Jesus had been buried and then raised on the third day (1 Cor 15:3–8). For him, it was only the perishable, physical body that had been buried while, in resurrection, the spiritual body was raised in glory (Myllykoski 2002: 68). Carrier (2005) develops further the view that Paul's idea of a spiritual resurrection was later turned into legends of Jesus having appeared to the disciples in flesh and blood. Lüdemann (2005), however, argues that, in 1 Cor 15:3–11, Paul actually tries to convince the Corinthians of the reality of bodily resurrection because the Corinthians, who were influenced by Gnosticism, had found it to be an incomprehensible idea. Be that as it may, the available historical evidence does not support the belief that Jesus was buried in an expensive tomb of the *arcosolium* type and that some of the disciples had found this tomb mysteriously empty.

2. Apparitions

It is often claimed that Christianity emerged from the disciples' visions or hallucinations of the risen Christ (Carrier 2005; also Lüdemann 1995; Wiebe 1997). Paul, for example, claims that his gospel is of divine origin (trans. New International Version): "I did not receive it from any man, nor was I taught it; rather, I received it by revelation from Jesus Christ" (Gal 1:12). However, in another context he says: "For what I received I passed on to you..." (1 Cor 15:3). The Greek words *paralambanō* and *paradidomai* used here are technical terms that refer to the handing on of rabbinical tradition. Consequently, Paul must be citing old tradition (Myllykoski 2002: 66). This contradicts his claim that he received his gospel directly as a revelation. For this and various other reasons, Price (2005) speculates that verses 3–11 are a later, post-Pauline interpolation. This, however, is not necessarily any more likely than its alternative (see Myllykoski 2002: 66–70).

In 1 Cor 15:3–8, Paul also claims that Jesus had appeared "to Peter, and then to the twelve." After that, he appeared "to more than five hundred of the brothers at the same time, most of whom are still living..." After appearing to James and the apostles, the Lord finally appeared to Paul himself. This list is not without problems; in some manuscripts, the number of twelve has actually been corrected to 11. Still more problematic is the claim about the 500 brothers about whom the gospels know nothing (Price 2005; cf. Barrett 1994: 341–42; Lüdemann 1994: 103–6; Luke 24:34; Acts 1:15). The most important issue is to identify Paul's psychological motive here. Price (2005: 88) sensibly asks why an eyewitness would appeal to a third hand list of other appearances. Matti Myllykoski (2002: 68), for his part, argues that Paul's intention here is to link himself to a chain of authorities who had seen the risen Lord.

It may be asked, however, whether such linking is necessary in the case where one really is an eyewitness. Chains of authority are usually important only when there is no direct connection to the ultimate, divine authority. Religious rituals, for example, consist of such chains. A priest can pronounce a couple man and wife because he has been ordained by a bishop who has been ordained by another bishop, and so on and so forth. The chain ends in Jesus Christ instituting the Church by ordaining Peter (McCauley and Lawson 2002: 18–30). In peoples' intuitions, it is a connection to the superhuman agent that is the most important factor determining the efficacy of the ritual (Barrett and Lawson 2001).

Thus, it is all the more astonishing that Paul's description of his revelatory experience is so stark (to put it mildly). He merely says that Jesus had "appeared" (*ōphthēs*) to him. On the basis of this brief remark alone, we cannot even be sure whether he is talking about a dream or a wakeful state. If, on the other hand, Paul implies that the Corinthians already knew everything about his revelatory experience, we may still wonder why no descriptions of it have survived in other sources. It is true that in Acts (9:3–9; 22:6–16; 26:12–18), we have more vivid descriptions of what happened on the road to Damascus, but they are mutually contradictory and seem to be based on fragmentary sources (see Price 2005: 88). We cannot rule out the possibility that Paul's alleged revelatory experience is only a rhetorical means of legitimating his authority. Thus, it seems rather artificial to seek the origins of Christianity in some special "experiences" (see Boyer 2001: 307–11).

However, some persons do have religious experiences which, in the words of neuropsychologist Ken Livingston (2005: 87), "reduce to particular patterns of activity in a large but reasonably well-defined portion of the central nervous system." Especially instability in the temporal lobes may cause vague feelings of presence and even visions, but these visions will always be shaped and interpreted by the concepts and beliefs the person in question knows prior to the experience (Proudfoot 1985; Sharf 1998; Pyysiäinen 2001: 109–39; Boyer 2001: 307–11). Buddhist mystics do not see the Virgin Mary, for example.

Thus, even if Paul really experienced some kind of altered state of consciousness (a micro-seizure in the temporal lobe), all inferences about it must have been made using concepts with which he was already familiar. Tradition makes sense of experience rather than being derived from it. Although a vision of the risen Christ may have convinced Paul of the fact that Jesus lives, it cannot explain why others found his proclamation plausible and appealing. Dramatic experiences and altered states of consciousness are relatively rare and cannot account for the spread of all the religious concepts and beliefs (Atran 2002). Hallucinatory visions of Christ presuppose early Christian beliefs rather than explain them. The emergence of Christianity thus cannot be explained without explaining why and how the relevant beliefs were successful in cultural selection; this, in turn, presupposes other arguments in addition to the idea of visions or hallucinations (see Pyysiäinen 2005).

Whereas Paul gives a mere dry list of persons to whom Jesus had appeared, the gospels present more vivid accounts of these appearances. As these accounts are known neither to Paul nor to the oldest gospel, Mark, they are likely to represent relatively late, legendary material. The earliest gospel, Mark, ends with the frightened women escaping from the empty tomb (Mark 16:8). The verses (16:9–20) that describe how Jesus appeared to the disciples and was taken into the heavens are a later addition to the text, repeating and applying Old Testament narratives about the patriarchs physically going to heaven (e.g., 2 Kings 2:11).

In Matthew (27:64), which was written a couple of decades after Mark, it is related how the chief priests and the Pharisees asked Pilate to give orders that the grave must be guarded for three days so that the disciples cannot come in the night to steal and carry away the body. Matthew (28:9–10, 20) then reports how Jesus appears to the women and later makes the simple promise to be with his followers "always, to the very end of the age," without any mention of an ascension into heaven. Luke (24:13–27, 36–37) has Jesus appear to the disciples who do not recognize him. When he reappears, the disciples regard him as a ghost. In the latest gospel, John (20:11–29), Jesus first appears to Mary Magdalene and then to the eleven who sit behind locked doors; Jesus shows his wounded hands and feet to convince Doubting Thomas that he really is of flesh and blood.

If the location where Jesus was buried was not known to the disciples, it is quite likely that traditional beliefs about ghosts were activated under proper circumstances (see Honko 1991). In the Greco-Roman world, the belief that the dead still somehow existed after death was common, albeit receiving many different expressions (see Fustel de Coulanges 1866: Book I; Cumont 1922; Hopkins 1983: 226–35; Walker 1985). The dead who have not been properly buried have been believed to haunt the living all over the world (Pentikäinen 1968, 1969; Johnston 1999). The ancient Israelite practice of commemorating the dead, caring for them and feeding them, is also well attested in ancient Near Eastern sources, although it has been debated whether the Israelites believed in the supernatural beneficent powers of the dead (Schmidt 1994). These kinds of beliefs seem to be fairly common everywhere and to be anchored in the way the human mind works in representing the idea of a dead agent (see Rosengren, Johnson, and Harris 2000; Bering 2002). In Luke's version of the legend, the disciples indeed regard Jesus as a ghost. Luke must have known that such spontaneous belief was a very likely outcome under these specific circumstances and thus used this motif in his account.

Jesus appearing to his followers after his death thus is best understood as a literary motif that was attention-grabbing and "contagious." It spread effectively in the form of narratives. If the disciples ever saw actual apparitions, it is precisely these kinds of narratives that would have made such apparitions possible. Although vague feelings of presence can be experienced irrespective of any traditional beliefs, it is these beliefs that give more precise content to experiences and also help trigger them (Pyysiäinen 2001: 109–30). If, on the other hand, by "experience" we mean everything "that happens to one and has an effect on the mind and feelings" (Räisänen 2000: 192), the concept no longer has much explanatory value and cannot help distinguish between visions and ordinary perception. In the light of Bering's findings (see below), the stories of Jesus still walking around would have had a natural appeal to the disciples' minds, without the mediation of "religious experience." As Parsons (2005: 437) puts it, "the postmortem 'sightings' of Jesus are no more remarkable than the similar reports about Elvis Presley or Jimmy Hoffa."

3. *Urban Legends and Dead Agents*

Let me introduce the following legend as an analogy. The grandmother of a family had died; the family wanted to have her buried in the family plot which was situated far away. It turned out that the cheapest way of transporting the corpse was to buy poor granny a train ticket in the sleeping compartment. The family then put the body on the top bunk in the sleeping car, explaining to the woman riding in the same compartment that granny was not feeling too well. But the woman should not worry as some relatives would pick her up at her destination. The woman, however, soon realized that granny was dead. She was afraid of being charged with murder and threw the body out of the door. At the destination, she explained to the astonished relatives that granny had left the train at the previous stop.

There are many different versions of the story about the "stolen grandmother." In some versions, the body really is stolen from a parked car while the family is having lunch. These kinds of stories are often referred to as "urban legends" or "contemporary legends": short, stereotyped reports of either appalling or amusing—but always unexpected—incidents (see Brunvand 1989; af Klintberg 1986). The stories spread like wildfire, with several versions of a theme rapidly being found all over the world. Such effective spread might be said to be due to two conditions: on the one hand, the story includes an expectation-incongruent element, such as a corpse in a sleeping compartment or a dead rat in a pizza; on the other hand, the events always take place in very familiar, everyday settings. Heath et al. (2001) have experimentally shown that legends tapping such basic emotions as surprise and disgust survive the best in cultural selection. People prefer to pass along legends that produce the highest level of disgust.

In most cases, it is not possible to find out how a particular version of the story had originated. Although ordinary human experiences of such things as corpses and trains form the natural basis of these stories, we usually cannot establish any straightforward link between a story and specific real-life events. It is not the case that the story about the stolen grandmother could be shown to have originated from what happened to this or that particular family.

The problem is the missing link connecting the first version of the story and some real event(s). Legends do not usually emerge from historical events without the mediation of other types of verbal accounts. For the most part, we are dealing with so-called "memorates," short personal reports of what happened to the narrator under specified circumstances. Memorates often gradually become schematized into legends and thus form part of the so-called "collective tradition" of a community (as distinguished from individual traditions). The collective tradition, in turn, forms models that guide people's experiences and their interpretation (Honko 1964; Pentikäinen 1968: 109–12). To quote Daniel Dennett (1993: 136; see also Pyysiäinen 2004: 147–59), since

> narratives are under continual revision, there is no single narrative that counts as the canonical version, the 'first edition' in which are laid down, for all time, the events that happened in the stream of consciousness of the subject, all deviations from which must be corruptions of the text.

In other words, our memories of what happened are constantly being updated and revised, it being impossible to get hold of any original version of a story.

To get back to our story, what would you think happened when the relatives could not find granny's body in the train? Did they really think that someone had stolen or destroyed the body? What if they had second thoughts and began to suspect that maybe granny was not dead, after all? Weird things do happen. In the many cases in which a person has simply disappeared for good, her or his relatives often hope against hope that the person in question is not really dead. As long as the body is not found, there is hope. Some do not even believe that Elvis Presley is dead.

The psychologist Jesse Bering (2002) has conducted some interesting empirical experiments on this. The subjects who had some kinds of religious beliefs were found to think that it was precisely desires and thoughts that continued after death whereas such states as thirst, illness or auditory perceptions were much more unlikely to continue. Even those subjects who regarded death as the final end considered desires, emotions and thoughts more likely to continue after death than the more bodily states.

Bering tested 84 students with different kinds of beliefs about the afterlife, including non-belief. The subjects were read two stories about a person who dies. Then their beliefs about the possible afterlife condition of the dead person were probed. Those who regarded death as the final end should have thought that no mental or bodily states continue after death whereas, for example, those who believed in reincarnation should have thought that all states continue, but this did not happen. All subjects regarded thoughts and emotions as being more likely to continue after death. The subjects clearly had some background intuitions about the afterlife that were not reducible to their explicit beliefs adopted from their culture.

We know, however, that the urban legend about the stolen grandmother is just a legend. There are no rituals or social institutions arranged around it and people do not organize their lives according to this belief. Although some may believe that there is a real event behind the legend, the belief is not taken very seriously. No one would kill or die because of this belief. In brief, the legend of the stolen granny does not involve religious belief (see Pyysiäinen 2003). The interesting question, however, is whether religious movements can, *in principle*, be organized around these types of legends. Unless we think that religions are formed only around true beliefs, it is obvious that a legend of this type could start a new religious movement.

Consider the alleged cases of a UFO crash at Roswell, New Mexico in 1947, and of a conspiracy in the background of the 9/11 events in New York in 2001. In 1947, an air balloon carrying military instruments came down at Roswell. A local newspaper published a tongue-in-cheek feature, explaining that a flying saucer had landed at Roswell. Rumors started to spread, and in 1980 they were presented as the truth in the book *The Roswell Incident* by Charles Berlitz and William Moore. Today, there are even museums in Roswell exhibiting crash-related artifacts, including pictures of extraterrestrials. Many people now believe that a UFO with aliens onboard really crashed at Roswell (Saler, Ziegler, and Moore 1997; Lewis 1995). What might have happened if we had had no means of finding a rational explanation and if true believers had been promised a life eternal (Carrier 2005: 174–75)? Likewise, many people firmly believe that the 9/11 events were maneuvered by the US government; they see every single detail as supporting this alleged conspiracy; no competing explanation seemingly can convince them of the numerous problems with their speculations (e.g., Griffin 2004). There is no such thing as bad publicity where conspiracy theories are concerned. As long as it is possible to make interesting inferences from a set of claims, many people will continue to do so, without much reflection (Boyer 2001; Barrett 2004).

Cognitive psychological arguments can help us explain the ways the human mind channels the cultural transmission of religious traditions. Stories of a certain kind become widespread because they have a natural appeal to the human mind. They are attention-grabbing and easy to recall; therefore they are contagious and get a head start in cultural selection. All kinds of concepts and beliefs compete for our attention; some win and some lose. Those that win are such that somemehow "fit" the human mind, as it were. We cannot help remembering and spreading around the most contagious stories. Cognitive psychology provides tools for finding those features of the mind that channel cultural transmission.

Underlying this view is a concept of culture and tradition which takes cultures and traditions to be statistical patterns in mental representations in a population. As Dan Sperber (1996: 97) puts it, culture is "the precipitate of cognition and communication in a human population." Thus, it is incorrect to oppose the cultural and the psychological; cultural patterns consist of mental representations of other people's mental representations. Cultures and traditions consist of beliefs (ideas, concepts, images, and so on) together with beliefs about the beliefs of others (and beliefs about the beliefs of others concerning the beliefs of others). Culture is shared knowledge in the sense of mental representations shared by many persons and having a long duration (Pyysiäinen 2005).

Concepts and beliefs are also used for some purpose (Saler 2001). Therefore, not only constraints of memory but also various kinds of practical matters contribute to the spread of concepts and beliefs. Ideas are not important because people believe in them; people rather believe in ideas that are important (Boyer 2001). God, for example, is not important because people believe in God; people instead believe in God because God is important for them. Deciding the truth value of religious beliefs is not a single and distinct mental operation. We do not decide whether a given belief is true before we start to employ it as a premise in reasoning. All that takes place is that given mental mechanisms send bits of information to other mental mechanisms, treating them as facts. These implicit processes produce in us various kinds of intuitions about how things are in the world. Explicit beliefs, such as "God exists," are attempts at justifying or even explaining these intuitions to ourselves. We do not start with explicit beliefs and only then try to adapt our behavior accordingly. We do not first reason that "God exists" and then try to figure out what consequences this should have for our behavior. That "God exists" is, instead, a plausible interpretation of intuitions guiding behavior (Boyer 2001: 298–306; see Pyysiäinen 2003).

Thus, we should look for the kinds of everyday inferences the disciples might have been able to make from the belief that the body of Jesus was not found and that Jesus may therefore not be dead after all. In other words, we should not look for some metaphysical reasons for believing that Jesus was risen; we are rather dealing with very practical issues of everyday life. "Christianity" did not emerge as a philosophy or a theology but as a social movement. Its rise should therefore not be studied only on the basis of theological texts and as a mere system of doctrines (Czachesz 2007; Martin 2005; see Stark 1997; Räisänen 1997: 1–16). Thus, both the formal properties of concepts and beliefs about the risen Christ as well as the possibility of making practical inferences on their basis contribute to the salience, memorability and spread of concepts and beliefs.

These practical inferences are related to the immediate situation the disciples faced, not to modern theological themes. The disciples formed a religious group that either had to break down with the death of its leader or find a way of developing a new organization. To Paul and his school, this meant finding a way of somehow legitimating their authority. There was hardly any other alternative for them than to ultimately trace the authority to the founder himself. Paul (or someone else writing in his name) did this by claiming that the risen Jesus had appeared to him, thus authorizing him to preach. In this way, the social dynamics of the new religious group have their roots in the ambiguous legends about the risen Jesus.

4. *Summary*

The point I have been trying to make is based on the fact that, in a historical explanation, we must make inferences concerning the motivations and intentions of persons: person X did Y because of Z (where Z involves a reference to the beliefs and desires of X). It is easy to see that explanations of the rise of Christianity have made extensive use of this type of explanation. It has, for example, been argued that because the timid disciples suddenly turned into brave preachers of the good tidings, they must have experienced something extraordinary. This is a psychological argument whether the scholar realizes it or not; yet it is mostly based on purely intuitive, folk-psychological reasoning. It is here that cognitive science can be of help. We need not rely on mere intuitive speculations on what the disciples must have felt, thought, and done. Instead, we can rely on empirically tested theories, the scope and limits of which can be explicated for the reader (Martin in this volume). I have here used as an example studies on how we think about dead agents. The point can be summarized as follows:

The physical status and spatial location of dead agents poses a difficult problem for the human cognitive system; we tend to think of dead agents as absent but existing agents (see Bering 2006). Additionally, the sight of a dead body is confusing: it still triggers the same automatic inferences about agency as it used to do, and yet we realize that the agentive properties have been decoupled from the body. Therefore, dead bodies are treated with utmost care and with the feeling that one is dealing with some uncanny mystery.

This is also reflected in the urban legend of the stolen grandmother. The legend is memorable because of the uncommon and disgust-provoking way of dealing with a dead body, resulting in a situation in which the family no longer knew where the dead granny was. I have tried to show that stories such as this one can become widespread without being based on any single dramatic event. It is not only "experiences" that call for a psychological explanation but also the ways in which stories spread.

Thus, the cognitive perspective can help us distance ourselves from the textualist paradigm of systematic theology and to rethink the idea of "tradition." Biblical and related texts are selective, literate crystallizations of sets of concepts, beliefs and stories that once were popular in a population. They are cultural artifacts. The rise of Christianity is not only a theological or a philosophical issue best studied through textual sources; it is rather a social and cultural process in which some ideas, stories and practices outperformed others in cultural selection. Aspects of this fact haven been emphasized in various ways by such scholars as István Czachesz (2007, this volume), Burton Mack (2001), Heikki Räisänen (2000), and Rodney Stark (1997), for example. They have pointed out the importance of the social sciences in the study of early Christianity. I have merely wanted to show that cognitive considerations can further extend these arguments (also Pyysiäinen in press); what is now needed are more attempts at applying the epidemiological models of cultural transmission to the development of early Christian beliefs and practices.

Acknowledgement

I want to thank Philip Esler, Luther Martin, Matti Myllykoski, Heikki Räisänen, and Vernon Robbins for valuable comments. The research for this paper was funded by the Academy of Finland (project 1-200827).

REFERENCES

Atran, Scott. 2002. "The Neuropsychology of Religion." In *Neurotheology*, edited by R. Joseph et al., 163–86. San Jose, Calif.: University Press, California.

Barrett, Charles K. 1994 (1968). *A Commentary to the First Epistle to the Corinthians*. London: A. & C. Black.

Barrett, Justin L. 1999. "Theological Correctness: Cognitive Constraint and the Study of Religion." *Method & Theory in the Study of Religion* 11: 325–39.

———. 2004. *Why Would Anyone Believe in God?* Walnut Creek, Calif.: AltaMira.

Barrett, Justin L., and Frank Keil. 1996. "Conceptualizing a Nonnatural Entity: Anthropomorphism in God Concepts." *Cognitive Psychology* 31: 219–47.

Barrett, Justin L., and E. Thomas Lawson. 2001. "Ritual Intuitions: Cognitive Contributions to Judgments of Ritual Efficacy." *Journal of Cognition and Culture* 1(2): 183–201.

Bering, Jesse. 2002. "Intuitive Conceptions of Dead Agents' Minds: The Natural Foundations of Afterlife Beliefs as Phenomenological Boundary." *Journal of Cognition and Culture* 2(4): 263–308.

———. 2006. "The Folk Psychology of Souls." *Behavioral and Brain Sciences* 29(5): 553–62.
Boyer, Pascal. 2001. *Religion Explained: The Evolutionary Origins of Religious Thought*. New York: Basic Books.
Brunvand, Jan Harold. [1986.] 1989. *The Mexican Pet: More "New" Urban Legends and Some Old Favourites*. Harmondsworth: Penguin.
Carrier, Richard C. 2005. "The Spiritual Body of Christ and the Legend of the Empty Tomb." In *The Empty Tomb: Jesus Beyond the Grave*, edited by Robert M. Price and Jeffery Jay Lowder, 105–231. Amherst, N.Y.: Prometheus Books.
Crossan, John Dominic. 1995. *Who Killed Jesus?* San Francisco, Calif.: HarperCollins.
Cumont, Franz. 1922. *Afterlife in Roman Paganism*. New Haven, Conn.: Yale University Press.
Czachesz, István. 2007. "The Transmission of Early Christian Thought: Toward a Cognitive Psychological Model." *Studies in Religion* 36: 65–84.
Dennett, Daniel C. [1991.] 1993. *Consciousness Explained*. Harmondsworth: Penguin.
Fustel de Coulanges, Numa Denis. 1866. *La cita antique*. Paris.
Griffin, David Ray. 2004. *The 9/11 Commission Report: Omissions and Distortions*. Redford, Mich.: Olive Branch Press.
Heath, Chip, Chris Bell, and Emily Sternberg. 2001. "Emotional Selection in Memes: The Case of Urban Legends." *Journal of Personality and Social Psychology* 81(6): 1028–41.
Honko, Lauri. 1964. "Memorates and the Study of Folk Beliefs." *Journal of the Folklore Institute* 1(1–2): 5–19.
———. [1962.] 1991. *Geisterglaube in Ingermanland*, Vol. I. Folklore Fellows Communications, 185. Helsinki: Academia Scientiarum Fennica.
Hopkins, Keith. 1983. *Death and Renewal*. Cambridge: Cambridge University Press.
Johnston, Sarah Iles. 1999. *Restless Dead: Encounters between the Living and the Dead in Ancient Greece*. Berkeley, Calif.: University of California Press.
Kirby, Peter. 2005. "The Case against the Empty Tomb." In *The Empty Tomb: Jesus Beyond the Grave*, edited by Robert M. Price and Jeffery Jay Lowder, 233–60. Amherst, N.Y.: Prometheus Books.
Klintberg, Bengt af. 1986. *Råttan i pizzan: Folksägner i vår tid* [The rat in the pizza: Folksayings in our time]. Stockholm: Norstedts.
Lewis, James R. 1995. *The Gods Have Landed: New Religions from Other Worlds*. Albany, N.Y.: State University of New York Press.
Livingston, Kenneth R. 2005. "Religious Practice, Brain, and Belief." *Journal of Cognition and Culture* 5(1–2): 75–117.
Lüdemann, Gerd. 1994. *The Resurrection of Jesus*. London: SCM Press.
———. 1995. *What Really Happened to Jesus: A Historical Approach to the Resurrection*. In collaboration with Alf Özen. Trans. by John Bowden. London: SCM Press.
———. 2005. "Did Gnosticism ever Exist?" In *Was There a Gnostic Religion?*, edited by Antti Marjanen, 121–32. Publications of the Finnish Exegetical Society 87. Helsinki: The Finnish Exegetical Society; Göttingen: Vandenhoeck & Ruprecht.
McCauley, Robert N., and E. Thomas Lawson. 2002. *Bringing Ritual to Mind: Psychological Foundations of Cultural Forms*. Cambridge: Cambridge University Press.
Mack, Burton L. 1988. *A Myth of Innocence: Mark and Christian Origins*. Philadelphia, Pa.: Fortress.
———. 2001. *The Christian Myth*. New York: Continuum.
Martin, Luther H. 2004. "Towards a Cognitive History of Religions." In *Unterwegs. Neue Pfade in der Religionswissenschaft / New Paths in the Study of Religions: Festschrift for Michael Pye*, edited by Christoph Kleine, Monika Schrimpf, and Katja Triplett, 75–82. München: Biblion.

———. 2005. "Performativity, Narrativity, and Cognition: 'Demythologizing' the Roman Cult of Mithras." In *Persuasion and Performance: Rhetoric and Reality in Early Christian Discourses*, edited by Willi Braun. Waterloo: Wilfrid Laurier University Press.
The *Mishnah*. [1933.] 1954. Translated by Herbert Danby. Oxford: Oxford University Press.
Myllykoski, Matti. 1991–1994. *Die Letzten Tage Jesu*. 2 vols. Annales academiae scientiarum fennicae, B 256 & 272. Helsinki: Academia Scientiarum Fennica.
———. 2002. "What Happened to the Body of Jesus?" In *Fair Play: Diversity and Conflict in Early Christianity: Essays in Honour of Heikki Räisänen*, edited by Ismo Dunderberg, Christopher Tuckett, and Kari Syreeni, 43–82. Leiden: Brill.
Parsons, Keith. 2005. "Peter Kreeft and Ronald Tacelli on the Hallucinatory Theory." In *The Empty Tomb: Jesus Beyond the Grave*, edited by Robert M. Price and Jeffery Jay Lowder, 433–52. Amherst, N.Y.: Prometheus Books.
Pentikäinen, Juha. 1968. *The Nordic Dead-Child Tradition*. Folklore Fellows Communications, 202. Helsinki.
———. 1969. "The Dead without Status." *Temenos* 4: 92–102.
Price, Robert M. 2005. "Apocryphal Apparitions: 1 Corinthians 15:3–11 as a Post-Pauline Interpolation." In *The Empty Tomb: Jesus Beyond the Grave*, edited by Robert M. Price and Jeffery Jay Lowder, 69–104. Amherst, N.Y.: Prometheus Books.
Proudfoot, Wayne. 1985. *Religious Experience*. Berkeley, Calif.: University of California Press.
Pyysiäinen, Ilkka. 2001. *How Religion Works: Towards a New Cognitive Science of Religion*. Leiden: Brill.
———. 2003. "True Fiction: Philosophy and Psychology of Religious Belief." *Philosophical Psychology* 16(1): 109–25.
———. 2004b. *Magic, Miracles, and Religion: A Scientist's Perspective*. Walnut Creek, Calif.: AltaMira.
———. 2005. "Intuition, Reflection, and the Evolution of Traditions." In *Moving Beyond New Testament Theology? Essays in Conversation with Heikki Räisänen*, edited by Todd C. Penner and Caroline Vander Stichele, 282–307. Publications of the Finnish Exegetical Society, 88. Helsinki: The Finnish Exegetical Society; Göttingen: Vandenhoeck & Ruprecht.
———. 2006. "No Evidence of a Specific Adaptation. A commentary on Bering." *Behavioral and Brain Sciences* 29(5): 483–84.
———. In press. "Reduction and Explanatory Pluralism in the Cognitive Science of Religion." In *Changing Minds: Religion and Cognition through the Ages*, edited by István Czachesz and Tamás Bíró. Groningen Studies in Cultural Change. Leuven: Peeters.
Räisänen, Heikki. [1997] 2000. *Beyond New Testament Theology*. London: SCM Press.
———. 1997. *Marcion, Muhammad and the Mahatma*. London: SCM Press.
Rosengren, Karl S., Carl N. Johnson, and Paul L. Harris, eds. 2000. *Imagining the Impossible: Magical, Scientific, and Religious Thinking in Children*. Cambridge: Cambridge University Press.
———. 2001. "On What We May Believe about Beliefs." In *Religion in Mind: Cognitive Perspectives on Religious Belief, Ritual and Experience*, edited by Jensine Andresen, 47–69. Cambridge: Cambridge University Press.
Saler, Benson, Charles A. Ziegler, and Charles B. Moore. 1997. *The UFO Crash at Roswell: The Genesis of a Modern Myth*. Washington, D.C.: Smithsonian Institution Press.
Sawicki, Marianne. 1994. *Seeing the Lord: Resurrection and Early Christian Practices*. Minneapolis, Pa.: Fortress.
Schmidt, Brian B. 1994. *Israel's Beneficent Dead: Ancestor Cult and Necromancy in Ancient Israelite Religion and Tradition*. Tübingen: J. C. B. Mohr (Paul Siebeck).
Sharf, Robert H. 1998. "Experience." In *Critical Terms for Religious Studies*, edited by Mark C. Taylor, 94–116. Chicago, Ill.: University of Chicago Press.

Sperber, Dan. 1996. *Explaining Culture: A Naturalistic Approach*. Oxford: Blackwell.
Stark, Rodney. [1996.] 1997. *The Rise of Christianity*. San Francisco: Harper.
Walker, P. W. L. 1990. *Holy City, Holy Places? Christian Attitudes to Jerusalem and the Holy Land in the Fourth Century*. Oxford: Clarendon Press.
Walker, Susan. 1985. *Memorials to the Roman Dead*. London: The Trustees of the British Museum.
Wiebe, Phillip. 1997. *Visions of Jesus: Direct Encounters from the New Testament to Today*. New York: Oxford University Press.

THE EMERGENCE OF EARLY CHRISTIAN RELIGION: A NATURALISTIC APPROACH

István Czachesz

This essay will assess some algorithmic models of social behavior for understanding religiosity and look for ways of applying such models to the emergence of early Christian religion. I will be operating especially within the theoretical framework of distributed, self-organizing, and dynamical systems.

Why do we need such an approach in the study of (early Christian) religion? For a long time, historians have been looking in vain for causal laws that explain the course of history (cf. Buchanan 2000; Casti 2003). We do not know rules that would enable us to predict the behavior of individuals or groups—not to mention whole societies or cultures. It seems that the development of history, culture, and society involve such complex interactions of underlying factors that predictive models of them cannot be constructed. Consequently, we cannot reconstruct the emergence of early Christianity as a chain of causal links. It does not mean, however, that there is nothing to say about the history or the emergence of religious movements. There are scientific methods to study complex and nondeterministic behavior: dynamical systems theory offers such an approach. In dynamical systems, the behavior of the whole is more than a sum of the behavior of the parts. In other words, the system displays emergent qualities. In this essay I propose ways to look at religion—and specifically early Christianity—from this perspective. In particular, I will put forward the hypothesis that religious ideas emerge as a necessary consequence of the sophisticated "flocking" rules of human societies.

First, I will outline the concept of distributed systems. Second, I will identify four major components of religion and explain why a distributed systems approach is needed. Third, I will give examples of applying such an approach to religion, including observations about early Christianity. I will conclude with some methodological observations.

1. What Are Distributed, Dynamical Systems? What is Distributed Knowledge?

In distributed systems, the behavior of the system is not centrally regulated; it rather emerges from the behavior of its individual parts. In other words, such systems are "self-organized" (cf. Resnick 1994; Clark 2001: 103–119). Originally the theory of "dynamical systems," or simply "systems theory," made use of differential equations to describe changes in complex, non-linear systems, the behavior of which cannot be explained as the sum of the behavior of their parts (e.g., Mainzer 1997; van Leeuwen 2005). Although the distributed systems discussed in this essay can also be examined from the point of view of classical systems theory, we call our systems "dynamical" primarily in the sense that their state is determined in every single moment through the interaction of their parts. Instead of looking for equations that describe the overall behavior of the system, we will focus on the elementary interactions among its parts. Knowledge in such a system is distributed: the parts obtain and store information about their environment and react accordingly. There is no central agent receiving information from the individual parts and deciding about their behavior. Finally, such systems can also be characterized as "stochastic": whereas the interactions among their elements can in principle be described by deterministic rules, their behavior on the whole is random.

Let us consider a few examples of simple distributed systems. Craig Reynolds (1987) simulated flocks of bird-like objects he baptized "boids" (from "bird-oids") using computer modeling. Each individual in the flock follows three simple rules of behavior. The rules are, in a decreasing order of priority (Reynolds 1987: 28):

(1) Collision Avoidance: avoid collisions with nearby flockmates
(2) Velocity Matching: attempt to match velocity with nearby flockmates
(3) Flock Centering: attempt to stay close to nearby flockmates

If we launch the system after assigning each boid a randomly chosen initial position and speed, after a short while a collective behavior emerges on the screen (Reynolds 2001). Reynolds (1987: 30) calls this an "eagerness" to participate in a flock-like motion. The same algorithm can be used to simulate the motion of schools of fish and herds.

In the boid model, the flock will reach a steady state ("relaxation") after a while, which is the result of a trade-off among the different constraints governing its behavior. The more variegated behavior of real flocks, Reynolds argues (1987: 31), is due to their interaction with the environment. In other words, realistic flock behavior involves "agent-agent" as well as "agent-environment" interactions. By adding obstacles to the simulation and a "steer-to-avoid" mechanism to the boids, the flock shows a particularly graceful obstacle-avoiding behavior. A nice example can be seen in the Disney movie "The Lion King" (1994), where a wildebeest stampede was animated using a similar flocking algorithm (Tiemann 1994; Reynolds 2001). Obstacles are not necessarily fixed in space. For example, in the "Cool School" model (Hooper 1999) a school of fish realistically attempts to avoid a whale as well as a number of smaller predator fish.

The behavior of a group of people can also be modeled using a flocking algorithm. Reynolds suggests (1987: 32) that the boids model could be used to simulate traffic patterns. Jessica Hodgins and her collaborators at the *Georgia Institute of Technology* have created various simulations of human motion, including groups of bikers avoiding an obstacle or riding through a bend (Brogan and Hodgins 1997; Hodgins 1998). The school of Tamás Vicsek at Eötvös University (Budapest) and Collegium Budapest modeled various types of group behavior (Helbing, Farkas, and Vicsek 2000; Farkas, Helbing, and Vicsek 2002). One of their models exemplifies the significance of distributed approaches for the study of critical real-life problems. Understanding the motion of crowds in corridors and fire escapes is crucial for the design of public buildings. For some two decades, various mathematical tools have been tested to model the motion of large crowds, none of which, however, yielded a satisfying solution (Helbing et al. 2001). Models based on the collective behavior of fluid and gas particles have already signaled a move toward a systems-theoretical approach. Yet a real breakthrough was achieved when scholars turned to the distributed paradigm, concentrating on the rules governing *individual* pedestrian motion. Dirk Helbing and his collaborators (Helbing, Farkas, and Vicsek 2000) used "flocking" rules to model the flow of crowds in panic situations. They have successfully simulated the deadly effects of impatience and herding when passing through fire-exits, the build-up of clogs at doors as well as in widenings (!), and the usefulness of pillars that prevent the formation of bottle-necks. Again, the overall behavior of these models emerged from the simple rules governing the individuals rather than from equations describing the whole, as was usual with earlier approaches.

Whereas research on flocking has yielded perhaps the most spectacular distributed simulations, there are also many other kinds of distributed models that have been developed in the past few decades. A particularly fruitful field of study has been the modeling of ant and termite societies. Following simple rules of behavior, ants collect food and termites build nests (Resnick 1994: 59–68, 75–81; cf. Nicolis and Prigogine 1989: 232–38; Mainzer 1997: 107–12). Mitchel Resnick (1987) has developed the very approachable StarLogo programming environment, in which various types of group behavior involving agent-agent and agent-environment interactions can be modeled. In connection with collective ant and termite behavior, we have to mention the field of ant robotics: instead of running computer simulations, these distributed models employ several robots that cooperate following simple behavioral rules (e.g., Wagner and Bruckstein 2001). For example, robot ants cluster around food, follow a leader, and play tag (www.ai.mit.edu/projects/ants). In such models, complex interactions occur between agents as well as between agents and the environment. There is no single centralized mechanism behind the phenomena: algorithms govern the individuals from whose behavior ant society as a whole emerges.

The examples have given us a taste of the potential of distributed models to produce spectacular group behaviors. But how is this all related to religion? In the next section of the essay, I will give an overview of the directions of the cognitive, empirically oriented study of religion and highlight issues that particularly invite the use of distributed models.

2. *The Need for a Distributed, Dynamical Systems Approach in the Cognitive Science of Religion*

Recent cognitive studies of religion have focused on four elements: religious experience, beliefs, texts and rituals. I will describe a model uniting the four elements (Fig. 1) and suggest that a distributed, dynamical systems perspective can substantially enhance our understanding of religion in all four areas.

Figure 1. Religion as a system of four components.

1. Religious experience
- elicited
- interpreted
- anticipated
- also hard-wired?

2. Belief system
- interprets experience
- intuitive/reflexive
- counter-intuitive
- "spontaneous pop-up"?

4. Rituals
- use texts
- elicit experience
- reinforce beliefs
- involve different memory systems? (modes theory)
- involve different roles of the divine? (ritual form theory)

3. Texts
- include literature, arts etc.
- interact with beliefs
- transmission supported by rituals
- how does innovation occur in transmission?

2.1. *Religious Experience*

Religious experience has been studied in the lab for decades (Wulff 1997: 169–204; Hood 2001; Livingston 2005). At the early stages (from the 1930s), physiological parameters have been recorded of subjects performing yoga, Zen meditation and Transcendental Meditation. More recently, Electro Encephalograph (EEG) and neuroimaging technology has been used (e.g., Azari et al. 2001; Livingston 2005). Religious experience has been actively elicited by isolation, drugs, hypnosis, sound and light effects, and a special swing called "the cradle of creativity." Among the many theories that the results of these experiments have generated, probably the best known is Michael Persinger's model of Medial Temporal Lobe religiosity (Persinger 1987; cf. Pyysiäinen 2003: 147–72). The temporal lobes are located at the lower part of both sides of the brain and contain brain areas involved in sound, speech, vision, remembering, and emotions. Persinger argues that this particular ensemble of brain areas—especially due to the involvement of the amygdala, responsible for emotions—made humans capable of feeling euphoria and depression, connecting these feelings with the experience of the self, which ultimately resulted in the experience of the terror of personal extinction. The biological capacity of the God Experience, Persinger suggests, was critical for the survival of the species inasmuch as without such a balance the phenomenon of the self could not be maintained. The God Experience is correlated with transient electric perturbations of the temporal lobe: when such *temporal lobe transients* (TLTs) occur, the innate feelings of the God Experience are displayed. TLTs and the God Experience can be elicited by various conditions, such as hypoxia (lack of oxygen) occurring at high altitudes or during yoga breathing; lack of blood sugar (achieved by starvation or fasting); release of stress hormones (e.g., changes of life style); as well as drugs, music, dance, and smells. The experience itself often involves a sense of profoundness without clear details. Visions, voices, and a sensation of flying are also frequent. Secondary properties of the God Experience include circumstantiality (excessive persistence with a topic), obsession-compulsion (repeated patterns of motor, word, or thought sequences), sobriety, euphoria, and the widening of affect (that is, the interpretation of everyday trivial circumstances as signs of the God Experience).

Without discussing Persinger's theory in detail, it is not difficult to realize that a puzzling variety of feelings and behaviors is associated with TLTs. Can all of these experiences be directly related with (only) religion? Are there perhaps other (non-religious) patterns of behavior that result from TLTs? Reacting to Persinger's theory, Vilayanur Ramachandran and Sandra Blakeslee pointed out (1998) that seizures of the Medial Temporal Lobe are well-known as a source of obsessive behavior. However, many of their patients with such epilepsy were obsessed not with religion but with writing, philosophy, or sex. I can see theoretically two solutions to this dilemma: either (1) different (religious vs. non-religious) sorts of experience result from different activations (e.g., activations involving different circuitries) of the same brain area; or (2) other conditions, such as one's mindset and belief systems, determine whether experience caused by TLTs (or more serious epilepsies) is understood as religious.

Religious experience seldom occurs spontaneously. A look at real-life religious systems shows that they induce as well as explain subjective experience. They elicit experience using techniques such as fasting, deprivation, music, dance, prayer, meditation, mass events, pilgrimage, architecture, art, and drugs. They also provide means to interpret (as well as anticipate) such experience, for example, as spiritual possession, journey of the soul, conversion, or works of the Holy Spirit. One component of the success of early Christianity was probably the efficiency with which it engaged religious experience and interpreted it, for example, as gifts of the Spirit, conversion, or dying and rising with Christ.

2.2. Belief System

We can thus safely assume that religious beliefs are needed for experience to be conceived of as religious. Simple beliefs can be studied on animal models. The simplest ways to learn about environmental clues are habituation and sensitization (Squire and Kandel 2003 [1999]: 24–28, 48–50; Eichenbaum 2002: 41–46). In habituation, the animal learns about the properties of a benign or unimportant stimulus that can be ignored; in sensitization, the animal learns about the properties of a harmful or threatening stimulus, and responds more vigorously to a variety of other stimuli as well (e.g., for some minutes after hearing a gunshot we will jump at hearing any noise). Sensitization and habituation are forms of non-associative learning. To associate two stimuli requires a more complex form of learning called classical conditioning (Squire and Kandel 2003 [1999]: 57–59; Eichenbaum 2002: 46–48). In operant conditioning, the subject learns about the relationship of a stimulus to the subject's behavior. For example, an animal learns to associate pressing a bar or a key with the delivery of food. Animals are also capable of learning from each other, which results in simple forms of cultural transmission (Hauser 2000: 115–40).

Humans also have beliefs acquired by observation. Following Dan Sperber (1996: 77–97), we can call them "intuitive beliefs." Most religious beliefs, in turn, belong to another sort: "reflective beliefs," which we learn from other people. Whereas both animals and humans are capable of cultural transmission, human cultures and the "reflective beliefs" sustained by them are evidently much more complex than those transmitted by animal societies. Some recent cognitive studies have questioned the importance of cultural transmission for religion. According to Pascal Boyer (1994: 227), "even if there was a completely random variation in religious representations, with every generation starting from scratch, certain types of representations would be favored." Jesse Bering (2002: 228; cf. Boyer 2003) goes a step further when he suggests that "implicit afterlife beliefs (...) would be characterized more or less as innate—piggybacking standard mental representational abilities specialized to human beings." His conclusion is rather straightforward: "Ghosts come from within, not without." Notwithstanding these opinions, we have good reasons to assign cultural transmission an important role in the survival and stability of religious concepts and rituals (see below). Whereas the mental representation of religious ideas is to some degree explained by the theory of counter-intuitiveness (Boyer 1994, 2001), a major challenge is to understand how ideas such as "omniscient god" or "eternal life" are mentally represented. Whereas the latter concepts, indeed, violate ontological expectations, both of them involve the cognitive element of a boundless quality ("omniscient" and "eternal") that is not explained (in fact, not even addressed) by the theory of counter-intuitiveness. The solution might be recursion (Czachesz forthcoming), which Marc Hauser, Noam Chomsky, and W. Tecumseh Fitch (2002) suggest is the only uniquely human feature of the language capacity. By recursion, we may be able to think about "knowledge" and "life" as being infinite. For example, some people know more than others, but some know even more: recursion enables us to infinitely re-apply this relation upon itself, until we arrive at the concept of "omniscience."

It has been proposed that supernatural beings are especially important in most religions. These beliefs seem to make use of various archaic mental structures (Boyer 2001: 171–77, 376): (1) the agent detection system, specialized for the identification of purposefully moving things, originally served to detect the presence of dangerous beasts and potential prey in the environment; (2) our theory of mind (see below) enables us to read other people's thoughts and feelings; (3) moral intuitions serve social interaction and successful cooperation. Consequently, when hearing of spirits and gods, we intuitively compare them to the unseen presence of predators and make conjectures about their perception, knowledge, and plans. Most importantly, we attribute them full knowledge of strategic information, that is, knowledge of "morally relevant aspects of what we do and what others do to us."

It is remarkable that all three mental tools identified by Boyer as underlying religious beliefs are in fact indispensable mechanisms serving interactions among human individuals. Such interactions, however, are the building blocks of dynamical social systems as well (cf. Semin and Smith 2002). We may hypothesize that if we can describe society in terms of dynamical systems, also sets of religious beliefs can be described by such a model.

2.3. *Texts*

"Texts" refer in a general sense to oral and written texts as well as other cultural artifacts. In Dan Sperber's terminology they are "public representations" (1996: 98–118; see below). Since we have not yet found a human civilization that does not produce texts (in the above sense), we can only make guesses about what religion would look like without cultural transmission. Would Mowgli have a human mind and be religious (i.e., display human religious behavior)? What we know about historical Mowglis (e.g., Ward 2002–2006), however controversial the evidence is, suggests that they do not think (and generally: do not behave) like humans. Human thought extends into the environment by means of texts and there seems to be no reason to bracket out this component from the investigation of religion.

Sacred texts, hymns, liturgy, religious vocabulary, and many other elements of religion are handed down from generation to generation. Such "public representations" regenerate a similar set of beliefs in the minds of the next generation. A major issue is how innovation occurs and whether one can speak of an evolution here (Rubin 1995; Pyysiäinen 2004: 147–59; Czachesz 2003; 2007). Beliefs are basically transmitted in two different ways. In some cases, the behavior of one individual (such as speech, mimics, or gestures) is read by another individual in whose mind internal representations are generated. At other times, some kind of medium (such as writing, art, or architecture) records the memories of one individual and these signs are read by another person. Expressed in the terminology of distributed systems, beliefs are transmitted either by agent-agent or by agent-environment interactions.

2.4. *Rituals*

Rituals utilize the material culture of religion (such as texts, art, and music) and elicit religious experience. Rituals also play an important role in the generation and fixation of religious beliefs by repetition. There are two major cognitive theories of ritual. Harvey Whitehouse (1995; 2000; 2004) has proposed the "modes of religiosity" theory which makes a distinction between "imagistic" and "doctrinal" forms of religion and establishes a connection between the sensory stimulation in a ritual and the ritual's performance frequency, connecting to them a number of other psychological and social variables. Robert McCauley and Thomas Lawson (2002), drawing on their ground-breaking study from 1990 (Lawson and McCauley 1990), put forward the "ritual form hypothesis," according to which both performance frequency and sensory stimulation are functions of how the role of supernatural agents is conceptualized in the ritual.

In terms of my religious systems model, the fixation of beliefs occurs by simultaneously generating religious experience and exposing believers to external representations such as art, music, hymns, and texts. Rituals, as I will argue below, may arise from simple behaviors, such as operant conditioning and flocking. Rituals, in conclusion, can be also described as dynamical systems driven by interactions between agents and the environment (ritual space and artifacts) as well as interactions among agents.

2.5. *Two Types of Distributed Systems in Religion*

In sum, we need a distributed systems approach in the study of religion for several reasons. Religion emerges from the interaction of a great number of participants with each other and their environment. Rituals are repetitive actions that emerge from these interactions. Texts (public representations) are environmental components that have been formed by the agents. Beliefs and experiences are generated by texts and rituals and describe the internal states of the agents. On a different level, however, also beliefs and experiences can be studied as distributed phenomena, inasmuch as they are emerging from the interaction of different parts within the human mind.

Although we are mainly using the "flocking" paradigm in this essay (due to its intuitive and approachable character), we have to notice that there are also other kinds of distributed systems. Whereas flocks consist of a great number of similar agents, other distributed systems contain fewer parts and the parts behave differently. For example, Andy Clark (2001: 112–17) distinguishes "emergence as collective self-organization" (such as flocking behavior) from "emergence of unprogrammed functionality." In the latter category, the participating elements are neither numerous nor similar, yet their interaction yields behaviors that are "not subserved by an internal state encoding the goals or how to achieve them." Both types of emergent behavior are finally characterized as "interactive complexity."

We can use this broader sense of distributed behavior to think about beliefs and experience. The human brain contains approximately 100 billion (10^{11}) nerve cells (neurons), and even a "piece of the brain the size of a grain of sand would contain one hundred thousand neurons" (Ramachandran and Blakeslee 1998: 8). Although neurons fall under many morphological types, they constitute large enough communities to model them by some kind of "flocking" approach (Clark's collective self-organization). A good example is the self-organizing synchronization of neurons to provide functions such as the circadian cycle, face-recognition, or even consciousness (Strogatz 2003: esp. 260–84). Large-scale synchronization of the brain is an underlying factor of epileptic seizures (Percha et al. 2005). Given that TLTs are microseizures of the brain, it would not be surprising if neural synchrony played an important role in religious experience (cf. Aftanas and Golocheikine 2001).

The human mind also produces the second kind of complexity, that is, Clark's "unprogrammed functionality." Most systems-theoretical approaches to cognition have in fact been proceeding in the latter direction (Port and Van Gelder 1995; recently Van Leeuwen 2005). Interactions among brain areas (anatomical units) or mental modules (functional units) result in emergent behaviors that are not programmed in any of the participating components. Rituals involving a small number of objects and participants may be also approached from this perspective. Belief systems may be excellent candidates to be studied from a distributed perspective in either sense (cf. Pinker 2005).

Finally, the model of religion that I have been outlining in this essay can also be approached as a distributed system, particularly in the sense of "unprogrammed functionality." Different components of religious systems engage in delicate interactions so that minor changes in the system can result in complex, unpredictable outcomes. The problem is remarkably similar to the issue of biological and cultural complexity (e.g., Oltvai and Barabási 2002; Denton 2004) and its detailed discussion has to be postponed to another occasion.

3. Some Applications of the Distributed Model to Religion and Early Christianity

In the third part of the essay, I will apply the distributed systems approach to various aspects of religion. I will primarily talk about religion in terms of the four components that I have discussed in the previous section. Nevertheless, it must be realized that defining religion is not an easy task. The four elements in my model can be used to describe other domains of human behavior, as well. Health care may be an example, as shown in the following diagram (Fig. 2). To the four components that have been identified already in religious systems I added here references to social networks (top of the diagram) and the natural environment (bottom of the diagram). In this essay, I do

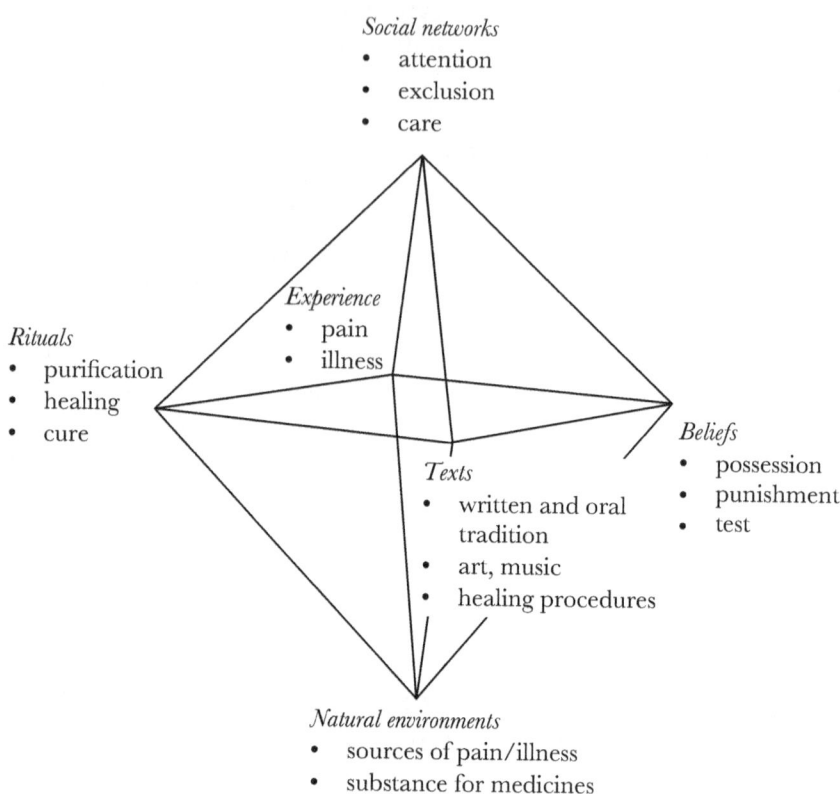

Figure 2. Health care as an example of cultural systems.

not make an effort to solve this issue (see recently Day 2005), but the solution might be that "religion" is a heuristic concept in the study of human behavior, which we will able to dismiss in the future.

3.1. *Religious Beliefs and Distributed Systems*

Distributed systems, as we have seen, offer a framework in which we can model social behavior with the help of a few simple rules of interaction between individuals (and the environment). In the examples which we have discussed hitherto, each agent interacted with a few agents in its physical neighborhood and all agents interacted with approximately the same number of neighbors.

In human societies, and often in animal societies, social networks are far more complex. The structures of the simplest human societies are largely shaped by the physical space they live in. The formation of villages and networks of villages follows geographical divisions. Even in the simplest human civilizations, however, people who never physically meet each other may know of each other and may influence each other's behavior. The village on the other side of the river or mountain, or even other people living at a longer distance, may be part of social reality without much, if any, physical exchange. Humans, and arguably some other species as well, can simulate the minds of other individuals even without a sensory input. Many children have imaginary companions (Taylor 1999; recently Hoff 2005). Furthermore, we can regard as real people of whom we read in novels or hear about in epic narratives, even if we think the characters were made up by the writers.

The mental tool we are using to achieve this is the so-called "theory of mind" (Frith and Frith 2005). The concept of the "theory of mind" has come under criticism recently (Leudar, Costall, and Francis 2004) and therefore it seems best to use it as a shorthand term for the above-mentioned abilities, rather than as a well-understood mental structure. At the base of this ability we probably find the mechanism of imitation (Brass and Heyes 2005; Byrne 2005), which occurs often without conscious knowledge or even against our will. One may think about the contagious nature of yawning, well-known in other species as well. "Mirror neurons" are thought to be responsible for this and similar phenomena, although the exact mechanisms are largely unknown as yet (Rizzolatti et al. 2002).

Whatever the neurological explanation may be, humans make simulations of the thoughts of other humans whom they do not see or hear, or even of other people they never knew. The organization of states relies on such mental abilities: leaders make assumptions of the behavior and reactions of their subjects and vice versa; large social groups are formed by individuals who never meet each other, or even never hear from each other. Wrong assumptions are often made, which in fact frequently results in social tension and unrest.

My suggestion is that religious ideas emerge as a necessary side-effect of the sophisticated "flocking rules" of human societies. The large-scale dynamics of human societies emerge as we make decisions based on interactions with our neighbors as well as on simulations of unknown, distant, and foreign human individuals. Some of the latter simulations are maintained in stabilized, stereotyped, and socially transmitted forms, such as national stereotypes. Ideas of supernatural agents are long-standing, stabilized, stereotyped, and socially transmitted simulations of distant or abstract persons. Supernatural agents, in fact, are often important family members, rulers, or distant, exotic people.

In terms of this hypothesis, there is little, if any, difference between abstract, distant social agents and supernatural ones. The major difference lies in the way secularized Western societies handle those ideas. However, in spite of this intended differentiation in Western societies, an appeal to ideas such as nation, social class, or monarch can evoke the same behavioral response as references to religious agents. In this framework, it also makes perfect sense that in Melanesian religious imagination foreign investors are identified with the tribal ancestors (Whitehouse 1995). In the framework of our flocking models, such ideas may be thought of as agents who follow the average behavior of a very large group of individuals. They may be imagined as "boids" with a very large mass and impetus. Individuals, in turn, adjust their behavior to those agents.

Elsewhere I have argued that the figure of Jesus in early Christian religion was extremely successful because it was shaped after the idea of ancestors, a widespread and attractive religious concept (Czachesz 2007). The risen Jesus is very similar to us humans, except that he is free of a body and is morally flawless. The frequent application of family metaphors to Jesus supports this reading. Relying on our arguments about the nature of religious ideas, we can add that Jesus' figure incorporates other widespread notions of abstract social agents inasmuch as he is thought about as Israel's Messiah and a monarch. I suggest that one of the major factors which enabled the formation of such a rich and flexible religious agent was the rapid as well as widespread circulation of the idea.

3.2. *Networks*

Although the work of Richard Dawkins and Dan Sperber have inspired much theorizing about the propagation of ideas, relatively little attention has been paid to a major factor in that process. I am referring here to social networks along which ideas (cultural bits) are transmitted. In the framework of distributed systems we can study also this phenomenon. We can use, for example, Uri Wilensky's NetLogo environment (Wilensky 1999–2007), which is based on Resnick's above-mentioned StarLogo, to experiment with the spread of messages in different social networks. In Wilensky's simple model, a message spreads in a society of randomly moving individuals (Fig. 3; I have modified the colors for

Figure 3. Spread of a message in NetLogo.

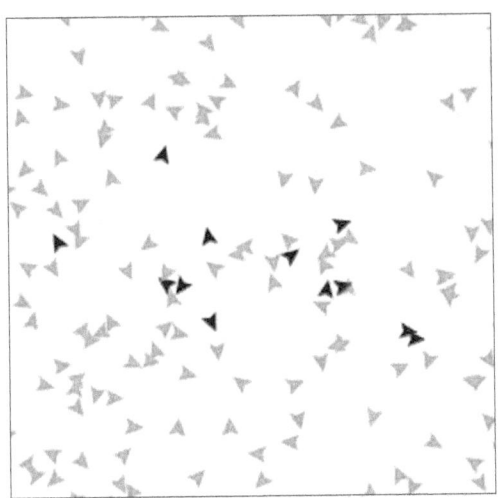

better visibility). When the simulation starts, only one agent is colored black, the one having the message. As other agents meet the "messenger," they turn black and become messengers themselves. The transmission of messages in real social networks is much more complicated than this. First, not everyone is equally interested in a given message. Second, not everyone meets the same number of people. Third, we learn, forget, and modify information. Finally, different messages spread along different networks (for example, we talk with different people about soccer, scholarship, and family life).

Recently network theory has made tremendous advance in understanding the underlying common mechanisms of various natural and artificial networks (Barabási 2002; cf. Buchanan 2002). Society can be easily modeled as a network, consisting of people and connections among them. A network can be described with a handful of parameters, such as its *diameter* (describing how quickly we get from someone to someone else on the network); its *degree distribution* (telling us whether there are very isolated or very popular individuals); and the strength of connections. This last feature was especially relevant for the spread of early Christianity (Czachesz forthcoming). Strong connections provide the backbone of networks and removing a few of them destroys the network structure: one may think of the royal family and its social connections in feudal societies. So-called weak links, in turn, can be removed in large numbers without immediate consequences;

yet various observations about natural and social networks suggest that these connections have an important stabilizing effect (Csermely 2006). Early Christians have created weak links in many different ways. They invested into charity; they regularly entertained visitors, such as teachers, prophets, and other wandering Christians; finally, a great number of women joined the movement, which added to it an extra networking potential, as compared with, for example, the male society of the Mithras cult. The diverse weak links helped to preserve the unity of the manifold movement in spite of the various debates and tensions that existed from the very beginning (Luttikhuizen 2002).

3.3. *Rituals*

Rituals are important locations for the generation of memories and for the reinforcement of existing ideas. Although this function of rituals has been appreciated (Lawson and McCauley 1990; Whitehouse 1995, 2000, 2004; McCauley and Lawson 2002), less attention has been paid to the mechanisms shaping the rituals themselves (e.g., Hinde 1999; Boyer 2001). I suggest that ritual may be approached as social behavior emerging in a distributed system.

An interesting example is the so-called "Mexican wave" seen in football stadia (Farkas, Helbing, and Vicsek 2002). A "Mexican wave" is a typical distributed behavior that emerges when a large number of spectators follow a few simple rules: when you see your second or third neighbor standing up, stand up yourself, raise your hands, and then sit down and lower your hands. Whether a wave emerges and spreads successfully, depends on how many spectators initiate it and where they sit in the stadium. Illés Farkas and his collaborators have successfully simulated the Mexican wave on the analogy of excitable media (Fig. 4), a model originally created to describe processes such as forest fires or wave propagation in heart tissue. People are regarded as excitable units that can be activated by an external stimulus: a distance- and direction-weighted concentration of nearby active people. Once activated, each unit follows the same set of internal rules to pass through the active (standing and waving) and refractory (passive) phases before returning to its original resting (excitable) state.

As I have noticed above, people display synchronized behavior in many different settings. Synchronization can be modeled in a distributed framework, by assigning simple rules to a number agents (e.g., Strogatz 2003: 55–59 and *passim*). Synchronized behavior is a source

Figure 4. The Mexican wave model.

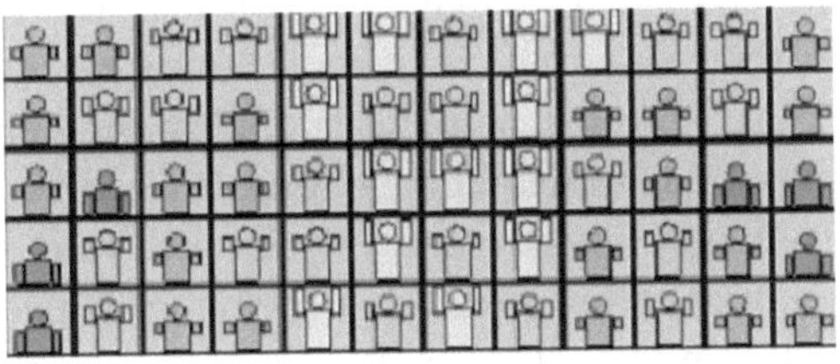

of joy and confidence, just think of marching, synchronized swimming, or dance. As Steven Strogatz has noticed, people often spontaneously fall into synchronicity. For example, sisters, roommates, close friends, or coworkers synchronize their menstrual periods. Eastern-European audiences synchronize their clap. Pedestrians synchronized their steps at the opening of the Millenium Bridge in London, putting the new bridge in danger. The Mexican wave is only one example of a wide range of synchronized behaviors.

It has to be noticed that joint action often involves complementary rather than identical behavior (Sebanz, Bekkering, and Knoblich 2006). However, synchronization spontaneously occurs even in such cases. Recent studies have shown that individuals working on mental tasks together non-consciously mimic each other's actions and synchronize rhythmical movements. Shall we replace the "theory of mind" with a "theory of body"? Do we synchronize our bodies so that we can read each other's minds? Communication experts have always warned us that our bodies tell more than our words. It seems that the long-standing interest in reading minds must be complemented (if not replaced) by a study of synchronizing bodies (cf. Gallese et al. 2004). Distributed models and rituals will occupy an important place in such a paradigm.

3.4. *Innovations*

The final issue to be mentioned is innovation. This is a very broad subject that is not exclusively related to religious behavior. In general, the success of the human species is largely dependent on its ability of inventing new forms of behavior and transmitting them without relying on genetic changes, which occur too slowly to follow fast changes in the environment (cf. Richerson and Boyd 2005). Still the subject is highly relevant for the study of early Christianity, which emerged as a set of successful innovations in the belief system, rituals, and institutions of first century (Jewish) religion.

The social dynamics of innovation include experimentation and imitation (cf. Kameda and Daisuke 2003). Individuals who experiment take a risk when they abandon the established ways of dealing with a situation. They may, however, sometimes find more efficient behaviors, and succeed where others fail. Still the majority is formed by so-called free-riders, who simply imitate the innovators. It is important that imitators do not only follow successful behavioral patterns, but also maladaptive ones. Any real-life society displays a balance of the two strategies, that is, innovation and free-riding. This can be excellently studied on a distributed model (Helbing, Farkas, and Vicsek 2000). Dirk Helbing with his collaborators has designed a model to discover how a group consisting of innovators and free-riders can escape from a smoke-filled room. Innovators tried to find fire-exits randomly, whereas free-riders just followed the innovators. The simulations have shown that the group succeeds in leaving the room within the shortest time if it includes both innovators and free-riders.

The application of such a model to religious innovation is complicated by the fact that we do not know what the fire-exits stand for in a religious system, that is, we do not yet exactly know what makes religion successful. If religion is functional in human society, the doors may stand for some optimal social effects. Even if religion is not functional we may be able to identify certain attractors, that is, optimal and therefore long-standing forms, which are approached by religious experimentation. Optionally, religion may turn out to be a set of social behaviors which appear to the rationalist mind as strange and irrational, without being substantially different from other similar but more favorably received behaviors, as I have suggested above. In this case, the attractors may be looked for by studying interactions with distant and abstract social agents (such as dead persons, monarchs, or nation) in a distributed system. If we succeed in finding algorithmic or mathematical models of religious innovation, we may be also able to minimize the emergence of socially destructive religious systems as well as the destructive use of existing forms of religiosity.

4. *Concluding Remarks*

A distributed systems approach bridges the gap between individual behavior and social phenomena. It helps to solve some fundamental difficulties of studying the social. Society has no behavior—individuals do; society has no knowledge—individuals do. Yet behavior and knowledge always present themselves as social realities. The same holds true for religion.

Finally, historians have the important task of supplying historical nuances to social theories and testing such theories against historical data. Religious systems and other social systems related to distant and invisible social agents may fulfill very different roles in different historical situations. Evolutionary approaches tend to bracket out historical differences as ones of secondary significance. For the student of the first century Mediterranean, the need for a historical perspective is obvious. Structurally similar social agents, such as ancestors, monarchs, nations, gods, and spirits, operate very differently at distant times and places. Therefore, the successful research strategy should integrate a systems-theoretical approach with well-informed historical differentiation.

REFERENCES

Aftanas, L. I., and S. A. Golocheikine. 2002. "Human Anterior and Frontal Midline Theta and Lower Alpha Reflect Emotionally Positive State and Internalized Attention: High-Resolution EEG Investigation of Meditation." *Neuroscience Letters* 310: 57–60.

Azari, Nina P. et al. 2001. "Neural Correlates of Religious Experience." *European Journal of Neuroscience* 13: 1649–52.

Barabási, Albert-László. 2002. *Linked: The New Science of Networks*. Cambridge, Mass.: Perseus Publishing.

Bering, Jesse M. 2002. "Intuitive Conceptions of Dead Agents' Minds: The Natural Foundations of Afterlife Beliefs as Phenomenological Boundary." *Journal of Cognition and Culture* 2: 263–308.

Boyer, Pascal. 1994. *The Naturalness of Religious Ideas: A Cognitive Theory of Religion*. Berkeley, Calif.: University of California Press.

———. 2001. *Religion Explained: The Evolutionary Origins of Religious Thought*. London: Vintage.

———. 2003. "Are Ghost Concepts 'Intuitive,' 'Endemic' and 'Innate'?" *Journal of Cognition and Culture* 3: 233–43.

Brass, Marcel, and Cecilia Heyes. 2005. "Imitation: Is Cognitive Neuroscience Solving the Correspondence Problem." *Trends in Cognitive Sciences* 9: 489–95.

Brogan, David C., and Jessica K. Hodgins. 1997. "Group Behaviors for Systems with Significant Dynamics." *Autonomous Robots* 4(1): 137–53.

Buchanan, Mark. 2000. *Ubiquity: The Science of History...or Why the World is Simpler Than We Think?* London: Weidenfeld & Nicolson.

———. 2002. *Small Worlds and the Groundbreaking Theory of Networks*. New York: W. W. Norton.

Byrne, Richard W. 2005. "Social Cognition: Imitation, Imitation, Imitation." *Current Biology* 15(13): R498.

Casti, John L. 2003. "How History Happens, or Why the Conventional Wisdom is Always Wrong." *Complexity* 8(6): 12–16.

Clark, Andy. 2001. *Mindware: An Introduction to the Philosophy of Cognitive Science*. Oxford: Oxford University Press.

Csermely, Péter. 2006. *Weak Links: Stabilizers of Complex Systems from Proteins to Social Networks*. Berlin: Springer.
Czachesz, István. 2003. "The Gospels and Cognitive Science." In *Learned Antiquity: Scholarship and Society in the Near-East, the Greco-Roman World, and the Early Medieval West*, edited by Alisdair A. MacDonald, Michael W. Twomey, and Gerrit J. Reinink, 25–36. Leuven: Peeters.
———. 2007. "The Transmission of Early Christian Thought: Toward a Cognitive Psychological Model." *Studies in Religion* 36, 65–84.
———. Forthcoming. "Complex Systems, Social Networks and the Success of Early Christian Religion." In *Changing Minds: Religion and Cognition through the Ages*, edited by István Czachesz and Tamás Bíró. Leuven: Peeters.
Day, Matthew. 2005. "The Undiscovered and Undiscoverable Essence: Species and Religion after Darwin." *Journal of Religion* 85: 58–82.
Denton, Trevor. 2004. "Cultural Complexity Revisited." *Cross-Cultural Research* 38: 3–26.
Eichenbaum, Howard. 2002. *The Cognitive Neuroscience of Memory: An Introduction*. Oxford: Oxford University Press.
Farkas, Illés, Dirk Helbing, and Tamás Vicsek. 2002. "Mexican Waves in an Excitable Medium: The Stimulation of this Motion Among Expectant Spectators Is Explained." *Nature* 419: 131–32.
Frith, Chris, and Uta Frith. 2005. "Theory of Mind." *Current Biology* 15(17): R644.
Gallese, Vittorio, Christian Keysers, and Giacomo Rizzolatti. 2004. "A Unifying View of the Basis of Social Cognition." *Trends in Cognitive Sciences* 8: 396–403.
Hauser, Marc D. 2000. *Wild Minds: What Animals Really Think*. New York: Henry Holt and Company.
Hauser, Marc D., Noam Chomsky, and W. Tecumseh Fitch. 2002. "The Faculty of Language: What Is It, Who Has It, and How Did It Evolve?" *Science* 298: 1569–79.
Helbing, Dirk, Illés Farkas, and Tamás Vicsek. 2000. "Simulating Dynamical Features of Escape Panic." *Nature* 407: 487–90.
Helbing, Dirk, Péter Molnár, Illés J. Farkas, and Kai Bolay. 2001. "Self-Organizing Pedestrian Movement." *Environment and Planning B: Planning and Design* 28: 363–83.
Hinde, Robert A. 1999. *Why Gods Persist: A Scientific Approach to Religion*. London: Routledge.
Hodgins, Jessica. 1998. Group Behavior. At: http://www.static.cc.gatech.edu/gvu/animation/Areas/group_behavior/group.html (accessed at March 1 2007).
Hoff, Eva V. 2005. "A Friend Living Inside Me—The Forms and Functions of Imaginary Companions." *Imagination, Cognition and Personality: The Scientific Study of Consciousness* 24(2): 151–90.
Hood, Ralph W. 2001. *Dimensions of Mystical Experiences: Empirical Studies and Psychological Links*. Amsterdam: Rodopi.
Hooper, David S. 1999. Cool School. At: http://www.kewlschool.com/ (accessed March 1, 2007).
Kameda, Tatsuya, and Daisuke Nakanishi. 2003. "Does Social/cultural Learning Increase Human Adaptability? Rogers's Question Revisited." *Evolution and Human Behavior* 24: 242–60.
Lawson, E. Thomas, and Robert N. McCauley. 1990. *Rethinking Religion: Connecting Cognition and Culture*. Cambridge: Cambridge University Press.
Leeuwen, Marco van. 2005. "Questions for the Dynamicist: The Use of Dynamical Systems Theory in the Philosophy of Cognition." *Minds and Machines* 15: 271–333.
Leudar, Ivan, Alan Costall, and Dave Francis, eds. 2004. "Theory of Mind: A Critical Assessment." Special issue of *Theory & Psychology* 14(5): 571–755.
Livingston, Kenneth R. 2005. "Religious Practice, Brain, and Belief." *Journal of Culture and Cognition* 5(1–2): 75–117.

Luttikhuizen, Gerard P. 2002. *De veelvormigheid van het vroegste christendom.* Delft: Eburon.
Mainzer, Klaus. 1997. *Thinking in Complexity: The Complex Dynamics of Matter, Mind, and Mankind.* 3rd ed. Berlin: Springer.
McCauley, Robert N., and Thomas E. Lawson. 2002. *Bringing Ritual to Mind: Psychological Foundations of Cultural Forms.* Cambridge: Cambridge University Press.
Nicolis, Grégoire, and Ilya Prigogine. 1989. *Exploring Complexity: An Introduction.* New York: W. H. Freeman.
Oltvai, Zoltán N., and Albert-László Barabási. 2002. "Life's Complexity Pyramid." *Science* 298: 763–64.
Percha, Bethany et al. 2005. "Transition from Local to Global Phase Synchrony in Small World Neural Network and Its Possible Implications for Epilepsy." *Physical Review E* 72: 031909.
Persinger, Michael. 1983. "Religious and Mystical Experiences as Artifacts of Temporal Lobe Function: A General Hypothesis." *Perceptual and Motor Skills* 57: 1255–62.
———. 1987. *Neuropsychological Bases of God Beliefs.* New York: Praeger.
Pinker, Steven. 2005. "So How *Does* the Mind Work." *Mind & Language* 20: 1–24.
Port, Robert F., and Timothy van Gelder. 1995. *Mind as Motion: Explorations in the Dynamics of Cognition.* Cambridge, Mass.: MIT Press.
Pyysiäinen, Ilkka. [2001] 2003. *How Religion Works: Towards a New Cognitive Science of Religion.* Leiden: Brill.
———. 2004. *Magic, Miracles, and Religion: A Scientist's Perspective.* Walnut Creek: AltaMira.
Ramachandran, V. S., and Sandra Blakeslee. 1998. *Phantoms in the Brain: Human Nature and the Architecture of the Mind.* London: Fourth Estate.
Resnick, Mitchel. 1994. *Turtles, Termites, and Traffic Jams: Explorations in Massively Parallel Microworlds.* Cambridge, Mass.: MIT Press.
Reynolds, Craig W. 1987. "Flocks, Herds, and Schools: A Distributed Behavioral Model." *Computer Graphics* 21(4): 25–34.
———. [1995] 2001. Boids: Background and Update. At: www.red3d.com/cwr/boids/ (accessed March 1, 2007).
Richerson, Peter J., and Robert Boyd. 2005. *Not by Genes Alone: How Culture Transformed Human Evolution.* Chicago, Ill.: University of Chicago Press.
Rizzolatti, Giacomo et al. 2002. "From Mirror Neurons to Imitation: Facts and Speculations." In *The Imitative Mind: Development, Evolution, and Brain Bases*, edited by Andrew N. Meltzoff and Wolfgang Prinz, 247–66. Cambridge: Cambridge University Press.
Rubin, David. 1995. *Memory in Oral Traditions: The Cognitive Psychology of Epic, Ballads, and Counting-out Rhymes.* New York: Oxford University Press.
Sebanz, Natalie, Harold Bekkering, and Günther Knoblich. 2006. "Joint Action: Bodies and Minds Moving Together." *Trends in Cognitive Sciences* 10(2): 70–76.
Semin, Gün R., and Eliot R. Smith. 2002. "Interfaces of Social Psychology with Situated and Embodied Cognition." *Cognitive Systems Research* 3: 385–96.
Sperber, Dan. 1996. *Explaining Culture: A Naturalistic Approach.* Oxford: Blackwell.
Squire, Larry R., and Eric R. Kandel. [1999] 2003. *Memory: From Mind to Molecules.* New York: Henry Holt and Company.
Strogatz, Steven. 2003. *Sync: The Emerging Science of Spontaneous Order.* New York: Hyperion.
Taylor, Marjorie. 1999. *Imaginary Companions and the Children Who Create Them.* New York: Oxford University Press.
Tiemann, Brian. 1994. "The Lion King:" Production Information. At: www.lionking.org/text/FilmNotes.html (accessed March 1 2007).
Vicsek, Tamás. 2001. "A Question of Scale." *Nature* 411: 421.
———. 2002. "The Bigger Picture." *Nature* 418: 131.
Wagner, Israel A., and Alfred M. Bruckstein. 2001. "From Ants to A(ge)nts: A Special Issue on Ant-Robotics." *Annals of Mathematics and Artificial Intelligence* 31(1): 1–238.

Ward, Andrew R. 2002–2006. FeralChildren.com: Isolated, Confined, Wolf and Wild Children. At: http://www.feralchildren.com (accessed March 1, 2007).

Whitehouse, Harvey. 1995. *Inside the Cult: Religious Innovation and Transmission in Papua New Guinea*. Oxford: Clarendon Press.

———. 2000. *Arguments and Icons: Divergent Modes of Religiosity*. Oxford: Oxford University Press.

———. 2004. *Modes of Religiosity: A Cognitive Theory of Religious Transmission*. Walnut Creek: AltaMira.

Wilensky, Uri. 1999. NetLogo. At: http://ccl.northwestern.edu/netlogo/ (accessed March 1, 2007). Center for Connected Learning and Computer-Based Modeling, Northwestern University, Evanston, Ill.

Wulff, David M. 1997. *Psychology of Religion: Classic and Contemporary*. 2nd ed. New York: John Wiley & Sons.

A COGNITIVE APPROACH TO RITUAL SYSTEMS IN FIRST-CENTURY JUDAISM

Kimmo Ketola

1. *Religious History and Ritual Systems*

A number of theories have recently been advanced which propose universally applicable types of religious systems, even proposing dynamic profiles of change and development by which these systems are characterized. The claim is that, all other things being equal, religions, by virtue of their inner logic alone, show characteristic patterns of development depending on a set of key features. For instance, sociologist Rodney Stark (1996) has made the case that if we want to provide adequate explanations of religious developments in history, such as the rise of Christianity, we also need to take into account what social science has found out about religious dynamics that is of general validity.

Here I shall only concern myself with the theoretical models advanced in the cognitive science of religion developed mainly since the early 1990s. The most prominent cognitive theories of religious systems that include predictions concerning religious socio-political organization are the theory of the two modes of religiosity, developed by Harvey Whitehouse (e.g., 1995, 2000, 2002a, 2002b, 2004a), and the theory of ritual form developed by E. Thomas Lawson and Robert N. McCauley (e.g., Lawson and McCauley 1990; McCauley and Lawson 2002). These theories were initially seen as competitors, and indeed they do produce competing predictions in a few cases. However, more recently there has been a growing emphasis on their fundamental commonalities (e.g., Lawson 2005). The discussion of the relative merits of each of these theories is ongoing (see Pyysiäinen 2001; Pyysiäinen and Anttonen 2002; Atran 2002; Whitehouse and McCauley 2005).

Cognitive approaches to religious socio-political organization are distinguished from sociological ones by the fact that, in them, religious systems are viewed as centering on rituals, rather than upon the ideological tension in which they exist in their broader socio-cultural environment. The cognitive approach recognizes that many of the religious rewards that inspire and motivate people to practice religion reside precisely in ritual (Atran 2002).

No doubt many rewards are gained from religious explanations of reality. Many rewards are also gained simply through belonging to social networks formed of like-minded people. Some rewards are only accessible through the coordinated action of a large social group and it is clear that religion fosters the formation of such collectivities. However, a powerful case can also be made for the view that it is primarily collective rituals that provide the foundations for all these rewards (Rappaport 1999; Sosis and Alcorta 2003; Atran 2002). According to this view, the ultimate sources of the rewards that motivate long-term practice and commitment most probably lie in rituals and practices rather than in doctrines. Ritual is also central to consolidating faith in the reality of religious claims in the minds of devotees. Rituals also often have a more directly utilitarian and this-worldly component to them, for example, in the form of healing (Pyysiäinen 2004a). Moreover, there are the simple and direct physical and psychological rewards that may come from ritual participation (Rappaport 1999).

The purpose of this essay is to examine religious developments and factionalism within Judaism in first-century Palestine in light of these theories. As Judaism is more concerned with orthopraxis than orthodoxy, this sort of analysis should prove especially illuminating and fruitful. Thus, I will examine the emergence of such groups as the Qumran community and the early Jesus movement and see whether they fit the patterns predicted by cognitive theory.

I should say at the outset that I am not a biblical specialist, and not even a historian. My field of expertise is in the cognitive study of contemporary religious movements. What I hope to be able to contribute to biblical scholarship is thus not a detailed examination of any textual or archaeological evidence. My study should be seen as an introduction to the basic outlines of the cognitive science of religion with regard to religious ritual systems and how such theories might be applied in biblical studies. In the following analyses, I therefore rely heavily on a few standard historical studies of the period, especially on E. P. Sanders' exemplary volumes (1985; 1992). However, since much of cognitive theorizing concerning religious rituals still rests upon many untested assumptions, I shall also take the opportunity to reflect on the adequacy of the theories in light of the material at hand.

2. *Ritual Life in First-Century Judaism*

Looking into the religious situation of first-century Judaism,[1] one is immediately struck by the importance of rituals for this particular religious system. Until the present day, Jewish identity has been shaped to a much larger extent by norms regarding practice than by adherence to a doctrine. Although first-century Judaism is today recognized among scholars as being very diverse in terms of competing ideological factions, a case can be made that, underlying all this diversity, there existed a deeply held consensus regarding certain ritual practices that effectively set the Jews apart from their neighbors (Sanders 1992).

The salience of the temple of Jerusalem to Jewish identity hardly needs emphasizing. The sacrificial cult at the temple was obviously a central part of ancient Jewish religion. It is evident that the sacrificial rituals at the temple were exceptionally intense and rousing events, at least during the three great pilgrim festivals of Passover (Hebrew, *Pesah*), Weeks (*Shavu'ot*) and Booths or Tabernacles (*Sukkot*) that the Bible required all Israelite males to attend.

Festivals were an integral part of ancient Jewish life and great multitudes of people seem to have attended these. Sanders has estimated that between 300,000 and 500,000 people attended these festivals, especially during Passover (Sanders 1992: 128). Sanders thinks it likely that Palestinian Jews, on average, attended one of the three festivals each year (Sanders 1992: 130).

Passover was undoubtedly the most important of these festivals, attracting the largest attendance and containing many emotionally highly rousing elements. The festival lasted eight days and it started with the sacrifice of the Passover lambs on the evening of the first day. Since one lamb was required for a group of ten people, Sanders estimates that approximately 30,000 lambs were sacrificed, requiring at least 10,000 priests. The man bringing the animal slaughtered it and the priest caught the blood, which was passed towards the altar. Then the worshipper carried out the whole lamb and roasted it. After night fell, it was eaten alongside unleavened bread and bitter herbs. (Sanders 1992: 125–38.)

---

[1] Here I follow Sanders (1992) and use this phrase to refer generally to the early Roman period (63 B.C.E.–66 C.E.).

Although the trip to Jerusalem may have been arduous, the Passover was a time for great rejoice and feasting. It combined piety with sumptuous eating, music, drinking, dancing and chatting with friends. Since the festival embodied the theme of national liberation—it commemorated the exodus from Egypt—it also often occasioned unrest and rioting. There were generally additional Roman troops present in the city during the festival in order to maintain peace (Sanders 1992: 128–38).

The second striking feature of this ritual system is its all-inclusive and centralized nature. The sacrificial practice of Judaism differed from that of the Greeks in that there was only one place for sacrifice, one temple (Sanders 1992: 49–50). Not only was the sacrificial cult centralized, but Judaism was also distinctive in the way in which it attempted to bring the entirety of life under religious control. Thus, in addition to the temple, there were two other foci of religious ritual life in Judaism in the first century: the synagogue and the home. The practices in these places were much more routinized and much less spectacular in nature. Jews of that time seem to have generally accepted the biblical requirement to constantly bear in mind the laws of God and this was achieved mainly by the twice-a-day prayers at home and the weekly study of scripture in the synagogue (Sanders 1992: 196–97).

The institution of the synagogue was essentially a house for prayer and reading scripture, although it served other communal functions as well. The origins of the institution are uncertain but by the first century it was so well established that authors of the time took it for granted (Sanders 1992: 198). Not much is known about activities in the synagogue; they probably included singing prayers and the reading and exposition of scripture. There is, however, only scant evidence for singing in unison (Sanders 1992: 208).

The emphasis on the individual adherence to the law sets ancient Judaism apart from many other religious systems of the time. The most obvious and universally kept set of laws consisted of the purity regulations. The majority of the laws were set for the purpose of keeping the temple in a state of ritual purity. The holy things were not to be handled in a ritually impure state caused, for example, by contact with semen, dead bodies or menstrual discharge. There is, however, some evidence that many people considered purity to be the proper state to be in, whether or not one was about to enter the temple (Sanders 1992: 218). The most essential means of purification was water and most impurities required bathing to eradicate, which ideally meant immersion in running water (Sanders 1992: 222). Another extensive set of rules regulated what Jews could and could not eat.

One further ritual requirement needs to be mentioned: Jewish families circumcised their sons. The practice was not uncommon in the Mediterranean world but it was nonetheless regarded as distinctively Jewish (Sanders 1992: 213). The conventional theological justification of the practice was that it was a sign of the covenant with Abraham and the election of Israel. The Torah (Gen 17:12; Lev 12:3) commands the Jews to circumcise boys on the eighth day after birth.

3. *The Cognitive Approach to Ritual Systems*

Within any particular religious tradition, one is likely find a multitude of different kinds of rituals and first-century Judaism was clearly no exception. The purpose of any general theory of ritual is to lay out the relevant distinctions which can provide some order in the immense variety of ritual phenomena. In cognitive analysis, the starting point is the effect of rituals on our senses and mind.

It is one of the most obvious but also most poorly researched aspects of ritual that it targets our physical senses in order to affect our emotions. A very brief perusal of the world's religions in this regard shows that no sensory modality is neglected in such attempts. There is an endless variety of means through which the orchestration of sensory stimuli—or its absence[2]—evokes the participants' feelings through the course of rituals. Such "sensory pageantry"—to use a term coined by McCauley and Lawson (2002)—can include sounds of musical instruments and song, tastes of food and drink, sightings of ritual objects and costumes, darkness and light, kinestethic sensations from dancing, kneeling, prostrating, and other bodily movements, haptic sensations of cold, wet, hot or dry environments or of pain and pleasure.

---

[2] McCauley and Lawson (2002) understand sensory stimuli and pageantry to be simple correlatives: the more stimulation, the more pageantry. However, there are rituals in which the emotions are evoked through an artificially arranged absence of any stimuli, as when participants are required to keep silent for an extended period or when they are kept in darkness. These simple maneuvers can, of course, have powerful emotional effects. Sensory pageantry could therefore be conceived as any means by which rituals alter our normal human stimulus environment, whether by an increase or a radical decrease of stimuli.

A lot has been written on the symbolic meanings of such ritual elements, but the more fundamental fact that they trigger various emotions and somatic states that can be experienced as highly satisfying or fulfilling, is often overlooked. While emotional arousal is an important issue behind sensory stimuli, McCauley and Lawson (2002) believe that a simple way to compare and measure such arousal is through the observable measurements of sensory pageantry. Accordingly, rituals can be described as situated somewhere along a continuum between low and high levels of sensory pageantry. Rituals of high levels of sensory pageantry may thus be assumed to evoke higher arousal in participants than rituals of low levels of sensory pageantry. In more mundane terms, some rituals seem to be highly intense, such as the sacrifice of 30,000 lambs in a spectacular festival attended by hordes of people, while others are very plain and ordinary—such as the daily immersion in a bath of clear and cool water, or the washing of the hands before eating, as practiced by Pharisees.

The other important dimension to be noted about rituals is the frequency of their performance. In terms of frequency, rituals can also be broadly classified in two distinct groups—the high-frequency ones and the low-frequency ones. Some rituals are repeated daily or weekly whereas some rituals are only done perhaps once in a lifetime, such as the Muslim pilgrimage to Mecca. These two types of frequencies have very different effects and demands on our memory; our ability to retain religious information is related to the frequency of our exposure to it.

With the help of these two variables we can map all different types of ritual into a two-dimensional space of ritual possibilities (see Fig. 1).

Most cognitive theorists agree that such a ritual space includes two major attractor positions where most rituals tend to be situated.[3] In corner A, there are low-frequency rituals of very high sensory pageantry. These tend to be capable of evoking religious intuitions and rousing religious motivations due to their higher levels of cognitive and sensory pageantry combined with emotional arousal. In the opposite corner D, there are high-frequency rituals accompanied with lower levels of sensory pageantry. These kinds of rituals, in turn, have the

---

[3] For extended discussion of this and more refined ways of mapping religious rituals, see McCauley & Lawson 2002; Whitehouse 2004a: 139–55. For counterexamples and a challenge to this claim, see Atran 2002: 157–59.

Figure 1. Potential rituals and the two attractor positions (adapted from McCauley and Lawson 2002: 43).

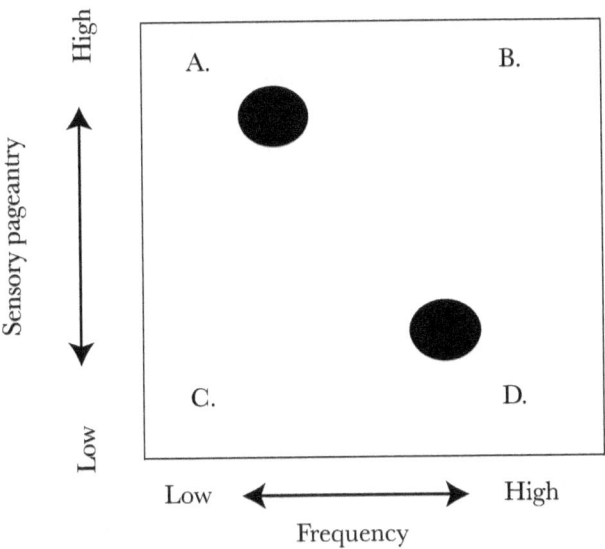

useful function of consolidating religious understandings and motivations through frequent repetition. According to most cognitive theories, these are the two basic types of rituals around which the majority of the world's religious traditions have been built, although the theories explain the fact quite differently.[4]

Thus, the broad argument presented here is that certain material, physiological and psychological factors constrain and limit religious ritual systems, which tend to converge towards certain attractor positions. Whitehouse further argues that these attractors involve distinguishable "modes of religiosity," that is, the "imagistic" and the "doctrinal." However, in view of the fact that many religious social organizations seem to be capable of involving both types of ritual systems quite easily, these expressions may be misleading. It is best to keep our theoretical

---

[4] Whitehouse's theory stresses the role of memory. In fact, he states that the bifurcation is very likely an adaptation to the constraints present in human memory in an attempt to transmit a religious tradition (2004a: 152). Thus, the transmission can be achieved in basically two ways: either through frequent repetition or through intense experience. Both result in lasting memories (Whitehouse 2002a, 2004a). McCauley and Lawson (2002: 113–23), in turn, explain the bifurcation as following the "ritual form," that is to say, whether the superhuman agent is connected to the agent's, instrument's or patient's role in the ritual's structural description (see below).

commitments to the minimum in this regard (cf. Boyer 2005). Thus, I shall opt for the theoretical language used by McCauley and Lawson involving simply different kinds of ritual systems. Whatever one's theoretical preferences in this regard, these factors are in any case the key to understanding the dynamic profiles of different religious ritual systems.

McCauley and Lawson (2002: 179–212) make an intriguing further statement, i.e., that religious ritual systems may be "unbalanced" in the sense of lacking rituals of one or the other attractor positions. According to their formulation, the balance of a religious ritual system depends on whether there exists both "special agent rituals" where the superhuman agents are conceived as acting upon humans and "special patient rituals" where humans act upon gods. One key claim of the theory of ritual form is that, all other things being equal, within a single ritual system, the special agent rituals always involve more sensory pageantry than the special patient rituals. They argue that the special agent rituals are of necessity infrequent ones because, when gods act, the consequences are conceived as permanent whereas when humans act, the results are impermanent. Furthermore, the high arousal can be explained as a means convincing the participants that something really important is going on. Thus, the infrequent, high arousal rituals are generally "special agent rituals" and the frequent, low arousal ones are "special patient rituals." (McCauley and Lawson 2002: 113–23.)

The Jewish ritual system around the first century does not seem to fit the pattern, however. From the point of view of the theory of ritual form, the Jewish ritual system would have to be described as an unbalanced system since there seem to have been no special agent rituals.[5] Festivals were most likely special patient rituals as all sacrifices are by definition special patient rituals.[6] Considering the amount of sensory pageantry present in these rituals, it seems that the ritual form hypothesis as presented by McCauley and Lawson may at least need some qualifications.

---

[5] Even circumcision is characterized as something the Jewish people are expected to do to honor the covenant (Gen 17: 9–14), rather than something that the priests are performing on boys on behalf of God.

[6] It must be kept in mind here that large religious ceremonies may well include several rituals, in the sense of the theory of ritual form. Thus, although sacrifices as such are special patient rituals, such acts may be included in larger ceremonial settings which may also include special agent rituals.

Whether the agentive properties of ritual really determine the amount the sensory pageantry is involved is, in any case, highly debatable on both conceptual and empirical grounds (Pyysiäinen 2001: 90–97; 2004b; 2005; Malley and Barrett 2003). Thus, it seems advisable to uncouple these two issues: the sensory pageantry of a ritual is not necessarily determined by the respective roles of gods and humans. Ritual systems may thus be balanced/unbalanced either with regard to the *form* of the rituals, that is, they may lack either special patient or special agent rituals, or in the sense of *ritual type*, determined simply by frequency and sensory pageantry (cf. Fig. 1.). Thus, first-century Judaism can be described as being unbalanced in terms of form and yet be described as balanced in terms of ritual type.

The situation is less problematic for the modes theory put forward by Whitehouse. The modes theory is built upon the assumption that different ritual systems (in terms of frequency and arousal) tend to produce distinct and identifiable socio-political formations. It is obvious that the sacrificial cult at the temple and especially the pilgrim festivals entailed high levels of sensory pageantry, thus boosting national loyalties and religious motivations. On the other hand, the regular twice-a-day prayers and the weekly attendance at the synagogue service entailed a very different ritual system involving low sensory pageantry and serving mainly in educating people in the religious law. It is important to note that lay people were indeed required to study the scripture (Sanders 1992: 198). However, the temple cult and the institution of the synagogue clearly contributed to the same socio-political formation of Judaism. In Whitehouse's terms, the situation could be seen as a case of "interacting modes of religiosity" (see Whitehouse 2000; 2004b). Both ritual systems contributed to the same Jewish identity.[7]

In summary, Jewish ritual life in first-century Palestine seems to represent a system that includes both low-frequency rituals with high sensory pageantry and high-frequency rituals of low sensory pageantry. However, in contrast to Lawson and McCauley's predictions, both of these main types of rituals seem to have been special patient rituals.

---

[7] However, the notion of interacting modes is problematic since it is far from clear what would count as counterevidence to the idea that ritual systems produce distinct modes of religiosity in the first place. Thus, I shall opt for the concept of balanced religious systems rather than interacting but essentially distinct modes. As far as I can see, the existence of two distinct and universally present modes has not been sufficiently demonstrated (see Whitehouse and Laidlaw 2004; Whitehouse and Martin 2004).

The role of the superhuman agents in these rituals does not seem to determine their type.

4. *The Dynamic Patterns*

Our second task is to see whether cognitive analysis can shed light on the religious socio-political formations within first-century Judaism. In a nutshell, the cognitive argument is that the type of ritual system on which the religious tradition maintains itself has consequences for the typical courses of change and development in the religious community in question. In the analysis of historical religious traditions, it is therefore of crucial importance to try to focus on the distinctive cultic communities and identify their most characteristic ritual practices. When such information is available, further hypotheses of the likely processes to have contributed to the evolution of religious communities can easily be made.

McCauley and Lawson (2002) have identified two broad patterns of religious change depending on whether the ritual system is balanced or unbalanced. Both the causes of religious splintering and their eventual outcomes are typically not the same in these types of systems. Again, their model is based upon the idea of formal properties of ritual systems. The system is balanced if the ritual system includes both special agent and special patient rituals whereas it is unbalanced if it lacks either the special agent or the special patient rituals. However, as the following discussion aims to show, the dynamic properties are really caused by the properties of ritual *types*, as determined by the frequency and sensory pageantry, and so one may use the model without committing oneself to the special assumptions of theory of ritual form.

The two most relevant cases here are the balanced system and the unbalanced system centering on rituals in the attractor position D (see Fig. 1). The major problem with the latter types of rituals is that they are often deficient in their power to motivate participation. Ritual systems based on only these types of rituals are therefore unstable because of the "tedium effect"[8] (McCauley and Lawson 2002: 192–201). This suggests two scenarios: first, in the case of excessive control over ritual expression and innovation, the motivation of participants may start to falter and

---

[8] On the "tedium effect," see Whitehouse 2000: 44–46; 2004a: 97–99.

the system may gradually start to lose adherents. Second, there may emerge various attempts at *ritual reform*, usually through incorporating elements of higher arousal into existing rituals. In extreme cases, the unbalanced systems of this type generate temporary splinter groups in which the existing rituals are invested with extraordinary amounts of sensory pageantry. Characteristically, participation in such revitalization movements does not change the participants' religious identity since there is no attempt to subvert these rituals. These revitalized rituals renew the motivation of the participants but after the most intense phase is over, participants often return to the parent system (McCauley and Lawson 2002: 200).

The balanced ritual systems, in turn, do not exhibit such fluctuations but are characterized by greater stability. As long as some of the rituals exhibit high levels of sensory pageantry, the level of motivation tends to remain high and the tedium effect may be effectively kept at bay. Similarly, as long as some of the rituals are frequently performed, they provide means for consolidating the religious conceptual systems into people's lives successfully. Provided that such ritual systems possess conceptual resources sufficient to ensure that the interpretations of the experiences engendered in high-arousal rituals do not deviate detectably from the prevailing tradition, such systems may be extraordinarily stable over a long period of time (McCauley and Lawson 2002: 181–82).

The most prominent causes of splintering in the balanced ritual systems appear to be conceptual and political, and very often they seem purely contingent. The reason for this is that the differences in opinion more likely result from the *interpretation* of rituals rather than their mode of performance (McCauley and Lawson 2002: 201–3).

McCauley and Lawson categorize different outcomes of splintering in the balanced systems into three typical scenarios: the new system may either (1) be destroyed along with its members; (2) dissolve with its participants surviving; or (3) the system may survive as an independent religious ritual system. In case it is not dissolved or destroyed, the system is in fact very likely to develop into an independent religious ritual system. In addition to successful resistance against suppression, other critical conditions for this development are that the new ritual system is also of the balanced type, and that it contains a greater amount of sensory pageantry as compared to the parent system (McCauley and Lawson 2002: 204–5).

However, there is always the possibility that the balanced systems begin to get out of balance through losing some of the sensory pageantry exhibited in rituals. Such *deflated balanced systems* may then become unstable, which sets the stage for other trajectories of change more typical of the unbalanced systems. McCauley and Lawson (2002: 209) list three typical scenarios of ritual development that may follow: (1) ritual intensification: splinter group movements may reenergize existing rituals of the infrequent, high-arousal type in the parent system; (2) ritual multiplication: splinter groups may permit additional performances of available rituals of the infrequent, high-arousal type; (3) ritual innovation: splinter groups may create completely new rituals accompanied with increased sensory pageantry (McCauley and Lawson 2002: 204–5).

In the following section, we shall examine which of these trajectories—characteristic of balanced, unbalanced or deflated balanced ritual systems—best characterizes the Jewish groups during the first century.

5. *Cultic Communities in First-Century Palestine*

Scholarship has recognized that Judaism of first-century Palestine was enormously diverse and dynamic (Sanders 1992; McClymond 2001). Competing factions, groups and sects were legion at that time. The most prominent groups seem to have been the Pharisees, the Sadducees, and the Essenes or Qumran community.[9] Other popular movements included the so-called "Fourth Philosophy" (essentially a religious tax resistance movement initiated by Judas the Galilean in 6 C.E.) and various anti-Roman resistance movements before and during the Jewish War 66–70, such as the Zealots and the Sicarii ("dagger men"). In addition, first-century Jewish society witnessed a plethora of individual prophetic figures, miracle workers and other holy men of popular Jewish religion, such as John the Baptist and Jesus (Sanders 1992: 13–29; McClymond 2001: 365–80; Vermes 2000: 230–49).

It has been argued that the Qumran community came into existence because of a perceived illegitimacy of the priestly practices. There

---

[9] The exact relationship of the Qumran community to the Essenes is under some dispute. The Qumran community may have been only a monastic settlement within a broader movement of Essenes which included married members. It may, however, also have been a splinter group of the Essene movement (see Sanders 1992: 342–45).

seems to have been a mixture of ritual and political reasons behind the protest. The community understood itself as the true temple and the people ordered their lives according to how they believed the temple ought to be managed and waited for the present temple leadership to be overthrown (McClymond 2001: 371). Some of the distinctive practices of the Qumran community were sharing of material possessions and strict regulations on ritual purity that normally applied only to the temple priests. Among the ritual practices of the community were communal meals and ritual bathing.

Closer to the religious mainstream were the "parties" of the Sadducees and the Pharisees. Here we see more clearly political issues at the root of these groups. The Sadducees and the Pharisees were the two contending groups vying for political favor among the rulers. The Sadducees were the leaders in Jerusalem from the age of the Maccabees, whereas the Pharisees replaced them as religious leaders after the Jewish War. Neither was a tightly organized group like the Essenes, however. The groups also had frequent doctrinal disputes with each other, largely over matters of ritual purity. Not much is known about the religious views of these groups. From the writings of Josephus, it appears, though, that the Pharisees were more strict in their observance of rules concerning ritual purity, while their religious views included popular traditions, like the idea of immortal soul, resurrection of the dead and eternal punishment for the wicked (McClymond 2001: 369–70). The Sadducees, on the other hand, held exclusively to the old law in matters of doctrine, but were otherwise more open to Hellenizing influences—sort of aristocratic intellectuals, perhaps.

If the above picture of the first-century groups is on the right track, the general causes of splintering in first-century Judaism were largely of a political and doctrinal nature, which is characteristic of balanced ritual systems. However, the Qumran community shows some evidence of developing alternative rituals in a self-sufficient ritual world of their own. According to the theory of ritual form, attempts at ritual reform should be rare in balanced systems whereas deflated balanced systems should be rife with innovation. The Qumran community and the Jesus movement constitute two important splinter groups providing further evidence in this regard. We shall have to look at these more closely to get some idea of the fundamental characteristics of the system.

6. *Were There Ritual Innovations?*

As Sanders (1992: 352) puts it, three things set the Qumran community apart from the rest of Judaism: food, purity and the temple. They adhered to a strict code of ritual purity that restricted their association with other people. They thought that only members of their community were destined for salvation; all other Jews were considered apostates. The members had sworn not to eat food prepared by non-members. They had a ritual calendar of their own, which meant that the community feasts were celebrated differently from the rest of Judaism. As a result of this, they—or at least some of them—lived in a self-enclosed world of their own. (Sanders 1992: 350-61; Vermes 1975: 42-44.)

It would therefore not be surprising if the Qumran community also developed ritual innovations to compensate for the loss of participation in the temple sacrifices and festivals. The most interesting development in this regard seems to be the institution of the so-called "Pure Meal," as Sanders translates the term, denoting the common meal partaken in the community. It was solely restricted to the members of the community. Novices were not allowed to participate until a year had passed. Misdeeds resulted in expulsion from the Pure Meal. To participate, one had to purify oneself by immersion in cold water and, according to Josephus, wear special clothes reserved solely for the meal. A priest always presided and was the first to bless the bread or the wine. It is, however, difficult to determine whether the Pure Meal took place in a special room that was forbidden to non-members and was treated as a sanctuary. (Sanders 1992: 352-61.)

There is some disagreement with regard to the frequency of meal. Sanders argues that this was not the same as the twice daily meal, but "a rite for special occasions, times when a group of sectarians ate the first fruits or bread or drank the new wine" (1992: 355, emphasis deleted). In contrast to the practice at Jerusalem, there were probably more than one first-fruits feast at Qumran. Another possibility is that the Pure Meals accompanied all solemn gatherings.

Following Sanders' overall reconstruction, we can thus conclude that the Qumran community regarded their community itself as a temple. Their codes of purity reflected the ones followed by the temple priesthood. It was a priestly practice to bathe before eating. Thus, the Qumranites aimed at the same level of purity that was required in the temple, if not exceeding it by adding a few extra rules. The community, in other words, seems to represent a kind of ritual intensification with some of their practices being completely new, such as the special Pure Meals. If such is the case, the development would be more characteristic of a deflated balanced type of ritual system.

In light of the Qumran practices, the movement that developed around the figure of Jesus is also quite intriguing. According to the Synoptic Gospels, Jesus was both a healer-exorcist and a prophetic preacher of the Kingdom of God. The practice of healing is especially noteworthy since religious healing is, in fact, a type of special agent ritual. In healing rituals, it is the supernatural agents who act on people suffering from various ailments. Healing cults are not, however, characteristic of religious elites. As Geza Vermes (2000) notes, Jesus was a charismatic holy man of a typically Near-Eastern type of popular religious figures, a "man of God," through whom ordinary people could come into contact with God. There seem to have been many similar figures in the first-century Near East (Vermes 2000). Such holy men have also been of profound importance in Islamic cultures up to the present day (Gellner 1981: 40–41). The baptisms performed by John the Baptist also point to the fact that there existed a popular demand for special agent rituals in first-century Judaism (Pyysiäinen 2004b; Uro forthcoming).

However, few such "men of God" have precipitated the development of organized religious movements in the way that Jesus did. It is therefore crucial to look at the ritual behavior that emerged in the movement around Jesus. If a charismatic person is simply one who is exceptionally committed to following the traditional religious norms, his or her behavior represents ritual intensification. Ritual intensifications of the unbalanced type rarely lead to full-scale new religions. However, if such intensification takes place in a deflated balanced system, it may more easily transform into a full-scale ritual innovation and thereafter lead to the formation of an independent religious movement.

The Jesus movement did eventually break out to form a new religious tradition, Christianity, and thus it is an especially interesting case to study. The controversy Jesus provoked may provide a pointer towards the nature of the rituals practiced among Jesus' followers.

It should be kept in mind that for a few decades after the crucifixion, the Jesus movement was composed mainly of Jews and they probably maintained all the outward marks of observant Jews (McClymond 2001: 433). James, the brother of Jesus, seems to have been a well-known figure in the Jerusalem Temple. As the biblical scholar Michael J. McClymond has observed: "These first followers of Jesus were pious adherents of

Judaism, who observed circumcision, the Sabbath, the dietary laws, festivals and fasts, and other traditions. If Jesus had clearly broken with these Jewish practices, then it is quite unlikely that his earliest followers would have continued them." (2001: 433) Indeed, much has been made of the Jewishness of Jesus in recent scholarship. As J. Andrew Overman and William Scott Green put it: "[T]he Jesus movement was a type of *Judaism* and was perceived as such by non-Jews" (Overman and Green 1992, cited in McClymond 2001: 375).

There were conflicts, however. Of special interest here is the practice of sharing meals with others. It does appear, for instance, that the primary conflict that the Jesus movement had with the Pharisees was precisely over eating habits. Sanders (1985) has claimed that there was no substantial conflict between Jesus and the Pharisees with regard to the Sabbath, food, and purity laws. However, the Gospels testify to a conflict concerning Jesus' sharing of meals with "sinners." These sinners were simply people who did not observe the Jewish law as strictly as the Pharisees would have it. Jesus seems to have had the most intimate shared meals with the most disreputable characters in society. Jesus incurred the wrath of the Pharisees by sharing meals with these outcasts (McClymond 2001: 435).

Bearing in mind what was taking place in the Qumran community, it is likely that the meals within the Jesus movement also had potent ritual significance. Unlike the Qumranites and the Pharisees, who shared communal meals among themselves, that is, among those deemed of equal purity, Jesus shared his meals with everybody. It has been suggested that this signifies a completely new concept of commensality tied with his view of the Kingdom of God (Crossan 1994). McClymond (2001: 394) summarizes the point aptly:

> Perhaps the most distinctive thing about Jesus' ministry [...] is his practice of open commensality in which different social groups—rich and poor, male and female, observant Jew and nonobservant—shared their meals in common. This was truly revolutionary, a ritual enactment of an inclusive kingdom that challenged existing social hierarchy.

All these facts seem to point towards the conclusion that first-century Judaism was indeed basically a balanced ritual system, one which was mostly characterized by doctrinal and political disputes rather than ritual ones. However, in view of the fact that the high arousal rituals were, in practice, out of reach for many ordinary people, especially for those living in the diaspora, the system was most likely in the process of becoming deflated. In such a situation, even quite an innocent attempt at ritual intensification, such as in the case of Jesus, would easily lead into theological disputes and full-scale splintering. When this had happened, the stage was set for a recognizably new kind of ritual to emerge among the followers of Jesus. Thus, important innovations took place around the special meals. In contrast to healing, where God is seen to act upon specific individuals and their ailments, the idea of a common meal, presided over by a superhuman agent, would in effect constitute a special agent ritual that transmits God's blessing to the entire group of participants. However, such an interpretation also constitutes a ritual innovation and a nucleus of a splinter group.

If this interpretation is correct, it would explain a number of salient features of the Jesus movement, and possibly even of the later development. It would explain the fact that Jesus, as a healer and prophet, would tend to gather a controversial ritual community around himself. In Qumran, the community was the new temple, in the case of Jesus, he declared *himself* to be the temple (Mark 14:58, 15:29; Matt 26:61, 27:40; John 2:19). This interpretation would explain why the meals gained such poignant meaning—and very likely increasing amounts of sensory pageantry—among his followers after the crucifixion. Even in his physical absence, Jesus was thought to be present in a special way at these meals. It would explain the fact that the sharing of bread and wine in common meals soon became the central act of commemoration of Jesus among his followers. The early Christians thought that Jesus' continued presence animated their eucharistic meals, even if healing and prophesying might have become less common quite early.

Thus, according to this line of thinking, there exists a crucial continuity from the very beginnings of Jesus' career through the Jesus movement to the early church in the form of common meals which, in the participants' eyes, may have gradually come to signify of the presence of the Kingdom of God. When and how such consensus on its meaning came to solidify is, of course, debatable, but without question, in the absence of such ritual innovation at some stage of its development, the Christian church would probably never have been born.

7. *Conclusion*

The analysis shows that first-century Judaism was highly unbalanced in *terms of form*. Apart perhaps from circumcision, which applied only to newborn males, there were no officially sanctioned special agent rituals available to the common people. Popular men of God, such as Jesus or John the Baptist, may have provided occasional outlets for people's yearnings for a more direct contact with God. Charismatic rural healer-prophets may always have been there to provide common people with experiences of being patients to God's direct acts. Normally, such charismatic figures are characteristic of unbalanced ritual systems, which do not create lasting groups around distinctive ritual innovations.

The most puzzling thing about this ritual system is that the rituals containing greatest amount of sensory pageantry apparently were not special agent rituals. This observation, if true, casts doubt on one of the central elements of Lawson and McCauley's theory. It seems advisable to conclude that the issue of balance in the *sense of form* (that is, balance in terms of special agent vs. special patient rituals) should be kept separate from the issue of balance in the *sense of ritual type*, determined by frequency and sensory pageantry alone. Thus, it is possible to observe that, by the first century, Judaism seems to have developed into a ritual system of the balanced type containing both infrequent high-arousal rituals and frequent low-arousal ones. The annual temple festivals with their high sensory pageantry seem to have been balanced with highly routine rituals in the synagogues and frequent prayers at home.

However, the evidence from the Qumran community and the Jesus movement suggests that it would be even more accurate to describe the Jewish ritual system around the time of Jesus as a *deflated* balanced system. Although firmly Jewish in their identity and in their acceptance of common Judaism, both the Qumran community and the Jesus movement may have inadvertently developed rudimentary forms of subversive ritual arrangements. They both developed a form of special communal meal with potent ritual and political significance in the context of purity-conscious and temple-centered Judaism. In the context of a (deflated) balanced system, even minor issues could have become contentious and therefore capable of triggering mutual hostilities between the splinter group and the rest of society. All the elements needed for the rapid development of independent ritual systems were thus in place. With the increasing separation of the Jesus movement from the rest of Judaism, the communal meal would eventually evolve through further incorporation of sensory pageantry into a central ritual expression of an entirely new religion, Christianity.

Acknowledgement

I thank Jutta Jokiranta, Petri Luomanen, Luther H. Martin, Ilkka Pyysiäinen, Tom Sjöblom and Risto Uro for helpful and encouraging comments on earlier versions of this paper. The research for this article was funded by the Academy of Finland (project 1-200827).

REFERENCES

Atran, Scott. 2002. *In Gods We Trust: The Evolutionary Landscape of Religion*. Oxford: Oxford University Press.
Boyer, Pascal. 2005. "A Reductionistic Model of Distinct Modes of Religious Transmission." In *Mind and Religion: Psychological and Cognitive Foundations of Religion*, edited by Harvey Whitehouse & Robert N. McCauley, 3-30. Walnut Creek, Calif.: AltaMira.
Crossan, John Dominic. 1994. *Jesus: A Revolutionary Biography*. San Fransisco, Calif.: HarperCollins.
Gellner, Ernest. 1981. *Muslim Society*. Cambridge: Cambridge University Press.
Lawson, E. Thomas. 2005. "Ritual Form and Ritual Frequency." In *Mind and Religion: Psychological and Cognitive Foundations of Religion*, edited by Harvey Whitehouse & Robert N. McCauley, 57-68. Walnut Creek, Calif.: AltaMira.
Lawson, E. Thomas, and Robert N. McCauley. 1990. *Rethinking Religion: Connecting Cognition and Culture*. Oxford: Oxford University Press.
Malley, Brian, and Justin Barrett. 2003. "Can Ritual Form Be Predicted from Religious Belief? A Test of the Lawson-McCauley Hypotheses." *Journal of Ritual Studies* 17(2): 1-14.
McCauley, Robert N., and E. Thomas Lawson. 2002. *Bringing Ritual to Mind: Psychological Foundations of Cultural Forms*. New York: Cambridge University Press.
McClymond, Michael J. 2001. "Jesus." In *The Rivers of Paradise: Moses, Buddha, Jesus, and Muhammad as Religious Founders*, edited by David Noel Freedman and Michael J. McClymond, 309-456. Cambridge: Eerdmans.
Overman, J. Andrew, and William Scott Green. 1992. "Judaism (Greco-Roman Period)." In *Anchor Bible Dictionary* 3:1027-54. New York: Doubleday.
Pyysiäinen, Ilkka. 2001. *How Religion Works: Towards a New Cognitive Science of Religion*. Leiden: Brill.
———. 2004a. *Magic, Miracles and Religion: A Scientist's Perspective*. Walnut Creek, Calif.: AltaMira.
———. 2004b. "Rituaalinen näkökulma kristinuskon syntyyn: kommentti Risto Uron artikkeliin." *Teologinen Aikakauskirja* 109: 562-67.
———. 2005. "Religious Conversion and Modal Dynamics." In *Mind and Religion: Psychological and Cognitive Foundations of Ritual*, edited by Harvey Whitehouse & Robert N. McCauley, 149-66. Walnut Creek, Calif.: AltaMira.
Pyysiäinen, Ilkka, and Veikko Anttonen, eds. 2002. *Current Approaches in the Cognitive Science of Religion*. London: Continuum.
Rappaport, Roy, A. 1999. *Ritual and Religion in the Making of Humanity*. Cambridge: Cambridge University Press.
Sanders, E. P. 1985. *Jesus and Judaism*. Philadelphia, Pa.: Fortress.
———. 1992. *Judaism: Practice and Belief 63 B.C.E.-66 C.E.* London: SCM Press

Sosis, Richard, and Candance Alcorta. 2003. "Signaling, Solidarity, and the Sacred: The Evolution of Religious Behavior." *Evolutionary Anthropology* 12: 264–74.
Stark, Rodney. 1996. *The Rise of Christianity: How the Obscure, Marginal Jesus Movement Became the Dominant Religious Force in the Western World in a Few Centuries.* Princeton, N.J.: Princeton University Press.
Uro, Risto. Forthcoming. "Towards a Cognitive History of Early Christian Rituals." In *Changing Minds: Religion and Cognition through the Ages*, edited by István Czachesz and Tamás Bíró. Groningen Studies in Cultural Change. Leuven: Peeters
Vermes, Geza. 1975. *The Dead Sea Scrolls in English.* 2nd edition. Harmondsworth: Penguin.
———. 2000. *The Changing Faces of Jesus.* London: Penguin.
Whitehouse, Harvey. 1995. *Inside the Cult: Religious Innovation and Transmission in Papua New Guinea.* Oxford: Clarendon Press.
———. 2000. *Arguments and Icons: Divergent Modes of Religiosity.* Oxford: Oxford University Press.
———. 2002a. "Modes of Religiosity: Towards a Cognitive Explanation of the Sociopolitical Dynamics of Religion." *Method & Theory in the Study of Religion* 14: 293–315.
———. 2002b. "Conjectures, Refutations, and Verification: Towards a Testable Theory of 'Modes of Religiosity.'" *Journal of Ritual Studies* 16(2): 44–59.
———. 2004a. *Modes of Religiosity: A Cognitivive Theory of Religious Transmission.* Walnut Creek, Calif.: AltaMira.
———. 2004b. "Theorizing Religions Past. In *Theorizing Religions Past: Archaeology, History, and Cognition*, edited by Harvey Whitehouse & Luther H. Martin, 215–32. Walnut Creek, Calif.: AltaMira.
Whitehouse, Harvey, and Luther H. Martin, eds. 2004. *Theorizing Religions Past: Archaeology, History, and Cognition.* Walnut Creek, Calif.: AltaMira.
Whitehouse, Harvey, and Robert N. McCauley, eds. 2005. *Mind and Religion: Psychological and Cognitive Foundations of Religion.* Walnut Creek, Calif.: AltaMira.
Whitehouse, Harvey, and James Laidlaw, eds. 2004. *Ritual and Memory: Toward a Comparative Anthropology of Religion.* Walnut Creek, Calif.: AltaMira.

GNOSTIC RITUALS FROM A COGNITIVE PERSPECTIVE

Risto Uro

1. *Studying Early Christian Rituals*

The analysis of early Christian rituals faces two major challenges. The first has to do with the theoretical basis of such an analysis and the second with the evidence to be analyzed or explained.

Scholars of early Christianity have generally approached their subject from theological or intellectualist perspectives, preferring belief to action, thought-world to social world, or myth to ritual. This is not to say that scholars have not been interested in the history of Christian liturgical texts and practices. Scholars of liturgy have typically traced the evolution of eucharistic and baptismal texts philologically, comparing ancient church orders and other liturgical traditions and trying to identify their most original forms as well as their background in Jewish ritual practices (Bradshaw 2002). The German history-of-religion school was fascinated by the influence of Hellenistic mysteries on early Christian myth and ritual (e.g., Reitzenstein 1927). More recently, especially New Testament scholars have begun to utilize sociological and anthropological models and perspectives in the study of early Christian texts. This has entailed some attempts to apply ritual theories developed in social or cultural anthropology, the most popular of which has been Victor Turner's analysis of the dialectics of structure and anti-structure in the ritual process (V. Turner 1969, 1974; for applications to early Christian data, see, e.g., Draper 2000; McVann 1991, 1994; Strecker 1999).

Nevertheless, in terms of theory, there is not a large body of scholarly literature on early Christianity utilizing the study of ritual in anthropology and comparative religion on which one could build a cross-disciplinary approach to studying early Christian rituals. The little that has been done in this regard is not always illuminating with regard to the actual ritual activities among the earliest Christians and the role these rituals played in the transmission of early Christian traditions. It seems justified to conclude that the study of early Christian rituals is still in its embryonic state and any attempts to develop theoretical approaches to them are consequently experimental. This essay is even doubly experimental since it seeks to test the applicability of a recent cognitive model, advanced by the anthropologist Harvey Whitehouse, on early Christian evidence. Cognitive approaches are themselves quite a novelty in the study of early Christianity and differ in many significant ways from more traditional approaches to ritual.

Although myth has often been preferred to ritual in the study of religion, or myth and ritual have been conjoined so that the latter has not been discussed without the former, recent approaches have emphasized that ritual should be studied in itself and for itself (Smith 1987: 103; Bell 1992: 16). This orientation creates a further problem for the study of early Christian ritual. If we want to study ritual in its own right, we immediately face the fact that the evidence we have for the ritual practices of the formative Christian groups, especially its first two hundred years or so, is at its best sparse and fragmentary. Of course, some theological interpretations of the rituals have remained and also a few passages that are more or less confidently identified as liturgical fragments. We also have some early church orders, such as the *Didache* (first or second century), *Apostolic Tradition* (early third century), and *Didascalia Apostolorum* (third century). These texts do not, however, yield a comprehensive picture of the ritual practices and the relationship between liturgical legislations (that is, church orders) and actual customs is far from being straightforward (Bradshaw 2002: 18–19). We do not have anything comparable to the ethnographic data based on fieldwork observations and interviews undertaken by anthropologists. No "thick description" of early Christian ritual systems is possible. This problem, of course, exists in the investigation of all ancient religions.

The latter challenge is further intensified if one focuses on what are usually called "gnostic" groups or movements among early Christians. The scholarly construct of "Gnosticism" is currently a subject of lively discussion (Williams 1996; King 2003; Marjanen 2005), but even without that, we are faced with huge problems in defining the evidence. We know even less of the community life of gnostic groups than of many other branches of Christianity which were not condemned as heretics by the church fathers. The knowledge we have often comes from the polemical writings of the early Christian heresiologists and should not be taken as disinterested observations or even as firsthand pieces of information, although parts of their accounts are obviously based on reading the books written by the heretics and even on personal contacts with them.[1] After the discovery of the Nag Hammadi texts, the material deriving from the gnostics themselves has increased dramatically, but only occasionally do we learn of the ritual practices in which the groups behind these texts were engaged (see, however, J. Turner 1994).

A Nag Hammadi text that has been most promising for ritual analyses is the *Gospel of Philip*, the third tractate of Codex II. Ever since its publication,[2] scholars have been intrigued by the gospel's numerous references to rituals and its complex discussions on their meanings and effects. Unfortunately, scholars have not been able to reach anything like a consensus on the ritual system(s) reflected in the gospel, since it presents highly symbolic and elusive exegeses and is quite uninformative about the actual practices. Nonetheless, however insufficient, the *Gospel of Philip*, together with some glimpses in other related texts and in the church fathers' works (first of all, in Irenaeus' *Adversus haereses*, Book I), constitutes the best "ethnographic" data available to us so far for an analysis of a ritual system of a Christian gnostic movement.

2. *The* Gospel of Philip *and the Valentinian Movement*

What makes it possible to speak of a movement here is the fact that most scholars classify the *Gospel of Philip* among the "Valentinian" writings. Valentinus was a Christian teacher who received his education and started his career in Alexandria, but spent at least fifteen years in Rome in the mid-second century. We know very little about his life and teaching. A few preserved fragments, however, give the impression of a learned person who composed letters, sermons and poems (Markschies 1992; Thomassen 2006). He eventually became a founder of what the church fathers call the "school of Valentinus," sometimes dividing it into two branches, an "Italic" or Western" school and an "Eastern" school. We know of several teachers, such as Ptolemy, Heracleion, Theodotus and Marcus (Mark), who were regarded as the disciples of Valentinus or were attached to the Valentinian school(s). Scholars have recently emphasized that the movement initiated by Valentinus indeed had the

---

[1] Irenaeus (ca. 180) says that his account is based on both conversations with some of the heretics and reading their books (*Haer.* 1, preface).
[2] The photographic edition: Labib 1956; the first translation into a modern language: Schenke 1959; and the first critical edition: Till 1963.

character of a philosophical school, or network of schools, rather than a distinct and exclusivistic religious sect (Layton 1987: 267; Markschies 1997; Dunderberg 2005a). In the early phase of the movement, the leaders could teach and act relatively freely in Christian communities and the adherents were not easily distinguished from other Christians (Dunderberg 2004). At some point, however, at least part of the movement became a clearly distinguishable group with their own rituals and meetings (Dunderberg 2004: 169–73). Irenaeus describes Marcosians, the adherents of the aforementioned Valentinian teacher Marcus (active ca. 160–180 C.E.), as practicing "redemption," a kind of second initiation for those who have "received perfect knowledge" (*Haer.* 1.21.1–5). We know that the movement continued to exist as a separate group for several centuries. A note of an incident concerning the burning of a Valentinian chapel in 388 has been preserved.[3] Valentians are mentioned among the lists of the heretical groups who were forbidden to assemble in the Roman Empire in the fifth century. The last report of them comes as late as from Canon 95 of the Trullan synod dated 692 (Layton 1987: 272). Whatever similarities there were between the philosophical schools and the Valentinian movement, I argue in this essay that Valentinians, from the late second century onwards, can best be described as a religious "splinter group" (Whitehouse's term) or a loose network of such groups that had partially separated themselves from the proto-orthodox churches represented (or envisioned) by Irenaeus, Hippolytus and other heresiologists (see also Green 1982).

Although most scholars assume that there is some relationship between the *Gospel of Philip* and the movement associated with Valentinus' name, scholars are far from being unanimous about the degree and nature of the gospel's reliance on Valentinian ideas and mythology. There are a few more or less obvious links to the texts that are usually labeled Valentinian. The one most often referred to is the bridal chamber (see the discussion below), which, according to Irenaeus, was the name of the "redemption" practiced by some Marcosians (*Haer.* 1.21.3; cf. also 1.13.3) and which appears frequently in the *Gospel of Philip*, sometimes in an indisputably ritual context (e.g., 67 [§ 68]; 69 [§ 76]). The gospel also contains a few other features that can be regarded as Valentinian, such as "Achamoth/Echmoth" as a name for

---

[3] This incident is mentioned in the correspondence between Ambrose, Bishop of Milan, and the emperor Theodosius (Ambrosius, *Ep.* 40–41).

Sophia or "Lower Sophia" (cf. *Gos. Phil.* 60 [§ 39]) and the role of Jesus as one who has come to correct the primordial separation resulting in death (*Gos. Phil.* 70 [§§ 78–79]; cf. 68 [§ 71]), as well as the idea of the divine syzygies or male-female pairs and the image of union with an angelic counterpart (cf. *Gos. Phil.* 58 [§ 26b]). These kinds of affinities make Schenke conclude that the *Gospel of Philip* was "compiled by a Valentinian for Valentinians, drawn from works many of which (if not all...) were Valentinian, used as a gospel first by Valentinian communities" (Schenke 1991: 186; see also Schenke 1997 and Thomassen 1997). Others have emphasized more strongly the incoherence of the gospel and the non-Valentinian character of many of its parts (e.g., M. Turner 1996) or preferred to read the gospel in its own right without any interpretative aid from other sources (Buckley 1988a).

Considering these alternative approaches, I adopt the moderate view that, although no a priori presumptions about the unity of either the gospel itself or the sources labeled Valentinian should be made, the other Valentinian sources should not be rejected as a potential framework for the interpretation of the ritual parts of the *Gospel of Philip*. It must be recognized, though, that "Valentinianism" is a theoretical construct based on generalizations of the church fathers and the often harmonizing reading of the sources (Desjardins 1990: 12). There is no reason to assume that exact copies of this construct existed in the minds of the adherents of the movement[4] or even that doctrinal unity was the primary concern of the Valentinian teachers (see below). Neither should we think that Valentinian ritual practices did not vary among different groups or evolve over the course of time. The assumption here is simply that, in certain texts, there is enough family resemblance for an analysis of ritual practices distinct from other Christian practices in some respects.

3. *Ritual in the* Gospel of Philip

The *Gospel of Philip* is a heterogeneous collection of various types of literature: aphorisms, ethical paraenesis, theological statements, polemic,

---

[4] Boyer (1994: 228–30, 259–61; see also Pyysiäinen 2001: 38–41) has called the idea that live religiosity could be understood as some kind of coherent dogma a "theologistic fallacy." Written theologies are not exhaustive catalogs of the beliefs of their responsive readers or audience.

narratives, biblical interpretations, and so on. Although it contains a few sayings of Jesus (e.g., 55–56 [§ 18]; 64 [§ 57]; 74 [§ 97]), the "gospel" is very different from another Nag Hammadi document, the *Gospel of Thomas*, which is a collection of dominical sayings. Some scholars have sought to identify some sort of organizing principle or structure in the whole text (Wilson 1962; Ménard 1967; Tripp 1982), but most speak of a florilegium or collection of various sources or excerpts which do not reveal any governing order (Schenke 1959: 2; Schenke 1991: 183; Layton 1987: 325; M. Turner 1996).

In spite of the fact that the material is heterogeneous and the line of thought often rambling and disjointed, scholars have ventured to reconstruct a single and coherent ritual system behind the gospel. In an early analysis, a key passage for identifying the rituals of the *Gospel of Philip* was seen in the statement on page 67 (§ 68): "The Lord [did] everything in a mystery: a baptism, a chrism, a eucharist, ransom, and a bridal chamber (*numphōn*)."[5] Segelberg interpreted this as a reference to "five gnostic sacraments" (1960: 191), a conclusion that has often been repeated in scholarly literature. Segelberg argued that three of these rites, baptism, chrism, and bridal chamber, together formed a complete gnostic initiation, while the Eucharist and redemption were repeated acts. Scholars also soon discovered that some passages suggested a hierarchy among these sacraments: the chrism is more powerful than baptism (*Gos. Phil.* 74 [§ 95]); the bridal chamber is compared to the holiest room in the temple of Jerusalem, "the holy of the holies" (*Gos. Phil.* 69 [§ 76]; cf. 84 [§ 125]), and is generally used as expressing the highest revelation.

Subsequent analyses of the gospel could not, however, confirm the initial observation about the five gnostic sacraments arranged in ascending order. The rest of the gospel does not seem to accord well with this scheme of the separate rituals or ritual acts gradually leading to a full initiation. "Redemption" (Copt. *sōte*; Gr. *lytrōn, (apo)lytrōsis*) is quite elusive. On page 69 (§ 76), it is associated with both baptism and the bridal chamber and nothing more is said about it in the gospel. "Chrism" (or anointing) was an integral part of the baptismal ritual in early Christianity, albeit the number of anointings and their place in the baptismal ritual varied from place to place. In the *Gospel*

---

[5] Unless otherwise noted, the English translations of the *Gospel of Philip* are from Isenberg 1989.

of Philip, chrism (or "fire" or "light") and baptism in water are also closely bound. "It is fitting to baptize in the two, in the light and the water; now the light is the chrism" (*Gos. Phil.* 69 [§ 75]; cf. also 57 [§ 25] and 67 [§ 66]). It is difficult to say whether the text presupposes two different rituals separated by time or whether the anointing was a part of the same initiation ritual which included both baptism with water and (post-baptismal) anointing with chrism (that is, with scented oil). In any case, the gospel places much emphasis on the latter ritual act. It is said to be superior to baptism because "it is from the word 'chrism' that we have been called 'Christians,' certainly not because of the word 'baptism'" (*Gos. Phil.* 74 [§ 95]). Moreover, scholars have had great difficulties in deciding whether the bridal chamber (*nymphōn*) and its cognate terms (*pastos, koitōn*) refer to a separate ritual (Schenke 1959: 6; Gaffron 1969; Buckley 1980, 1988b), to some sort of earthly marriage (Williams 1986; Deconick 2001), to the whole initiation process (Pagels 1997; Thomassen 2006: 341), or to no ritual act at all (cf. Layton 1987: 226).

A number of scholars have pointed out that there is little or nothing in the gospel that is incompatible with the ritual practices presupposed in such non-gnostic writings as the *Didache*, Justin's *First Apology* and *Apostolic Tradition* (Pagels 1997: 282–83; see also Desjardins 1987 and Thomassen 2006: 398). In *Philip*, baptism is clearly an act of immersion (*Gos. Phil.* 64 [§ 59]) preceded by the divestiture of clothing (75 [§ 101]). The pronunciation of the threefold name ("father, son, holy spirit") over the catechumen is probably also presumed (67 [§ 67]). Various anointings, the kiss of peace at the end of the ceremony (cf. 59 [§ 31]) (Penn 2002), and the Eucharist with bread and (mixed) wine[6] are all ritual elements of the baptismal liturgy that were widely attested in early Christianity. The *Gospel of Philip* gives deeper meanings to these acts and makes much of their symbolic potentiality, but it is not easy to elicit from these interpretations a ritual procedure radically different from those described in the aforementioned non-gnostic writings.

On the other hand, there are at least two considerations which should make us cautious about concluding that the *Gospel of Philip* simply presents an original, spiritual interpretation of the baptism-chrism-Eucharist

---

[6] To mix water with wine was a standard procedure in celebrating the Eucharist. Compare *Gos. Phil.* 75 [§ 100] with Justin, *1 Apol.* 65 and Irenaeus, *Haer.* 1.13.1; 5.13. This corresponds to the usual Greek custom of drinking mixed wine.

initiation cycle common in most second- and third-century Christian communities[7] without giving any clues to specifically Valentinian ritual innovations and confrontations with other Christian groups. The first has to do with the polemical references found in the gospel, the second with the use of the language of the bridal chamber.

To begin with, there is an interesting passage that reveals a denial of the efficacy of baptism in certain cases:

> If anyone goes down into the water and comes up again without having received anything, and says, "I am a Christian," he has borrowed the name at the interest. But if he receives the Holy Spirit, he possesses the name as a gift. He who has received a gift does not have it taken away. But one who has received something at interest, it will be demanded back from him. So it happens with us, when anyone submits to a mystery. (*Gos. Phil.* 64 [§ 59])[8]

This passage can be compared with other passages which emphasize the necessity of baptizing "in two," that is, both with water and chrism (see above), and elucidate that it is precisely chrism baptism that makes the baptized person Christian, not the water baptism alone (74 [§ 95]). Such claims that some people do not really receive the Holy Spirit at baptism and that it is necessary to baptize in "light and water" (69 [§ 75]) to make a person a real Christian can easily be read as an attack against some people who do receive the name as a loan with interest and whose ritual practices do not place a similar emphasis on baptizing "in two." A passage from Irenaeus' *Adversus haereses* (1.6.4) confirms that Valentinians indeed had an identity that separated them from other, "less perfect" Christians. In addition to false doctrines, Irenaeus writes, they

> indulge in other foul and godless practices, against which we guard ourselves because of fear of God and do not sin even in thought or word. For this they run us down as uncultured and ignoramuses. Themselves, however, they extol by calling themselves perfect and the children of election. Indeed, they say that we receive grace for use only, and so it will be taken away; they, however, have grace as a proper possession, which came down from above, from the unspeakable and unnameable conjugal couple, and so it will be increased for them. For this reason, they say,

---

[7] One should not, of course, presume a liturgical unity in late second- and early third-century *non*-Valentinian churches. For the diversity of baptismal practices, see Bradshaw 2002: 144–70.

[8] Trans. from Schenke 1991.

they must always and in every way put into practice the mystery of the conjugal union.⁹

Irenaeus' words show how easily the language of borrowing grace/the name of a Christian could be used polemically against outsiders. Used polemically, the passage on *Gos. Phil.* 64 effectively attacks not only the "borrowers of the name," but also those who baptized them. To suggest that a baptism presided over by a local bishop does not necessarily give the gift of the Holy Spirit is a serious accusation indeed.

On another occasion, Irenaeus urges his readers to suspect those presbyters "who stand apart from the principle of succession, and gather in any place whatsoever (*et quocunque loco*), regarding them either as heretics with evil intentions, or as schismatics, puffed up with themselves, or as hypocrites..." (Pagels 2002: 369). This indicates that there were some presbyters among Irenaeus' opponents (Valentinians) and that these opponents gathered in meetings unauthorized by the developing central leadership of the church. Pagels infers from Irenaeus' mention of the heretical presbyters that Valentinians were not "an anticlerical movement." Hippolytus, writing circa two decades later than Irenaeus, suggests that the leaders among Marcosians were "bishops" (*Haer.* 6.41.4–5). Nonetheless, it is probably justified to argue that Valentinianism did not incline toward organizing itself as a movement under centralized, translocal leadership with fixed liturgies and doctrines. Irenaeus was puzzled by how unstable the doctrines of the Valentinians were and "how...they do not say the same things about the same subject, but contradict themselves in regard to things and names" (*Haer.* 1.11.1). As for their rituals, Irenaeus sarcastically observes that "there are as many redemptions as there are mystery-teachers of this doctrine" (*Haer.* 1.21.1). Even though Irenaeus certainly exaggerates the diversity of the Valentinian doctrines and practices to drive home his case, his criticism may still be based on the fact that there were Valentinians who did not show much concern for either orthodoxy or orthopraxy and, unlike another second-century deviant group, the Marcionites, did not aim at establishing church-like universal organizations. The material collected in the *Gospel of Philip* fits particularly well into such a context. This description is in agreement with Green who states that "Valentinian offshoots were localized and lacked associational links to a regional or universal community" (1982: 113).

---

⁹ Trans. from Unger and Dillon 1992.

Although notoriously difficult to interpret, the language of the bridal chamber may be taken as another indication of the ritual innovations and the splinter group situation reflected in the *Gospel of Philip*. Irenaeus writes that the Valentinians "must always and in every way put into practice the mystery of the conjugal union" (*Haer.* 1.6.3). Later, when Irenaeus describes various forms of "redemption" practiced by Marcosians (or Valentinian groups in general), he states: "Some of them prepare a bridal chamber and complete the mystic teaching with invocations on those who are being initiated. What was performed by them, they assert, is a spiritual marriage after the likeness of the conjugal unions on high" (1.21.3). In the *Gospel of Philip*, the bridal chamber and its cognates are present with such frequency that the bridal chamber has been seen as the central theme of the whole writing.

It must be recognized that the use of the imagery of the bridal chamber and, more generally, the nuptial/sexual imagery as a metaphor for salvation are widely attested in non-Valentinian Christian writings as well as in other religious texts of antiquity (Zimmermann 2001; Lapinkivi 2004; Nissinen and Uro in press). There are, however, reasons to believe that, for the Valentinians, the language of the bridal chamber was not just one metaphor among others but a characteristic feature of their theological and ritual parlance (Uro in press). As noted above, scholars' interpretations of the different uses of the bridal chamber vary greatly and it may be impossible to reach an agreement about the meaning and the content of the imagery in the *Gospel of Philip*. What seems to be relatively certain, however, is that the gospel envisions at least two bridal chambers: the "great" celestial bridal chamber (*Gos. Phil.* 71 [§ 82]; see also 84–86 [§§ 125–127]) and a "mirrored bridal chamber," which could be understood as a kind of worldly counterpart of this celestial bridal chamber. Moreover, the bridal chamber imagery is, on several occasions, associated with some ritual procedures, especially with chrism (*Gos. Phil.* 67 [§ 66]; 67 [§ 67]; 74 [§ 95]; cf. 84 [§ 125]) but also with other rituals (see 67 [§ 66]; 67 [§ 68]; 69–70 [§ 74–79]).

There is also a peculiar expression "child/children of the bridal chamber," which appears several times in the gospel. "It is from water and fire and light that the child of the bridal chamber came into being" (67 [§ 66]); see also 72 [§ 87]; 76 [§ 102]; 86 [§ 127]). This expression is clearly an epithet for those who have passed through some sort of initiation, those who have "received the truth in images" (86 [§ 127]). It is interesting that a similar phrase occurs in a second century inscription found on the Via Latina in Rome. The inscription has been reconstructed by Lampe as follows (Lampe 2003):

> Co[brothers] of the bridal chambers, celebrate with torches the [ba]ths for me;
> They hunger for [ban]quets in ou[r rooms],
> [la]uding the Father, and praising the Son;
> Oh, may there be flow[ing] of the only spring and of the truth in the very place (or then).

"Lauding the Father and praising the Son" suggests that this inscription derives from a Christian family or group. If so, it represents one of the earliest Christian epigraphic documents (Lampe 2003: 300). It also shows, provided that Lampe's emendation is correct, that there were Christians in Rome who identified themselves as the "brothers" of the "bridal chamber(s)" and this status was connected with special kinds of rituals ("[ba]ths") celebrated for each individual. It is further arguable that the ritual ablutions of this group were somehow different from the baptism described by Justin, Irenaeus and Hippolytus. The plural "[ba]ths" celebrated for the "I" of the inscription does not quite fit the singular baptism assumed by the church fathers. Although we are far from being able to make a certain conclusion, the most probable hypothesis is that the group was Valentinian and they understood themselves as the "brothers" or "children" of the "bridal chamber(s)," just like the people who used the *Gospel of Philip*.[10]

4. *Valentinians and the Imagistic Mode of Religion*

What can be sketched from the very fragmentary and sparse evidence in the *Gospel of Philip* and related texts, then, is an early Christian splinter

---

[10] Lampe (2003: 298–307) presents a strong case for the Valentinian origin of the inscription. Another second-century marble, a memorial to Flavia Sophe, has been found on the Via Latina and contains two inscriptions. The first of them may also reveal signs of Valentinian ritual and theology:
> Longing for the fatherly light, O sister bride, my Sophe,
> In the ablutions of Ch[rist] anointed with imperishable holy balsam,
> You have hastened to gaze upon the divine countenances of the Aeons,
> Upon the great angel of the great counsel, the true Son,
> You have gone [to] the bridal chamber and ascended to the...fatherly...

For the Valentinian nature of this inscription, see Lampe 2003: 308–13 and Dunderberg, 2004: 170–73.

group that was initiated by Valentinus and active in the latter half of the second century and early third century (in some remnants possibly later). Although in the beginning, the members of the movement had not completely separated themselves from the major churches—hence Irenaeus' problem that it was not always easy to tell who was a "Valentinian"—there is ample evidence that, at some point, some of them had established their own ritual communities with revised practices or perhaps also completely new ritual innovations. Although the Valentinians understood themselves as (true) Christians, they had developed a group identity of their own that could be seen in the use of such expressions as "the children" or "co-[brothers] of the bridal chamber."

From the perspective of ritual studies, one could focus on several aspects of the "ethnographic" data extracted from the sources by means of historical analysis. One could, for example, pursue the old path by emphasizing the parallelism between the Valentinian cosmological myth (versions of which have been preserved in the sources) and the ritual language of the bridal chamber (which remains elusive and obscure). The ritual re-enacts the myth (Segal 1998). Many scholars accordingly argue that the Valentinians both re-enacted and anticipated the great cosmological marriage in celebrating the bridal chamber ritual (J. Turner 1994: 162). One could, furthermore, continue to analyze the symbolic interpretations of the *Gospel of Philip* and to explore or decode the web of meanings woven by the collector of the disparate sayings and traditions. Such a task is, of course, endless since symbols are inherently open-ended and multivalent (Sperber 1995; Pyysiäinen 2001: 43–44). A more recent approach is to take ritual as embodied power negotiation (Bell 1992). Following this cue, one could investigate the power relations between the centralized church leadership envisioned by Irenaeus and the antihierarchical stance of the local Valentinian offshoots to see how these relations are reflected in the ritual practices of the respective movements.

I am not denying the usefulness of any of these approaches. I have, however, chosen a quite different theoretical framework which is based on recent advances in the cognitive science of religion (Andresen 2001; Pyysiäinen and Anttonen 2002; Tremlin 2006). Cognitive theories of ritual have been developed, seeking to provide testable explanations for divergent patterns of ritual transmission and to show how these patterns might account for varied profiles of religious systems (Lawson and McCauley 1990; McCauley and Lawson 2002; Whitehouse 1995, 2000, 2004; Pyysiäinen 2004: 135–46). Like all cognitive theories of religion, these theories of ritual boldly claim to be universal since they are based on the scientific theories about the cognitive mechanisms of the human mind, which have remained nearly unchanged irrespective of historical and cultural changes. Cognitive approaches, thus, promise to contribute to the ongoing discussion on the use of social-scientific models in the study of early Christianity (Elliott 1986; Esler 1995; Horrell 1996; Lawrence and Aguilar 2004).

Among the cognitive theories of ritual, Harvey Whitehouse's "modes of religiosity" theory is the most useful for our purposes in embracing *both* psychological *and* sociopolitical factors of religious activity (but see also McCauley and Lawson 2002: 179–212). Whitehouse suggests that religions have two "attractor positions" around which they tend to coalesce. These are called "imagistic" and "doctrinal" modes. At the heart of the theory is the observation that low frequency, often painful or dramatic rituals, such as initiation rites in many tribal cultures, are codified in what psychologists call episodic memory. In contrast, frequently repeated rituals are codified in semantic memory.[11] Whitehouse notes that a clustering of sociopolitical features has been recognized in numerous theories (e.g., in Max Weber's routinized and charismatic religious forms and Victor Turner's "structure" and "communitas"), but what is new about the theory of modes of religiosity is the way it places these features together in a single model that explains the clustering in terms of cognitive and psychological causes. The key features of the doctrinal and imagistic modes can be illustrated by Table 1 cited from Whitehouse's *Modes of Religiosity* (p. 74).

It seems clear that, according to the theory, the form of early Christianity championed by Irenaeus and his followers was strongly developing toward the doctrinal mode. This is not to say that early Christian baptism, as an once-in-a-lifetime experience, could not create strong and lasting memories in the episodic memory of those who passed through the ritual. Fasting and all-night vigils preceding baptism probably facilitated this process. However, the long pre-baptismal preparation of the initiates—three years according to the *Apostolic Tradition*—and especially regular attendance at Sunday services and listening to sermons and reading of written texts effectively contributed to encoding

---

[11] To explain briefly, semantic memory consists of general knowledge about the world, episodic memory of special events in a person's life experience. The distinction was first suggested by Tulving 1972.

Table 1. Contrasting Modes of Religiosity (Whitehouse 2004: 74).

Variable	Doctrinal	Imagistic
Psychological Features		
1. Transmissive frequency	High	Low
2. Level of arousal	Low	High
3. Principal memory system	Semantic schemas and implicit scripts	Episodic/flashbulb memory
4. Ritual meaning	Learned/acquired	Internally generated
5. Techniques of revelation	Rhetoric/logical integration, narrative	Iconicity, multivocality, multivalence
Sociopolitical Features		
6. Social cohesion	Diffuse	Intense
7. Leadership	Dynamic	Passive/absent
8. Inclusivity/exclusivity	Inclusive	Exclusive
9. Spread	Rapid/efficient	Slow/inefficient
10. Scale	Large scale	Small scale
11. Degree of uniformity	High	Low
12. Structure	Centralized	Noncentralized

religious knowledge in semantic memory. There is no doubt that much of the religious knowledge acquired by an average church member was learned, not internally generated (cf. number 4 in Whitehouse's table). The church fathers clearly intended to create a standardized "orthodoxy," a body of Christian doctrines that would be universally accepted in all churches (in reality, people's beliefs and practices naturally varied a great deal), and a strong centralized organization, which could withstand both outside attacks and internal schisms.

How should one place Valentinian groups in Whitehouse's "modes theory"? As a splinter group that was not totally separated from the proto-orthodox church, the Valentinian movement may be seen as representing the same doctrinal mode as its parent church and using similar strategies of teaching and frequently performed rituals (e.g., the Sunday Eucharist). We may assume that many of the members of the movement attended regular worship and Eucharist with other Christians. The teachings of the Valentinian leaders may therefore be taken simply as a form of orthodoxy set against another orthodoxy. To a certain degree, this may have been the case. In his treatise against the Valentinians, Tertullian blames them for the "officiousness with which they guard their doctrine." He also criticizes the length of the period of instruction that preceded the initiation into Valentinian communities—as much as five years (Tertullian, *Val.* 1.1–4).[12] However, Tertullian's further discussion suggests that the Valentinians he knew were not hard-line dogmatists who were eager to convince everyone of the rhetorical and logical power of their doctrines.

> If you propose to them inquiries sincere and honest, they answer you with stern look and contracted brow, and say, "The subject is profound." If you try them with subtle questions, with the ambiguities of their double tongue, they affirm a community of faith (with yourself). If you intimate to them that you understand *their opinions*, they insist on knowing nothing themselves. If you come to a close engagement with them they destroy your own fond hope of a victory over them by a self-immolation. Not even to their own disciples do they commit a secret before they have made sure of them. They have the knack of persuading men before instructing them; although truth persuades by teaching, but does not teach by first persuading. (*Val.* 1.16–18 *ANF*)

Tertullian's caricature is meant to make fun of his Valentinian competitors. But caricatures often contain a seed of truth. There is nothing inherently implausible in Tertullian's description that the Valentinians (like many other religious groups in Late Antiquity, including many forms of Christianity) spoke of deeper mysteries that were not openly revealed to outsiders or neophytes. The references to the bridal chamber would certainly have strengthened the sense of a secret mystery. It may have been this aura of secrecy that attracted people to the Valentinian teachers, not only the substance of their teaching. This indicates a different technique of revelation than what Tertullian regards as appropriate ("truth persuades by teaching").

My conclusions here suggest that Valentinian groups were at least partially moving from the doctrinal mode toward the imagistic mode of religiosity.[13] Although there is no doubt that Valentinians were capable of producing sophisticated theological treatises (cf., e.g., *Ptolemy's Letter to Flora*, and the *Treatise on the Resurrection*), the *Gospel of Philip* shows that the teaching related to the Valentinian initiation could be "iconistic,"

---

[12] It is, however, possible that the five-year catechesis refers only to the Eleusinian mysteries to which Tertullian compares the Valentinian initiation. See Thomassen 2006: 388.

[13] It should be emphasized that Whitehouse does not argue that pure types of imagistic and doctrinal modes can be found in the real world, but rather that there is "a tendency for religious systems to gravitate toward divergent attractor positions" (Whitehouse 2004: 76).

that is, based on multivalent images and metaphors (such as the bridal chamber) and lacking in authoritative canonical interpretation (cf. number 5 in Whitehouse's table). If the *Gospel of Philip* was used in the preparation for baptism, it hardly contributed to creating uniform ideas about the meaning of the sacraments in the minds of the catechumens. Instead, the gospel would probably have fostered an aura of secrecy and excitement with regard to the coming initiation. Equipped with impressionistic and rousing images, the neophytes would probably not end up having very similar religious representations *after* the ritual either. The truth could then be more a matter of personal reflection on the shared ritual than a matter of confessing orthodox beliefs (cf. number 5 in the table).

There is some evidence (albeit all coming from the opponents) that the level of arousal (number 2) was higher among the Valentinians than what was habitual in the churches guided by Irenaeus and Hippolytus. Both church fathers condemn the "magical tricks" of Marcus in the celebration of the Eucharist (e.g., the transubstantiation of wine into the blood of Grace through the prayer of invocation),[14] which may imply that there were dramatic and rousing elements in Valentinian rituals. Although laden with negative expressions, Irenaeus' description of the glossalalia of Marcosian women contains many realistic features: "...she becomes puffed up and elated by those words [of Marcus], her soul becomes aroused at the prospect of prophesying, her heart beats faster than usual. She dares idly and boldly to say nonsensical things and whatever happens to come to mind..." (*Haer.* 1.13.3).

There are also a few sociopolitical features in Valentianism which match Whitehouse's imagistic mode rather than the doctrinal one. I argued above that Valentinian splinter groups were localized and lacked associational links to a regional or universal community. This can be contrasted with the proto-orthodox churches, which were developing toward a more centralized organization (number 12 in the table). Relatively speaking, the Valentinian groups may have been more exclusive than their mother church as they distinguished themselves, the "pneumatic seed," from the rest of "psychic" Christians (number 8). If Tertullian's description of heretics who blur the distinction between laity

---

[14] Irenaeus, *Haer.* 1.13.2. Cf. also Hippolytus, *Haer.* 6.39.1–42.2.

and clergy truly depicts the Valentinian community life, it is justified to call their version of leadership less "dynamic" (number 7).[15]

Other features are hazier, however. It is possible to speculate that the social cohesion (number 6) among the selected group of Valentinian "perfects" or "spirituals" was more intense than among other Christians, but we should not underestimate the mutual solidarity among Irenaeus' fellow Christians, who had experienced violent persecutions by the Roman authorities (see Pagels 2002: 348). As for the spread of Valentinian ideas and practices (number 9), it can hardly be considered slow since, at the end of the second century, branches of Valentinus' "school" were found in both Western and Eastern parts of the Roman Empire. In the long run, however, the proto-orthodox churches were more successful.

The major difficulty in contrasting Valentinian and orthodox Christian groups as "imagistic" and "doctrinal" in the sense of Whitehouse's theory is the issue of ritual frequency (number 1 in the table). Since most of this analysis has concentrated on the Valentinian initiation, we cannot make a simple distinction between repetitive orthodox practices and less frequent Valentinian rituals. Whatever ritual actions constituted the Valentinian initiation, it was probably not different from other early Christian initiations in terms of frequency. Even if it was a process of several ritual actions (cf. the "baths" in the Via Latina inscription cited above), it was not different in principle from the baptism stipulated, for example, in the *Apostolic Tradition*, since that was also a process that lasted several days or weeks or even years depending on how one demarcates the ritual. It is reasonable to assume that Valentinian and other Christian rituals discussed above were all initiatory rituals, usually performed only once in person's lifetime (although people in antiquity could be—and sometimes were—initiated into several mysteries). The frequency hypothesis has received severe criticism (McCauley 2001; Pyysiäinen 2001: 77–142; Atran 2002: 149–73; see also Ketola in this volume) and it has been argued that Whitehouse's theory stands or falls on this hypothesis (McCauley and Lawson 2002: 104–16). McCauley and Lawson's alternative theory is based on ritual form which consists of agent, patient, action and instrument. McCauley and Lawson argue

---

[15] See *Prescription against Heretics* 41: "...it is doubtful who is a catechumen, and who a believer; they have all access alike...today one man is their bishop, tomorrow another; today he is a deacon who tomorrow is a reader; today he is a presbyter who tomorrow is a layman. For even on laymen do they impose the functions of priesthood." (*ANF*)

that rituals in which culturally postulated, superhuman agents are associated with the agent of a ritual (special-agent rituals) are performed infrequently, are not reversible and usually involve all kinds of sensory pageantry and arousal. Early Christian baptism was a special-agent ritual and thus its form predicts that it was regarded as irreversible by the believing community. This theory helps us to understand the severity of the claim implied in the *Gospel of Philip* that some people do not receive the Holy Spirit at baptism (*Gos. Phil.* 64 [§ 59]; see the discussion above). But its application to Valentinian groups has a problem similar to that of the frequency hypothesis. The analysis only shows that the Valentinians may have performed a different version of the Christian initiation but did not change its form in terms of McCauley and Lawson's theory. The initiation remained a special-agent ritual as did initiations into mysteries in general (Gragg 2004: 81).

Although the level of frequency or the form of the ritual does not change when we move from the communities of Irenaeus to those of his opponents, it is possible to argue that Valentinians strongly *intensified* the imagistic aspects of the early Christian initiation. Several considerations discussed above support this conclusion. Perhaps the failure with respect to the ritual frequency is not fatal for the application of the model (see also Pyysiäinen 2001: 77–144, but compare a more critical assessment in Pyysiäinen 2006). Emotional provocation in an initiation ritual may cause the memories of the ritual episode to be encoded in episodic memory as special, "mystical" events. These memories can, however, be interpreted according to the prevailing doctrinal schemata (Pyysiäinen 2004: 140), as may have happened in the churches which followed Irenaeus' guidelines. Irenaeus' Valentinian opponents, in contrast, may have relied on a different pattern of codification, at least if the *Gospel of Philip* gives any glimpse of their sacramental teaching. Religious experiences were not overwritten by doctrinal interpretations but rather they were left open to what Whitehouse calls "spontaneous exegetical reflection." The modes of religiosity theory predicts that such a cognitive processing has an array of consequences for the social morphology of religious traditions. It seems that the analysis of the Valentinian movement confirms many of these predictions (see also Leopold 2004), although no perfect fit can be achieved between the theory and historical evidence. I would assume that such a fit can seldom be reached (see also the discussion on Whitehouse's theory in the introduction).

There are apparent problems in locating "proto-orthodoxy" and Valentinianism in diametrically opposite modes of religiosity as if these modes were exhaustive and exclusive (see also Laidlaw 2004: 8). As argued above, the historical evidence does not support such an exclusive distinction between the Valentinian and non-Valentinian Christian groups. Moreover, Whitehouse has himself stressed that there are many religions that corporate *both* imagistic *and* doctrinal modes of operation (Whitehouse 2000: 125–46).[16] His ethnography among the Mali Baining in Papua New Guinea demonstrates that doctrinal movements (such as the Pomio Kivung and Paliau movements) often generate sporadic outbursts of splinter-group activity which includes imagistic features, but does not lead to a complete break with the parent movement. Whitehouse even argues that the mainstream movements could not survive without these intermittent outbursts of imagistic practices that revived the religious commitment and overall cohesion of the members and reduced the "tedium effect."

We also have to assume a lot of interplay between imagistic and doctrinal practices among the second- and early third-century Christian groups. It may not be justified to speak of a contrast between the *mainstream* orthodox churches and Valentinian sects or splinter groups since, at least in the period in question, it was more a matter of competitive versions of Christianity than of a dominant church/divergent sect dichotomy. But it is quite reasonable to argue that, as a doctrinal religion, Christianity needed imagistic practices to survive and various second-century movements arose to fill this need. Valentinians were one such group, which may have formulated Christian beliefs and practices in the imagistic direction. Our historical data is too fragmentary to allow us to conclude whether the imagistic practices of the Valentinian groups remained strong enough to form a clear alternative to formative orthodox churches.

Cognitive theories of ritual are still in their infancy. Whether different patterns of codification, ritual frequency, or ritual form play a causative role in the formation of religious movements is debated.[17] For a scholar

---

[16] The reliance on "interacting modes of religiosity" (Whitehouse 2004: 75–77), however, raises the question of what would falsify Whitehouse's hypothesis (Pyysiäinen 2006: 346).

[17] For a critique of causal explanation in Whitehouse's theory, see, e.g., Wiebe 2004.

of early Christian religion, however, even these pioneering cognitive theories can open a whole set of new questions which may ultimately lead to new hypotheses about "orthodoxy" and "deviancy" as well as about the evolution of Christianity in general. These new hypothesis will be built on the old ones and add cognitive explanations to cultural and political analyses.

Acknowledgement

I am grateful to Michel Desjardins, Ismo Dunderberg, and Antti Marjanen, who read various versions of this essay and gave valuable comments. Parts of this study have been published in M. Nissinen and R. Uro, eds, *Sacred Marriage: Divine-Human Sexual Metaphor from Sumer to Early Christianity*. Winona Lake, Ind.: Eisenbrauns. I thank Eisenbrauns for allowing the use of the essay in this volume.

REFERENCES

Andresen, Jensine, ed. 2001. *Religion in Mind: Cognitive Perspectives on Religious Belief, Ritual, and Experience*. Cambridge: Cambridge University Press.

Atran, Scott. 2002. *In Gods We Trust: The Evolutionary Landscape of Religion*. Oxford: Oxford University Press.

Bell, Catherine. 1992. *Ritual Theory—Ritual Practice*. Oxford: Oxford University Press.

Boyer, Pascal. 1994. *The Naturalness of Religious Ideas: A Cognitive Theory of Religion*. Berkeley, Calif.: University of California Press.

Bradshaw, Paul F. 2002. *The Search for the Origins of Christian Worship: Sources and Methods for the Study of Early Liturgy*. London: SPCK.

Buckley, Jorunn Jacobsen. 1980. "A Cult-Mystery in the Gospel of Philip." *Journal of Biblical Literature* 99: 569–81.

———. 1988a. "Conceptual Models and Polemic Issues in the Gospel of Philip." In *Aufstieg und Niedergang der römischen Welt* II, 25.5, edited by Hildegaard Temporini and Wolfgang Haase, 4167–94. New York: de Gruyter.

———. 1988b. "'The Holy Spirit as a Double Name': Holy Spirit, Mary, and Sophia in the Gospel of Philip." In *Images of Feminine in Gnosticism*, edited by Karen L. King, 211–27. Studies in Antiquity and Christianity. Philadelphia, Pa.: Fortress.

DeConick, April D. 2001. "The True Mysteries: Sacramentalism in the Gospel of Philip." *Vigiliae Christianae* 55: 225–61.

Desjardins, Michel R. 1990. *Sin in Valentianism*. SBLDS 108. Atlanta, Ga.: Scholars Press.

———. 1987. "Baptism in Valentianism." Paper presented at the Annual Meeting of the SBL, Boston.

Draper, Jonathan A. 2000. "Ritual Process and Ritual Symbol in Didache 7–10." *Vigiliae Christianae* 54: 121–58.

Dunderberg, Ismo. 2004. "Valentinian Teachers in Rome." In *Christians as a Religious Minority in a Multicultural City: Modes of Interaction and Identity Formation in Early Imperial*

Rome, edited by Jürgen Zangenberg and Michael Labahn, 157–74. London: T&T Clark International.

———. 2005a. "The School of Valentinus." In *A Companion to Second-Century Christian "Heretics,"* edited by Antti Marjanen and Petri Luomanen, 64–99. Supplements to Vigiliae Christianae, 76. Leiden: Brill.

———. 2005b. "Valentinian Views about Adam's Creation: Valentinus and the Gospel of Philip." In *Lux Humana, Lux Aeterna: Essays on Biblical and Related Themes in Honour of Lars Aejmealeus*, edited by Antti Mustakallio, Heikki Leppä and Heikki Räisänen, 509–27. Publications of the Finnish Exegetical Society, 89. Helsinki: The Finnish Exegetical Society; Göttingen: Vandenhoeck & Ruprecht.

Elliott, John H. 1986. "Social-Scientific Criticism of the New Testament: More on Methods and Models." *Semeia* 35: 1–33.

Esler, Philip F., ed. 1995. *Modelling Early Christianity: Social Scientific Studies of the New Testament in Its Context*. London: Routledge.

Gaffron, Hans-Georg. 1969. "Studien zum koptischen Philippusevangelium unter besonderer Berücksichtigung der Sakramente." Ph.D. diss., Rheinische Friedrich-Wilhelms-Universität zu Bonn.

Gragg, Douglas L. 2004. "Old and New in Roman Religion: A Cognitive Account." In *Theorizing Religions Past: Archeology, History, and Cognition*, edited by Harvey Whitehouse and Luther H. Martin, 69–86. Walnut Greek, Calif.: AltaMira.

Green, Henry A. 1982. "Ritual in Valentinian Gnosticism: A Sociological Interpretation." *Journal of Religious History* 12: 109–24.

Horrell, David G. 1996. *The Social Ethos of the Corinthian Correspondence: Interests and Ideology from 1 Corinthians to 1 Clement*. Studies of the New Testament and Its World. Edinburgh: T&T Clark.

Isenberg, Wesley W. 1989. "[Translation of] The Gospel of Philip." In *Nag Hammadi Codex II,2–7 together with XIII,2*, Brit. Lib. Or.4926(1), and P.Oxy. 1, 654, 655*. Vol. 1: *Gospel According to Thomas, Gospel According to Philip, Hypostasis of the Archons, and Indexes*, edited by Bentley Layton, 143–215. Nag Hammadi Studies, 20. Leiden: Brill.

King, Karen L. 2003. *What Is Gnosticism?* Cambridge, Mass.: The Belknap Press of Harvard University Press.

Labib, Pahor, ed. 1956. *Coptic Gnostic Papyri in the Coptic Museum at Old Cairo*. Cairo: Cairo Government Press.

Laidlaw, James. 2004. "Introduction." In *Ritual and Memory*, edited by Harvey Whitehouse and James Laidlaw, 1–9. Walnut Greek, Calif.: AltaMira.

Lampe, Peter. 2003. *From Paul to Valentinus: Christians at Rome in the First Two Centuries*. Minneapolis, Minn.: Fortress.

Lapinkivi, Pirjo. 2004. *The Sumerian Sacred Marriage in the Light of Comparative Evidence*. State Archives of Assyria Studies, 15. Helsinki: Neo-Assyrian Text Corpus Project.

Lawrence, Louise J. and Mario I. Aguilar, eds. 2004. *Anthropology and Biblical Studies: Avenues of Approach*. Leiden: Deo.

Lawson, Thomas E. and Robert N. McCauley. 1990. *Rethinking Religion: Connecting Cognition and Culture*. Cambridge: Cambridge University Press.

Layton, Bentley. 1987. *The Gnostic Scriptures*. Garden City, Mich.: Doubleday.

Leopold, Anita Maria. 2004. "Syncretism and the Interaction of Modes of Religiosity: A Formative Perspective on Gnostic-Christian Movements in Late Antiquity." In *Theorizing Religions Past: Archeology, History, and Cognition*, edited by Harvey Whitehouse and Luther H. Martin, 105–21. Walnut Greek, Calif.: AltaMira.

Marjanen, Antti, ed. 2005. *Was There a Gnostic Religion?* Publications of the Finnish Exegetical Society, 87. Helsinki: The Finnish Exegetical Society; Göttingen: Vandenhoeck & Ruprecht.

Markschies, Christoph. 1992. *Valentinus Gnosticus? Untersuchungen zur valentinianishcen Gnosis mit einem Kommentar zu den Fragmenten Valentin*. Wissenschaftliche Untersuchungen zum Neuen Testament, 65. Tübingen: Mohr Siebeck.

———. 1997. "Valentinian Gnosticism: Toward the Anatomy of a School." In *The Nag Hammadi after Fifty Years: Proceedings of the 1995 Society of Biblical Literature*, edited by John D. Turner and Anne McGuire, 401–38. Nag Hammadi and Manichaean Studies, 44. Leiden: Brill.

McCauley, Robert N. 2001. "Ritual, Memory, and Emotion: Comparing Two Cognitive Hypotheses." In *Religion in Mind: Cognitive Perspective on Religious Belief, Ritual and Experience*, edited by Jensine Andresen, 115–40. Cambridge: Cambridge University Press.

McCauley, Robert N. and Thomas E. Lawson. 2002. *Bringing Ritual to Mind: Psychological Foundations of Cultural Forms.* Cambridge: Cambridge University Press.

McVann, Mark. 1991. "Rituals of Status Transformation in Luke-Acts: A Case of Jesus the Prophet." In *The Social World of Luke-Acts: Models for Interpretation*, edited by Jerome H. Neyrey, 333–60. Peabody, Mass.: Hendrickson.

———. 1994. "Reading Mark Ritually: Honor-Shame and the Ritual of Baptism." In *Transformations, Passages, and Processes: Ritual Approaches to Biblical Texts*, edited by Mark McVann, 179–98. Semeia, 67. Atlanta, Ga.: Scholars Press.

Ménard, Jacques E. 1967. *L'Évangile selon Philippe*. Strasbourg: Université de Strasbourg.

Nissinen, Martti, and Risto Uro, eds. In press. *Sacred Marriage: Divine-Human Sexual Metaphor from Sumer to Early Christianity.* Winona Lake, Ind.: Eisenbrauns

Pagels, Elaine. 1997. "Ritual in the Gospel of Philip." In *The Nag Hammadi Library after Fifty Years: Proceedings of the 1995 Society of Biblical Literature Commemoration*, edited by John D. Turner and Anne McGuire, 280–91. Nag Hammadi and Manichaean Series, 44. Leiden: Brill.

———. 2002. "Irenaeus, the 'Canon of Truth,' and the Gospel of John: 'Making Difference' through Hermeneutics and Ritual." *Vigiliae Christianae* 56: 339–71.

Penn, Michael. 2002. "Performing Family: Ritual Kissing and the Construction of Early Christian Kinship." *Journal of Early Christian Studies* 10: 151–74.

Pyysiäinen, Ilkka. 2001. *How Religion Works: Towards a New Cognitive Science of Religion.* Cognition and Culture, 1. Leiden: Brill.

———. 2004. *Magic, Miracles, and Religion: A Scientist's Perspective.* Walnut Greek, Calif.: AltaMira.

———. 2006. "Memories: Religion and Cultural Transmission." *Anthropological Quarterly* 79: 341–53.

Pyysiäinen, Ilkka and Veikko Anttonen, eds. 2002. *Current Approaches in the Cognitive Science of Religion.* London: Continuum.

Reitzenstein, Richard. 1927. *Die Hellenistische Mysterienreligionen.* Leipzig: Teubner.

Schenke, Hans-Martin. 1959. "Das Evangelium nach Philippus: Ein Evangelium der Valentianer aus der Funde von Nag-Hamadi." *Theologische Literaturzeitung* 84: 1–26.

———. 1991. "The Gospel of Philip." In *New Testament Apocrypha*. Vol. 1: *Gospels and Related Writings*, edited by Wilhelm Schneemelcher and Robert McL. Wilson, 179–87. Cambridge: Clarke.

———. 1997. *Das Philippus-Evangelium (Nag-Hammadi-Codex II,3)*. Texte und Untersuchungen 143. Berlin: Akademie Verlag.

Segal, Robert A., ed. 1998. *The Myth and Ritual Theory: An Anthology.* Malden, Mass.: Blackwell.

Segelberg, Eric. 1960. "The Coptic-Gnostic Gospel according to Philip and Its Sacramental System." *Numen* 7: 189–200.

Smith, Jonathan Z. 1987. *To Take Place: Toward Theory in Ritual.* Chicago, Ill.: The University of Chicago Press.

Sperber, Dan. [1975] 1995. *Rethinking Symbolism.* Cambridge: Cambridge University Press.

Strecker, Christian. 1999. *Die liminale Theologie des Paulus: Zugänge zur paulinischen Theologie aus kulturanthropologischer Perspektive*. Forschungen zur Religion und Literatur des Alten und Neuen Testaments, 185. Göttingen: Vandenhoeck & Ruprecht.
Thomassen, Einar. 1997. "How Valentinian Is the Gospel of Philip?" In *The Nag Hammadi Library after Fifty Years: Proceedings of the 1995 Society of Biblical Literature Commemoration*, edited by John D. Turner and Anne McGuire, 251–79. Nag Hammadi and Manichaean Studies 44. Leiden: Brill.
———. 2006. *The Spiritual Seed: The "Church" of the Valentinians*. Nag Hammadi and Manichaean Studies, 60. Leiden: Brill.
Till, Walter C. 1963. *Das Evangelium nach Philippos*. Patristische Texte und Studien 2. Berlin: de Gruyter.
Tremlin, Todd. 2006. *Minds and Gods: The Cognitive Foundations of Religion*. New York: Oxford University Press.
Tripp, D. H. 1982. "The 'Sacramental System' of the Gospel of Philip." In *Studia Patristica XVII*, edited by Elisabeth A. Livingstone, 251–60. Oxford: Pergamon Press.
Tulving, Endel. 1972. "Episodic and Semantic Memory." In *Organization of Memory*, edited by E. Tulving and W. Donaldson, 381–403. New York: Academic Press.
Turner, John D. 1994. "Ritual in Gnosticism." *Society of Biblical Literature Seminar Papers* 33: 136–81.
Turner, Martha Lee. 1996. *The Gospel according to Philip: The Sources and Coherence of an Early Christian Collection*. Nag Hammadi and Manichaean Studies, 38. Leiden: Brill.
Turner, Victor. 1969. *The Ritual Process: Structure and Anti-Structure*. Chicago, Ill.: Aldine.
———. 1974. *Dramas, Fields, and Metaphors: Symbolic Action in Human Society*. Cornell Paperbacks, 151. Ithaca, N.Y.: Cornell University Press.
Unger, Dominic J. and John J. Dillon, eds., 1992. *St. Irenaeus of Lyons: Against the Heresies*. Ancient Christian Writers, 55. New York: Newman.
Uro, Risto. In press. "The Bridal Chamber and Other Mysteries: Ritual System and Ritual Transmission in the Valentinian Movement." In *Sacred Marriages: Divine-Human Sexual Metaphor from Sumer to Early Christianity*, edited by Martti Nissinen and Risto Uro. Winona Lake, Ind.: Eisenbrauns.
Whitehouse, Harvey. 1995. *Inside the Cult: Religious Innovation and Transmission in Papua New Guinea*. Oxford: Clarendon.
———. 2000. *Arguments and Icons*. Oxford: Oxford University Press.
———. 2004. *Modes of Religiosity: A Cognitive Theory of Religious Transmission*. Walnut Greek, Calif.: AltaMira.
Wiebe, Donald. 2004. "Critical Reflections on the Modes of Religiosity Argument." In *Theorizing Religions Past: Archeology, History, and Cognition*, edited by Harvey Whitehouse and Luther H. Martin, 197–214. Walnut Greek, Calif.: AltaMira.
Williams, Michael A. 1986. "Use of Gender Imagery in Ancient Gnostic Texts." In *Gender and Religion: On the Complexity of Symbols*, edited by Caroline Walker Bynum, Stevan Harrell and Paula Richman, 196–227. Boston, Mass.: Beacon.
———. 1996. *Rethinking "Gnosticism:" An Argument for Dismantling a Dubious Category*. Princeton, N.J.: Princeton University Press.
Wilson, Robert McL. 1962. *The Gospel of Philip: Translated from the Coptic Texts, with Introduction and Commentary*. London: Mowbray.
Zimmermann, Ruben. 2001. *Geschlechtermetaphorik und Gottesverhältnis: Traditionsgeschichte und Theologie eines Bildfelds in Urchristentum und antiker Umwelt*. Wissenschaftliche Untersuchungen zum neuen Testament. 2. Reihe, 122. Tübingen: Mohr Siebeck.

PART TWO

CONCEPTUAL BLENDING IN EARLY CHRISTIANITY

CONCEPTUAL BLENDING IN THE *EXEGESIS ON THE SOUL*

Hugo Lundhaug

1. *Introduction*

The Nag Hammadi tractate the *Exegesis on the Soul* (NHC II,6) sets the stage for its ten manuscript pages of scriptural exegesis with the following statement: "The wise of old gave the soul a feminine name. Indeed, in her nature she is a woman. She even has her womb" (*Exeg. Soul* 127.19–22).[1] In this essay, I will focus on what Frederik Wisse has called "a difficult and perhaps not entirely successful metaphor" (Wisse 1975: 73) in this text, that of the womb of the soul. I will try to show its rhetorical function and its relation to other related conceptual metaphors in the tractate, especially that of the soul as a woman. In doing so, I will outline the way in which *the Exegesis on the Soul* sets in motion a number of complex and intertwined conceptual blends.

The *Exegesis on the Soul* takes the form of a mythical narrative interspersed with commentaries, more or less oblique allusions, and, uniquely among the Nag Hammadi texts, quite a few direct and lengthy scriptural quotations. The storyline describes the soul, personified as a woman, and her life of prostitution/fornication (*porneia*) after her fall from heaven into a material body, and her subsequent repentance once she realizes her predicament. Upon hearing the soul's weeping and pleas for forgiveness, her Father, with whom she lived in her original existence in heaven, takes pity on her and provides her with salvation in the form of a husband. The soul's original heavenly existence was "male-female," and the (re)union between the soul and her savior-husband re-establishes this original pair and leads to the soul's ascent back into heaven.

Although the narrative itself, of fall, repentance, and salvation, is rather simple, it is not presented in a simple manner. It is especially the text's intricate and often implicit construction of conceptual

---

[1] I use the Coptic text established by Layton (1989). All translations from the Coptic are my own.

and intertextual blends that causes interpretive problems. Take, for instance, the following description of the cries of the fallen soul and her salvation:

> But when she understands the afflictions she is in and when she cries out to the Father and when she repents, then the Father will have mercy on her and he will turn her womb from the things of the outside and again he will turn it inside, and the soul will receive her part. (*Exeg. Soul* 131.16–22.)

"I do not understand this figure of speech, of itself and in the present context," admits William C. Robinson (1970: 115) with regard to this rather unusual anatomical imagery. In the present essay, I shall delve into the poetics of the *Exegesis on Soul* and investigate the function of this and related metaphors in the tractate.

2. *A Cognitive Approach*

As Philip Eubanks points out in a recent article, "[t]he best place to begin analyzing discourses is often with its salient metaphors and metonymies. One important advantage of this approach is that it helps us to locate a discourse's principal and most rhetorically potent ideas" (Eubanks 2005: 195). As Eubanks emphasizes, however, it is not enough just to *identify* key metaphors and metonymies. What is needed is a thorough analysis of the *function* of such devices in discourse. "If we are to infer cognition from people's culturally embedded language," Eubanks adds, "we must examine that language with tools that permit us to see intertextual relationships, to make judgments about intent and reception, and to notice widespread, subtle patterns of communication" (Eubanks 2005: 195–96).

In my analysis of the poetics of the *Exegesis on the Soul*, I will employ theories developed within the emerging interdisciplinary field of cognitive poetics (Stockwell 2002; Gavins and Steen 2003), most prominently Gilles Fauconnier and Mark Turner's theory of *conceptual blending*, also known as *conceptual integration, mental binding*, or simply *blending theory* (Fauconnier and Turner 1998, 2002; Coulson and Oakley 2000). Let us now take a brief look at the theory.

Mark Turner describes the basic idea of conceptual blending as "the mental operation of combining two mental packets of meaning...selectively and under constraints to create a third mental packet of meaning that has new, emergent meaning" (Turner 2002: 10). In part, blending theory builds on *conceptual metaphor theory*, a theory that crucially regards metaphor as a mode of thinking, fundamental to our everyday thought, rather than as a manner of speaking (Lakoff and Johnson 1980; Lakoff 1993; Kövecses 2002). The basic idea of conceptual metaphor theory is that a more concrete conceptual domain provides elements and structure allowing us to conceptualize a more abstract one, as is the case, for example, with the commonly used metaphor LIFE IS A JOURNEY, where the concept of a journey helps us to think about the more abstract concept of life.

Blending theory also draws crucially upon Fauconnier's previous research into mental space theory (Fauconnier 1994, 1997; Sweetser and Fauconnier 1996). As Todd Oakley has pointed out, the creation and understanding of narratives also depends "on our capacity to create and exploit webs of mappings between mental spaces" (Oakley 1998: 327). In Fauconnier and Turner's definition, mental spaces are "small conceptual packets constructed as we think and talk, for purposes of local understanding and action" (Fauconnier and Turner 1996: 113, 1998: 137, 2002: 40). It can be described as a short-term cognitive construct that depends on other more stable long-term knowledge structures (Kövecses 2002: 227–28), but "the crucial characteristic of a mental space," as Eve Sweetser puts it, "is that there can be systematic cognitive mappings between it and other mental spaces, with consequences for (inter alia) reference" (Sweetser 1999: 135). Mental space theory, then, is a general model for the description of "interconnections between parts of complex conceptual structures" (Sweetser 1999: 134–35).

Blending theory operates with a minimum of four mental spaces, that is, a minimum of two input spaces, plus a so-called generic space that contains the abstract structure common to the two input spaces, and a blended space made up of elements and structure projected from the two input spaces as well as elements and structure emerging from within the blend itself.[2] It is important to note, however, that the number of possible input spaces is in principle infinite.

A conceptual blend depends upon cross-space mappings of counterpart relations between input spaces, and projection of elements and structure from these into a blended space. This projection is selective,

---

[2] See the figure in Fauconnier and Turner 2002: 46.

which means that only some of the features of the input spaces are actually projected to the blended space. In the blend itself, the elements projected into it are integrated and combined but structure and elements may also emerge that have no counterparts in the input spaces, and inferences may be projected back to them. Thus, in addition to describing the projections and cross-space mappings between mental spaces, blending theory also accounts for so-called emergent structure. The basic mechanisms of blending theory apply regardless of whether new structure emerges from the blending process or not, and regardless of the nature of the conceptual integration in question.

It should be noted that once the conceptual integration network has been established, mental work is not done exclusively within the blended space. Rather, the network is utilized as a whole. As Fauconnier and Turner (1996: 113) put it:

> We know the connection of the blend to the input spaces, and the way that structure or inferences developed in the blend translates back to the input spaces. We work over all four spaces simultaneously, but the blend gives us structure, integration, and efficiency not available in the other spaces.

The process of running the blend may also call up new input spaces, recruit new structure, elements, and frames, and contribute to the creation of new blends. Indeed, the blended space may itself become an input space in another conceptual integration network.

Moreover, the generic space may serve to prime intertexts and concepts in long term memory that exhibit the same generic feature or features, which in turn facilitates the recruitment of further input spaces from these primed intertexts or concepts. The primary function of the generic space is that of cohesion. Elements and abstract structure that are common to the input spaces are projected to this space. The generic space may also facilitate the recruitment of further input spaces to the blend. In the words of Seana Coulson: "The ability to reframe something at a higher level of abstraction (as in a representation evoked in the generic space of a frame network) may serve as a retrieval cue for frames which would have been otherwise unavailable" (Coulson 1997: 298). Coulson is here discussing the so-called frame network, but the principle holds true for any kind of network. It should be noted, however, that in more complex *conceptual integration networks*, with more than two input spaces, all input spaces need not share the same generic space, although having a shared generic space makes the network as a whole more cohesive.

The texts and concepts which share more features with the generic space are especially prone to be called up to working memory, where the process of blending takes place. Further input spaces, cued by the running of the blend, may also be recruited to the network from other texts as well as from project elements and structure of the blend. The notion of "priming" is important here (Tulving and Schacter 1990; Schunn and Dunbar 1996; Hogan 2003). Bob Snyder defines priming as "[a] process whereby the recall of a particular memory causes the low-level activation of other associated memories (a context), without this process necessarily becoming conscious." This again "makes it more likely that some of those semiactivated memories will also be recalled" (Snyder 2000: 262).

3. *The Soul is a Woman*

Perhaps *the* most important premise for the overall rhetoric of the *Exegesis on the Soul* is the fact that the soul is presented as a woman. This is referred to in various ways throughout the tractate and introduced in anatomical terms in its very first lines, where we learn that the soul is a woman in her "nature" (*physis*) and that she has a womb (*Exeg. Soul* 127.19–22, quoted above). From the perspective of conceptual metaphor theory, we have here a mapping of elements and structure from the more concrete source domain of WOMAN onto the more abstract target domain of SOUL. This is thus the first expression of the conceptual metaphor THE SOUL IS A WOMAN. This metaphor serves as the rhetorical backbone of the text, and helps its readers to conceptualize the rather abstract topic of the internal life and struggles of the soul in terms of more concrete biological and cultural knowledge of women, i.e., in terms of features drawn from what we may regard as the *Idealized Cognitive Model* (ICM) of WOMAN (Lakoff 1987).[3]

---

[3] In the words of Raymond Gibbs, an ICM is "a prototypical 'folk' theory or cultural model that people create to organize their knowledge." They "are idealized and don't fit actual situations in a one-to-one correspondence but relate many concepts that are inferentially connected to one another in a single conceptual structure that is experientially meaningful as a whole" (Gibbs 1994: 58). Often, concepts are defined by a set of metaphors, each highlighting different aspects of the ICM. Lakoff refers to this as ICM clustering. Even when a concept is defined by a cluster of cognitive models, however, it is psychologically easier to grasp as a single concept, than as the sum of its constituents (Lakoff 1987: 74–76, 203).

As Raymond Gibbs has pointed out, concepts and categories are highly flexible (Gibbs 2003: 31–32). ICMs such as WOMAN, that are made up of different, sometimes contradictory, elements, should thus be viewed as temporary and context-dependent mental representations (see Gibbs 2003: 33). This means that when the reader encounters the metaphorical source ICM of WOMAN in the *Exegesis on the Soul*, he or she draws upon concrete knowledge of specific parts of that ICM, depending on the context and depending on his or her prior "real-world" and textual knowledge and experience. Concepts, Gibbs has argued, are thus "temporary constructions in working memory constructed on the spot from generic and episodic information in long-term memory," rather than stable long-term memory structures (Gibbs 2003: 32).

Of course, like most ICMs, that of WOMAN is also culturally contingent (cf. Kövecses 2005); the exact composition of this ICM in the *Exegesis on the Soul*'s late antique *Sitz im Leben* is impossible for us to retrieve. This does not leave us totally in the dark with regard to its possible metaphorical entailments, however. At least to some extent, common embodied experience and retrievable intertextual connections make it possible for us to discern a good number of metaphorical entailments that may be postulated as plausible for late antique readers as well.

In the example given above, we saw that the *Exegesis on the Soul* specifically highlights one such entailment that follows from the overarching metaphor THE SOUL IS A WOMAN, namely the detail that the soul has a womb. The emphasis on this metaphorical entailment at this point in the tractate serves a dual purpose. It is not only used as an argument for the soul's femaleness, but more importantly it sets the stage for the further rhetorical exploitation of this very aspect of the source ICM at a later stage in the narrative (cf. Sevrin 1983: 84–85).

The temporary and contextual character of metaphorical meaning construction (see Gibbs 2003) is important. Since any given source input will only highlight certain aspects of the target, we often find that inputs from several different source domains, or ICMs, which may even be mutually contradictory, are used to highlight different aspects of the same target depending on context, rhetorical or otherwise. That is, different metaphors are used at different times to illuminate the same target domain or ICM so that different aspects of it may be brought to mind. These phenomena, which are also commonly used as rhetorical devices in the *Exegesis on the Soul* and other Nag Hammadi texts, are referred to by Zoltán Kövecses respectively as the "range of the target" and the "scope of the source" (Kövecses 2000, 2005: 121–23).

Throughout the *Exegesis on the Soul*, the basic metaphor THE SOUL IS A WOMAN draws on different aspects of this source ICM to create a number of lower level conceptual metaphors like THE SOUL IS A VIRGIN, PROSTITUTE, BRIDE, WIFE, SISTER, MOTHER and DAUGHTER. In terms of blending theory, this may be described as the WOMAN ICM being drawn upon to supply different mental input spaces, at different points throughout the *Exegesis on the Soul*, corresponding to various such stereotypical female roles. Elements and structure of each of these are at different times blended with elements from the "target" input THE SOUL. I shall now take a closer look at the function of some of these lower level metaphors of the overarching conceptual metaphor THE SOUL IS A WOMAN.

In the *Exegesis on the Soul*, the soul starts out as a virginal daughter properly obedient to her father (127.22–25), but this state of affairs changes dramatically with her fall:

> But when she fell down to a body and came to this life, she fell into the hands of many robbers, and the wanton men tossed her into each others hands and they [...]. Some used her [by force], while others did this by way of deceit with a gift. In general they defiled her, and she [...her] virgin[ity]. And she prostituted herself in her body and she gave herself to everyone, and whomever she was about to embrace she considered to be her husband. (*Exeg. Soul* 127.25–128.4.)

In this account there are several notable contrasts in relation to the soul's original state. At this fallen stage the soul is no longer a virgin. She is defiled, not only against her will, but also willingly, believing each and every man to be her husband. Both aspects are important for the further development of the narrative. First, her many false husbands at this stage stand in direct opposition to the one who is later referred to as "her perfect husband" (*Exeg. Soul* 137.6–7) and "true bridegroom" (132.15). Secondly, her victimization at the hands of "robbers" and "wanton men" shows her weakness and vulnerability away from the safety provided by her father and her husband and brother. The *Exegesis on the Soul* describes the earthly adulterers as both seducing and forcing her, and they make her be a slave for them as if they were her faithful husbands and her true masters (128.7–17). The terms "husband" and "master" are closely linked and strengthen the aspects of power and submission in the activation of the MARRIAGE ICM, which are subsequently highlighted when the text later alludes to Gen 3:16 LXX/ 1 Cor 11:3/Eph 5:23 in its statement that "the master of the woman is her husband" (*Exeg. Soul* 133.9–10).

Now, how do we interpret the description of the soul's fallen state as opposed to her pre-existent life in heaven? Robinson has argued that "the narrative revels in condemning sex" (Robinson 1970: 105) and speaks of the original state of the soul as an "asexual state (virginity and androgyny)," in contrast to its fallen state, "characterized by sexual identity (female or male)" (Robinson 1989: 137). It is "sexuality in itself" that in Robinson's view is the soul's problem (Robinson 1989: 137, 1970: 114), and he comes to the conclusion that "deliverance would entail restoration of the original state of asexuality" (Robinson 1989: 137). I would argue that this interpretation misses the rhetorically important contrast between the soul as a lone female and the soul as the female part of a male-female pair, and likewise the contrast between her one true spouse and her many false husbands or adulterers. In her fall, the soul, the female part, leaves her true male partner, and thus ends up consorting with false ones. Salvation consequently entails reunification with the former. The *Exegesis on the Soul* also makes clear that there is, in fact, such a thing as legitimate (comm)union for the soul, but it is strictly that which involves Christ, her true spouse and savior. Communion with others is described as adultery, fornication, or prostitution. The soul's metaphorically female identity is thus essential for the narrative and the overall rhetoric of the text. The metaphorical entailments of describing the soul as male would be quite different and certainly not compatible with this.

Perhaps the single most curious feature of the *Exegesis on the Soul* is the way it uses the imagery of the soul's womb to describe important aspects of her fallen state and the nature of salvation. The notion that the soul has a womb is in itself not unique to this tractate. In the *Legum allegoriae* of Philo of Alexandria, we find the notion that the soul has a womb which may give birth to good things as a result of God implanting virtues in it (*Leg.* 3.180). As we shall see, the *Exegesis on the Soul* develops the metaphor in a similar direction, but also significantly extends its usage, exploiting some of its metaphorical entailments in novel ways.

A case in point is when the tractate contrasts the state of the womb of the fallen soul with that of a proper woman, stating that

> the womb of the body is on the inside of the body like the other internal organs, but it is to the outside that the womb of the soul turns, like the genitals of the male, which are on the outside. (*Exeg. Soul* 131.23–27.)

This is an important rhetorical move. By describing the womb of the soul as in a significant way resembling male genitalia, the *Exegesis on the*

Soul infers male characteristics to the soul in her fallen state. It is here worth noting that certain medical theories in antiquity presented the male and female genitals as being analogous, the one being like the other turned inside out (Smith 1988: 354–55). Thus, as the tractate points out, when turned the wrong way the womb resembles male genitals. This allows for the presentation of the soul not only as an immoral woman, but also as having transgressed gender-boundaries. As Richard Smith has argued, the way in which the narrative also portrays the soul as actively seeking out partners herself is in many ways in the manner of a male. The image of the external male genitalia-like womb serves to highlight the male aspects of this behavior (Smith 1988: 354), while simultaneously presenting it as an inherently unnatural kind of behavior for the soul. After all, the womb is not supposed to be on the outside resembling male genitals. The result is that both the soul's actions and her physiology violates category boundaries, and in the final analysis it results in her having paradoxically both male and female characteristics in her fallen state. She is, in a sense, both a female prostitute and a male fornicator. The imagery of the inverted womb reinforces this blend since it is still a womb (female), but resembles male genitalia.

It should be noted that on the level of the metaphorical source, the *Exegesis on the Soul* does not directly condemn sexuality per se, but only illicit sexuality, i.e., that which amounts to prostitution/fornication (*porneia*) or adultery (*moicheia*). Should we, then, understand *porneia*, as it is used in the *Exegesis on the Soul*, as a metonym for sexuality in general (cf. Robinson 1970, 1989), or should we rather see it as having a *metaphorical* target referent? The tractate actually seems to stress the point that its prostitution imagery does not refer primarily to bodily prostitution or actual sexual infidelity, but rather, by way of metaphor, to the soul's relationship with the material world in general, sexual immorality being merely one of its bodily manifestations:

> But concerning this prostitution (*porneia*) the apostles of the Savior commanded: "Guard yourselves against it. Purify yourselves of it" (cf. Acts 15:20, 29; 21:25; 1 Thess 4:3; 1 Cor 6:18; 2 Cor 7:1), speaking not only about the prostitution (*porneia*) of the body, but rather that of the soul. Therefore the apostles [write to the churches] of God, in order that [prostitution (*porneia*)] of this sort might not happen among [us]. But the great [struggle] concerns the prostitution (*porneia*) of the soul. From it comes the prostitution (*porneia*) of the body as well. (*Exeg. Soul* 130.28–131.2.)

The prostitution of the body is thus explicitly contrasted with the prostitution of the soul. The two are indeed linked, the one being presented as the cause of the other, but they are also clearly distinguished. Note also that it is in fact the *porneia* of the body that is linked to the *porneia* of the soul. Nowhere does the *Exegesis on the Soul* equate *porneia* with sexuality as such. Whatever its underlying views may be concerning the latter, the text emphasizes that it is making an argument that relates specifically to the soul. This point is further strengthened when the tractate proceeds by quoting 1 Cor 5:9–10 together with Eph 6:12, explaining that "Paul" is "speaking spiritually:"

> Therefore Paul, writing to the Corinthians, said: "I wrote to you in the letter: 'Do not mix with prostitutes,' by no means (meaning) the prostitutes of this world or the greedy or the robbers or those who worship idols, since then you would need to leave the world" (1 Cor 5:9–10). Thus he is speaking spiritually, for "the struggle is for us not against flesh and blood" (Eph 6:12), according to him, "but against the rulers of this darkness and the spirits of wickedness" (Eph 6:12). (*Exeg. Soul* 131.2–13.)

According to the *Exegesis on the Soul*, then, "Paul" should not be taken to refer primarily to bodily prostitution in 1 Cor 5:9–10, but rather to the prostitution of the soul. We are thus invited to read the imagery metaphorically. It seems clear that the soul can choose between associating with worldly matters, described metaphorically as prostitution/fornication (*porneia*), or with the Savior. We thus get the metaphorical blends ASSOCIATING WITH WORLDLY THINGS IS AN ILLICIT SEXUAL RELATIONSHIP and ASSOCIATING WITH CHRIST IS A LEGITIMATE SEXUAL RELATIONSHIP, which are intimately connected to the overarching metaphor CHRISTIAN LIFE IS A MARRIAGE WITH CHRIST, a full analysis of which is beyond the scope of this essay.

4. *Baptism is Washing*

A necessary step on the way to the soul's marriage with Christ, however, is baptism. The *Exegesis on the Soul* introduces baptism in a rather unique way, utilizing the womb imagery that is such an integral part of the metaphor THE SOUL IS A WOMAN in this text:

> Therefore, when the womb of the soul turns itself by the will of the Father to the inside, she is baptized and immediately she is cleansed of the defilements of the outside, this which was pressed upon her, like [garments, when they are dirty,] are lifted into the [water and are] turned until their dirt [is out] and they are purified.[4] The purification of the soul

---

[4] I follow Layton's reconstruction of the Coptic text (Layton 1978).

is to receive once again her [new]ness of her original nature, and to turn herself again. This is her baptism. (*Exeg. Soul* 131.27–132.2.)

The soul is described as being washed like a garment in the waters of baptism. In this way a connection is made between the cleansing of the soul and the ritual act of baptism, by means of the metaphorical blend BAPTISM IS WASHING.[5] Moreover, in likening the baptism of the soul to the washing of clothes in water, the *Exegesis on the Soul* also invokes the well-known metaphor of the soul as a garment. Let us take a closer look at the blend that is created by this passage (See Figure 1).

In this conceptual integration network, water, cleansing, and immersion are found in both inputs and are fused in the blend. We see that there are mappings of counterpart relations between soul and garment and between sins and dirt. In the blend, the concrete relationship between the garment and the dirt in the washing input structures the understanding of the relationship between the ritual act of baptism and the effect this has upon the soul. Thus, in baptism, the sins are removed from the soul like dirt, and the soul is turned like a garment.

Importantly, the two counterpart-relations mentioned above are also identical with two conventional early Christian metaphors, namely SIN IS DIRT and THE SOUL IS A GARMENT. The use of the BAPTISM IS WASHING metaphor in this way thus also primes the reader's memory of other well-known uses of the motif of the soul as a garment, and brings to mind the richness of the garment-metaphor with its wider implications and its diverse use in early Christian literature, particularly in connection with baptism (see Layton 1978; Brock 1982).

The soul is metaphorically a garment in the BAPTISM IS WASHING blend. An interesting effect, however, is caused by the range of the target ICM SOUL in this tractate. The soul is a garment, but it is first and foremost a woman. The *Exegesis on the Soul* utilizes this double metaphorical identification of the soul in its description of baptism by blending the metaphors THE SOUL IS A WOMAN and THE SOUL IS A GARMENT within the overall BAPTISM IS WASHING blend. This is facilitated by a metonymic tightening (Fauconnier and Turner 1998: 171; Turner and Fauconnier 2000) of the projection from the source ICM of WOMAN which causes a shift from THE SOUL IS A WOMAN, to THE SOUL IS A WOMB, by way of the metonymy THE WOMB FOR THE WOMAN. The subsequent blending

---

[5] This, it may be remarked, can be regarded as a metonymically motivated metaphor (cf. Radden 2003), since an element of washing in water is a part of the ritual of baptism.

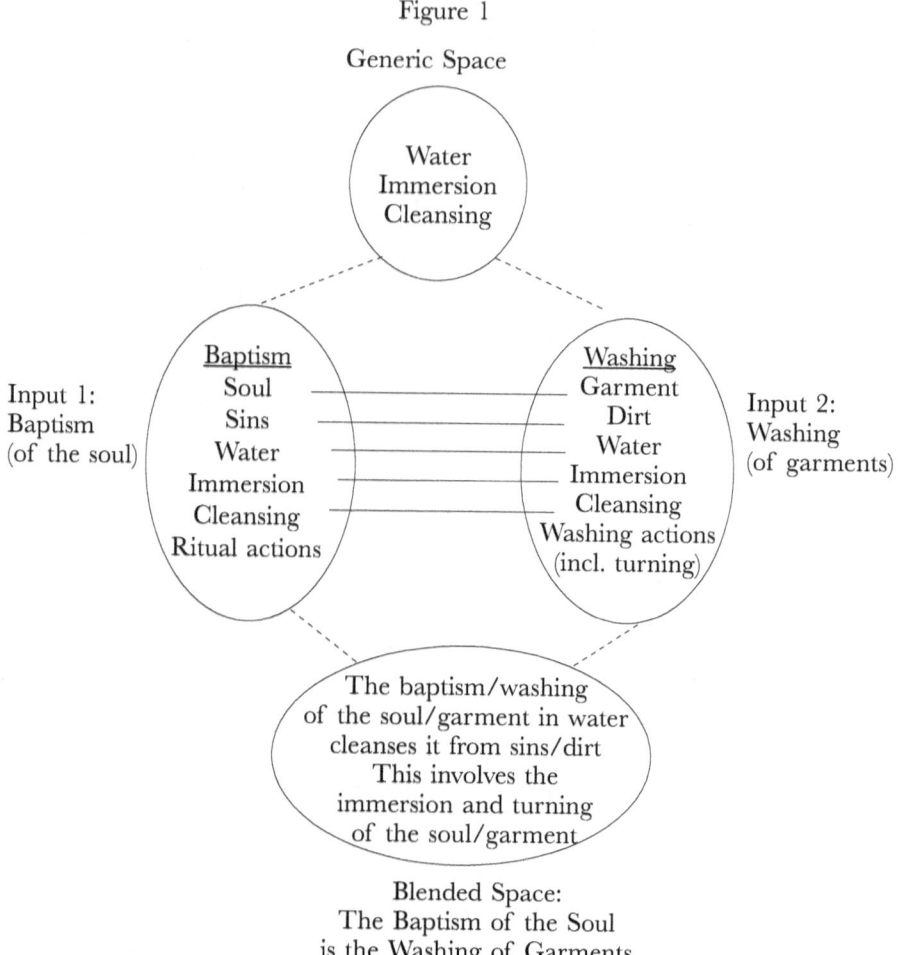

Figure 1

Blended Space:
The Baptism of the Soul
is the Washing of Garments

of the latter with THE SOUL IS A GARMENT, creates a temporary fusion in the blend of the image of the womb with that of the garment, a fusion which only exists in the blended space. This blended space can further be conceived of as existing within the BAPTISM IS WASHING blend as it is constructed in the *Exegesis on the Soul* (see Figure 2).

When this blend is interpreted within the framework of the real world knowledge of the WASHING ICM, that in the washing of garments, the garments are often turned inside out, the implication is that the baptism of the soul involves the washing and turning of the—now mentally fused—womb/garment in water. We thus see how the basic metaphor BAPTISM IS WASHING, when it also involves the two metaphors THE SOUL

CONCEPTUAL BLENDING IN THE *EXEGESIS ON THE SOUL*

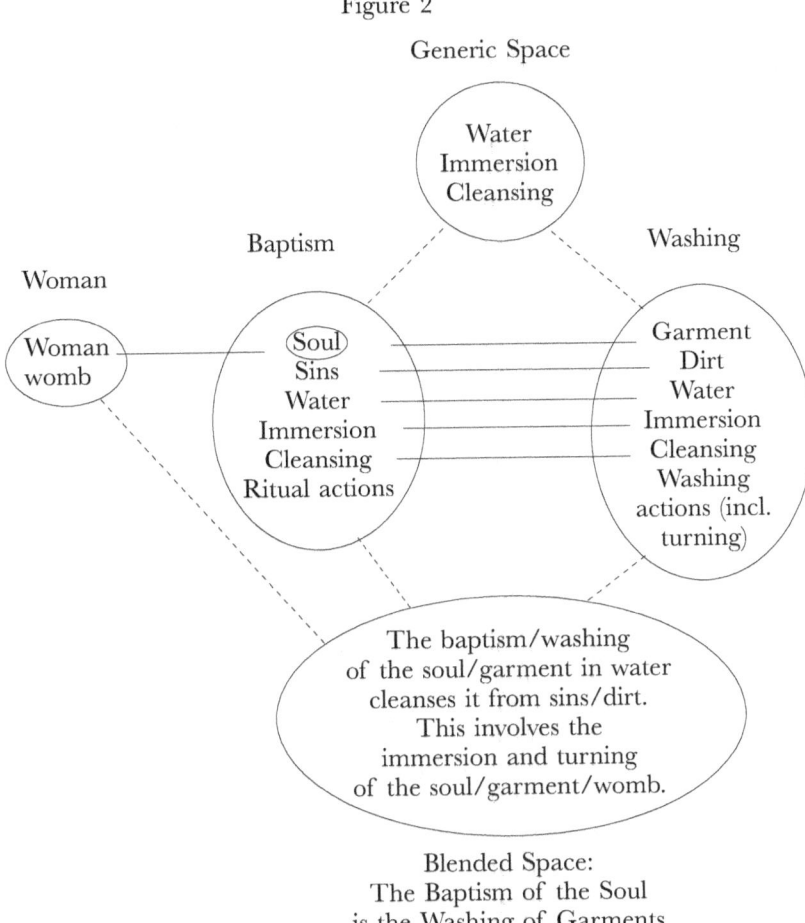

Figure 2

Blended Space:
The Baptism of the Soul
is the Washing of Garments

IS A GARMENT and THE SOUL IS A WOMAN, can produce, by elaboration in the process of blending, such creative imagery as the turning inside-out of the womb of the soul in baptism. This is facilitated by the exploitation of certain potential entailments of one of the basic metaphors underlying the *Exegesis on the Soul*, namely THE SOUL IS A WOMAN, in a surreal but suggestive blend. It is moreover a creative elaboration that is subsequently utilized in the unfolding narrative.

The image of the turning of the womb is a striking way to describe the transformation of the characteristics of the soul from male into female, but this use of the womb-imagery also functions to highlight certain aspects of the rhetorically important inside versus outside dichotomy. The outside is connected with matter, deception, unimportance, pollution, and down, whereas the inside is connected with positive things like spirit, truth, importance, purity, and up. This outside-inside dichotomy plays an important part in the tractate's rhetoric of conversion and redemption. The womb of the soul is a central point of reference in all this, showing "the outside" as bad and "the inside" as good, and conversion as the turning of the soul's womb from the outside to the inside. Moreover, the rhetoric of naturalness is an important one in the *Exegesis on the Soul*, and it is made clear that the natural and proper direction of the womb is toward the inside. We may recall the opening lines of the tractate, where it is pointed out that the soul is female "in her nature," which is further explicated by the fact that she has a womb (127.21–22). It is thus not natural for the soul to resemble a man by having its womb on the outside.

In her baptism, the soul is described as being cleansed of its sins, renewed, and turned into a proper female, and hence as becoming a proper bride for the upcoming wedding with Christ. The cleansing and turning of the womb in baptism is thus a necessary precondition for the soul's unification with the Savior and sets the stage for further metaphors of salvation later on in the narrative, especially those which are connected to the ICMs of MARRIAGE and PROCREATION.

5. *Birth and Rebirth*

Salvation is in the *Exegesis on the Soul* linked with the imagery of birth. This is again connected to the reception of the Savior's seed, for the tractate stresses that "since she is a woman" she is "unable to bear children on her own." Significantly, the state of the soul's womb is connected to the soul's receptivity of good or bad seed and her ability to bear children. While on the outside, the womb of the soul is polluted and the soul receives bad seed and produces children that are sick and stupid (128.21–26). Only after the womb is cleansed and turned toward the inside can the soul receive good seed from the Savior and produce good children (133.34–134.6). This is described as "the great perfect marvel (*thauma*) of birth" (134.4–5), recalling John 3, with its discussion of rebirth through water and spirit, and especially John 3:7 ("Do not marvel that I said to you, 'You must be born anew'").

The necessity for the soul not only to give birth but also to be reborn is explicitly affirmed by the *Exegesis on the Soul*, which states that "the soul will be saved through the rebirth" (134.28–29). The use of this phrase

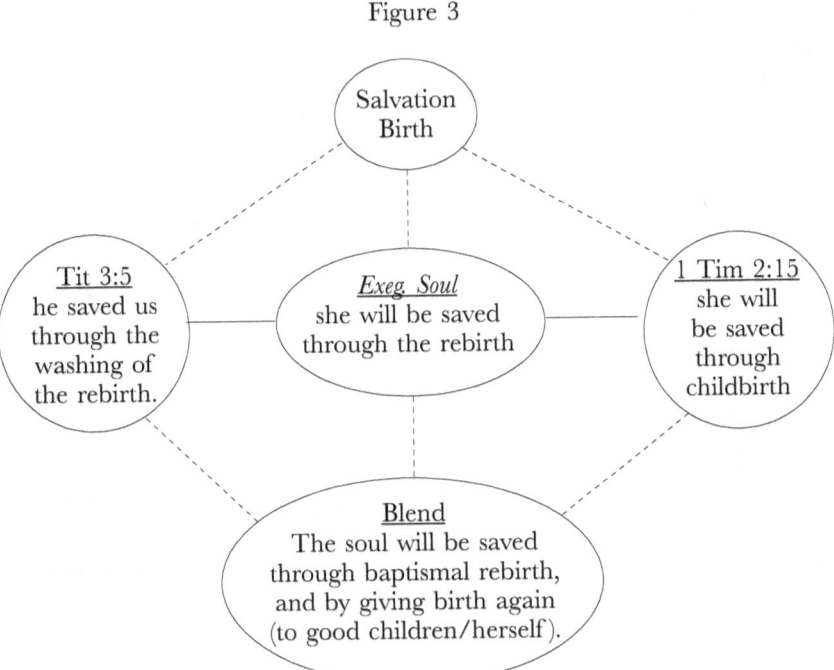

Figure 3

is interesting, since the way "rebirth" is used here may be understood not only to refer to the soul being reborn but also to her giving birth again, which is partly achieved through an intertextual blend involving Titus 3:5 and 1 Tim 2:15 (see Figure 3). The duality that the soul must both give birth again and become reborn gains yet another dimension with the tractate's statement that "it is necessary for the soul to give birth to herself and become once again as she was before" (*Exeg. Soul* 134.6–8). The renewal of the soul is, as we have seen, connected to her baptism, and baptism is also connected to the soul's rebirth by way of the blend shown in Figure 3. Although the reference to baptism is not made explicit in *Exeg. Soul* 134.6–8, it is present in the Titus 3:5 input space and may easily be called upon by the readers of the passage when they "run the blend," assuming that they know and recognize Titus 3:5. Moreover, when 1 Tim 2:15 is also taken into account, we may interpret the *Exegesis on the Soul* as describing the soul's necessary baptismal rebirth that leads to her renewed ability to give birth—to good children and/or herself—all of which may be given several metaphorical interpretations.

The *Exegesis on the Soul* refers to ritual actions at several points throughout the tractate, both overtly and rather more allusively. As

Majella Franzmann has pointed out, however, it is often difficult to know whether ritual terminology in the Nag Hammadi material is used metaphorically or to refer directly to actual ritual practice (Franzmann 1996: 36). With regard to the passage discussed above, where the purification of the soul is described in terms of the washing of garments, the concluding statement that "this is her baptism" (*Exeg. Soul* 132.2), can be interpreted to indicate either that the description pertains to what happens to the soul in the ritual of baptism (cf. Yarnold 2001), or that the baptism of the soul is a metaphor for something else, for instance, mental or spiritual processes (see Segelberg 1977: 60; Wisse 1975: 79). Both possibilities are attested in our early Christian sources. This means that depending on the postulated hypothetical context, and on the reader, we may interpret the various references to baptism in the *Exegesis on the Soul* strictly literally, or as either the target or the source in metaphorical blends. This also nicely illustrates a point that, for example, Patrick Colm Hogan has made of rejecting the existence of literal or metaphorical utterances per se, and acknowledging only literal and metaphorical *interpretations* (Hogan 2003: 91).

6. *Summary and Conclusion*

The *Exegesis on the Soul* frames its discourse on the Christian life and the importance and significance of the sacraments with an allegorical narrative of the fall and redemption of the soul portrayed as a woman. This creates ample opportunity for the tractate to utilize a whole range of rich and interlinking metaphors together with corresponding scriptural and other literary intertexts. We have seen that by expanding upon the idea that the soul is female, the tractate draws upon aspects of female anatomy and literary descriptions and discussions of female transgression and prostitution, as well as traditional female roles in marriage and procreation, for its conceptual blends.

The soteriological metaphor of "becoming male" was prevalent in early Christian literature (Vogt 1991), and as Marvin Meyer puts it, "[r]arely does a religious text from antiquity and late antiquity recommend that one become female" (Meyer 2002: 107). The *Exegesis on the Soul* is thus an interesting departure from this pattern. Here it is a requirement for the salvation of the soul that she becomes a proper woman and wife. By exploiting the related metaphorical entailments, the tractate emphasizes the proper power relationship between the soul and Christ. Analogous to the way a good wife should submit herself to the rule of her husband, which seems to be the common cultural assumption presupposed by this text, the soul should submit to the authority and rule of Christ. The effectiveness of this symbolism stems from the tractate's opening premise that the soul is female and a common cultural understanding of the role of the wife in relation to her husband in marriage. When the soul is turned into a proper woman, it is quite "natural" for her to receive her proper husband and submit herself to his rule (cf. Williams 1988: 15). Moreover, the metaphors of sexuality and procreation also rely upon the soul's female nature.

But does the fact that the soul is a woman in the *Exegesis on the Soul* mean that the tractate is only concerned with the souls of women, as Madeleine Scopello has argued? Interpreting the imagery of the soul as a woman literally rather than metaphorically, Scopello uses the text as evidence for "the historical and social reality of women in the gnostic communities," and claims that the author of the *Exegesis on the Soul* was probably a woman, since in her view "the sexual accounts of a text such as the *Exegesis on the Soul* are more probably ascribed to a woman than to a man" (Scopello 1988: 87–90). The overall rhetoric of the tractate, however, seems rather to imply that the soul is metaphorically female regardless of the gender of the body it inhabits (cf. Good 1988: 38–39).

Frederik Wisse claims that "[o]nly celibacy would be consistent with the teaching of the tractate" (Wisse 1975: 78). But although a celibate life would in no way contradict what we have found in our reading of the *Exegesis on the Soul*, bodily celibacy is not necessarily assumed. Robinson's conclusion that the tractate's main concern is to condemn sexuality, requires the identification, by metonymy, of illicit sex, i.e., *porneia* and *moicheia*, with sex in general in the rhetoric of the *Exegesis on the Soul*. However, there does not seem to be compelling reasons for doing so. On the contrary, to take what the tractate says about the prostitution of the soul to simply signify the sinfulness of sex seems to go against the argument the tractate makes on the basis of 1 Corinthians and Ephesians, discussed above. Moreover, the restoration of the soul to its original state does not seem to entail a restoration to asexuality, but rather to a state of perpetual union with "her perfect husband" (*Exeg. Soul* 137.6–7). What is stated in the *Exegesis on the Soul* is the need for the soul to turn its back on worldly things and embrace life with him. The soul is supposed to be faithful to Christ, but whether a celibate bodily life is the only way to achieve such chastity of the soul, while hardly unattested in early Christian sources, is not a question that is answered by the text itself. In the final analysis, it is up to the reader and his or her interpretive community to decide what kind of life would be consistent with the tractate's view of the soul. (Fish 1980).

However this may be, the examples given above nicely illustrate Seana Coulson and Todd Oakley's statement that, "even though cognitive models in blended spaces are occasionally bizarre, the inferences generated inside them are often useful and lead to productive changes in the conceptualizer's knowledge base and inferencing capacity" (Coulson and Oakley 2005: 1514–15).

REFERENCES

Brock, Sebastian P. 1982. "Clothing Metaphors as a Means of Theological Expression in Syriac Tradition." In *Typus, Symbol, Allegorie bei den östlichen Vätern und ihren Parallelen im Mittelalter*, edited by Margot Schmidt, 11–38. Eichstätter Beiträge, 4. Regensburg: Friedrich Pustet.

Coulson, Seana. 1997. "Semantic Leaps: The Role of Frame-Shifting and Conceptual Blending in Meaning Construction." Ph.D. Diss., University of California, San Diego.

Coulson, Seana, and Todd Oakley. 2000. "Blending Basics." *Cognitive Linguistics* 11(3–4): 175–96.

———. 2005. "Blending and Coded Meaning: Literal and Figurative Meaning in Cognitive Semantics." *Journal of Pragmatics* 37(10): 1510–36.

Eubanks, Philip. 2005. "Globalization, '*Corporate Rule*,' and Blended Worlds: A Conceptual-Rhetorical Analysis of Metaphor, Metonymy, and Conceptual Blending." *Metaphor and Symbol* 20(3): 173–97.

Fauconnier, Gilles. 1994. *Mental Spaces: Aspects of Meaning Construction in Natural Language*. Cambridge: Cambridge University Press.

———. 1997. *Mappings in Thought and Language*. Cambridge: Cambridge University Press.

Fauconnier, Gilles, and Mark Turner. 1996. "Blending as a Central Process of Grammar." In *Conceptual Structure, Discourse and Language*, edited by Adele E. Goldberg, 113–30. Stanford, Calif.: CSLI Publications.

———. 1998. "Conceptual Integration Networks." *Cognitive Science* 22(2): 133–87.

———. 2002. *The Way We Think: Conceptual Blending and the Mind's Hidden Complexities*. New York: Basic Books.

Fish, Stanley. 1980. *Is There a Text in This Class? The Authority of Interpretive Communities*. Cambridge, Mass.: Harvard University Press.

Franzmann, Majella. 1996. "The Concept of Rebirth as the Christ and the Initiatory Rituals of the Bridal Chamber in the *Gospel of Philip*." *Antichthon* 30: 34–48.

Gavins, Joanna, and Gerard Steen, eds. 2003. *Cognitive Poetics in Practice*. London: Routledge.

Gibbs, Raymond W., Jr. 1994. *The Poetics of Mind: Figurative Thought, Language, and Understanding*. Cambridge: Cambridge University Press.

———. 2003. "Prototypes in Dynamic Meaning Construal." In *Cognitive Poetics in Practice*, edited by Joanna Gavins and Gerard Steen, 27–40. London: Routledge.

Good, Deirdre J. 1988. "Gender and Generation: Observations on Coptic Terminology, with Particular Attention to Valentinian Texts." In *Images of the Feminine in Gnosticism*, edited by Karen L. King, 23–40. Studies in Antiquity and Christianity. Philadelphia, Pa.: Fortress.
Hogan, Patrick Colm. 2003. *Cognitive Science, Literature, and the Arts: A Guide for Humanists*. New York: Routledge.
Kövecses, Zoltán. 2000. "The Scope of Metaphor." In *Metaphor and Metonymy at the Crossroads: A Cognitive Perspective*, edited by Antonio Barcelona, 79–92. Topics in English Linguistics, 30. Berlin: Mouton de Gruyter.
———. 2002. *Metaphor: A Practical Introduction*. Oxford: Oxford University Press.
———. 2005. *Metaphor in Culture: Universality and Variation*. Cambridge: Cambridge University Press.
Lakoff, George. 1987. *Women, Fire, and Dangerous Things: What Categories Reveal About the Mind*. Chicago, Ill.: University of Chicago Press.
———. 1993. "The Contemporary Theory of Metaphor." In *Metaphor and Thought*, edited by Andrew Ortony, 202–51. Cambridge: Cambridge University Press.
Lakoff, George, and Mark Johnson. 1980. *Metaphors We Live By*. Chicago, Ill.: University of Chicago Press.
Layton, Bentley. 1978. "The Soul as a Dirty Garment (Nag Hammadi Codex II, Tractate 6, 131:27–34)." *Muséon* 91: 155–69.
———. 1989. "The Expository Treatise on the Soul: Critical Edition." In *Nag Hammadi Codex II,2–7 Together with XIII,2*, Brit. Lib. Or.4926(1), and P. Oxy. 1, 654, 655*. Vol. 2: *On the Origin of the World, Expository Treatise on the Soul, Book of Thomas the Contender*, edited by Bentley Layton, 144–68. Nag Hammadi Studies 21. Leiden: Brill.
Meyer, Marvin W. 2002. "Gospel of Thomas Logion 114 Revisited." In *For the Children, Perfect Instruction: Studies in Honor of Hans-Martin Schenke on the Occasion of the Berliner Arbeitskreis für koptisch-gnostische Schriften's Thirtieth Year*, edited by Hans-Gebhard Bethge, Stephen Emmel, Karen L. King, and Imke Schletterer, 101–11. Nag Hammadi Studies 54. Leiden: Brill.
Oakley, Todd V. 1998. "Conceptual Blending, Narrative Discourse, and Rhetoric." *Cognitive Linguistics* 9(4): 321–60.
Radden, Günter. 2003. "How Metonymic Are Metaphors?" In *Metaphor and Metonymy in Comparison and Contrast*, edited by René Dirven and Ralf Pörings, 407–34. Berlin: Mouton de Gruyter.
Robinson, William C., Jr. 1970. "The Exegesis on the Soul." *Novum Testamentum* 12: 102–17.
———. 1989. "The Expository Treatise on the Soul: Introduction." In *Nag Hammadi Codex II,2–7 Together with XIII,2*, Brit. Lib. Or.4926(1), and P. Oxy. 1, 654, 655*. Vol. 2: *On the Origin of the World, Expository Treatise on the Soul, Book of Thomas the Contender*, edited by Bentley Layton, 136–41. Nag Hammadi Studies 21. Leiden: Brill.
Schunn, Christian D., and Kevin Dunbar. 1996. "Priming, Analogy, and Awareness in Complex Reasoning." *Memory & Cognition* 24(3): 271–84.
Scopello, Madeleine. 1988. "Jewish and Greek Heroines in the Nag Hammadi Library." In *Images of the Feminine in Gnosticism*, edited by Karen L. King, 71–90. Studies in Antiquity and Christianity. Philadelphia, Pa.: Fortress.
Segelberg, Eric. 1977. "Prayer Among the Gnostics? The Evidence of Some Nag Hammadi Documents." In *Gnosis and Gnosticism: Papers Read at the Seventh International Congress on Patristic Studies (Oxford, September 8th–13th 1975)*, edited by Martin Krause, 54–69. Nag Hammadi Studies 8. Leiden: Brill.
Sevrin, Jean-Marie. 1983. *L'Exégèse de l'ame (NH II, 6): Texte établi et présenté*. Bibliothèque copte de Nag Hammadi, Section "Textes," 9. Québec: Les Presses de l'Université Laval.

Smith, Richard. 1988. "Sex Education in Gnostic Schools." In *Images of the Feminine in Gnosticism*, edited by Karen L. King, 345–60. Studies in Antiquity and Christianity. Philadelphia. Pa.: Fortress.
Snyder, Bob. 2000. *Music and Memory: An Introduction*. Cambridge, Mass.: MIT Press.
Stockwell, Peter. 2002. *Cognitive Poetics: An Introduction*. London: Routledge.
Sweetser, Eve. 1999. "Compositionality and Blending: Semantic Composition in a Cognitively Realistic Framework." In *Cognitive Linguistics: Foundations, Scope, and Methodology*, edited by Theo Janssen and Gisela Redeker, 129–62. Cognitive Linguistics Research 15. Berlin: de Gruyter.
Sweetser, Eve, and Gilles Fauconnier. 1996. "Cognitive Links and Domains: Basic Aspects of Mental Space Theory." In *Spaces, Worlds, and Grammar*, edited by Gilles Fauconnier and Eve Sweetser, 1–28. Cognitive Theory of Language and Culture. Chicago, Ill.: University of Chicago Press.
Tulving, Endel, and Daniel L. Schacter. 1990. "Priming and Human Memory Systems." *Science* 247(4940): 301–6.
Turner, Mark. 2002. "The Cognitive Study of Art, Language, and Literature." *Poetics Today* 23(1): 9–20.
Turner, Mark, and Gilles Fauconnier. 2000. "Metaphor, Metonymy, and Binding." In *Metaphor and Metonymy at the Crossroads: A Cognitive Perspective*, edited by Antonio Barcelona, 133–45. Topics in English Linguistics 30. Berlin: de Gruyter.
Vogt, Kari. 1991. "'Becoming Male': A Gnostic and Early Christian Metaphor." In *Image of God and Gender Models in Judaeo-Christian Tradition*, edited by Kari Elisabeth Børresen, 172–87. Oslo: Solum.
Williams, Michael Allen. 1988. "Variety in Gnostic Perspectives on Gender." In *Images of the Feminine in Gnosticism*, edited by Karen L. King, 2–22. Studies in Antiquity and Christianity. Philadelphia, Pa.: Fortress.
Wisse, Frederik. 1975. "On Exegeting 'The Exegesis on the Soul.'" In *Les Textes de Nag Hammadi: Colloque du Centre d'Histoire des Religions (Strasbourg, 23–25 octobre 1974)*, edited by Jacques-É. Ménard, 68–81. Nag Hammadi Studies, 7. Leiden: Brill.
Yarnold, Edward. 2001. "The Body-Soul Relationship Mainly in Connection with Sacramental Causality." In *Ascetica, Gnostica, Liturgica, Orientalia: Papers Presented at the Thirteenth International Conference on Patristic Studies Held in Oxford 1999*, edited by Maurice F. Wiles and Edward Yarnold, 338–42. Studia Patristica, 35. Leuven: Peeters, 2001.

CONCEPTUAL BLENDING AND EARLY CHRISTIAN IMAGINATION

Vernon K. Robbins

1. *Introduction*

The emergence of early Christianity during the first century C.E. is a truly remarkable phenomenon. The literature this movement produced during its first seventy years of existence exhibits profound creativity in the context of traditional cultures, which are known for their conservative nature. Years ago, scholars like Amos Wilder (1964) observed that there were amazingly "new" formulations of phrases and words in New Testament literature. There has, however, been only limited progress in our understanding of how this "newness" emerged. Many scholars have exhibited and discussed the wide reaching diversity in traditions, concepts, and practices among different groups of early Christians. There have been only a few attempts, however, to develop modes of analysis and interpretation that show what one might call the "inner workings" of visualizations, conceptualizations, and orientations in the context of this diversity.

Ilkka Pyysiäinen has done some very interesting thinking about this in a paper entitled "Intuition, reflection, and the evolution of traditions." For my purposes, his discussion of "selection," "guided variation," and "biased cultural transmission" are very helpful (Pyysiäinen 2005: 289–92). His discussion feeds naturally into analyses of "partial mapping" and other things in *conceptual integration theory* (alternatively called *conceptual blending theory*), which I will discuss below. Pyysiäinen also observes the presence of "pre-narrative" as frameworks that guide reproduction (Pyysiäinen 2005: 290). István Czachesz (2007) also has presented some very helpful concepts in "Toward a Cognitive Psychology of Early Christian Transmission." In the context of three alternative approaches to religion in cognitive science, Czachesz discusses schema theory, and introduces four "scripts" upon which he thinks early Christian literature relies: martyrdom script; gospel script; healing script; and divine call script (Czachesz 2003). In my view, this is a very promising approach, especially when it is correlated both with "serial recall," when scripts serve as underlying story-grammars to narrative (Czachesz 2003: 21), and with "the cognitive relevance hypothesis of Christology," which Czachesz describes as "the early Christian conceptualization of Jesus adapted to the economy of the mind by closely approaching the archaic idea of ancestors" (Czachesz forthcoming).

In the context of various new approaches to religion from the perspective of cognitive science on brain and mind, my approach is especially informed by Conceptual Blending (or Conceptual Integration) Theory and Critical Spatiality Theory. Instead of four scripts (Czachesz), my socio-rhetorical analysis exhibits six rhetorical dialects (called rhetórolects) that blend dynamically with one another in first century Christian discourse. Each of the rhetorolects emerges in embodied cognition through interaction with specifically located contexts that provide picturing based on seeing places and spaces through social and cultural experiences. This aspect of discourse I call rhetography, namely evoking pictures through pictorial expression (Robbins forthcoming a). Each rhetorolect is nurtured in the mind through cultural frames that evoke story-lines containing a sequence of pictures in the context of pictorial narration. Each rhetorolect also contains reasonings, which I call their rhetology, namely "assertions," "supports," and "juxtapositions" of thoughts that evoke "meanings" in the context of images, actions, feelings, and so forth. Gilles Fauconnier and Mark Turner's *The Way We Think* (2002) and Seana Coulson's *Semantic Leaps* (2001) have been especially helpful in my analysis and interpretation of the dynamic and complex conceptual blending that occurs among the six rhetorolects that have emerged in my socio-rhetorical analysis.[1] An excellent Afterword in the 2003 publication of George Lakoff and Mark Johnson, *Metaphors We Live By* (2003) explains the relation of Conceptual Blending (Integration) Theory to conceptual metaphor theory. The first programmatic conceptual blending interpretation of a New Testament passage in a socio-rhetorical framework has now been completed and will be forthcoming soon as a published book (von Thaden 2007).

The six rhetorolects that have emerged in my analysis are: *wisdom, prophetic, apocalyptic, precreation, miracle,* and *priestly* rhetorolect. One of the challenges is to discover how these rhetorolects blend with one

---

[1] I am especially grateful to Robert von Thaden and Bart B. Bruehler, two Ph.D. graduates from Emory University who have advanced the use of Conceptual Integration Theory and Critical Spatiality Theory for interpreting early Christian texts in their dissertations.

another. Perhaps certain blends of two, or perhaps three, rhetorolects create "emergent blend structures" (Fauconnier and Turner 2002) that are especially generative in early Christian discourse. We are just beginning to find our way with these things. This essay gives a preview of blending in early Christian miracle discourse. But first a little more introduction to the six rhetorolects.

2. *A Basic View of Early Christian Rhetorical Dialects (Rhetorolects)*

In the context of socio-rhetorical analysis and interpretation of early Christian literature during the 1990s (Robbins 1996a,b), very different modes of argumentation began to appear, creating exceptional challenges for analysis and interpretation of all the different kinds of discourse in the New Testament, as well as in other early Christian literature. In the context of inductive analysis of portions of all the writings in the New Testament and some Christian writings outside the New Testament, six major kinds of discourse began to emerge. In 1996, it was decided that six discourses functioned as rhetorical dialects that interacted dynamically with one another to create the Christian discourse that existed by 100 C.E. In addition, I decided to follow the advice and example of Benjamin H. Hary, a sociolinguist at Emory University, to shorten the phrase "rhetorical dialect" to "rhetorolect" (Robbins 1996c). After changes in the names of three of the rhetorolects over a period of eight years, the names have emerged as: *wisdom, prophetic, apocalyptic, precreation, miracle,* and *priestly*. In each of the rhetorolects, pictorial narration and reasoning associated with particular social, cultural, and religious locations have emerged as highly significant. Focus on these locations is producing more detailed analysis of the social, cultural, and ideological aspects of socio-rhetorical interpretation (Robbins 1996a). It became obvious, first of all, that a major characteristic of early Christian discourse emerges from the patterns with which it creates enthymematic argumentation out of pictorial narration and reasoning related to people's bodies, households, villages, synagogues, cities, temples, kingdoms and empires (Robbins 1998, 2002, 2006). In other words, the cognitions and reasonings were emerging from "lived experiences" in specific places in the first century Mediterranean world. This has led to the use of "critical spatiality theory" in socio-rhetorical interpretation (Bruehler 2008). This area of study, located in the field of cultural geography studies, builds in particular on writings by Henri

Lefèbvre (1991), Robert D. Sack (1986, 1997), Pierre Bourdieu (1989), Edward W. Soja (1989, 1993, 1996), and Stephen Toulmin (1990). James W. Flanagan has been especially instrumental in bringing critical spatiality theory into biblical study (Flanagan 1999, no date; Gunn and McNutt 2002). In 1991, Robbins used Robert D. Sack's *Human Territoriality* for socio-rhetorical analysis of "images of empire" in Acts (Robbins 1991a) and T. F. Carney's *The Shape of the Past* (1975) for the social location of the implied author of Luke-Acts (Robbins 1991b). Jerome H. Neyrey has applied strategies for interpreting the social location of the implied author to Jude and 2 Peter (Neyrey 1993), Luke's social location of Paul (Neyrey 1996), the Gospel of John (Neyrey 2002a, 2002b), and to Paul's writings (Neyrey 2003). Since 2000, Roland Boer (2000) has written an important study on "the production of space" in 1 Samuel 1–2, Michael McKeever (2000) an analysis of "refiguring space in the Lukan passion narrative," Claudia V. Camp (2002) an important essay on "storied space" in Sirach, Victor H. Matthews (2003) an important discussion of physical, imagined, and "lived" space in ancient Israel, and Thomas B. Dozeman (2003) an essay on Ezra-Nehemiah.

Socio-rhetorical interpretation is using critical spatiality theory together with cognitive theory about conceptual blending to analyze and interpret the nature of early Christian discourse. Here the foundational work is Fauconnier and Turner's *The Way We Think*.[2] The merger of conceptual blending theory with critical spatiality theory is clarifying the relation of social places to cultural, ideological and religious spaces in the six primary early Christian rhetorolects. According to Fauconnier and Turner (2002: xv, 279): "Conceptual integration always involves a blended space and at least two inputs and a generic space." To these insights, Seana Coulson (2001) in particular has added the insight that organizing, cultural frames are continually operative, either as background or foreground, in conceptual blending. Socio-rhetorical analysis and interpretation of rhetorolects proceeds, therefore, on the presupposition that places and spaces dynamically inform conceptual blending through the presence of cultural frames which this essay calls rhetorolects. Rhetorolects organize pictures of people and loca-

---

[2] The use of this book for socio-rhetorical commentary is the result of an e-mail by L. G. Bloomquist on Dec. 4, 2002, which called attention to the relation of conceptual blending theory to early Christian blending of rhetorolects, which was a topic of discussion at the Rhetoric of Religious Antiquity meetings prior to the AAR/SBL sessions at Toronto in November, 2002.

Figure 1. Conceptual Blending of Frames and Spaces in Rhetorolects.

Cultural Frames (Rhetorolects)	Conventionally organized mental domains in Mediterranean culture and tradition
Generic Spaces	Conceptual mental spaces
Experienced Spaces (Firstspace)	Experiences of the body in social places
Conceptualized Spaces (Secondspace)	Sensory-aesthetic and cognitive experiences creating cultural, religious, and ideological places
Spaces of Blending (Thirdspace)	Debate, reconciliation, elaboration, and avoidance in relation to cultural, religious, and ideological places

tions together in ways that nurture special cultural memories. Certain words and phrases evoke these memories in a manner that frames the reasoning about topics the discourse introduces to the hearer. As the discourse creates pictures in the mind of special social, cultural, religious, and ideological places, it creates movements in the mind of association, dissociation, admiration, dislike, love, anger, courage, fear, etc. Figure 1 presents an abstract table that displays the presence of cultural frames (rhetorolects), generic spaces (highly multiple cognitive activities), experienced spaces (firstspace/input 1); conceptualized spaces (secondspace/input 2); and spaces of blending (thirdspace) that are dynamically related to one another in early Christian rhetorolects.

People's words and phrases evoke conventional discourse frames (rhetorolects) that invite pictures of spaces and actions that exist in cultural memory. Sensory-aesthetic experiences of the body in various social places—like household, village, city, synagogue, kingdom, temple, and empire—in the world are the "firstspace" contexts in which people develop and perpetuate special pictures and memories in their minds. People activate cognitive and conceptual abilities to interpret these social places and actions as "secondspace" cultural, religious, and ideological places. In addition, people use processes of part-whole, similar-dissimilar, opposite, etc. to relate pictures, actions, and reasonings (in "generic" spaces) to one another. In the context of these activities, people negotiate their daily lives in ongoing contexts of sensory-aesthetic experiences which are "thirdspace" "spaces of blending." Socio-rhetorical interpreters are accepting the challenge of analyzing and interpreting six rhetorolects that function as organizing, cultural frames that blend places and spaces in special networks of reasoning and argumentation: wisdom, prophetic, apocalyptic, precreation, miracle, and priestly (Robbins forthcoming b). Figure 2 below presents an initial display of important places and spaces in the six primary early Christian rhetorolects.

Early Christian wisdom rhetorolect blends human experiences of the household, one's interpersonal body, and the geophysical world (firstspace) with the cultural space of God's cosmos (secondspace). In the lived space of blending (thirdspace), God functions as heavenly Father over God's children in the world, whose bodies are to produce goodness and righteousness through the medium of God's wisdom, which is understood as God's light in the world. In this context, wisdom rhetorolect emphasizes "fruitfulness" (productivity and reproductivity). The goal of wisdom rhetorolect is to create people who produce good action, thought, will, and speech with the aid of God's wisdom.

Early Christian prophetic rhetorolect blends the speech and action of a prophet's body in an experiential space of God's kingdom on earth (firstspace) with conceptual space of God's cosmos (secondspace). The reasoning in the rhetorolect presupposes that the prophet has received a divine message about God's will. The prophet speaks and acts in contexts that envision righteous judgments and actions by kings, who should be God's leaders who establish justice on the earth. As a result of the nature of God's message, the prophet regularly experiences significant resistance, and often explicit rejection and persecution. In the space of blending (thirdspace), God functions as heavenly King over his righteous kingdom on earth. The nature of prophetic rhetorolect is to confront religious and political leaders who act on the basis of human greed, pride, and power rather than God's justice, righteousness, and mercy for all people in God's kingdom on the earth. The goal of prophetic rhetorolect is to create a governed realm on earth where God's righteousness is enacted among all of God's people in the realm with the aid of God's specially transmitted word in the form of prophetic action and speech.

Early Christian apocalyptic rhetorolect blends human experiences of the emperor and his imperial army (firstspace) with God's heavenly temple city (secondspace), which can only be occupied by holy, undefiled people. In the space of blending (thirdspace), God functions as a heavenly emperor who gives commands to emissaries to destroy all the evil in the universe and to create a cosmic environment where holy

Figure 2. Blended Spaces and Locations in Early Christian Rhetorolects.

Cultural Frames (Rhetorolects)	Wisdom	Prophetic	Apocalyptic	Precreation	Miracle	Priestly
Social, Cultural, & Physical Realia (1st Space)	Household, Vegetation, Living Beings	Political Kingdom	Political Empire, Imperial Temple, Imperial Army	Political Empire & Emperor's Household	Human Body & Unexpected Phenomena & Transformations in the natural world	Altar, Temple & Temple City
Visualization, Conceptualization, & Imagination of God's World (2nd Space)	God as Father-Creator (Progenitor), Wisdom (light) as Mediator, People as God's children, Jesus as God's Son	God as King, God on kingly throne in heavenly court, Selected humans as prophets and kings, Selected people as God's kingdom, Jesus as Prophet-Messiah selected and sent by God	God as Almighty (Pantokratōr), Jesus as Son of Man, King of King and Lord of Lords	God as Eternal Emperor-Father, Jesus as God's Eternal Son	God as Transforming Power, Selected humans as agents of God's transforming power, People as healed and transformed by God, Jesus as Healer & Miracle-Worker	God as Holy and Pure, God on priestly throne in heavenly temple, Selected humans as priests, People as God's holy & pure priestly community (assembly, city, kingdom), Jesus as Priest-Messiah

Figure 2 (*cont.*)

Spaces of Mental Conception (Generic Spaces)	Cause-effect, change, time, identity; intentionality; representation, part-whole Formal argumentative topics: opposites, grammatical forms of the same word, correlatives, more and less, time, turning back upon the opponent, definition, varied meanings, division, induction, previous judgment, parts, consequence, contrast, openly and secretly, analogy, same result, before and after, purpose as cause, for and against, implausible probabilities, contradictions, cause of false impression, cause and effect, better, doing contrary to what has been done, mistakes, meaning of a name.[3]				
Ongoing Bodily Effects and Enactments: Blending in Religious Life (3rd Space = Space of Blending)	Human body as Producer of Goodness & Righteousness	Human body as Distributor and Receiver of justice (food, bodily needs, honor)	Human body as Receiver of resurrection & eternal life in a "new" realm of well-being	Human body as Receiver of eternal life through friendship (belief & loyalty) with God's eternal Son	Human body as Healed and amazingly Transformed	Human body as Giver of sacrificial offerings and Receiver of beneficial exchange of holiness and purity between God and humans

---

[3] Aristotle, *Rhetoric* 2.23.1–29 (1397a–1400b); Kennedy 1991: 190–204.

bodies experience perfect well-being in the presence of God. Apocalyptic rhetorolect, then, features destruction of evil and construction of a cosmic environment of perfect well-being. The goal of this blending is to call people into action and thought guided by perfect holiness. The presupposition of the rhetorolect is that only perfect holiness and righteousness can bring a person into the presence of God, who destroys all evil and gathers all holiness together in God's presence. Apocalyptic redemption, therefore, means the presence of all of God's holy beings in a realm where God's holiness and righteousness are completely and eternally present.

Early Christian precreation rhetorolect blends human experiences of a deified emperor (like the Roman emperor) and his household (firstspace) with a philosophically conceptualized cosmos (secondspace), with the presupposition that God has the status in non-time and non-space of a loving heavenly emperor with a household populated by loving people. The result of this philosophically utopian blending is the presence of the loving Emperor Father God in God's heavenly household before all time and continually throughout God's "non-time." God's Son existed with God during "non-time" before time began with the creation of the world. This "eternal" Son does what His Father asks him to do, and heirs and friends of the eternal emperor and his eternal son receive eternal benefits from their relation to this eternal household. In the space of blending (thirdspace), God functions as heavenly Emperor Father who possesses eternal blessings He will give to people as a result of his love for the world and the people in it. People may enter into this love by believing, honoring, and worshipping not only God but also his eternal Son and members and friends whom God sends out with a message of eternal blessings. Precreation rhetorolect, then, features love that is the source of all things in the world and the means by which people may enter into God's eternal love. In this rhetorolect, God's light is love that provides the possibility for entering into eternal love, rather than being limited to light that is the basis for the production and reproduction of goodness and righteousness. The goal of the blending in precreation rhetorolect is to guide people towards community that is formed through God's love, which reflects the eternal intimacy present in God's precreation household.

Early Christian miracle rhetorolect has a primary focus on human bodies afflicted with paralysis, malfunction, or disease. In this context, a malfunctioning body becomes a site of "social geography." Miracle rhetorolect features a bodily agent of God's power who renews and restores life, producing forms of "new creation" that oppose powers of affliction, disruption, and death. The "location" of importance for early Christian miracle rhetorolect, therefore, is a "space of relation" between an afflicted body and a bodily agent of God's power (firstspace). In this rhetorolect, there is no focus on any particular social, cultural, political, or religious "places" on earth. A bodily agent of God's power, wherever it may be, is a "location" where God can function as a miraculous renewer of life (secondspace). A major goal of miracle rhetorolect is to effect extraordinary renewal within people that moves them toward speech and action that produces communities that care for the well-being of one another (thirdspace).

Early Christian priestly rhetorolect blends human experiences in a temple or other place of worship (firstspace) with a concept of temple city and God's cosmos (secondspace). Reasoning in priestly rhetorolect presupposes that ritual actions benefit God in a manner that activates divine benefits for humans on earth. In the space of blending (thirdspace), people make sacrifices by giving up things that give them well being in the form of giving them to God. Food, possessions, and money may be offered up to God, but also honor through thanksgiving, prayer, hymns, and worship. Some of these things may be given to God by giving them to other people on earth, or by allowing other people to take things like honor or fame away without protest. The greatest sacrifice people can offer to God, of course, is their entire life. Usually, in contrast, a person gives up only certain highly valued things in life. Early Christian priestly rhetorolect features thanksgiving, praise, prayer, and blessing in contexts regularly perceived to be sacrificial in intent and practice. By the end of the 1st century C.E. much, though not all, Christian priestly rhetorolect was somehow related to Jesus' death on the cross. Priestly rhetorolect features beneficial exchange between God and humans in a context of human sacrificial action. The goal of the conceptual blending is to create people who are willing to give up things they highly value in exchange for special divine benefits that come to them, because these sacrifices are perceived to benefit God as well as humans. In other words, sacrificial actions by humans create an environment in which God acts redemptively among humans in the world.

The inclusion of conceptual blending theory and critical spatiality theory in socio-rhetorical interpretation allows an interpreter to construct a topology of spaces in early Christian rhetorolects and to interpret the rhetorical power of the blending of spaces in these rhetorolects.

Since each of the rhetorolects presents social, cultural, religious, and ideological language, story-telling, and argumentation that evoke specific pictures, emotions, cognitions and reasonings, each rhetorolect made vital contributions in distinctive ways to a new culture of discourse that was emerging during the first century. Since many of the social places present in early Christian discourse (like household, village, places of sacred ritual, city, etc.) continue to exist to the present day in some reconfigured form, early Christian discourse continually functions anew in places believers perceive to be similar in social, cultural and religious function. Some believers locate their thinking primarily in one rhetorolect at a time, blending aspects of other rhetorolects into this one rhetorolect for very specific purposes. Other believers locate their thinking in a particular blend of multiple rhetorolects, inviting selective aspects of other rhetorolects in implicit, subtle and nuanced ways. The variations produce a dynamic conceptual, cognitive, and verbal system of Christian discourse that is highly adaptive to multiple contexts and cultures. Figure 3 below exhibits the dominant social, cultural and ideological rhetoric internal to each rhetorolect.

Dynamic blending of the six early Christian rhetorolects created a richly variegated culture of early Christian discourse by the end of the first century. Believers blended each rhetorolect dynamically with the other rhetorolects either by blending multiple rhetorolects into one dominant rhetorolect or by blending particular rhetorolects together in a particularly forceful manner. The dynamics of these blendings

Figure 3. Rhetoric internal to each Rhetorolect.

Wisdom	Prophetic	Apocalyptic	Precreation	Miracle	Priestly
Speech of God, Christ, and believers produces fruitfulness	God calls people, including Christ, to call and exhort people to be a righteous kingdom	Christ's initial coming produced a new beginning and Christ's return will produce a new world	God's and Christ's primordial existence produces eternal life in believers	God's power working in and/or through Christ and believers produces bodily transformation	Sacrifice by Christ and believers produces glorification of God and holy benefit for believers

throughout the verbal culture of early Christianity produced a continually increasing combination of cognitions, reasonings, picturings, and argumentations. This interactive process continued in Christian discourse throughout the centuries, and it continues in our present day. The following Figure shows the spaces where double-domain blending could occur. There is a potential for thirty double-domain blends in the following table. The blending in early Christian discourse is so dynamic, however, that multiple blends of various kinds appear. For this reason, there will be no attempt in this essay to fill the following table simply with double-domain blends, like wisdom and prophetic, wisdom and apocalyptic, wisdom and precreation, and so forth.

3. Wisdom Blends with Prophetic, Priestly, and Apocalyptic Rhetorolect in 2 Peter 1:5–8

Instead of attempting to fill the table in Figure 4 with dual-domain blends, like prophetic wisdom or apocalyptic wisdom, the discussion below exhibits two samples of blending in early Christian discourse.

Figure 4. Potential Double-Domain Blends in Early Christianity Discourse.

	Wisdom	Prophetic	Apocalyptic	Precreation	Miracle	Priestly
Blended Wisdom Rhetorolect	X					
Blended Prophetic Rhetorolect		X				
Blended Apocalyptic Rhetorolect			X			
Blended Precreation Rhetorolect				X		
Blended Miracle Rhetorolect					X	
Blended Priestly Rhetorolect						X

After this discussion, a final section of the essay will analyze and discuss the nature of some of the blending in early Christian miracle rhetorolect.

First is a display and brief discussion of the blending of wisdom rhetorolect with priestly, prophetic, and apocalyptic rhetorolect in 2 Peter 1:5–11. Christian wisdom rhetorolect is present in 2 Pet 1:5 as it features people's production of the virtues of excellence, self-control, piety, and love.

Figure 5. Wisdom Rhetorolect in 2 Peter 1:5–8.

> [5]For this very reason, be earnest to supplement your faith (*pistis*) with excellence (*aretē*), excellence with knowledge (*gnōsis*), [6]knowledge with self-control (*enkrateia*), self-control with steadfastness (*hypomonē*), steadfastness with piety (*eusebeia*), [7]piety with kinship affection (*philadelphia*), kinship affection with love (*agapē*). [8]For when you possess these and increase in them, they will keep you from being ineffective (*argos*) and unfruitful (*akarpos*) in the knowledge (*epignōsis*)[4] of our Lord Jesus Christ.

The list in 2 Pet 1:5 moves in a progression from faith to love. Some of the virtues are widespread in the Greco-Roman world, like excellence, self-control, piety, and kinship affection (Neyrey 1993: 154). The list is framed with the Christian virtues of faith at the beginning and love at the end. This framing gives the list its dialectical, religious quality in the Mediterranean world. In contrast to this list, Seneca, *Ep.* 85:2 begins with prudence (*prudens*) and ends with being happy (*beatus*), while Cicero, *Leg.* 1.7.22 begins with foresight (*providum*) and ends with "full of reason and prudence" (*plenum rationis et consilii*). It is characteristic of early Christian wisdom rhetorolect to present a sequence that either begins with faith and ends with love (Rom 5:1–5; 1 Cor 13:13) or begins with love and ends with faith (Eph 4:2–5). Instead of including hope (*elpis*), which often is in early Christian lists that feature faith and love,[5] 2 Pet 1:5–8 includes steadfastness, like 2 Thess 1:4. Early Christian wisdom rhetorolect in 2 Pet 1:5–8, then, manifests itself in a triadic framework of faith, steadfastness, and love, into which it inserts knowledge,

---

[4] Neyrey (1993: 150) translates this "for the acknowledgment."
[5] Rom 5:1–5; 1 Cor 13:13; Eph 4:2–5; 1 Thess 1:3; 5:8; Rom 12:6–12; Eph 1:15–18; Col 1:4–5.

excellence, self-control, piety, and kinship affection. This list presents a new framework for well-known and widespread Mediterranean virtues, blending them into a "Christian" rhetorolect that, on the one hand, sounds familiar and, on the other hand, emphasizes the key Christian topoi of faith and love at the beginning and the end.

2 Pet 1:9–10 introduce prophetic and priestly rhetorolect into the wisdom rhetorolect of 1:5–8.

Figure 6. Triple-Blended Wisdom Rhetorolect in 2 Peter 1:9–10.

Wisdom/Prophetic/Priestly	⁹For anyone who lacks these things is short-sighted and blind, and is forgetful of the cleansing of past sins. ¹⁰Therefore, brothers and sisters, be all the more eager to confirm your call (*klēsis*) and election (*eklogē*), for if you do this, you will never stumble.

2 Pet 1:9–10 continue in the mode of wisdom rhetorolect, with 1:9 instructing its hearer/reader with an additional rationale ("for") and 1:10 following with a conclusion ("therefore"). Vs. 9, however, features language characteristic of prophetic discourse when it speaks of blindness[6] that causes shortsightedness. This prophetic discourse blends with priestly discourse when it refers to the cleansing of past sins, "which probably refers to a ritual such as baptism or some other *mikvoth* or washing rite" (Neyrey 1993: 154). 2 Pet 1:10 continues with prophetic rhetorolect when it exhorts the hearers to confirm their call and election.[7] After the exhortation, vs. 10 presents a rationale that uses language of stumbling like Philo uses to describe the result of deception (*Leg. All.* 3.66) (Neyrey 1993: 162). Vs. 10, then, continues a blend of prophetic and wisdom rhetorolect that could bring the thought sequence to an end.

Instead of ending with a blend of wisdom, prophetic, and priestly rhetorolect, 2 Pet 1:11 presents a rationale containing argumentation of early Christian apocalyptic rhetorolect.

---

[6] Isa 42:7, 16, 18, 19; 43:8; 59:10; cf. 29:18; 35:5; 61:1 (LXX).
[7] See *kaleō* and *eklektos* in LXX Isaiah and Jeremiah.

Figure 7. Blended Wisdom Rhetorolect in 2 Peter 1:11.

Wisdom/Apocalyptic	¹¹For in this way, entry into the eternal kingdom of our Lord and Savior Jesus Christ will be richly provided for you.

If 2 Pet 1:11 continued in a prophetic mode, it would refer to the believer's inheritance in the kingdom of God. Instead, it promises a specifically Christian apocalyptic outcome: entrance into the eternal kingdom of our Lord and Savior Jesus Christ. Those who live according to the wisdom listed in 1:5–8, will not simply be happy, full of reason and prudence, or guided by love, but they will become participants in the glorious, eternal kingdom of God's heavenly Messiah Jesus. The concept of Christ's eternal kingdom is new to apocalyptic in the Mediterranean world, featuring a special emphasis of Christian apocalyptic rhetorolect. The rhetorical argumentation in 2 Pet 1:5–11 reaches its climactic point not in the goals of wisdom, priestly, or prophetic rhetorolect either separately or blended together. Rather, the argumentation creates a sequence that blends early Christian wisdom, priestly, and prophetic rhetorolect into early Christian apocalyptic rhetorolect. The end result is multiple-scope blending (Fauconnier and Turner: 279–98) that reconfigures widespread Greco-Roman wisdom discourse into a highly complex conceptual system of Christian reasoning, argumentation, and exhortation. The goal of these verses is to produce human bodies filled with "knowledge of God and the Lord Jesus Christ." The aim of exhortation and argumentation is to set the hearer's sights on virtues that move beyond the goals of the moral philosophers in the Mediterranean world toward goals articulated by early Christian wisdom, prophetic, priestly, and apocalyptic discourse. No one discourse, however, is sufficient to articulate the goals the early Christians envision. Blending these discourses together in their own particular "dialectical" manner, early Christians presented a system of reasoning and believing that moved hearers beyond the conceptual systems of the moral philosophers into a religious system of belief focused on the eternal kingdom of God's heavenly Messiah Jesus.

4. *Precreation Blends with Apocalyptic and Priestly Rhetorolect in Col 1:15–20*

Next we come to blended precreation rhetorolect in early Christian discourse. Christian precreation rhetorolect features God's eternal divinity working through Christ's primordial nature. Col 1:15–20 blends precreation rhetorolect with apocalyptic and priestly rhetorolect as the discourse unfolds. Col 1:15–17 presents a view of "the Lord Jesus Christ" (1:3, cf. 1:1–2, 4), God's beloved Son (1:13), before the creation of the world. In this primordial environment, God is invisible. If an interpreter brackets the statement about "thrones, dominions, principalities, or powers" in 1:16, these two verses evoke a precreation frame that is so powerful that no other frame tends to come into view.

Figure 8. Precreation Rhetorolect in Col 1:15–17.

> [15]He is the image (*eikōn*) of the invisible (*aoratos*) God, the firstborn (*prōtotokos*) of all creation; [16]for in him all things in the heavens and on earth were created, things visible (*orata*) and invisible (*aorata*) [...], all things have been created through him and for him. [17]He himself is before (*pro*) all things, and in him all things hold together.

Col 1:15 makes two assertions about God's Son in relation to the invisible God. First, there is a statement that concerns seeing. God's Son is not invisible like God, but is "the image" of the invisible God. Seeing is a central focus of wisdom discourse. But the seeing in 1:15 is not focused on the created world: the sun, moon, and stars in their orbits; the animals in their ordered activities; and the days, weeks, months, and seasons that order time in the realm of human experience. Rather, the seeing is a seeing in the mind: an act of "imagining" Christ as an "image" of something invisible. The verses do not describe what primordial Christ, the image of "invisible" primordial being, actually looks like. "The author is not interested in any mythological elaboration of what is 'before' time. God is not subject to human categories of time" (Kuschel 1992: 334). The presence of Christ in non-time with invisible God is a way of talking about the priority of Christ over all things except invisible, eternal God.

Second, there is in 1:15 a statement that appears to be temporal, an assertion about Christ in relation to time. Christ is the firstborn of all creation. The word "firstborn" (*prōtotokos*) would seem to imply that

Christ was a created being, the first being "born" like other created beings. This means that "firstborn" here refers to "a process within God, a 'before' in God himself, before the world was created" (Kuschel 1992: 334). Around 323 C.E., Arius argued, using this and other scripture to support his view that:

> The one without beginning established the Son as the beginning of all creatures... He [the Son] possesses nothing proper (*idios*) to God, in the real sense of propriety, for he is not equal to God, nor yet is he of the same substance (*homoousios*)... there exists a Trinity in unequal glories, for there subsistencies (*hypostases*) are not mixed with each other... The Father is other than the Son in substance (*kat' ousian*) because he is without beginning (Arius, *Thalia* in Athanasius, *On the Councils of Ariminum and Seleucia* 15; quoted in Ayres 2004: 55).

In response to this assertion, "the church fathers interpreted the 'born' (*tokos*) in the sense of 'begotten' (as a begetting within God) and the 'first' (*proto*) in the sense of a temporal 'before' (*pro*)" (Ayres 2004: 55). This meant that the Son was not actually "created" by God but came forth within God prior to the creation of the world (Dunn 1989: 189). Col 1:16 introduces an emphasis that all things in heaven and earth, visible and invisible, were created in, through, and for the "firstborn image" of the invisible God. Then Col 1:17 asserts that this image of God is before all things and all things hold together in him. This precreation imagery focuses on the Son as the mediator of all things in such a manner that he is not only superior to all things but also the inner linking network that holds all things together. Such a focus within precreation imagery appears to be a blend of early Christian precreation and wisdom rhetorolect. This blend integrates the concept of a primordial "image Son" with the concept of an ordered and interconnected world that exhibits the wisdom through which God created the world (cf. Sir 43:26; Lohse 1971: 52).

In early Christian wisdom rhetorolect, God's wisdom is available to humans both through careful observation of how God's created world works and through teaching by God's Son when he was on earth. Early Christian wisdom rhetorolect focuses on the "visible" powers in heavens: sun, moon, and stars; the animals in their ordered activities; and the days, weeks, months, and seasons that order time in the realm of human experience. The wisdom evoked in Col 1:15–17 is beyond this "ordinary" wisdom that is based on things that are visible in God's created world. The wisdom in Col 1:15–17 is "precreation wisdom,"

wisdom that comes only through "seeing with the mind's eye" into the primordial realm of God's invisible, divine being that lies outside the created order. Only "precreation" discourse has the capacity to evoke such a conceptual frame within the mind and to fill this frame with "precreation" information.

Col 1:18 introduces a new frame with a counter-image of "firstborn from the dead," and this frame causes the reference to "thrones, dominions, principalities, or powers" and "for him" in 1:16 to move into the foreground.

Figure 9. Apocalyptic Rhetorolect in Col 1:16, 18.

> [16]...whether thrones or dominions (*kyriotētos*) or principalities (*archai*) or powers (*exousiai*)—all things have been created...for him...[18][...] he is the beginning, the firstborn (*prōtotokos*) from the dead, so that he might come to have (*hina genētai*) first place (*prōteuōn*) in everything.

Col 1:18 introduces the concept of "firstborn from the dead." This phrase was nurtured into language in early Christian apocalyptic rhetorolect.[8] As Lohse (1971: 56) asserts:

> he is the "beginning" as the one who is the "first-born from the dead" (*prōtotokos ek tōn nekrōn*) through whom the eschatological event has been initiated. As the first one who has arisen from those who have fallen asleep, he is the first fruit (*aparchē*) who guarantees the future resurrection of the dead (1 Cor 15:20, 23). Thus he is the "Originator of Life" (*archēgos tēs zōēs*; Acts 3:15), the "first to rise from the dead" (*prōtos ex anastaseōs nekrōn*; Acts 26:33) and the "firstborn of the dead and ruler of the kings on earth" (*ho prōtotokos tōn nekrōn kai archōn tōn basileōn tēs gēs*; Rev 1:5).

In first century Christian discourse, the apocalyptic story-line about the end of the world included God's resurrection of Christ from the dead into heaven, Christ's establishment of his (Christ's) kingdom by putting all his enemies under his feet, including death (1 Cor 15:25–26), and then Christ's handing of his kingdom over to God (1 Cor 15:24, 27–28). This imagery of the heavenly Christ's authority, power, and rule from the heavens (1 Cor 15:24) naturally evokes an apocalyptic, rather than a precreation, understanding of the "thrones, dominions, principalities, or powers" and "for him" in Col 1:16. As Eduard Lohse

---

[8] See 1 Pet 1:3–5 for the way Christ as firstborn of the dead becomes a means for new birth in believers; Elliott 2000: 331–38.

indicates, this visual language is at home in apocalyptic discourse. In 2 En 20:1, Enoch reports "and I saw there (i.e., in the seventh heaven) a very great light and fiery troops of great archangels, incorporeal forces, and dominions and orders and governments, cherubim and seraphim, thrones and many-eyed ones, nine (ten) regiments...."[9] Early Christian apocalyptic rhetorolect brings invisible powers in the heavens into human sight through "seers" who are shown "the things in the heavens" that bring about the end time. Early Christian apocalyptic focus on the end of time emphasized the "heavenly ruling power" both of God and Christ. Some of the most natural cultural imagery for power in Mediterranean antiquity was "thrones" and "dominions" (lordly [*kyriotētes*] realms). Early Christianity added "principalities" (*archai*) from language for rulers (*archontes*), and it added authorities (*exousiai*). In the context of an emphasis on the end time, the "for him" (*eis auton*) in Col 1:16 would now focus on Christ's ownership of all creation through his rule over it before he hands it to God at the end of time.

In Col 1:15–18, then, there are two images of Christ, and they are what W. J. T. Mitchell (1994) calls "dialectical images" that introduce "multistability." The counterplay of precreation and apocalyptic in Col 1:15–18 is like Ludwig Wittgenstein's "Duck-Rabbit" and Norma Scheidemann's "My Wife and My Mother-In-Law" (Mitchell 1994: 46–47). At first some people may see the duck and the wife while others immediately see the rabbit and the mother-in-law.[10] When the others mention the rabbit and the mother-in-law the first group may be able to see them also, and vice versa. Since the word *eschatos* (last), which would clearly evoke conceptuality of the end time, is not present anywhere in Colossians, many people, like the early Arians readily see a precreation frame in the context of the language that uses *pro* (1:17), *proteuō* (1:18), and *prōtotokos* (1:15, 18) in Colossians (Dunn 1989:

---

[9] Lohse 1971: 51n.133. Cf. *T. Levi* 3:8: in heaven "there are thrones (*thronoi*) and powers (*exousiai*) in which they always offer praise to God"; 2 En 61:10: "...all the host of the heavens, and all the holy ones above, and the host of God, the Cherubim, Seraphin and Ophannin, and all the angels of *power*, and all the angels of *principalities*, and the Elect One, and the other *powers* on the earth (and) over water..."

[10] According to Mitchell (1994: 51), a focus on one frame in a context of multistability is a result of "the mind's eye" or one's "mental eye:" "The Duck-Rabbit, and multistable images in general, reveal the presence of the 'mind's eye' roving around this storeroom, interpreting the pictures, seeing different aspects in them. The bodily eye simply transmits information: 'the image on the retina does not change' (p. 282), and the identity of the observer, his 'difference' from viewers, is located in the mental eye: 'physical eyes see alike, but...mental eyes reflect their own individualities' (p. 277)."

189–90). In contrast, the presence of reference to "thrones, dominions, principalities, or powers" along with "firstborn from the dead" could immediately evoke an apocalyptic frame of meaning for some people. The natural conclusion is that "the expression 'firstborn' (*prōtotokos*) could be understood in a great variety of ways in the first century: as a statement about the pre-existent or about the exalted Christ, i.e. as a predicate of origin or exaltation. Both interpretations would have stood side by side without any attempt to reconcile them" (Kuschel 1992: 334).

Within time, however, "dominant culture" (Robbins 1996a: 168–74; 1996b: 86–89) interpretation has come to insist that apocalyptic conceptuality controls the reasoning in Col 1:15–20. In modern times it has become conventional to argue that "firstborn of all creation" (Col 1:15) is properly understood as "an exalted predicate" rather than a reference to a process of begetting within God prior to the creation of the world. As Karl-Josef Kuschel puts it: "the statement about Christ as 'firstborn of all creation' is meant to be understood in terms of a thoroughgoing eschatology... [E]schatology is the motive force and the interpretation of protology" (Kuschel 1992: 335). He elaborates this position by arguing that there is

> no need to develop the thought of the text by making the *prōto* [of *prōtotokos*] into a *pro*; only in this way is there no need to make the second part of the word, the *tokos*, independent, "in that it is meant to imply begetting within God." By contrast, an interpretation of the "firstborn" as a predicate of exaltation makes it unnecessary to divide the word into its components. (Kuschel 1992: 334–35.)

Thus, modern interpreters regularly remove the multistability within the two images by making eschatology (apocalyptic) the dominant frame. A primary result of this dominant culture interpretation is to make the concept of "firstborn before all creation" metaphorical: "'(like a) firstborn (over) all creation' rather than 'firstborn before all creation'" (Kuschel 1992: 335). This interpretation essentially changes the wording of the text, but a widespread group of interpreters accept the interpretation, because their goal is to establish "stability" in New Testament language. "Metastability" is unacceptable, in their view, in the context of "scientific" (*wissenschaftliche*) interpretation of New Testament discourse.

There may, in fact, be a third frame of meaning at work in Col 1:15–20. Some of the wording in Col 1:18–20 appears to be early Christian priestly rhetorolect, a conceptual frame that introduces Christ as a mediator who enacts beneficial exchange between God and humans.

Figure 10. Priestly Rhetorolect in Col 1:18–20.

> [18]He is the head of the body, the church; [...]. [19]For in him all the fullness of God was pleased to dwell, [20]and through him God was pleased to reconcile to himself all things, whether on earth or in heaven, by making peace through the blood of his cross.

Col 1:18–20 blend theology and Christology with ecclesiology. The ecclesiology in this passage does not emerge out of early Christian wisdom rhetorolect that uses imagery about the body that a young child can understand (cf. 1 Cor 12:1–31). Rather, it blends "philosophical" wisdom language about the cosmos with hierarchical priestly language. The priestly language in Col 1:18–20 is sacrificial, asserting that "peace" occurs "through the blood" of the Son's cross. As Kuschel states, "For the author... Christ's blood is not spilt by dispute and violence which cries out for vengeance. For him, Christ's blood (in analogy to the Old Testament sacrifices) is blood which 'makes peace'" (Kuschel 1992: 336). Interpreters often miss how this priestly frame may become an additional (perhaps competitive) conceptual "map" for the passage. Once the priestly frame comes into view, the form of the entire passage as a "hymn to Christ" gains in importance. As Lohse asserts: the "interpretive phrase: through the blood of his cross (*dia tou haimatos tou staurou autou*)... gives a new direction to the train of thought. A 'theology of glory,' which might view the consummation as already achieved, is corrected by the 'theology of the cross' (cf. 2:14f.). Peace has not been established in an other-worldly drama but rather in the death of Jesus Christ" (Lohse 1971: 60). While interpreters regularly recognize early Christian priestly rhetorolect in the language about the blood of the cross, they often do not correlate this conceptuality with the hierarchical nature of the church as it is described in Col 1:18.

The presence of the priestly frame introduces a conceptual hierarchy, with God at the top, humans at the bottom, and the priest and the material substance of the cosmos in a position of mediation between God and humans. The priest functions as the mediator who oversees beneficial exchange between God and humans by receiving material substances of the cosmos from humans and manipulating these substances appropriately in relation to the divine. This leads to a special relation of the priest to the material substances of the cosmos. During the Hellenistic period, two things of great importance set the stage for early Christian priestly rhetorolect about Christ's death on the cross in relation to the cosmos. First, various philosophical and religious writings, from Plato to Iranian Pahlavi literature, wrote about the cosmos as a living body in which the sky, the heaven, or Zeus is the head and the lower parts of the body are the earth (Lohse 1971: 53–55). Second, the precious material substances of the vestment of the high priest are "cosmologized."[11] In other words, the high priest becomes the "cosmological mediator" between humans and God in language that has an uncanny relation to Col 1:15–20. In the words of Philo of Alexandria:

> ...the high priest should have in evidence upon him an image (*eikona*) of the all (*tou pantos*), that so by constantly contemplating it he should render his own life worthy of the sum of all things, secondly that in performing his holy office he should have the whole universe (*pas ho kosmos*) as his fellow-ministrant (*sylleitourgei*). And very right and fit it is that he who is consecrated to the Father of the world (*to ton hierōmenon tōi tou kosmou patri*) should take with him also that Father's son (*ton huion*), the all (*to pan*), for the service of the Creator and Begetter (*gegennēkotos*). (Philo, *Spec. Leg.* 1.96; trans. Colson and Whitaker, Loeb Classical Library)

To this Philo adds that "the high priest of the Jews makes prayers and gives thanks not only on behalf of the whole human race but also for the parts of nature, earth, water, air, fire" (1.97). Then in *Spec. Leg.* 2.192 "Philo describes Tishri as the 'feast of trumpets' and says that it signifies the ending of wars and thanksgiving to 'God, the peace-maker and peacekeeper, Who destroys factions both in cities and in the various parts of the universe'" (Hay 2000: 64). In Hellenistic Judaism, then, the Mediterranean focus on the cosmos as a living body blends in a special way with the priest in the context of sacrificial worship. While the focus in Col 1:20 on the Lord Jesus Christ as the Son who made "peace through the blood of his cross" is Greek language spoken as a noticeable "rhetorical dialect" during the first century, the conceptual blending of the priest, and especially the high priest, with the cosmos as a living body with a head and lower body parts is significantly present in Mediterranean culture. Thus, it is likely that triple-domain blending is occurring when the Son as the "head" of the body, the church, rec-

---

[11] See the beginnings of this tradition in the vestments of the Aaronic priests in Exod 28.

onciles all things to himself and makes peace through his blood on the cross in this context. With this language the Son is not only primordial image and eschatological ruler but also cosmological priest who enacts beneficial exchange between God and all created things, including the heavens, the earth, and humans.

Thus, the overall discourse of Col 1:15–20 introduces three cultural frames: precreation, apocalyptic, and priestly. While the presence of the multistability of precreation and apocalyptic is well-known and recognized in New Testament scholarship, the presence of the priestly frame is significantly contested. Ernst Käsemann focuses on the "specifically Christian" nature of the statements "of the church" (*tēs ekklēsias*, v. 18a) and "through the blood of his cross" (*dia tou haimatos tou staurou autou*, v. 20) to differentiate the message of the hymn from "the suprahistorical, metaphysical drama of the Gnostic redeemer" (Hay 2000: 45). In a context of interpreting Käsemann's approach, Lohse asserts that "the term 'to reconcile' (*apokatallaxai*, v. 20) does not allude, even remotely, to a connection with Jewish conceptions of sacrifices and of the great Day of Atonement..." (Hay 2000: 46). When interpreters are concerned to distinguish between "truly Christian" and gnostic or Arian points of view in the discourse, they may not only push the precreation frame into the background with an emphasis on the apocalyptic frame of meaning for the discourse, but they may virtually ignore or directly dismiss the priestly frame in the hymn.

Thus, in the context of precreation imagery in Col 1:16–17, graphic visual language about thrones (*thronoi*), dominions (*kyriotētes*), principalities (*archai*), and powers (*exousiai*) introduces graphic visual language that, in modern times, regularly brings apocalyptic discourse into a position of dominance over the reasoning in the discourse.[12] While the language of "firstborn" is a common term in each domain that establishes a "cross-domain correlation" (Lakoff and Johnson 2003: 245) between precreation imagery and apocalyptic imagery, still interpreters may insist that the apocalyptic imagery is dominant. In the context of the

---

[12] Cf. 1 Cor 8:5: "Indeed, even though there may be so-called gods in heaven or on earth—as in fact there are many gods and many lords..." It is noticeable that characteristic apocalyptic language, namely *apokalyptō* (to reveal) and *apokalypsis* (revelation) never occur in Colossians. Rather, *phaneroō* (to manifest: 1:26; 3:4[2]; 4:4) and mystery (*mysterion*: 1:26, 27; 2:2; 4:3), language that is highly characteristic of precreation rhetorolect occurs in Colossians.

multistability of the precreation-apocalyptic blend, the cosmological-priestly blend in 1:18–20 introduces a significantly new direction to the train of thought. It is possible, however, that interpreters may remain so focused on one dominant constellation of imagery in the passage that they will ignore, or explicitly dismiss, the priestly frame in 1:18–20. One of the reasons interpreters are able to do this is the topos of power, which functions as a bridging topos among all three domains: Christ's power to create all things, rule over all powers in the heavens and on earth, and make peace through his blood on the cross. Since power is so central to apocalyptic discourse, it can be natural to allow the apocalyptic frame to rule over the other frames, much like God's and Christ's rule puts all things in submission to it.

Multiple blendings of early Christian rhetorolects created a vibrant, interactive system of Christian discourse by the end of the first century C.E. This system of discourse was able to address issues and topics concerning individual human bodies, households, villages, synagogues, cities, temples, kingdoms, empires, the created world, and even God's primordial realm. The ability of this discourse to address microcosmic details about individual bodies on earth as well as macrocosmic details about God's primordial realm prepared Christianity not only to function in a context where it became the official religion of the Roman Empire but also to function potentially in multiple contexts in any culture anywhere in the world. This discourse was able to do this, because it was interactive with topoi that address issues, concerns, emotions, insights, knowledge, and mysteries that cover a spectrum reaching from mundane daily activities to the widest reaches of God's unknown realm of being. To be sure, there are many topics and issues first century Christian discourse did not address. Nevertheless, the spectrum was so wide-reaching that it successfully launched a new culture of discourse in the Mediterranean world that expanded and became continually more nuanced and complex throughout twenty centuries in the history of the world.

5. *Frames and Characters in Early Christian Miracle Discourse*

Once an interpreter sees that rhetorolects blend dynamically in early Christian discourse, the question emerges how one may use Fauconnier and Turner's synthetic discussion of Conceptual Integration Theory to begin to display some of the inner processes of blending in this discourse. Here we can do no more than raise certain issues and point toward a few phenomena to begin a discussion.

One of the issues that immediately surfaces is Fauconnier and Turner's discussion of the relation of frames to character in blending processes within each rhetorolect and in processes whereby rhetorolects blend with one another. On the one hand, earlier statements in this essay have identified rhetorolects as cultural frames. Fauconnier and Turner describe a frame in the context of explaining a simplex network. According to them, "An especially simple kind of integration network is one in which human cultural and biological history has provided an effective frame that applies to certain kinds of elements as values, and that frame is in one input space and some of those kinds of elements are in the other input space" (Fauconnier and Turner 2002: 120). For an example, they use the "readily available frame of human kinship," which is "*the family*, which includes roles for father, mother, child, and so on" (Fauconnier and Turner 2002: 120). For our example, we would like to use the readily available frame of miracle rhetorolect, which includes a person who is ill, a healer, and often someone who enables the ill person to receive a miraculous healing from the healer. In contrast to the family frame, which "prototypically applies to human beings" (Fauconnier and Turner 2002: 120), the miracle frame regularly juxtaposes human beings and a personage (perhaps somehow "partially divine") who has access to special powers to perform miraculous deeds, i.e. deeds of power (*dynamis*). If there is an integration network with one mental space containing only this frame, and another space containing a special personage, Jesus, and people trying to touch him for healing, then a simplex network is present. Luke 6:19 is an example: "And all in the crowd were trying to touch him [Jesus], for power came out from him and healed all of them."

When we conceive of Jesus as healer of people who touch him, we have created a blend in which some of the structure of the miracle frame is integrated with the elements Jesus and people touching him. This, according to Fauconnier and Turner, is a simplex network. There is a cross-space mapping between the input spaces that is a "frame-to-values connection" (Fauconnier and Turner 2002: 120). In this instance the role healer connects to the value Jesus and the role ill person who is healed connects to the value "people trying to touch him." Our initial attempt to display this is in Figure 11.

According to Fauconnier and Turner: "In a simplex network, the relevant part of the frame in one input is projected with its roles, and

Figure 11. Miracle Rhetorolect: Healing

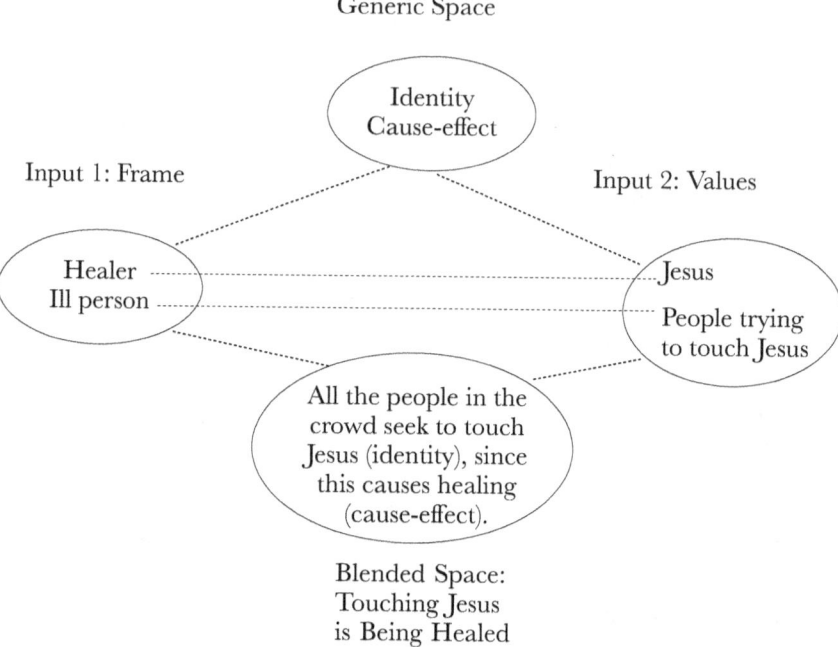

the elements are projected from the other input as values of those roles within the blend. The blend integrates the frame and the values in the simplest way" (Fauconnier and Turner 2002: 120). The sentence asserting that "All in the crowd were trying to touch Jesus, because power came out from him and healed them all" prompts the blend that Jesus is the healer of people in the crowd: "X (Jesus) is the Y (healer) of Z (people in the crowd)."

An initial challenge for socio-rhetorical interpreters attempting to display the blending of early Christian rhetorolects with one another will be to identify the nature of the simplex networks internal to each rhetorolect. When Fauconnier and Turner introduce the family frame, they use an example that features father and daughter. There are, of course, many more roles in the family frame. One immediately thinks of mother and son. But how many more roles might there be? Surely mother-in-law (Mark 1:30), father-in-law, daughter-in-law, son-in-law, grandfather, and grandmother will also be roles in the family frame. Could there also be others, like tutor or servant? In other words, if a frame is "readily available," how does one negotiate roles that may be readily available in the family frame in the first century Mediterranean world that may not be readily available in the 21st century family in, e.g., American "Western" or African culture.

Moving back to miracle rhetorolect, will an initial challenge be to identify all the roles in first century Mediterranean healings, like those who bring ill people to a healer, those who mediate with a healer so that an ill person is healed without ever coming into contact with Jesus, etc.? Will a second challenge be to identify miracle working of all kinds, in which healing is only one frame, but there are also other frames like stilling storms, feeding small amounts of food to large crowds of people, walking on water, cursing a fig tree, etc.? How, then, does one negotiate "frames" in an analysis of early Christian rhetorolects in particular, and in early Christian discourse more generally?

Another issue in blending is the relation of frames to character. After extended analysis and discussion of frames in simplex, mirror, single-scope, and double-scope networks, Fauconnier and Turner discuss "Identity and Character" in chapter twelve (Fauconnier and Turner 2002: 249–67). In this chapter, Fauconnier and Turner assert that identity and character are "an equally important aspect of the way we think," alongside our ability to think with frames (Fauconnier and Turner 2002: 251). Character is so transportable across different frames, and frames so transportable across different characters, that "we are able to extract regularities over different behaviors by the same person to build up a generic space for that person—a personal character" (Fauconnier and Turner 2002: 251–52). Also, "we are able to extract regularities over different behaviors by many people to build up a generic space for a kind of behavior" (Fauconnier and Turner 2002: 252). These appear to be important issues to identify, analyze, and interpret in the context of "rhetorolect interpretation."

Let us return to Luke 6:19 and include the preceding verse with it:

> [18]They had come to hear him and to be healed of their diseases; and those who were troubled with unclean spirits were cured. [19]And all in the crowd were trying to touch him, for power came out from him and healed all of them.

According to Luke 6:18, people have come both to hear Jesus and to be healed of their diseases. There are, then, two frames and two character-types at work in these two verses. The two frames are wisdom and miracle rhetorolect, and the two character-types are teacher (sage) and healer.

Now a series of questions immediately emerges. Is one frame somehow dominant over the other in this sequence? Verse 19 only emphasizes healing. Luke 6:20–49, however, introduce a long "sermon on the plain" by Jesus, in which there is no reference to healing. Or *is* there reference to healing in Luke 6:20–49? Is the presence of the poor in the kingdom of God a form of healing blended with wisdom (6:20)? Is the filling of the hungry and the laughter of the weeping a form of healing blended with wisdom (6:21)? Are the actions of loving your enemies, doing good to those who hate you, blessing those who curse you, praying for those who abuse you, offering the other cheek, giving your coat as well as your shirt, and giving to every one who begs (6:27–30) all instances of wisdom rhetorolect blended with miracle rhetorolect? In other words, are these examples of "healed minds" producing "healed actions"?

In terms of frames, the issue will concern the blending of the frames of wisdom and miracle rhetorolect. Put in terms of character, does the blending become more complex? It is quite clear at the outset that the character types apply to Jesus, who functions both as teacher and healer. What about those who are healed? Do healed people become agents of a blend of teaching and healing? In other words, if healed people are restored to fully functioning human beings, what kind of beings are they perceived to be? Have they been changed in any way from the kind of person they were before they became ill, or have they simply been restored to that previous person? Or is the "previous person" completely unimportant in relation to the "new picture" of the person? Is the new person a blend not only of the frame but also of character? In other words, do the healed people somehow become teachers and healers? If not, why not? Can frames but not characters blend in those who are healed? One thinks immediately about disciples, where not only the frames but also the characters appear to blend, so that disciples are sent out as apostles both to teach and to heal.

The relation of frame to character, then, appears to be a highly important issue in analysis and interpretation of conceptual blending in early Christian discourse. At one point, Fauconnier and Turner list five character types: saint, diplomat, hooker (prostitute), mediator, and conqueror. Then they say: "Construing *prostitute* as just a general frame, we can investigate character by asking how such a character would perform in that frame." Then they ask how "Mother Teresa, Margaret Thatcher, Cleopatra, or Bill Clinton would operate within the prostitute frame." They observe that Mother Teresa's character (saint) might reveal itself in acceptance of "the sacrifice with fortitude, by never complaining, by trusting God." But "the frame cannot impinge upon her character, for 'To the pure, all things pure.'" Therefore, character will prevent her from ever becoming a prostitute (p. 253). In the case of Mary Magdalene, they suggest, there is a requirement of a change in character from prostitute to saint (Fauconnier and Turner 2002: 253). This is a very important discussion for early Christian discourse. The six rhetorolects I have introduced suggest that Jesus somehow fills both the frames and the roles internal to wisdom, apocalyptic, precreation, prophetic, miracle, and priestly rhetorolect. But how does Jesus operate within each frame? Then how do his followers operate within each frame? Let us think a little more about this in respect to the roles of Jesus in early Christian discourse.

One of the key aspects of early Christian discourse is its presentation of Jesus as a character who is transportable over many different frames and activities. The transportability has certain limits, but the nature of the different frames is truly remarkable, since a significant number of the frames have counterfactual relationships to one another. There are frames that present Jesus with seemingly unlimited power, juxtaposed with frames that present Jesus with power so limited that people are able to kill him and bury him. There are frames that limit Jesus to a human personage born on earth, and frames that present Jesus as a cosmic being who existed "before all other things were created." There are frames that limit Jesus to a human personage who "loves even his enemies," and frames that present Jesus as destroying people on earth with a two-edged sword that comes out of his mouth. There are frames that present Jesus as "a friend of prostitutes and tax-collectors," and there are frames that present Jesus as the perfect, holy high priest in the heavens. On the one hand, the rhetorolects blend Jesus with six major "character types": sage; prophet; end-time seer and judge; eternal being; miracle worker; and priest. On the other hand, the rhetorolects blend Jesus with six major cultural frames: wisdom; prophetic; apocalyptic; precreation; miracle; and priestly. In and of itself, then, early Christian discourse focuses on Jesus in highly complex, creative, and counterintuitive ways. How should interpreters negotiate the relation of frames to character in socio-rhetorical analysis and interpretation of the dynamic blending of the rhetorolects in relation to Jesus in early Christian discourse?

The next question, then, concerns followers of Jesus. How do followers of Jesus operate within the six frames of wisdom, prophetic, apocalyptic, precreation, miracle, and priestly rhetorolect? Here there may be some surprises. It would appear, at first blush, to be counter-intuitive for followers of Jesus to operate in a precreation frame. God obviously existed before the creation of the world. Christians make the amazing assertion that Jesus existed with God prior to the creation of the world. Believers, however, certainly could not exist before the creation of the world, could they? Well, perhaps they did, but can we be sure? Ephesians 2:10 says: "For we are what he has made us, created in Christ Jesus for good works, which God prepared beforehand to be our way of life." I do not feel competent at this point to analyze and display the complex conceptual blending in this verse. Nor is there space to go into all the details that are involved here. So I will be content with a few observations and questions. The beginning of the verse emphasizes that the believer is God's workmanship, what God has made us (*poiēma*). But then the verse features an unusual concept of being "created in Christ Jesus." Many scholars have observed the unusual nature simply of being "in Christ" (*en christōi*), and some have tried to explain the concept in relation to participation of an initiate in a god who plays a central role in a mystery religion. This verse moves a step beyond this concept by asserting that a believer has been "created in Christ Jesus." What kind of a concept of creation is this? How are believers created in Christ Jesus and when are they created in Christ Jesus?

The presence of the verb "prepared beforehand" (*proētoimasen*) opens the possibility of believers having been created in Christ before the creation of the world. Thus, precreation rhetorolect may be an important frame in the blend. Perhaps, however, the term precreation is too temporally constructed to describe the blend. Perhaps the point is creation in "God's non-time," namely in "eternity," which lies beyond temporal boundaries. In this instance, the "beforehand preparation" is really a way of referring to something that is present eternally in "the mind" of God, which is "beforehand" for all human beings but in no way is structured by time. In other words, the unusual verb to "pre-prepare" is a way to try to speak about something that existed always, outside the boundaries of time, in God's "plans" for creation. Creation, then, started time, but this does not mean that God or Christ are somehow limited to created time. God created believers in Christ beyond the boundaries of time. In this way, believers operate in God and Christ's "precreation" time, which does not exist only before time but always.

But perhaps this is not what the verse says. Another important part of Ephesians 2:10 is the prepositional phrase "for good works" (*epi ergois agathois*), which points to the goal of wisdom rhetorolect. The verse appears to emphasize that it is "good works" that God prepared beforehand. So, perhaps the emphasis on "beforehand" does not apply to "being created in Christ," which occurs later in time, but to "for good works" which always existed in the "plans" of God for creation. So perhaps precreation rhetorolect only provides a frame that blends with God in this verse, but the frame does not blend either with Christ Jesus, since the creation in Christ occurs after creation, or believers "who walk in the good works" God has prepared beforehand.

I have introduced Ephesians 2:10 and precreation rhetorolect to illustrate that one must be prepared for highly counterintuitive blendings in early Christian discourse. There might be ways, however, we could analyze, display, and interpret how the rhetorolects work in relation to God, to Jesus, and to believers.

Another interesting moment in Fauconnier and Turner's discussion of identity and character arises when they discuss redemption, restoring honor, vengeance, vendetta, and curse. They assert that, from a frame point of view, these cultural categories are "mirror networks": a person succeeds in the later situation (Fauconnier and Turner 2002: 259). In the blend, the earlier and later situation "become one, and the character (if not the behavior) of the protagonist comes from the later input, thus providing in the blend and in the generic space a stable and good character from which the earlier input space is merely an unfortunate deviation" (Fauconnier and Turner 2002: 259). Perhaps the blend of wisdom and healing discussed above in Luke 6 could be approached with this insight. Being healed is a type of redemption, where the earlier event of being ill blends with the later event of being healed. The later event only has meaning with respect to the earlier event, but the later event determines the meaning of both events. Perhaps most, if not all, of the guiding cultural categories in the rhetorolects are mirror blends of this sort with respect to believers. For wisdom rhetorolect, the presence of wisdom that enables a person to produce good fruits of righteousness has meaning only in relation to an early event when a person did not have this wisdom. For apocalyptic rhetorolect, the presence of a holy or unholy life that either gives a person access to heaven or assigns a person to destruction has meaning in relation to an earlier event when a person received holiness or did not receive it. What would this tell us about Christianity if a majority of its cultural categories were "mirror networks"?

6. Conclusion

This essay has proposed that early Christian discourse achieves special dynamics and creativity through extensive processes of embodied conceptual blending. Six major early Christian rhetorolects function as rich cultural frames for early Christian discourse: wisdom, prophetic, apocalyptic, precreation, miracle, and priestly. Each rhetorolect either blends or competes with other rhetorolects either individually or in combination with one or more of the others. A special challenge of the blending in early Christian discourse concerns the processes of blending in each rhetorolect and processes by which rhetorolects blend and compete with each other. One of the major issues in these processes is the relation of frames to identity/character. How do frames and character work in conceptual blending with respect to God, to Jesus, and to believers? The character Jesus is highly transportable throughout the six rhetorolects, albeit in some instances in highly counterintuitive ways. One of the tasks must be to exhibit how Jesus operates in each of these cultural frames, and perhaps in other frames as well. But another major question is how both God and believers operate in the six major cultural frames. It appears that believers operate in highly similar ways to Jesus in certain frames. Do believers operate in some frames in highly different ways than Jesus? If so, how do they operate in different ways and why do they seem to operate in these different ways? Likewise, do believers operate in some frames in ways highly similar to God? Or do believers usually act in ways highly different from God? How many surprises are there for how believers operate in certain frames? Some ways that seem highly counterintuitive may, in fact, be quite well developed conceptually already during the first century. This essay suggests that we have much work ahead of us. Perhaps, however, this work can show us some things we could not even think about before, or perhaps could not think about in fruitful ways. If this essay helps us to take even some small steps forward in our understanding of the remarkable creativity underlying early Christian discourse, it will have been worth the effort.

REFERENCES

Ayres, Lewis. 2004. *Nicaea and its Legacy: An Approach to Fourth-Century Trinitarian Theology.* Oxford: Oxford University Press.
Boer, Roland 2000. "Sanctuary and Womb: Henri Lefebvre and the Production of Space." Paper presented to the AAR/SBL Constructions of Ancient Space Seminar, 2000. Online: http://www.cwru.edu/affil/GAIR/papers/2000papers/Boer.html.
Bourdieu, Pierre. 1989. "Social Space and Symbolic Power." *Sociological Theory* 7: 14–25.
Bruehler, Bart B. 2008. *The Public, the Political, and the Private: The Literary and Social-Spatial Functions of Luke 18:35–19:48.* Ph.D. diss., Emory University.
Camp, Claudia V. 2002. "Storied Space, or, Ben Sira 'Tells' a Temple." In *"Imagining" Biblical Worlds: Studies in Spatial, Social and Historical Constructs in Honor of James W. Flanagan.* Edited by David M. Gunn, and Paula M. McNutt, 64–80. Journal for the Study of the Old Testament Supplement Series, 359. Sheffield: Sheffield Academic Press.
Carney, Thomas F. 1975. *The Shape of the Past: Models and Antiquity.* Lawrence, Kans.: Coronado Press.
Coulson, Seana. 2001. *Semantic Leaps: Frame-Shifting and Conceptual Blending in Meaning Construction.* Cambridge: Cambridge University Press.
Czachesz, István. 2003. "The Gospels and Cognitive Science." In *Learned Antiquity: Scholars and Society in the Near-East, the Greco-Roman World, and the Early Medieval West,* edited by A. A. MacDonald, M. W. Twomey and G. J. Reinink, 25–36. Leuven: Peeters.
———. 2007. "The Transmission of Early Christian Thought: Toward a Cognitive Psychological Model." *Studies in Religion* 36, 65–84.
———. Forthcoming. "Metamorphoses in Early Christian Imagination: A Cognitive-Psychological Approach." In *Proceedings of the Jewish Pseudepigrapha & Christian Apocrypha Section at the SBL International Meeting in Groningen,* The Netherlands, July 25–28, 2004, edited by P. Piovanelli. Turnhout: Brepols.
Dozeman, Thomas B. 2003. "Geography and History in Herodotus and in Ezra-Nehemiah." *Journal of Biblical Literature* 122(3): 449–66.
Dunn, James D. G. 1989. *Christology in the Making: A New Testament Inquiry into the Origins of the Doctrine of the Incarnation.* Second edition. Grand Rapids: Eerdmans.
Elliott, John H. 2000. *1 Peter.* Anchor Bible, 37B. New York: Doubleday.
Fauconnier, Gilles and Mark Turner. 2002. *The Way We Think: Conceptual Blending and the Mind's Hidden Complexities.* New York: Basic Books.
Flanagan, James W. 1999. "Ancient Perceptions of Space/Perceptions of Ancient Space." *Semeia* 87: 15–43. Online: http://www.cwru.edu/affil/GAIR/papers/jwf-papers/CBA2000/CBA.html.
———. no date. Constructions of Ancient Space: A website at: http://guildzone.org/.
Gunn, David M., and Paula M. McNutt, eds. 2002. *"Imagining" Biblical Worlds: Studies in Spatial, Social and Historical Constructs in Honor of James W. Flanagan.* Journal for the Study of the Old Testament Supplement Series, 359 Sheffield: Sheffield Academic Press.
Hay, David M. 2000. *Colossians.* Abingdon New Testament Commentaries. Nashville: Abingdon Press.
Kuschel, Karl-Josef. 1992. *Born Before All Time? The Dispute over Christ's Origin.* New York: Crossroad.
Lakoff, George, and Mark Johnson. 2003. *Metaphors We Live By.* Chicago, Ill.: University of Chicago Press.
Lefèbvre, Henri. [1974] 1991. *The Production of Space.* Translated by Donald Nicholson-Smith. Oxford: Blackwell.
Lohse, Eduard. 1971. *Colossians and Philemon.* Hermeneia. Philadelphia, Pa.: Fortress.

McKeever, Michael C. 2000. "Refiguring Space in the Lukan Passion Narrative." Paper presented to the AAR/SBL Constructions of Ancient Space Seminar, 2000. Online: http://www.cwru.edu/affil/GAIR/papers/2000papers/mckeever.htm.
Matthews, Victor H. 2003. "Physical Space, Imagined Space, and 'Lived Space' in Ancient Israel." *Biblical Theology Bulletin* 33: 12–20.
Mitchell, W. J. Thomas. 1994. *Picture Theory: Essays on Verbal and Visual Representation*. Chicago, Ill.: University of Chicago Press.
Neyrey, Jerome H. 1993. *2 Peter, Jude*. Anchor Bible 37C: 32–42, 128–42. New York: Doubleday.
———. 1996. "Luke's Social Location of Paul: Cultural Anthropology and the Status of Paul in Acts." In *History, Literature, and Society in the Book of Acts*, edited by B. Witherington, III, 251–79. Cambridge: Cambridge University Press.
———. 2002a. "Spaces and Places, Whence and Whither, Homes and Rooms: 'Territoriality' in the Fourth Gospel." *Biblical Theology Bulletin* 32: 60–74.
———. 2002b. "Spaced Out: 'Territoriality' in the Fourth Gospel." *Hervormde Teologiese Studies* 58:632–63.
———. 2003. "The Social Location of Paul." In *Fabrics of Discourse: Essays in Honor of Vernon K. Robbins*, edited by D. B. Gowler, L. G. Bloomquist, and D. F. Watson, 126–64. Harrisburg, Pa.: Trinity Press International.
Philo Alexandrianus. [1929] 1991. *Legum allegoriae*. Philo, Vol. I, tr. & ed. by F. H. Colson and G. H. Whitaker. Loeb Classical Library. Cambridge, MA: Harvard University Press.
———. [1958, 1960] 1984, 1989. *De specialibus legibus*. Philo, Vol. VII–VIII, tr. & ed. by F. H. Colson. Loeb Classical Library. Cambridge, MA: Harvard University Press.
Pyysiäinen, Ilkka. 2005. "Intuition, Reflection, and the Evolution of Traditions." In *Moving Beyond New Testament Theology? Essays in Conversation with Heikki Räisänen*, edited by Todd C. Penner and Caroline Vander Stichele, 282–307. Publications of the Finnish Exegetical Society, 88. Helsinki: The Finnish Exegetical Society; Göttingen: Vandenhoeck & Ruprecht.
Robbins, Vernon K. 1991a. "Luke-Acts: A Mixed Population Seeks a Home in the Roman Empire." In *Images of Empire*, edited by L. Alexander, 202–21. Sheffield: JSOT Press. Online: http://www.religion.emory.edu/faculty/robbins/Pdfs/MixedPopulation.pdf.
———. 1991b. "The Social Location of the Implied Author of Luke-Acts." In *The Social World of Luke-Acts: Models for Interpretation*, edited by Jerome H. Neyrey, 305–32. Peabody, Mass.: Hendrickson.
———. 1996a. *The Tapestry of Early Christian Discourse: Rhetoric, Society and Ideology*. London: Routledge.
———. 1996b. *Exploring the Texture of Texts: A Guide to Socio-Rhetorical Interpretation* Harrisburg, Pa.: Trinity Press International.
———. 1996c. "The Dialectical Nature of Early Christian Discourse." *Scriptura* 59: 353–62. Online: http://www.religion.emory.edu/faculty/robbins/dialect/dialect353.html.
———. 1998. "From Enthymeme to Theology in Luke 11:1–13." In *Literary Studies in Luke-Acts: A Collection of Essays in Honor of Joseph B. Tyson*, edited by R. P. Thompson and T. E. Phillips, 191–214. Macon, Ga.: Mercer University.
———. 2002. "Argumentative Textures in Socio-Rhetorical Interpretation." In *Argumentation in Biblical Texts: Essays from the 2000 Lund Conference*, edited by A. Eriksson, T. H. Olbricht, and W. Übelacker, 27–65. Emory Studies in Early Christianity, 8. Harrisburg, Pa.:Trinity Press International. Online: http://www.religion.emory.edu/faculty/robbins/Pdfs/LundArgument.pdf
———. 2006. "Enthymeme and Picture in the Gospel of Thomas." In *Thomasine Traditions in Antiquity: The Social and Cultural World of the Gospel of Thomas*, edited by Jon

Ma. Asgeirsson, April D. DeConick, and Risto Uro, 175–207. Nag Hammadi and Manichaean Studies, 59. Leiden: Brill.
———. Forthcoming a. "Rhetography: A New Way of Seeing the Familiar Text." In *The Legacy of George A. Kennedy's Rhetorical Interpretation* (provisional title), edited by Duane F. Watson and C. Clifton Black.
———. Forthcoming b. *The Invention of Christian Discourse*, Vol 1: *Wisdom, Prophetic, and Apocalyptic Discourse*. Blandford Forum, UK: DEO Publishing.
Sack, Robert D. 1986. *Human Territoriality: Its Theory and History*. Cambridge: Cambridge University Press.
———. 1997. *Homo Geographicus: A Framework for Action, Awareness, and Moral Concern*. Baltimore Md.: Johns Hopkins University Press.
Soja, Edward W. 1989. *Postmodern Geography: The Reassertion of Space in Critical Social Theory*. New York: Verso.
———. 1993. "Postmodern Geographies and the Critique of Historicism." In *Postmodern Contentions: Epochs, Politics, Space*, edited by J. P. Jones, III, W. Natter, and T. R. Schatzki, 113–36. New York: Guildford.
———. 1996. *Thirdspace: Journeys to Los Angeles and Other Real-and-Imagined Places*. Cambridge, Mass.: Blackwell.
Toulmin, Stephen. 1990. *Cosmopolis: The Hidden Agenda of Modernity*. Chicago, Ill.: University of Chicago Press.
Thaden, Robert von. 2007. *The Wisdom of Fleeing Porneia: Conceptual Blending in 1 Corinthians 6:12–7:7*. Ph.D. diss., Emory University.
Wilder, Amos. 1964. *The Language of the Gospel: Early Christian Rhetoric*. New York: Harper and Row.

PART THREE

SOCIO-COGNITIVE APPROACHES TO CHRISTIAN
ORIGINS AND EARLY JUDAISM

THE SOCIOLOGY OF KNOWLEDGE, THE SOCIAL IDENTITY APPROACH AND THE COGNITIVE SCIENCE OF RELIGION

Petri Luomanen

1. Introduction

The cognitive science of religion emerged among scholars of comparative religion at the beginning of the 1990s. This multidisciplinary approach draws on cognitive science, cognitive and developmental psychology, neuroscience, evolutionary biology and anthropology. Since the cognitive scientists of religion have already developed some theories for the study of religion,[1] it is reasonable to apply these while developing a cognitive approach to Christian origins and early Judaism. This strategy makes it possible to evaluate and develop cognitive scientific theories of religion through the analysis of biblical and related materials.[2]

Some scholars' linguistic, literary and rhetorical approaches to early Christian tradition also share with some cognitive scientists of religion the interest in built-in language learning, grammatical structuring, and metaphor creation propensities of the mind. For instance, biblical literary critics, cognitive neuroscientists and some cognitive scientists of religion all regard Noam Chomsky as one of the pioneers of their discipline. In this area of study, the basic properties of the innate language module provide a starting point for the analysis of religious language and practices.[3]

---

[1] Thus far, the approach has been applied in the study of the foundations and transmission of religious concepts (Boyer 2002a), religious rituals (Lawson and McCauley 1990, 2002), "epidemics" of religious beliefs in cultures (Sperber 1996), and the role of memory systems and emotions in the transmission of religious ideas (Whitehouse 2004)—to name a few of the areas of study that have also become known among scholars of early Christianity. For an overview of the approach, see the Introduction to this volume.

[2] Some pioneering attempts have already been made—and more will be presented in the present volume—in order to apply similar theories to the study of early Christianity. See, Uro 2004; Czachesz 2007, and the essays in Part I in this volume.

[3] Lawson and McCauley 1990: 60–83; Gazzaniga, Ivry and Mangun 2002: 17–18; cf. the essays in Part II in this volume.

Another incentive for consulting the same disciplines as the cognitive scientists of religion comes from the recent application of social psychological theories in the study of the New Testament. As indicated in the Introduction to this volume, the so-called *social identity approach* has a built-in cognitive interface that can be highlighted and developed by keeping up with the latest results of cognitive psychology, neuroscience and other related disciplines. This strategy may also help to shed more light on some cognitive aspects of group behavior. Because the social identity approach belongs to the field of social psychology, it is able to draw on the long and well documented research on social cognition. Thus far, this area has received only limited attention within the cognitive study of religion.[4]

The main goal of this essay is to sketch a methodological roadmap for the application of the cognitive approach in conjunction with the social-scientific analysis of biblical and related materials. Therefore, the focus is on research history and methodological issues. The essay consists of four main sections.

In the first section, I discuss Peter Berger and Thomas Luckmann's sociology of knowledge. Berger and Luckmann's theory (1966) is often connected to phenomenology and social constructionism. It emphasizes the social determinants of knowledge and may therefore appear as a critical alternative to the cognitive study of religion which is interested in the innate cognitive functions of the mind.

The second section of this essay casts more light on the relationship between the social identity approach and the cognitive study of religion. Because the background and the basic concepts of the social identity approach have already been presented in the Introduction to this volume, I introduce some additional features of the approach and provide further examples of its connections with the cognitive science of religion.

The third main section connects the social psychological discussion more directly with the physiological properties of the brain, demonstrating how cognitive neuroscience may help to validate social psychological theorizing.

In the concluding section, I expound briefly on the application of some of the methodological insights developed in the previous sections.

---

[4] An important exception is Boyer 2002a: 327–40. For further on these questions, see below.

Because this essay focuses on theoretical issues, the example will not include detailed argumentation. It only seeks to delineate some guidelines for future research. The other essays in Part III of this volume (by Esler, Hakola and Jokiranta) serve as further examples of socio-cognitive approaches to early Judaism and early Christianity.

2. *The Sociology of Knowledge*

2.1. *Berger and Luckmann's Sociology of Knowledge within the Social Sciences*

Peter L. Berger and Thomas Luckmann's classic study *The Social Construction of Reality: A Treatise in the Sociology of Knowledge* (1966) has established its position as one of the classics of sociology. Like all classics, it is clearly a product of its own time. The theory was originally framed at the end of 1960s in a period when the sociology of knowledge had lost its attraction among social scientists.

The roots of the sociology of knowledge are usually traced back to Marx' view according to which a person's consciousness is determined by his/her social being. In addition to Marxism (in its original form, not as interpreted by "latter-day Marxists"), Berger and Luckmann find the roots of their discipline in Nietzschean ideas and in Wilhelm Dilthey's historicism. The beginning (and sometimes the end) of the sociology of knowledge as a distinct sub-area within sociology is usually connected to Karl Mannheim. However, Berger and Luckmann also emphasize the role of Max Scheler in "inventing" the discipline. Scheler made a distinction between *ideal factors* ("Idealfaktoren") and *real factors* ("Realfaktoren") but emphasized the independent character of the ideal factors. Real factors only regulate the historical conditions under which the ideal factors can appear in history but they cannot affect ideal factors' contents. Mannheim was more radical and stressed that human thought is always influenced by social context and its ideologizing influence. However, in his view, the socially unattached intellectuals are best positioned to overcome such limitations. (Berger and Luckmann 1966: 17–22; Marshall 1998: 343).

In Berger and Luckmann's view, the sociology of knowledge had been too much concerned with ontological and epistemological questions. They wanted to redefine the scope of the sociology of knowledge by bracketing the ontological and epistemological questions and approaching the subject from an empirical point of view:

> The sociology of knowledge must first of all concern itself with what people "know" as "reality" in their everyday, non- or pre-theoretical lives. In other words, common-sense "knowledge" rather than "ideas" must be the central focus of the sociology of knowledge. (Berger and Luckmann 1966: 25.)

When directing their attention to the "common-sense world of everyday life" Berger and Luckmann were especially drawing on Alfred Schutz. Another important source for inspiration had been George Herbert Mead and other American symbolic interactionists. (Berger and Luckmann 1966: 25–29.)

Berger and Luckmann's theory succeeded in reviving interest in social prerequisites of knowledge. When it showed the importance of the social construction of knowledge for all sociological research it also—paradoxically—contributed to the decline of the sociology of knowledge as a separate sociological subdiscipline (Aittola and Raiskila 1994: 227). However, in a broader sense—not as a clearly definable subdiscipline—the sociology of knowledge keeps feeding various branches of sociological research by calling attention to formation, preservation and transmission of knowledge. Consequently, some of the topics—like the analysis of collective (or social) memory—that are regarded as part of the "new sociology of knowledge," have also been in the focus of recent sociologically oriented research on Jewish and Christian traditions.[5]

Because Berger and Luckmann's theory largely depends on Alfred Schutz, the founder of phenomenological sociology, it is usually considered as an example of the phenomenological approach (see Marshall 1998: 493; Aittola and Raiskila 1994: 213). If such a characterization is used, it should be kept in mind that Berger and Luckmann's phenomenology is not merely interpretative in character. They do not just confine themselves to the description of peoples' everyday knowledge, but they also seek to *explain* the formation of meanings and institutions in social interaction. Nevertheless, they always examine these processes

---

[5] Swindler and Arditi 1994: 308–10. One of the recent contributions in this area of study is Eviatar Zerubavel's *Time Maps* (2003). Interestingly, the theory developed in Zerubavel's earlier book *Social Mindscapes: An Invitation to Cognitive Sociology* (1997) seems to come quite close to Berger and Luckmann's approach. For research on social memory, see the Introduction to this volume and Esler's essay in Part III.

from the viewpoint of an individual and this exemplifies their critical stance towards functionalism.[6]

Although the sociology of knowledge as a separate discipline has not had a very prominent position within sociology, Berger and Luckmann's treatise has had another kind of lasting effect because it introduced the term "constructionism" to the sociological vocabulary. Consequently, their work is considered as one of the first contributions to the field of *social constructionism* (Marshall 1998: 609). However, it should be noted that Berger and Luckmann themselves subscribe to social constructionism only insofar as it refers to the appreciation of culture in the development of social institutions. They reject the forms of social constructionism that depict all interpretations of reality as equally valid or propose that there is no reality outside the interpretations (Berger 2001: 190–91. Luckmann's comment in a collection that commemorates Berger's scholarly work is very revealing: "Who in heaven or hell, more likely hell, invented (social) 'constructivism'?" (Luckmann 2001: 23). Overall, Berger and Luckmann's theory is considered—including the authors themselves—as incorporating both the Weberian and the Durkheimian approaches to sociology.

Berger and Luckmann understand society entirely as a human product. However, there is a dialectic process between society and its human producers since society profoundly shapes the way in which people experience their everyday reality. Berger and Luckmann (1966: 78–79; Berger 1967: 3–4) describe this dialectic of the social world in terms of *externalization, objectification* and *internalization*. Externalization refers to the human creation of the social world while objectification and internalization are concerned with its consolidation and transmission to succeeding generations. When Berger and Luckmann described the latter two phases of the dialectical process, they used three terms, *everyday life, legitimation* and *symbolic universe,* which have become quite influential among New Testament scholars. Although these terms are often used by biblical scholars, their meaning in the context of Berger and Luckmann's theory may not have been always fully understood.

According to Berger and Luckmann, *everyday life* is reality that does not need any additional verification. Its facticity is immediately experienced.

---

[6] Aittola and Raiskila 1994: 217–20. Berger and Luckmann (1966: 208) consider "the standard functionalist explanations in the social sciences a theoretical legerdemain."

Its phenomena are prearranged in patterns that seem to be independent of one's apprehension of them, and it is constituted by objects that have been designated as objects before one's appearance on the scene (Berger and Luckmann 1966: 35–37). *Symbolic universes*, for their part, emerge in the processes of habitualization and institutionalization. Habitualization spontaneously produces institutions that need to be made objectively available to persons who were not involved with the production of the institutions in the first place. When the institutional order is transmitted to other generations, it needs to be explained and justified, i.e., *legitimized*. Berger and Luckmann distinguish four levels of legitimation. The first level contains simple statements like "This is how things are done." The second level contains rudimentary theoretical propositions. The third level contains explicit theories. The symbolic universes represent the fourth and most comprehensive level of legitimation. Symbolic universes can be spoken about only in symbolic language, that is, in the language that refers to realities other than those of everyday experience. They are bodies of theoretical tradition that integrate the whole of historical society, the biography and experiences of an individual into a meaningful whole. In short, the symbolic universe "puts everything in its right place." (Berger and Luckmann 1966: 110–22.)

2.2. *The Sociology of Knowledge and the Study of Early Christianity: A Brief History*

Wayne A. Meeks' article "The Man from Heaven in Johannine Sectarianism" (1972) is known as the first New Testament contribution that made use of Berger and Luckmann's study. Meeks' main argument was that the Gospel of John provided a new "symbolic universe" for the sectarian Johannine community. As such, it "legitimated" the group's isolation from the larger society (Meeks 1972: 70). Only one year after the publication of the *Social Construction of Reality*, Berger had applied the sociology of knowledge to religion in his book *Sacred Canopy: Elements of Sociological Theory of Religion* (1967). This became one of the theoretical foundations for another pioneering work in the social-scientific study of the Bible, John Gager's *Kingdom and Community* (1975). Since some aspects of Berger's *Sacred Canopy* were also used by some other developers of the social-scientific approach to early Christianity (Kee 1980; Theissen 1993a, 1993b),[7] it is clear that the sociology of knowledge was one of the formative theoretical approaches in the beginnings of the social-scientific study of early Christianity.[8] However, several other theoretical models were also used at this early stage and Berger and Luckmann's study was by no means the only approach that these pioneers were applying. Furthermore, the key concepts of their sociology of knowledge, such as symbolic universe and legitimation, had not yet found their way into the common parlance of New Testament scholars.

The sociology of knowledge gained more attention in the late 1980s and the early 1990s when concepts derived from Berger and Luckmann's treatise started to find their way into a growing number of New Testament studies. One of the books which inspired and convinced others of the benefits of Berger and Luckmann's conceptualizations was Philip Esler's *Community and Gospel in Luke-Acts* (1987). Since similar approaches were soon applied to the other synoptic Gospels (Overman 1990; Syreeni 1990; Luomanen 1998)[9] and Paul (Watson 1986; MacDonald 1988; Pickett 1997), the entire field of New Testament scholarship became familiar with Berger and Luckmann's terminology, albeit sometimes only superficially. After the renaissance of the late 1980s and the early 1990s, Berger and Luckmann's theory has not received quite as much attention but it has been applied to some studies—even quite recently, almost forty years after its initial publication (Adams 2000; Fuglseth 2005).

David Horrell (2001: 146–48) has aptly described the reasons why Berger and Luckmann's sociology of knowledge was embraced by New Testament scholars. First, Berger and Luckmann's sociology offers a non-reductionist sociological approach to the New Testament. Although Berger and Luckmann regard all knowledge—including religious—as

---

[7] References are to the English translation of Theissen's collected essays. The original articles were published in German in the 1980s.

[8] The earliest influences of Berger and Luckmann's work on New Testament studies are summarized well by Horrell 2001. For Berger's relation to theology, see Dorrien 2001.

[9] Thanks to Esler and others, Kari Syreeni, in particular (1990: 127–31), I also came across Berger and Luckmann's theory at the beginning of 1990s when I was preparing my doctoral dissertation on the Gospel of Matthew. I found Berger and Luckmann's theory useful for my task and the concepts derived from their theory—in a slightly modified form—ended up playing a central role in my investigation (Luomanen 1998).

a human product, they give full credence to its phenomenological objectivity without reducing it to a mere reflection of socio-economic relationships. Second, the contents of the symbolic universe closely resemble the "body of theoretical tradition" that biblical scholars are most familiar with, namely theology. However, it provides a new twist for theological reflection by explicitly combining the symbolic universe (= "theology") with everyday social practices. It brings theology down to earth by integrating it more closely with ethics as well as concrete norms and practices that regulate social relationships.

Horrell also directs critical questions at Berger and Luckmann's theory and its application within New Testament studies (1996: 39–45; 2001: 148–51). In Horrell's view, Berger and Luckmann's concept of legitimation does not allow enough causality for ideologies or religious traditions to establish social practices. This is because they see legitimation as a post-practice activity which seeks to find grounds for already existing practices. Horrell also thinks that Berger and Luckmann emphasize the objectivity of social order so much so that it blinds one to the fact that social reality is being continuously reproduced and transformed. Thus, Berger and Luckmann's approach leads one to portray change as threat. Finally, Horrell agrees with Giddens (whose approach he endorses) that Berger and Luckmann's approach "completely lacks a conception of the critique of ideology."

Berger (2001: 197) has admitted that the way in which the term "legitimation" was used in his earlier work was subject to the kind of criticism Horrell presents but he rejects Horrell's other critical points. Berger points out that legitimation is problematic only as a term and he has attempted to use it more cautiously later on. His intention was not to depict religion as a *post festum* phenomeneon, a derivative of preexisting social structures. Horrell's second criticism seems to closely resemble the criticism biblical scholars—following general social-scientific discussion—have leveled against functionalism and structuralism.[10] It is, indeed, hard to find any justification for this sort of criticism because Berger and Luckmann clearly take a critical stance towards functionalism (see above). The same applies to the last critical point that

---

[10] Theissen, who explicitly drew on functionalist sociology in his *Soziologie der Jesusbewegung* (1985), has often been criticized for this sort of too static approach (Horsley 1989; Arnal 2001) but even in his case, the criticism is not fully justified (cf. Theissen 1993c: 254–56; Luomanen 2002).

Horrell has borrowed from Giddens. Giddens' (and Horrell's) criticism is more indicative of his own concerns than Berger and Luckmann's possible defects. Berger and Luckmann's phenomenology of the legitimation of social order is equally open to readings that see the process of social consolidation from the viewpoint of the retainers as it is to readings that seek to identify with those who are not ready to comply with preexisting social orders.

Although Berger and Luckmann's sociology of knowledge places the individual at the center of sociological theorizing and depicts a dialectical relation between the individual's externalization and internalization of social order, it pays little attention to possible indigenous qualities of the mind in this dialectical process. Instead, it characterizes the mind almost like an empty shell with certain input and output qualities that partly effect the dialectical process but which do not have any significant effect on the contents or form of what is being externalized or internalized. There are no innate cognitive functions that would have effects on the sociological formations.

> Humanness is socio-culturally variable. In other words, there is no human nature in the sense of a biologically fixed substratum determining the variability of socio-cultural formations. There is only human nature in the sense of anthropological constants (for example world-openness and plasticity of instinctual structure) that delimit and permit man's socio-cultural formations. But the specific shape into which this humanness is moulded is determined by those socio-cultural formations and is relative to their numerous variations. While it is possible to say that man has a nature, it is more significant to say that man constructs his own nature, or more simply, that man produces himself. (Berger and Luckmann 1966: 67.)

Because Berger and Luckmann's treatise dates from the 1960s, it would be unfair to blame them for not paying enough attention to present trends in cognitive sciences. However, it is clear that although Berger and Luckmann themselves reject the extreme forms of social constructionism, their theory—as they themselves present it—does not leave much room for innate cognitive functions that would constitute the basis for the communication of a shared understanding of reality. Because their theory emphasizes the active human construction of social reality but brackets the analysis of innate cognitive properties that would affect the externalization and internalization, it is no wonder that their theory has given rise to extremely relativistic ideas about knowledge.

The cognitive approach appeared on the scene at approximately the same time as Berger and Luckmann's sociology of knowledge became more popular within New Testament studies. However, in contrast to the cognitive approach that is "still going strong" the analytical potential of Berger and Luckmann's theory seems to be exhausted. Nevertheless, it is still helpful in describing the dynamics of externalization, objectification and internalization/legitimation. Furthermore, it has certainly left its mark on the discipline—"legitimation" and "symbolic universe" were adopted in the diction of the field (though often used without a very clear connection to Berger and Luckmann's theory). Yet Berger and Luckmann's theory has not recently inspired much new research. Thus, it can be considered as "background technology"[11] even within New Testament research. Leading social-scientifically oriented researchers are directing their attention to other, more promising theories, such as the social identity approach.

3. *The Social Identity Approach and the Cognitive Science of Religion*

3.1. *Social Identity Theory, the Search for Coherence and Personalization*

As an overall theory, the social identity approach stands closer to symbolic interactionism and conflict theories than to the structural-functionalist tradition in that it sees social reality as being in constant flux (Hogg and Abrams 1988: 14–17; cf. Tajfel 1981: 131 and Marshall 1998: 657–59). According to Tajfel:

> Much of what happens to us is related to the activities of groups to which we do or do not belong; and the changing relations between these groups requires constant readjustments of our understanding of what happens and constant causal attributions about the why and the how of the changing conditions of our life. (Tajfel 1981: 131.)

In the context of the above quotation, Tajfel discusses three processes that are involved with an individual's adjustment to his/her social context: *categorization, assimilation and search for coherence*. Since categorization has already been discussed in the Introduction to this volume, I shall not elaborate on that subject here. Regarding assimilation, it suffices to note that, in social psychological language, the term refers to the learning of social information that cultures have generated over a long period of time. This, of course, includes a host of given categories and

---

[11] I owe this characterization to Philip Esler.

stereotypes that children learn in the communities where they are raised (Berger and Luckmann would call this "internalization" or "socialization"; cf. 1966: 149–66). In this context, the most interesting of the three aspects of social readjusting is the search for coherence.

Although Tajfel's view on the basic need for cognitive coherence seems valid as a general principle, it is important to keep in mind—and here cognitive science can supplement Tajfel's approach—that the renewal of cognitive structures proceeds more through patching than through total cognitive revolutions. Rather than starting from scratch, new information is integrated into the existing cognitive structures and old structures are modified only to the extent that is necessary (cf. Bless, Fiedler and Strack 2004: 67–68; Wilkes 1997: 157–62, 209–10, 294–96). In general, human cognition is consistent only as far as it needs to be consistent.[12]

In Tajfel's opinion, it is possible to distinguish two types of changes which may challenge the integrity of an individual's self-image: changes within a group, i.e., *intragroup changes* and changes between groups, i.e., *intergroup changes*. In both cases, the individual needs to build a cognitive structure that provides him/her with a satisfactory explanation of the changes with which he/she is faced (Tajfel 1981: 137). One central means in this process is *personalization*: the reasons for changes are traced back to *personal characteristics of individuals or to group characteristics that are perceived to be inherent and immutable* (Tajfel 1981: 138–39; italics added).[13] From the cognitive science point of view, this might be seen as an example of the function of the innate agent detection system (cf. Boyer 2002b: 73–77; Barrett 2002: 94–96) and *essentialist thinking* (Gil-White 2001; Boyer 2002: 329–34; further on this below). Notably,

---

[12] These socio-cognitive considerations about consistency have direct bearing on some hotly debated issues within New Testaments studies. Theological analysis of the New Testament books, especially Paul's epistles, has incited debates concerning their theological consistency. From a cognitive perspective, it seems clear that Paul, who wrote his letters in response to certain developments in the congregations he was addressing or to promote his own missionary plans, is quite unlikely to have retained consistency throughout all his epistles. At best, we could expect him to evince only some sort of situational consistency, a stance from which he argues in a particular historical setting. For an overview of the debate concerning Paul's consistency, see Räisänen 2001: 94–96.

[13] Tajfel makes a distinction between two kinds of causal explanations that can be used to account for the changes in the status quo: (1) situational explanations that are not directly connected to the groups involved (such as natural catastrophes); and (2) the tendency to attribute the causes of changes to *group or personal characteristics*.

Lakoff and Johnson (1980: 33–34) also list *personification* as one of the fundamental ontological metaphors which simplify abstract phenomena in the world by representing them in human terms. It is not too hard to find examples of this in our everyday life. In particular, we have all become familiarized with the stereotyped group characteristics attributed to minority groups in our own societies. At the end of this essay, I discuss some examples of personalization in Christian heresiologies.

3.2. *Prototypes and Exemplars in Social Categorization*

Philip Esler has pioneered the use of the social identity approach in the study of New Testament (Esler 1998, 2003). Among the key concepts he adopted from the social identity approach in his study on Paul's letter to the Romans were *prototypes* and *exemplars* (on the relation of these two, see below). In Esler's perspective, Paul used Abraham as a prototype who serves as the foundation for a new common ingroup identity for both Judean[14] and non-Judean Christians in Rome (Esler 2003: 171–94).

Because of the cognitive roots of the social identity approach, it is also possible to pose more in-depth questions about the cognitive role of prototypes and exemplars in social categorizations. This kind of deeper cognitive analysis might lend further credence to social-scientific analysis by showing that when models fit the data, this is not because of some accidental correspondence but because of the innate and universal cognitive functions of the mind (cf. the Introduction to this volume).

Tajfel and his colleagues showed that categorization of visual stimuli and accentuation of differences between visually observed categories have regularities that also characterize the formation of cognitive representations of social groups and intergroup relations. Thus, Tajfel showed a clear correspondence between perceptual judgments and the formation of social stereotypes. For Tajfel, it was important to realize that such negative phenomena as prejudice and stereotyping of outgroups cannot be understood without analyzing the cognitive processes that produce them:

---

[14] Esler prefers to use the term "Judean" instead of "Jewish" because, for him, it better captures the original geographical overtones of the Greek term. See, Esler 2003: 63–74.

> The principal argument is...that the etiology of intergroup relations cannot be properly understood without the help of an analysis of their cognitive aspects, and also that this analysis cannot be derived from statements about motivation and about instinctive behaviour (Tajfel 1981: 131). It is important and *useful*...that a consideration of prejudice as a phenomenon in the minds rather than in the guts of people should take precedence...(Tajfel 1981: 142).

This cognitive aspect in Tajfel's (and Turner's) *social identity theory* is further developed in John Turner's *self-categorization theory*.[15] The original mission of Turner's theory was to cast light on the psychological basis of group formation but its most important contribution in the field of the social identity approach has turned out to be a new cognitive perspective on social categorization (Oakes, Haslam and Turner 1998: 75). While Tajfel described the cognitive representations of groups mainly in terms of categorization, accentuation and stereotyping, Turner has introduced the concept of prototypicality (or prototypes) in the discussion of social perception.

Turner and his colleagues have taken their cue from Eleanor Rosch who had studied the cognitive representation of semantic categories in a series of experiments in the 1970s. The results of Rosch's experiments challenged the classic Aristotelian view according to which membership in a category is defined by a set of critical features shared by all members of the category. The experiments rather showed that, in practice, membership in a category is judged on the basis of a degree of similarity to the *prototype* (the best example) of the category in question. Consequently, members of a category vary in their degree of typicality. This also effects how easily they are classified: the closer the stimulus is to the prototype, the faster it is categorized. For instance, American subjects see robins as more typical representatives of the bird category than ostriches. On the other hand, the invocation of the category prototype by the category name negatively affects how quickly two examples of "poor" members of the category were recognized as belonging to the same category. This probably happens because, in this case, a simple matching task (verification if the two examples share certain features) is replaced by two separate verifications through the prototype and this takes more time. Thus, instead of being clearly defined closed entities, categories are more like "fuzzy sets" where

---

[15] For the relation of these theories, see the Introduction to this volume.

members of a category are tied together through "family resemblance." Furthermore, Rosch's experiments also showed that categories vary in their relative inclusiveness so that superordinate categories are more inclusive than basic/intermediate categories and subordinate categories are less inclusive than the basic/intermediate categories. (Rosch 1975: 193–96, 203–5, 224–27; Oakes, Haslam and Turner 1998: 75–76.)

In short, Rosch's experiments showed that there is a relative inclusiveness across categories and a relative prototypicality within categories. Self-categorization theory makes use of both these aspects. Following Rosch, self-categorization theory assumes three levels of abstraction for self-categories: interpersonal (subordinate level; self as an individual), intergroup (intermediate/basic level; self as a group member) and interspecies (superordinate level; self as a human being). Self-categorization theory also assumes that prototypicality plays a key role in judgments about group memberships. (Oakes, Haslam and Turner 1998: 76–80).

Social psychologists and cognitive scientists have disputed the role of prototypes and their relation to exemplars in (social) categorization. While earlier research focused on the role of preconceived categories and schemata ("prototypes"; cf. Tajfel's research) in social categorizations, the function of exemplars (information about specific group members) started to gain more attention at the beginning of 1990s (cf. Smith and Zárate 1992). Various social psychological models of intergroup perception have tried to determine the conditions under which people are engaged either with prototype representations or exemplar representations of ingroups and outgroups. For instance, it has been suggested that the salience of a group might have an effect on whether the prototype or the exemplar mode of representation is activated. Since salience is often connected to relative group sizes, it would follow that more salient small groups are represented predominantly by prototypes while less salient large groups evoke the exemplar representation mode (Mullen, Rozell and Johnson 1996). It is not possible to go into the details of this discussion here. In the following, I only briefly describe the stance of the self-categorization theorists[16] and introduce some neuroscientific experiments that may help to understand how prototypes and exemplars are processed in the brain.

---

[16] For an overview of the positions, see Oakes, Haslam and Turner 1998.

There has been a tendency among some social psychologists to take social prototypes as *fixed cognitive structures*, abstract representations of ideal group members. Membership in the category is assessed on the basis of perceived similarity to the prototype. For instance Brewer, who was among the first to draw on Rosch's studies, has argued for the character of prototypes as picture-like images of the ideal category member (Brewer 1988). Some social psychological approaches to leadership have also assumed that possible leaders are assessed on the basis of their similarity to the prototype of the ideal leader (Frazier and Lord 1988).

However, Medin (1989) has pointed out that, if prototypes are understood as fixed invariable cognitive structures, the assessment of the membership in a given category is reduced to the simple attribute matching task. Comparison to necessary and sufficient attributes (the classic approach) is replaced with comparison to the attributes of the prototype.[17] According to Medin, "Prototype theories...fail to reflect the *context sensitivity* that is evident in human categorization. Rather than getting at the character of human conceptual representation, prototypes appear to be more of a caricature of it" (Medin 1989: 1472; emphasis added).[18] Since there are also other cognitive researchers that have emphasized the contextual variability of judgments of prototypicality (Barsalou 1987), the self-categorization theorists have insisted that prototypes must not be understood as fixed cognitive structures. Instead, prototypicality always depends on the judgmental context. Turner and his colleagues also argue that this is the original "Roschian" view of prototypicality (Oakes, Haslam and Turner 1998: 76). Because

---

[17] Interestingly, Gil-White 2001 supports his argument about the human tendency to process "ethnies" as essences of natural kinds by defending the "classic" categorization model. In his view, people would resort to the classic matching when making decisions about memberships in the category of natural kinds. Even if this would work for "ethnies," which I doubt, it is clear that the assumption fails to do justice to the context sensitivity of most social categorizations.

[18] Medin and his colleagues argue for the "background theories" the perceivers have about the world. These theories have a crucial role in determining which categories hang together as meaningful wholes. Because Medin studies general category formation, his approach is more comprehensive than what needs to be developed in the context of social ingroup and outgroup categorizations. From the viewpoint of Medin's approach, social categorization can be understood as an example of one meaningful whole that is held together by the assumption that humans tend to form groups and act according to their group memberships. However, Medin's theory shares with self-categorization theory the idea of categorizations as contextual variables (see below).

prototypes are perceived as contextual variables, they prefer to speak about *prototypicality* instead of (fixed) prototypes.

In self-categorization theory, the dynamic character of social comparisons is formalized in the principle of *meta-contrast*. According to the meta-contrast principle, "a given set of items is more likely to be categorized as a single entity *to the degree that differences within that set of items are less than differences between that set and others within the comparative context*" (Oakes, Haslam and Turner 1998: 77). Consequently, the most prototypical member of a group is the one whose position minimizes intragroup differences and maximizes intergroup differences (Oakes, Haslam and Turner 1998: 80; Marguez, Páez and Abrams 1998: 127).[19] Notably, the theory assumes that the most prototypical position and relative prototypicality of the members is being constantly monitored and recalculated according to shifting comparative contexts. For example, the prototypical communist in the context of fascists is different from the prototypical communist in the context of liberal democrats (Oakes, Haslam and Turner 1998: 80).

Although self-categorization theorists themselves do not explicitly use the term "exemplar" in their discussion, it seems clear that the calculations of prototypicality have to be based on real-life exemplars of ingroup and outgroup members or exemplars that have become otherwise salient in the comparative context, such as historical or fictitious group members.[20] Similarities and differences are not observed across randomly chosen representatives but within a set of exemplars that are (initially) thought to be relevant representatives of the ingroup and the outgroups. This brings us back to the question of how prototypes and exemplars are related to each other in social categorizations and whether we should regard prototypes or exemplars as more important in

---

[19] Self-categorization theory has further formalized the calculation of the meta-contrast by the *meta-contrast ratio* which is the average perceived intercategory difference divided by the average perceived intracategory difference. The flexibility and the context sensitivity of prototypicality as it is postulated in a self-categorization framework makes the approach different from simple theorizing in the terms of group "entitativity," at least in the form that entitativity approach is presented by Gil-White 2001 (cf. Hamilton, Sherman and Sack's comment on Gil-White 2001). Thus, Gil-White's criticism of entitativity theories does not apply to self-categorization theory or related social psychological theorizing (cf. Rothbart and Taylor's comment on Gil-White 2001).

[20] In some contexts, exemplars may also include historical or fictitious persons. These are particularly important if the user of the social identity approach wishes to include a discussion of historical perspective. See Cinnirella 1998: 231–32; Esler 2003: 22–24, 172–78.

judgments about group memberships. A possible answer to this question may come from neurological laterality experiments (see below).

3.3. *Essences and Coalitional Calculations*

Before moving on to the discussion of how prototypes and exemplars are possibly processed in the brain, it is appropriate to note that cognitive scientists of religion have also discussed the problems of social categorization.[21] However, this has happened mainly in terms of *essence* concepts and *coalitional calculations*. For Boyer, essentialism is closely related to prototypes: the essentialist system is triggered in the brain when three conditions are met: (1) living things seem to have common external features, that is, a prototype; (2) living things are thought to be born of other members of the same category; (3) and reproduction is possible only within the category. When the essentialist system is triggered, groups are explicitly pictured as having natural qualities. Members of the group are thought to share some inherited eternal propensities (Boyer 2002: 328–29; cf. above Tajfel's understanding of personalization). However, Boyer thinks that, in the case of social categorizations, essentialist thinking is only a derivative. Essence-based understandings "are *the concepts we spontaneously use to describe intuitions that are in fact not about social categories but about coalitions.*" Thus, Boyer assumes that, in the brain, there is a sort of coalitional calculator of which people are not aware. The costs and benefits of these computations are then translated into essence based discourse which makes it easier for people to deal with them. (Boyer 2002: 330–31.)

Boyer proceeds to analyze the behavior of modern fundamentalist movements in this theoretical framework. He suggests that the persecution of deviant ingroup members by fundamentalists is to be understood as a powerful message about the costs of possible defection (Boyer 2002: 336–40). The phenomenon Boyer describes here, a more severe treatment of ingroup than outgroup defectors, is often also treated in social psychological studies, but termed there as the "black sheep effect" (e.g., Marques, Páez and Abrams 1998: 129–31).

---

[21] Racial categorizations, in particular, have been discussed (for instance, Sperber 1996: 143–46; see also Cosmides, Tooby and Kurzban 2003, cited in the Introduction to this volume) but the case differs from "intraracial" group formations.

Because the concepts and terms in social psychological and cognitive science discourses are different, it is not easy to relate these two discourses to each other—although it seems obvious that they are dealing with the same subject matter. A more detailed discussion of their relation has to be saved for another occasion. I shall restrict myself here to some basic observations on two similarities and one obvious difference. First, both the self-categorization theory and Boyer's model presume a social calculus that is not directly accessible from conscious reflection. In the self-categorization theory, this is the meta-contrast principle (and ratio) and in Boyer's model, it is coalitional computations. Second, consequently, both theories depict the two related concepts—the prototypes of the self-cataegorization theory and the essences of Boyer's model—as derivatives. They are not starting points for social categorization but a secondary reflection of more subtle processes. Third, the obvious difference lies in the character of what is calculated. While Boyer's model presumes a calculation of the *costs and benefits* of social relations, the self-categorization theory's meta-contrast ratio computes the observed *similarities and differences* in intragroup and intergroup relations. From the perceived differences and similarities are then thought to "flow, amongst other things, attraction and dislike, agreement and disagreement, cooperation and conflict" (Oakes, Haslam and Turner 1998: 80).

It is clear that a much more elaborate discussion would be needed in order to reach a fair judgment about the strengths and weaknesses of these slightly different approaches to social categorization. However, on the basis of this rather restricted comparison, I am inclined to take the meta-contrast calculus of the self-identification theory as a more subtle approach to social catergorization than Boyer's coalitional computations. The meta-contrast approach allows for a larger variety of psychological motives to affect the cohesion of social groups. Boyer's model, with its emphasis on the simple computation of costs and benefits, gives an instrumental and rational slant on social relations that usually host a multitude of social and psychological motives.[22]

---

[22] Of course, it is possible to qualify coalitional computations by assuming that these involve not just rational or utilitarian choices but also computations of intuitive emotional and affective gains. As a matter of fact, since Boyer assumes that the computation is unconscious (not a result of conscious reflection), he may have something like this in mind. However, if this kind of qualification is necessary, it shows that the idea of coalitional computations as such is a rather robust tool for the analysis of social interaction. For the function of intuitive and reflective information processing

On the other hand, the idea of essentialist thinking captures very well the tendency of individuals and groups to picture their (hostile) outgroups in terms of living things. It is quite possible that the ease with which people engage themselves with this kind of discourse betrays an innate module in the mind that becomes activated under certain perceptual conditions. The module in question may simply be a general living-things module (cf. Atran's comment on Gil-White 2001) and it is not necessary to presume any coalitional calculations behind this.

4. Prototypes and Exemplars in the Brain

4.1. Evidence from Laterality Experiments

In this last theoretical section, I proceed to discuss how prototypes and exemplars are possibly processed in the brain. The discussion is directly connected with the social psychological discourse that was introduced in the previous sections. However, since essentialist thinking is closely connected to prototypes, the discussion may also partly bear on the question of which mechanisms in the brain participate in essentializing processes.[23]

Laterality studies are conducted with split-brain patients whose left and right hemispheres have been disconnected (usually as an extreme means to prevent violent epileptic seizures), patients who have lesions either in the left or in the right hemisphere, and with healthy subjects by directing stimuli only to the left hemisphere (from the right visual field) or to the right hemisphere (from the left visual field). These studies indicate that the left hemisphere may rely on prototypical representations while the right hemisphere seems to be more adept at exemplar modes or representation.

---

systems in the brain, see Pyysiäinen 2005. For the closely related distinction conscious vs. unconscious processing, see Gazzaniga, Ivry and Mangun 2001: 660–71.

[23] There is a discussion among neuroscientists that bears more directly on the issue of essentialist thinking and thinking in terms of natural kinds but it is not possible to go into the details of that debate here. Neuroscientists have conducted several experiments in order to locate areas in the brain that would be involved with processing information on living things vs. nonliving things or living things vs. man-made tools, the latter being presented as an alternative to the first distinction. In the naming of these living/nonliving/man-made things, the left temporal lobe especially seems to play a crucial role. Gazzaniga, Ivry and Mangun 2002: 221–26, 355–60. Cf. below the role of the left hemisphere in the formation of prototypes.

For instance, Marsolek (1995; cited here according to Gazzaniga, Ivry and Mangun 2002: 435–36) conducted a laterality experiment with normal subjects. He created eight prototypes of abstract line drawings and eight sets of variations on these prototypes. During a training period, the subjects were shown the variations (not the prototypes) and were trained to categorize them. In the test phase, the stimuli were presented either in the left or in the right visual field. When the subjects were shown the variations, their judgments were faster when the variations were processed by the right hemisphere (presented in the left visual field). On the other hand, when they were presented with the previously unseen prototypes, their judgments were faster when the stimuli were processed by the left hemisphere (presented in the right visual field). Thus, it seems that the left hemisphere had "correctly" abstracted the form of the prototypes from the exemplars and was therefore able to recognize them faster. The right hemisphere, for its part, had stored the information about the exemplars as they were shown and was therefore faster when dealing with them.

The ability of the left hemisphere to engage in categorization, interpretation and theory construction is attested in many neurological processing systems, including perception, memory and language. As a matter of fact, the specialization of the left hemisphere in these areas is probably connected to the fact that language processing is located in the left temporal lobe and language development requires highly developed categorization skills. (Gazzaniga, Ivry and Mangun 2002: 436.)

Although the left hemisphere is better at category formation and interpretation, the right hemisphere is faster and more accurate in tasks demanding identification of previously confronted stimuli. When split-brain patients were asked whether or not they had seen a series of stimuli in the set that they had studied for the experiment, their right hemisphere was able to correctly identify the previously seen items and reject the ones that were not seen. However, the left hemisphere of these patients tended to falsely identify items that were not seen in reality but which resembled those that the subjects were shown, presumably because the left hemisphere found these correct in the light of the schema/prototype it had created. (Gazzaniga, Ivry and Mangun 2002: 672–75.)

In the light of the laterality experiments, the left hemisphere appears as an interpreter that goes beyond simply observing the facts by creating theories that assimilate the observations into comprehensive wholes. In the right hemisphere, the observational accuracy remains high because it is not engaged in these kinds of interpretative operations. In an intact brain, these two systems operate in concert allowing highly developed category formation and theorizing without sacrificing veracity. (Gazzaniga, Ivry and Mangun 2002: 436–47, 672–75.)

4.2. The Social Identity Approach in the Light of Laterality Experiments

The significance of the lateratility experiments for the social identity approach lies in the fact these prove the existence of two different cognitive systems in the brain for the processing of prototypes and exemplars. Furthermore, they show that, in a normal brain, these are not two mutually exclusive modes of processing but form a dual system that enables flexible, context (exemplar) sensitive categorizing and theorizing. Thus, it seems worthwhile to develop the social identity approach in terms of theorizing with both exemplars and prototypes. For instance, *exemplars* could be termed as observed ingroup and outgroup members as well as culturally transmitted descriptions of the possible past, present and future members of ingroups and outgroups. Exemplars can contribute to categorical judgments either "on line," as present observations or through memory retrieval. The context of the social categorization affects the relative salience of the exemplars to be taken into account and it also cues the memory retrieval of previously stored exemplars with their associative emotional and other characteristics.[24]

The term *prototype* could be reserved for the products of the categorizing and generalizing activity of the left hemisphere. This use of the term *prototype* would be fully consistent with the way in which prototypicality is presently defined by self-categorization theorists: prototypicality is profoundly context dependent and dependent on the individual who accomplishes the social calculus in terms of the meta-contrast principle. By definition, it is possible to discuss shared group prototypes only as approximations of averages of individually calculated prototypicalities since groups as such do not possess memories or conduct assessments of prototypicalities. This line of theorizing would not allow for the

---

[24] The third main assumption of Smith and Zárate's exemplary based model (1992) is that "a range of social and motivational factors including individual differences, the perceiver's past experiences, the self-schema, the current social context, in-group/outgroup dynamics, and the like, which are known to affect social judgment, do so by shaping the perceiver's attention to stimulus dimensions and therefore influencing exemplar retrieval and use."

direct communication of prototypes since prototypicalities are always assessed/calculated by individuals in certain, irreproducible contexts (individuals are, though, deeply affected by their group memberships). However, exemplars are more easily accessible to social entrepreneurs who may try to effect the assessment of prototypicalites by manipulating the character and salience of relevant past, present and future exemplars.

The above considerations about terminological distinctions between exemplars and prototypes are suggestive; it is clear that, in practice, similar context sensitive analyses of prototypicalities can be made without such clear-cut terminological distinctions between exemplars and prototypes.[25] More important is that although the above considerations are not intended to be an exhaustive analysis of the cognitive aspects of social categorizations, the above reasoning—together with examples presented in the Introduction to this volume—should make clear the benefits of trying to combine social psychological theorizing with cognitive (neuro)science.

5. *An Example: Towards a Socio-Cognitive Study of Early Christian Heresiologies*

Heresiology[26] as a genre is a perfect target for socio-cognitive analysis. Heresiologies were written and used precisely for the kinds of purposes that the social identity approach is designed to expose: categorization of outgroups, accentuation of differences between the ingroup and the outgroups and the search for subjective cognitive coherence.

Personalizing—or essentializing—strategy is widespread in heresiological treatises. One instance of these sorts of cognitive operations can be found in Epiphanius' description of the Ebionites. Epiphanius was a bishop of Salamis who wrote a description and refutation of "heresies"

---

[25] For instance, Esler (2003: 172–75) makes a distinction between exemplars and prototypes. However he also seems to suggest some overlap between the two concepts: exemplars refer to historical persons, but if the person proves to be fictitious, then one could term him/her a prototype. Nonetheless, irrespective of the terminology, Esler's analysis of the prototypes Paul uses in Romans is highly context sensitive.

[26] From the mid-second century onwards the church fathers started to write heresiologies where they aimed at confuting the doctrines of their main adversaries. The oldest heresiology that has survived into our days is Ireanaeus' *Adversus haereses* (ca. 175–185 C.E.). However, Irenaeus' treatise is based on an earlier heresiology by his teacher Justin the Martyr, who is usually regarded as the creator of the genre within Christianity.

(*Panarion*) in the late fourth century. There he attacks Ebion, the supposed leader of a Jewish-Christian "heresy" of the Ebionites:

> But he is making a completely false accusation—this dreadful serpent with his poverty of understanding. For "Ebion", translated from Hebrew to Greek, means "poor". For he is indeed poor, in understanding, hope, and actual fact, since he takes Christ for a mere man... I suppose the poor, wretched person got the name from his father and mother by prophesy. (*Pan.* 30.17.1; trans. Williams 1987)

This quotation exemplifies personalization on two levels. The first level of personalization is the very notion that the sect was founded by an individual. Epiphanius had inherited this idea from some of his predecessors (Tertullian, Origen, Eusebius) but the first references to the Ebionites do no have any information about a person called Ebion. Therefore, modern scholars agree that the person is fictitious. Originally, the term must have been a self-designation of Jewish Christians who saw themselves as poor and humble servants of God.

The invention of the person Ebion is often explained by referring to the fact that since many of the "heresies" were founded by individuals, it was natural to think that the Ebionites were also followers of a certain Ebion. While there is nothing wrong with this logic, the cognitive approach helps us to better understand why Ebion was eventually "incarnated." It is not simply a question of standardizing the heresiological discourse. The simple underlying motive is that it is easier for the brain to deal with persons rather than abstract doctrines.

The second instance of personalization in the example can be seen in the personal qualities that Epiphanius attributed to Ebion. The "heretical" doctrine of the Ebionites is traced back to the low intellectual skills of the supposed founder of the sect. Notably, Epiphanius argues that these qualities were immutable since the name was based on prophesy. This coheres neatly with Tajfel's description of the effects of personalization (see above). Furthermore, Epiphanius' characterization of Ebion as "this dread serpent" addresses the same cognitive living-things module that processes personalization, adding strong negative emotions to the prototype his readers were to compute on the basis of this description.

Another interesting example of heresiological fiction is Epiphanius' description of the Nazarenes. Space does not allow for a detailed discussion here but I have argued elsewhere that Epiphanius' description of the Nazarenes (*Panarion* 29) is his own fiction that he composed on the basis of scattered information about early Jewish Christians that he was able to collect from the Acts of the Apostles and Eusebius's *Ecclesiastical History* (Luomanen 2005, 2007). The "heresy" of the Nazarenes was created because that helped Epiphanius to depict the earliest stages of the history of Jewish Christianity in more concrete terms and to confute doctrines that appeared to him as an unbearable mixture of Judaism and Christianity.

In the light of the above developed distinction between *exemplars* and *prototypes*, the main characteristics of Epiphanius' heresiological discourse can be described as follows. Epiphanius was a social *entrepreneur* who sought to manipulate the boundaries around his own Christian group by creating such exemplars of outgroup members that would maximize the difference between the members of his ingroup and the (imagined) members of the outgroups. The doctrinal disputes behind the heresiological accounts were quite abstract and, as such, not easily communicable. Furthermore, like many of the church fathers, Epiphanius did not often know personally any adherents of the movements he was criticizing and therefore did not have any first-hand knowledge about the groups and the factual practices he was discussing. In the absence of real-life *exemplars* of the adherents of the movements, he was bound to base his judgments on *prototypical* cognitive representations he had developed in his mind. These gave form to fictitious quasi-exemplars through which he tried to make the discussion comprehensible for his readers.[27] Paradoxically, it follows that, in some respects, the fictitious exemplars that are not overburdened with the constraints of empirical reality may give us a better glimpse of Epiphanius' prototypes and self-understanding—provided we correctly perceive their character as self-reflections.

In conclusion, I find the cognitive approach to prototypes and exemplars significant for historical research in two respects. First, the distinction between exemplars and prototypes helps us to better conceptualize the relationship between the historical sources and the social psychological reality behind them. Although there is no one-to-one relationship between the exemplars in the sources and the prototypes in the minds of the ancient writers/readers—we can never exactly know what the ancients had in their minds—we know that there is a formative connection between the exemplars and the prototypes. Moreover, we also know that the cognitive mechanism in the brain that computed the prototypes from the exemplars has remained practically

---

[27] For fictitious *exemplars*, see Cinnirella 1998: 231–32.

the same during the past two millennia. Thus, we have some means to approximate the past prototypes that had a significant impact on social identities and intergroup relations.

Second, the dynamic character of the prototypes has significant consequences regarding the character of concepts and models that can be used in the reconstruction of (ancient) social realities. If the generative factors of social reality have a deeply dynamic nature, that is, group norms and boundaries, prototypes, social and self-identities, etc. are being constantly monitored, reconstructed, redefined and reassured, it follows that all the attempts to form "objective" etic descriptions of these realities can—paradoxically—use only models and concepts that allow for variations.

This need for conceptual flexibility is being constantly challenged by two discourses that strive for inflexibility and rigid definitions of group boundaries and norms. On the one hand, the fuzzy character of the ultimate social reality is problematic—from the emic point of view—for all human parties involved but especially for social entrepreneurs who seek to enhance their control over their ingroup. Their discourse, of which the Christian heresiologies are but one example, seeks to create order in what to them may appear as chaos. On the other hand, the fuzzy social reality does not easily surrender to classic scientific discourse with its striving for categorical definitions that are based on necessary and sufficient attributes.

A lot of time and ink has been wasted because due attention has not been rendered to differences among these three viewpoints. A prime example of this is the "definition" of Jewish Christianity. A great variety of definitions have been proposed—mostly from the classic "necessary and sufficient" point of view—and none of these has satisfied large number of scholars. Rigid categories always tend to ignore some aspects that are crucial in some situations. If not, that is only because the category has been defined in such general terms that it has become practically obsolete. The same applies, *mutatis mutandis*, to several other discussions, especially in the humanities, about "terms extremely difficult to define." There will be no end to these frustrating disputes unless scholarly communities start to see that the real problem lies in the discrepancy between the classic "accurate" scientific categories and the fuzzy social reality. Once this is realized, I am convinced that more and more "terms extremely difficult to define" will find more satisfactory dynamic conceptualizations. For instance, in the case of Jewish Christianity, rigid definitions could be abandoned in favor of a more dynamic approach which maps out *Jewish-Christian profiles*, mixtures of degrees of Jewishness and Christianity. Judgments about these can be reached through the study of *indicators of Jewish Christianity*, a set of key characteristics of Judaism and Christianity, in conjunction with observations about the effect of these indicators on social borders and social identification.[28]

6. *Conclusion*

The above discussion provided examples of two sociological theories, Berger and Luckmann's sociology of knowledge and the social identity approach, both of which have been applied in the study of early Christianity. They both originated in the 1960s and the 1970s and deal with the acquisition, maintenance and transmission of knowledge about social phenomena. However, they differ in their present applicability—in particular regarding their ability to link up with the cognitive approach to religion. Because Berger and Luckmann's theory has not inspired much new research, their sociology of knowledge seems to represent "background technology." Nevertheless, the obsolete outlook of the sociology of knowledge is partly misleading since the kinds of problems Berger and Luckmann helped to crystallize have become standard questions in various branches of sociology. Thus, the sociology of knowledge—though not necessarily termed as such—still keeps feeding the imagination of sociologically oriented biblical scholars. One example of this is the present interest in social memory (cf. Introducion and Esler's essay in this volume) which is also considered one of the main topics of the "new sociology of knowledge."

For scholars coming from an ideology- and theology-centered research tradition, Berger and Luckmann's theory provided a rather gentle application of sociology because of its emphasis on the symbolic universe

---

[28] For the definition of Jewish Christianity and for the more flexible approach, see Luomanen 2003: 265–69; 2007. Originally, I ended up developing the more flexible definition simply because the rigid, traditional approach was clearly a dead end. In developing the approach, I was inspired by Murray's (1990) "spectrum" definition. The study of Jewish-Christian profiles differs from Murray's approach in that it combines the study of indicators with observations about the indicators' impact on social border marking. The first version of the approach was published in Myllykoski and Luomanen 1999. It was not until I wrote this essay that I realized the compatibility of this approach with the results of neuroscientific research on (social) categorization.

as the overriding means of legitimation. The ease with which scholars have adopted the concept as part of their standard vocabulary raises the question whether it is only the term that has changed—from "theology" to "symbolic universe"—while the actual contents of the analysis has not changed so much. On the other hand, it is clear that the analysis of early Jewish and Christian traditions can never become pure sociology. As long as Christianity and Judaism remain living religions, there will always be theologically relevant and interesting questions that occupy the minds of researchers who are studying the foundational traditions of these religions. Moreover, the material available does not easily lend itself to purely sociological analysis. There is a host of questions connected to the analysis of (often historically layered) ancient texts that also have to be sorted out before it is possible to present views about the social setting of the people who authored these documents.

The same also applies to the cognitive approach to early Christianity. The study of cognition will not provide a magic key to the correct interpretation of ancient texts. The above review suggests that it is reasonable to study cognition in conjunction with the culture and social setting where the individual mind is nurtured. Berger and Luckmann's view according to which "man produces reality and thereby produces himself" (Berger and Luckmann 1966: 204) is still valid. Despite the fact that Berger and Luckmann's theory itself does not much allow for innate predispositions in the human "production of reality," the viewpoints their theory offers for the analysis of the enculturation of an individual mind still prove quite helpful.

The cognitive approach can contribute to the study of Christian origins especially by providing scientifically tested information and systematically formulated theories about the functions of the mind. Quite often scholars supplement their historical constructions with psychological assumptions about "reasonable" or "natural" human responses and strategies. Instead of doing these reconstructions instinctively, on the basis of gut feelings alone, it would be better if we could also use some systematically formulated and tested theories. Even now it is possible to validate some cognitive and social psychological conceptualizations with neuroscientific experiments. In the future, there will be more and more possibilities for this due to new and better brain imaging techniques that are being developed.

From the very beginnings of Christianity, philosophy has been one of the disciplines through which Christian thinkers have reflected on their religious beliefs and practices. However, today, philosophers are becoming more and more aware of the challenge of the cognitive science of religion to such philosophical (Platonic) traditions that ignore the embodied character of the mind. The results of cognitive science are showing how deeply our intellects are rooted in the physiological properties of our brains. Disembodied souls are truly getting their flesh and bones back again. Theologians should have no reason to distance themselves from this development. Certainly, "theology in the flesh" is not alien to the Jewish–Christian tradition—though some profoundly Hellenized versions of Christian (and Jewish) theologizing will surely find it discomforting.[29] What we would need are theories that are capable of bringing together both the cognitive and the social approaches to early Christianity (cf. Pyysiäinen 2003: 73–74). The social identity approach seems to be one good candidate for such a task because of its built in cognitive interface.

REFERENCES

Adams, Edward. 2000. *Constructing the World: A Study in Paul's Cosmological Language.* Edinburgh: T&T Clark.

Aittola, Tapio, and Vesa Raiskila. 1994. "Jälkisanat." In Peter L. Berger and Thomas Luckmann. *Todellisuuden sosiaalinen rakentuminen.* Trans. Vesa Raiskila, 213–31, 248–52. Helsinki: Gaudeamus, 1994. [Post Script in Finnish translation of Berger and Luckmann's *Social Construction of Reality.*]

Arnal, William E. 2001. *Jesus and the Village Scribes: Galilean Conflicts and the Setting of Q.* Minneapolis, Minn.: Fortress.

Atran, Scott. 2001. Comment on Francisco J. Gil-White, "Are Ethnic Groups Biological 'Species' to the Human Brain? Essentialism in Our Cognition of Some Social Categories." *Current Anthropology* 42: 537–38.

Barrett, Justin L. 2002. "Dumb Gods, Petitionary Prayer and the Cognitive Science of Religion." In *Current Approaches in the Cognitive Science of Religion*, edited by Ilkka Pyysiäinen and Veikko Anttonen, 93–109. New York: Continuum.

Barsalou, Lawrence W. 1987. "The Instability of Graded Structure: Implications for the Nature of Concepts." In *Concepts and Conceptual Development: Ecological and Intellectual Factors in Categorization*, edited by Ulrich Neisser, 101–40. Cambridge: Cambridge University Press.

Berger, Peter L. 1967. *The Sacred Canopy: Elements of a Sociological Theory of Religion.* Garden City, N.Y.: Doubleday.

———. 2001. "Postscript." In *Peter Berger and the Study of Religion*, edited by Linda Woodhead with Paul Heelas and David Martin, 189–98. London: Routledge.

Berger, Peter L., and Thomas Luckmann. 1966. The *Social Construction of Reality: A Treatise in the Sociology of Knowledge.* London: Allen Lane.

---

[29] Cf. Lakoff and Johnson 1999 (*Philosophy in the Flesh: The Embodied Mind and Its Challenge to Western Thought.* New York: Basic Books).

Bless, Herbert, Klaus Fiedler, and Fritz Strack. 2004. *Social Cognition: How Individuals Construct Social Reality*. Hove: Psychology Press.
Boyer, Pascal. 2002a. *Religion Explained: The Human Instincts that Fashion Gods, Spirits and Ancestors*. London: Vintage.
———. 2002b. "Why Do Gods and Spirits Matter at All?" in *Current Approaches in the Cognitive Science of Religion*, edited by Ilkka Pyysiäinen and Veikko Anttonen, 68–92. New York: Continuum.
Brewer, Marilynn B. 1998. "A Dual Process Model for Impression Formation." In *Advances in Social Cognition, Vol. 1*, edited by Thomas K. Strull and Robert S. Wyer, 1–36. Hillside, N.J.: Erlbaum.
Cinnirella, Marco. 1998. "Exploring Temporal Aspects of Social Identity: The Concept of Possible Social Identities." *European Journal of Social Psychology* 28: 227–48.
Cosmides, Leda, John Tooby, and Robert Kurzban. 2003. "Perceptions of Race." *Trends in Cognitive Sciences* 7(4): 173–79.
Czachesz, István. 2007. "The Transmission of Early Christian Thought: Toward a Cognitive Psychological Model." *Studies in Religion* 36: 65–84.
Dorrien, Gary. 2001. "Berger: Theology and Sociology." In *Peter Berger and the Study of Religion*, edited by Linda Woodhead with Paul Heelas and David Martin, 26–39. London: Routledge.
Esler, Philip. 1987. *Community and Gospel in Luke-Acts: The Social and Political Motivations of Lucan Theology*. Society for New Testament Studies Monograph Series 57. Cambridge: Cambridge University Press.
———. 1998. *Galatians*. New Testament Readings. London: Routledge.
———. 2003. *Conflict and Identity in Romans: The Social Setting of Paul's Letter*. Minneapolis, Pa.: Fortress.
Frazier, S. L., and R. G. Lord. 1988. "Stimulus Prototypicality and General Leadership Impressions: Their Role in Leadership and Behavioral Ratings." *Journal of Psychology* 122: 291–303.
Fuglseth, Kåre Sigvald. 2005. *Johannine Sectarianism in Perspective: A Sociological, Historical, and Comparative Analysis of Temple and Social Relationships in the Gospel of John, Philo and Qumran*. Supplements to Novum Testamentum 119. Leiden: Brill.
Gager, John G. 1975. *Kingdom and Community: The Social World of Early Christianity*. Englewood Cliffs, N.J.: Prentice-Hall.
Gazzaniga, Michael S., Richard B. Ivry and George R. Mangun. 2002. *Cognitive Neuroscience: The Biology of the Mind*. Second Edition. New York: W.W. Norton & Company.
Gil-White, Francisco J. 2001. "Are Ethnic Groups Biological 'Species' to the Human Brain? Essentialism in Our Cognition of Some Social Categories." *Current Anthropology* 42: 515–54.
Hamilton, David L., Steven I. Sherman, and Jeremy D. Sack. 2001. Comment on Francisco J. Gil-White, "Are Ethnic Groups Biological 'Species' to the Human Brain? Essentialism in Our Cognition of Some Social Categories." *Current Anthropology* 42: 540–41.
Hogg, Michael A., and Dominic Abrams. 1988. *Social Identifications: A Social Psychology of Intergroup Relations and Group Processes*. London: Routledge.
———. 1999. "Social Identity and Social Cognition: Historical Background and Current Trends." In *Social Identity and Social Cognition*, edited by Dominic Abrams and Michael A. Hogg, 1–25. Malden, Mass.: Blackwell.
Horrell, David G. 1996. *The Social Ethos of the Corinthian Correspondence: Interests and Ideology from 1 Corinthians to 1 Clement*. Studies of the New Testament and Its World. Edinburgh: T&T Clark.
———. 2001. "Berger and New Testament Studies." In *Peter Berger and the Study of Religion*, edited by Linda Woodhead with Paul Heelas and David Martin, 142–53. London: Routledge.

Horsley, Richard A. 1989. *Sociology and the Jesus Movement*. New York: Crossroad.
Kee, Howard C. 1980. *Christian Origins in Sociological Perspective*. London: SCM Press.
Lawson, E. Thomas, and Robert N. McCauley. 1990. *Rethinking Religion: Connecting Cognition and Culture*. Cambridge: Cambridge University Press.
———. 2002. Bringing Ritual to Mind: Psychological Foundations of Cultural Forms. Cambridge: Cambridge University Press.
Lakoff, George, and Mark Johnson. 1980. *Metaphors We Live By*. London: University of Chicago Press.
———. 1999. *Philosophy in the Flesh: The Embodied Mind and Its Challenge to Western Thought*. New York: Basic Books.
Luckmann, Thomas. 2001. "Berger and His Collaborator(s)." In *Peter Berger and the Study of Religion*, edited by Linda Woodhead with Paul Heelas and David Martin, 17–25. London: Routledge.
Luomanen, Petri. 1998. *Entering the Kingdom of Heaven: A Study on the Structure of Matthew's View of Salvation*. Wissenschaftliche Untersuchungen zum Neuen Testament 2, 101. Tübingen: Mohr Siebeck.
———. 2002. Review of William E. Arnal, *Jesus and the Village Scribes: Galilean Conflicts and the Setting of Q. Catholic Biblical Quarterly* 64: 751–52.
———. 2003. "Where Did Another Rich Man Come From? The Jewish-Christian Profile of the Story About a Rich Man in the 'Gospel of the Hebrews' (Origen, *Comm in Matth.* 15.14)." *Vigiliae Christianae* 57: 234–75.
———. 2005. "The Nazarenes." In *A Companion to Second-Century Christian "Heretics,"* edited by Antti Marjanen and Petri Luomanen. Supplements to Vigiliae Christianae 76. Leiden: Brill.
———. 2007. "Ebionites and Nazarenes." In *Jewish Christianity Reconsidered*, edited by Matt Jackson-McCabe, 81–118. Minneapolis, Minn.: Augsburg Fortress.
MacDonald, Margaret Y. 1988. *The Pauline Churches: A Socio-historical Study of Institutionalization in the Pauline and Deutero-Pauline Writings*. Cambridge: Cambridge University Press.
Medin, Douglas L. 1989. "Concepts and Conceptual Structure." *American Psychologist* 44: 1469–81.
Meeks, Wayne A. 1972. "The Man from Heaven in Johannine Sectarianism." *Journal of Biblical Literature* 91: 44–71.
Myllykoski, Matti, and Petri Luomanen. 1999. "Varhaisen juutalaiskristillisyyden jäljillä." *Teologinen Aikakauskirja 104*: 327–48. [English abstract: "On the Trail of Early Judaeo-Christianity," p. 321.]
Marques, José M., Dario Páez, and Dominic Abrams. 1999. "Social Identity and Intragroup Differentiation as Subjective Social Control." In *Social Identity: International Perspectives*, edited by Stephen Worchel et al., 124–41. London: Sage Publications.
Marshall, Gordon, ed. 1998. *A Dictionary of Sociology*. Oxford: Oxford University Press.
Mullen, Brian, Drew Rozell, and Craig Johnson. 1996. "The Phenomenology of Being in a Group: Complexity Approaches to Operationalizing Cognitive Representations." In *What's Social About Social Cognition? Research on Socially Shared Cognition in Small Groups*, edited by Judith L. Nye and Aaron M. Brower, 205–29. London: Sage Publications.
Murray, R. P. R. 1990. "Jewish Christianity" In *A Dictionary of Biblical Interpretation*, edited by R. J. Coggins and J. L. Houlden. London: SCM Press.
Oakes, Penelope, S. Alexander Haslam, and John C. Turner. 1998. "The Role of Prototypicality in Group Influence and Cohesion: Contextual Variation in the Graded Structure of Social Categories." In *Social Identity: International Perspectives*, edited by Stephen Worchel et al., 75–92. London: Sage Publications.
Overman, J. Andrew. 1990. *Matthew's Gospels and Formative Judaism: The Social World of the Matthean Community*. Minneapolis, Minn.: Fortress.
Pickett, Raymond. 1997. *The Cross in Corinth: The Social Significance of the Death of Jesus*. Journal for the Study of New Testament Suppelment Series 143. Sheffield: Sheffield Academic Press.

Pyysiäinen, Ilkka. 2002. "Introduction: Cognition and Culture in the Construction of Religion." In *Current Approaches in the Cognitive Science of Religion*, edited by Ilkka Pyysiäinen and Veikko Anttonen, 1–13. New York: Continuum
———. [2001] 2003. *How Religion Works: Towards a New Cognitive Science of Religion.* Leiden: Brill.
———. 2005. "Intuition, Reflection and the Evolution of Traditions." In *Moving Beyond New Testament Theology? Essays in Conversation with Heikki Räisänen*, edited by Todd Penner and Caroline Vander Stichele, 282–307. Publications of the Finnish Exegetical Society 88. Helsinki: Finnish Exegetical Society; Göttingen: Vandenhoek & Ruprecht.
Rosch, Eleanor. 1975. "Cognitive Representations of Semantic Categories." *Journal of Experimental Psychology* 104: 192–233.
Rothbart, Myron, and Marjorie Taylor. 2001. Comment on Francisco J. Gil-White, "Are Ethnic Groups Biological 'Species' to the Human Brain? Essentialism in Our Cognition of Some Social Categories." *Current Anthropology* 42: 544–55.
Räisänen, Heikki. 2001. *Challenges to Biblical Interpretation: Collected Essays 1991–2001.* Biblical Interpretation Series 59. Leiden: Brill.
Smith, Eliot R., and Michael A. Zárate. 1992. "Exemplar Based Model of Social Judgment." *Psychological Review* 99: 3–21.
Sperber, Dan. 1996. *Explaining Culture: A Naturalistic Approach.* Cambridge, Mass.: Blackwell.
Swindler, Ann, and Jorge Arditi. 1994. "The New Sociology of Knowledge." *Annual Review of Sociology* 20: 305–29.
Syreeni, Kari. 1990. "Between Heaven and Earth: On the Structure of Matthew's Symbolic Universe." *Journal for the Study of the New Testament* 40: 3–13. Uro, Risto. 2004. "Eksegetiikka ja kognitiivinen uskontotiede." *Teologinen Aikakauskirja* 109: 549–61. [English abstract: "Biblical Studies and the Cognitive Approach to Religion," p. 514]
Tajfel, Henri. 1981. *Human Groups and Social Categories: Studies in Social Psychology.* Cambridge: Cambridge University Press.
Theissen, Gerd. 1985. *Die Soziologie der Jesusbewegung: Eine Beitrag zur Entstehungsgeschichte des Urchristentums.* München: Chr. Kaiser Verlag.
———. 1993a. "Sociological Research into the New Testament: Some Ideas Offered by the Sociology of Knowledge for a New Exegetical Approach." In Gerd Theissen, *Social Reality and the Early Christians: Theology, Ethics, and the World of the New Testament*, 1–29. Edinburgh: T&T Clark.
———. 1993b. "Christology and Social Experience: Aspects of Pauline Christology in the Light of the Sociology of Knowledge." In Gerd Theissen, *Social Reality and the Early Christians: Theology, Ethics, and the World of the New Testament*, 187–201. Edinburgh: T&T Clark.
———. 1993c. "Sociological Theories of Religion and the Analysis of Early Christianity." In Gerd Theissen, *Social Reality and the Early Christians: Theology, Ethics, and the World of the New Testament* 231–56. Edinburgh: T&T Clark.
Watson, Francis. 1986. *Paul, Judaism and the Gentiles: A Sociological Approach.* Society for New Testament Studies Monograph Series 56. Cambridge: Cambridge University Press.
Whitehouse, Harvey. 2004. *Modes of Religiosity: A Cognitive Theory of Religious Transmission.* Walnut Creek, Calif.: AltaMira.
Wilkes, A. L. 1997. *Knowledge in Minds: Individual and Collective Processes in Cognition.* Hove: Psychology Press.
Williams, Frank. (trans.) 1987. *The Panarion of Epiphanius of Salamis: Book I (Sects 1–46).* Nag Hammadi Studies 35. Leiden: Brill.
Zerubavel, Eviatar. 1997. *Social Mindscapes: An Invitation to Cognitive Sociology.* Cambridge, Mass.: Harvard University Press.
———. 2003. *Time Maps: Collective Memory and the Social Shape of the Past.* Chicago, Ill.: The University of Chicago Press.

"REMEMBER MY FETTERS": MEMORIALISATION OF PAUL'S IMPRISONMENT

Philip F. Esler

In three of the pseudo-Pauline letters—Colossians, Ephesians and 2 Timothy—"Paul" writes as someone who is imprisoned and in chains. The penultimate statement in what is probably the earliest of them, Colossians, indicates that this is not just an incidental feature but bears upon how these texts should be interpreted: "Remember my fetters" (*mnēmoneuete mou tōn desmōn*; 4:18). Why does the author of Colossians say this? And why does he and the authors of Ephesians and 2 Timothy establish a dramatic framework for their communications in which "Paul" appears as a chained prisoner? Although this is a question not usually asked—thus Paul as prisoner is not one of the six images mentioned by Boer (1980) as noteworthy in Pauline literature after his death, nor does Margaret MacDonald notice it in her discussion of Boer (1988: 123–26)—the purpose of this essay is to provide a fresh answer to it. Since I accept the position held by a majority of New Testament scholars that Paul was not the author of Colossians, Ephesians and the Pastoral Epistles,[1] any explanation offered must relate to the circumstances that obtained for the Christ-movement after Paul's death (or, far less probably, to the period shortly before he died). Reasonable evidence exists, that Paul, like Peter, died in Rome in the mid to late 60s, in spite of occasional expressions of scepticism.[2]

---

[1] For arguments in favour of this position, see Dunn 1996: 35–39 (for Colossians); Lincoln 1990: lix–lxxiii (for Ephesians) and Hanson 1982: 2–11 (for the Pastoral Epistles). But note Luke Johnson's interesting recent defence of the authenticity of the Pastorals (Johnson 1996: 4–33). Richard Bauckham (1988) has helpfully outlined the character of pseudo-apostolic letters in relation to genuine ones.

[2] See Bauckham 1992 on much of the evidence for the death of Peter in Rome. One sceptic on Peter's death in Rome is Michael Goulder (2004), but his case is undermined by his failure to take seriously the archaeological evidence for a rather elaborate memorial to Peter on the Vatican Hill as early as 150–160 (see, Guarducci 1984, 1989; Toynbee and Perkins 1956) or the evidence for the presence of Peter and Paul in Rome in Ignatius of Antioch's *Letter to the Romans* which was written about 110 C.E. (see 4.2–3). The fact that no other city contested the claim of the Roman

In line with the theme of the present volume I will seek to employ a social psychological and cognitive science approach to socio-religious phenomena (in the latter respect under the influence of Boyer 2001 and Pyysiäinen 2001 and 2004). I will pursue my topic in the following way. First, I will review the relevant data in Colossians, Ephesians and 2 Timothy, pointing especially to the themes of imprisonment and memory in these texts. Secondly, I will offer a brief explanation of how social identity theory and the largely sociological notions of collective memory assist us to understand this material, yet ultimately fail to deal with the important question of how memories are transmitted. Thirdly, I will set out some cognitive-scientific perspectives on memory, especially autobiographical memory, and apply these perspectives to the three texts. Fourthly, and finally, I will conclude by reviewing what we have learned from this exercise and what avenues for future enquiry it has opened up.

1. *Outlining the Data: Colossians, Ephesians, 2 Timothy and Memory*

1.1. *Paul as Prisoner in Colossians, Ephesians and 2 Timothy*

We begin with Colossians because that is likely to be the oldest of the three texts under consideration and because most scholars believe that the author of Ephesians utilised it in the course of composing that work. Colossians purports to be by "Paul, an apostle of Christ Jesus through the will of God, and Timothy, my brother" (1:1) and is addressed to "the holy and faithful brothers in Christ in Colossae" (1:2). Like Paul's genuine letter to the Romans, Colossians purports to be a letter to a community that Paul himself did not found. Later on it emerges that Paul was also not the founder of the congregation at Laodicea; yet still he strives for the Christ-followers in both places (2:1).

As he writes, "Paul" is bound, that is, in prison (*dedemai*; 4:3). "Paul" notes that others (Judean fellow-workers of his) with him are sending greetings, including Aristarchus, his fellow prisoner (*synaichmalōtos*) (4:10–11). For many critics, the details in Colossians amount to a strong case for Colossians being authentically Pauline. They usually

---

church that Peter and Paul died and were buried in Rome is a very significant piece of evidence for the authenticity of this claim.

call in aid the similarities to the personal details provided in his letter to Philemon (where seven of the individuals mentioned in Colossians 4 appear),[3] which Paul also co-writes with Timothy and is a prisoner (*desmios*) as he does so (Phlm 1), but without mentioning his place of imprisonment. Yet these similarities can also be interpreted on the basis that a pseudonymous writer after Paul mined the letter to Philemon, a genuine writing of Paul and written from prison, for historical details that could allow him to make the fictional framework of his work more convincing.

Most critics (see Lincoln 1990: lxvi–lxxiii.) consider that Ephesians draws upon and therefore was written later than Colossians and most probably not by Paul. Ephesians contains far less information about its putative setting than Colossians. And what is the position of "Paul" as he writes? As in Colossians, there is emphasis on his being a prisoner. Twice "Paul" designates himself as "the prisoner" (Eph 3:1: "the prisoner [*ho desmios*] of Christ"; 4:1: "the prisoner [*ho desmios*] in the Lord"), not, it must be stressed, "a prisoner." Not only does this usage seem more plausible after Paul's death,[4] but it is difficult to avoid the conclusion that the anonymous author wants to present Paul as the paradigmatic prisoner for Christ. This theme re-emerges in a prominent place, as in Colossians, toward the end of the letter, when "Paul" states that "I am an ambassador in chains" (*presbeuō en halysei*) on behalf of the mystery of the Gospel (Eph 6:19–20).

With 2 Timothy we find the author (anonymous to most, but to some the authentic Paul) creating a dramatic situation that is rich in detail in a manner similar to Colossians. The author quickly begins to build up a picture of "Paul" as prisoner. This motif starts in 2 Tim 1:8, where "Paul" implores Timothy not to be ashamed of bearing witness to the Lord "nor of me, his prisoner" (*ton desmion autou*), a usage which is very similar to the expression "the prisoner of Christ/the Lord" in Eph 3:1 and 4:1. He suffers for the gospel (1:13). He is in chains (1:16) and now, quite clearly, Rome is the site of his imprisonment (1:17). He is wearing fetters (*desmoi*) like a criminal, but the word of God is not fettered (*dedetai*; 2:9). "Paul" wants Timothy to share in his suffering (2:3; *synkakopathēson*). In 2 Tim 3:11 "Paul" mentions his previous trials and

---

[3] See Dunn 1996: 274–88 for a discussion of the individuals mentioned.
[4] I am grateful to Professor Larry Hurtado of the University of Edinburgh for drawing my attention in a conversation we had on Ephesians in 2004 to the importance of the *ho* preceding *desmios* on both occasions.

then adds, "Indeed all who wish to live piously in Christ Jesus will be persecuted" (3:12). He is already at the point of being sacrificed (4:6), although he has survived an earlier trial (4:17), which has allowed him to proclaim the gospel to all the non-Judeans. Luke Johnson (1996: 38–41) has questioned the usefulness of the widespread scholarly tendency to regard 2 Timothy as a "farewell discourse" on the basis that Paul's death is only intimated and another literary form, "paraenetic," fits the evidence better. Yet, if Paul's death does not weigh heavily over this work his imprisonment most certainly does and requires interpreters to pay it close attention.

1.2. *Explicit Memory-Language in Colossians, Ephesians and 2 Timothy*

Several explicit references to memory occur in these texts, even though the absence of such language would not necessarily invalidate an approach sensitive to anamnetic concerns, since phenomena can exist in texts even without explicit labelling. In Colossians there is one such reference, but the extremely significant one noticed above: the statement in the very prominent, penultimate clause in the letter: "Remember my fetters" (*mnēmoneuete mou tōn desmōn*; 4:18). This provides an assertion of this theme that is emblematic for this letter and, it is submitted, for Ephesians and 2 Timothy.

In Ephesians memory crops up explicitly twice. First, "Paul" states that he never ceases remembering (*mneian poioumenos*) them in his prayers (1:16), a sentiment very similar to that of Paul himself expressed in 1 Thessalonians (1:2) and Romans (1:9). This is not some empty banality but rather an illustration of how the historical Paul sought to maintain interpersonal contact with fellow Christ-followers even when he was physically absent from them. The author of Ephesians appreciates the importance of this outlook and practice and accordingly repeats it here. Yet it is also probable that in attributing this work to Paul he was seeking to re-establish Paul's presence in memory, even though the apostle was now ontologically separated from them in death.[5] The second reference to memory in Ephesians is at 2:11, where "Paul" exhorts the addressees to remember (*mnēmoneuete*) their condition as non-Judeans (2:11), when they were alienated from the covenants enjoyed by Judeans, without hope and without God (2:12). Here memory serves as the vehicle to

---

[5] For the power of memory to allow us to stay in touch with our dead, see Esler 2005a: 217–28.

drive home the horrors of their state before the acquisition of their new identity and destiny in Christ. The author's point is that memory of the past must condition their sense of the present; they exist in a temporal continuum where past, present and future comprise an integrated experiential framework.

There is an even richer lode of memory-language in 2 Timothy, with six instances. Four of these occur, with emphatic positioning, in vv. 3–6. "Paul" holds a memory (*echō...mneian*) of Timothy constantly in his prayers (1:3). He remembers his tears (1:4). He has remembrance (*hypomnēsin*) of Timothy's sincere faith (1:5) and he reminds (*anamimnēskō*) him to rekindle the gift of God that came to him with the laying on of hands (1:6). Later in the letter he directs Timothy to remember (*mnēmoneue*) Jesus Christ (2:8) and to remind (*hypomimnēske*) other Christ-followers (2:14) of the message set out in 2:11–13. It is hard to avoid the conclusion that in 2 Timothy "Paul," as a figure devoted to remembering, shows the way for other Christ-followers to be like him.

2. *The Contribution of Social Identity Theory and Collective Memory*

2.1. *Social Identity Theory and Colossians, Ephesians and 2 Timothy*

In the last decade I have frequently employed social identity theory in seeking to make sense of the meanings biblical texts communicated to their original audiences (see Esler 1998 and 2003). I am reliant upon the understanding of social identity originally developed by Henri Tajfel, John Turner and others at Bristol University in the 1970s and 1980s and which is still flourishing.[6] Building on research that indicated that merely allocating individuals to groups resulted in the manifestation of group phenomena such as ingroup favouritism and discrimination against outgroups, Tajfel proposed that social identity was that aspect of a person's identity which derived from belonging to a group.

At a general level, it is worthwhile considering the Christ-followers for whom the unknown authors of Colossians, Ephesians and 2 Timothy composed these texts (no doubt to be presented orally) as members of groups (probably local cells of the Christ-movement) who derived an

---

[6] See Tajfel 1978, 1981; Tajfel and Turner 1979. An important source for this research is the *European Journal of Social Psychology*.

important part of their identity from belonging to such a group. They contain much data that differentiates social reality into the ingroup of loyal Christ-followers and a number of outgroups, either those who have not turned to Christ (Colossians and Ephesians) or those who once did but have now abandoned or corrupted their commitment (2 Timothy). The first group designation for the addressees of Colossians is "the holy people and faithful brethren in Colossae" (1:2). All others are simply "those outside" (4:5). In Ephesians the addressees are described as "the holy ones who are also faithful in Christ Jesus" (1:2).[7] On several occasions the author mentions the exalted nature of such an identity (for example, 1:7-8, 11-14); it represents transition from death to life (2:1-2). They must be people of light, not of darkness (4:6-14). The outgroups are "the sons of disobedience" (2:2). In 2 Timothy there is also a pronounced ingroup/outgroup contrast, but now the outgroup comprises people who were once ingroup members, but have deviated from the true path. In 2 Timothy the group differentiation is no longer between Christ-followers and non-Christ-followers, but between loyal Christ-followers and other members of the movement who have left the right path.

2.2. *Persecution and the Strength of Group-Affiliation*

Although Tajfel and Turner (1979) recognised that members might leave a group, it is also clear that certain aspects of the environment might heighten a sense of group-belonging. This commonly occurs where a group is suffering some form of persecution and the members cannot leave or choose not to do so. Here the social identity derived from belonging to such a group will become more salient than in the absence of persecution. Various types of harassment and persecution seem to have characterised the Christ-movement from its very beginnings (as in Mark 4:17 and 13:9, several incidents in Acts, 1 Thess 2:14 and so on). Members of the movement were occasionally imprisoned, tried and executed. On the assumption that the works with which we are concerned were written after Paul's death in the mid to late 60s, they were all directed toward people who would have been aware not only of occasional and intermittent imprisonment of this type, but also of Nero's major action

---

[7] See the commentaries for the complexities of this designation, especially the issue of whether it initially contained a locative reference.

against Christ-followers in Rome after the fire in the capital in July 64 C.E. This culminated in a large number of them being executed in various horrific ways, as recounted by Tacitus (*Annales* 15.44). Thus, the motif of imprisonment—that is a basic aspect of the three pseudo-Pauline letters in our gaze—would have been part of the experience of their addressees and (a negative yet powerful) part of the identity they obtained from belonging to the Christ-movement, with pronounced cognitive, emotional and evaluative elements.

We must account for the fact, however, that there is no reference in Colossians and Ephesians to the addressees experiencing persecution. In 2 Timothy, on the other hand, "Paul" twice urges "Timothy" to share in his suffering, in both cases (1:8; 2:3) using a word only found here in the New Testament (*synkakopatheō*). Later he widens the sentiment to one of general application: "All who wish to live piously will be persecuted" (3:12). When the author predicts "difficult times" in the "last days" (3:1), he does not include persecution in his account of these difficulties (3:2–9), yet such behaviour is closely consonant with the references to those who are "inhuman," "implacable," "fierce" and "haters of good" in 3:3. These data are explicable on the basis that Colossians and Ephesians were the earliest of the three texts, written either before the pace of persecution had picked up or by authors sensitive to the need to avoid anachronism by not having "Paul" allude to phenomena not characteristic of his time.

Yet we are dealing with texts attributed to Paul, a great figure from the recent past of the Christ-movement and this particular feature demands close attention, first from existing scholarly methodology and then in connection with two further elements of social identity theory: group prototypes and the function of time and temporal progression in building group identity.

2.3. *Paul, Social Identity, Prototypes and Time*

Some Current Scholarly Approaches to the Figure of Paul
David Meade has argued, from a viewpoint of traditional historical criticism, that both Ephesians and 2 Timothy present Paul as an "archetype" of orthodoxy and orthopraxis, of teaching and ethics (1986: 116–57). Ephesians promotes the maximum continuity between Paul and his later followers by presenting the apostle as the steward of the mystery (1:9; 3:3, 4, 9; 5:32; 6:19; Meade 1986: 148). Meade interprets

Eph 3:3–4 as meaning that the author is seeking to relate his message to the mystery that Paul himself had desired, using the same means of a letter to do so, with the mystery in Ephesians being linked to the unity of the church, ecclesiology rather than the Christology of Colossians (1986: 149–51). Meade proposes that the author depicts Paul as a prisoner to identify the composition of the work with the last period of Paul's life, and thus as attempting "to secure the heritage of Paul after his passing" (1986: 153). In relation to the Pastorals, Meade notes that the author takes such pains to identify with Paul and his associates in order to preserve sound teaching. Paul is now *the* authority in this area. It is highly significant that both 1 and 2 Timothy present Paul as a foundational example of "orthodoxy" and "orthopraxis," uniquely using the word *hypotypōsis* (1 Tim 1:16; 2 Tim 1:13). In Phil 3:17 (and cf. 2 Thess 3:9) the historical Paul had asked the Philippian Christ-followers to become fellow-imitators of him and regard him as a *typos*. In 1 and 2 Timothy Paul becomes the *hypotypōsis*. The Pastorals have "typological intent" in which Paul becomes paradigmatic of discipleship (1986: 122–30). Paul's representatives, such as Timothy, have the task of not only reproducing Pauline doctrine but also his style of discipleship (1986: 128).

Yet there are problems with Meade's approach. In line with current scholarship, he considers that the totality of religious phenomena can be subsumed under the headings of teaching and ethics. But this is simply reductionist in relation to the reality of the socio-religious phenomena we have before us, in which experience and affective and evaluative states play significant roles. He also overlooks the function of memory in these works. We require a theoretical framework that brings into play all of these dimensions.

Margaret MacDonald (especially 1988 and 2000: 186–87) has applied to the picture of Paul in Colossians the ideas of sociologist Max Weber, who suggested that the death of a charismatic leader created a crisis of leadership in the movement that could threaten its very existence. To prevent this, those who assumed authority had to legitimate their position in terms of the authority once borne by the charismatic leader. She considers that something similar may be at work in Colossians. There may be something to this suggestion, but it leaves untouched the remarkable statement in the last verse: "Remember my fetters" (Col. 4:18). Let us see how social identity theory, especially when developed in the area of collective memory, offers a way forward in understanding Paul's imprisonment and the emphasis on remembering it.

Social Identity and Group Prototypes and Exemplars

Social identity theorists have shown that groups frequently link their identities to outstanding figures from the past who are dead but whose remembrance lives on among the members. These may either be *prototypes* (made up or imagined figures) or *exemplars* (real persons from history). The group will regard a figure from the past as a group prototype or exemplar if he or she represented the group identity to the maximum extent (Haslam 2001: 66). Winston Churchill and Charles de Gaulle are exemplars, respectively, for the British and the French. The group will often appeal to such a prototype or exemplar in difficult or ambiguous times to remind them of who they are or ought to be. Such a figure will endorse the value of belonging to the group and also, at times, provide a model of what to believe and how to act if one is to manifest the identity of the group. Among first century Judeans, Abraham fulfilled such a role (see Luke 3:8). The very different pictures Paul paints of Abraham in Galatians, on the one hand, and Romans on the other, shows how the memory of such a figure could be contested between and within groups (Esler 2006 and 2003: 171–94).

The authors of Colossians, Ephesians and 2 Timothy all present Paul as an exemplar of the Christ-movement, that is, as a real person characteristic of its identity. The author of each of these works wants his audience to regard Paul as someone who is maximally representative of what it means to be a Christ-follower in order to push them to adopt a particular view on certain issues pertinent to their present situation.

In all three texts "Paul" begins by introducing himself as an apostle of Jesus Christ. This brings him close to Christ and his gospel in a most intimate way. In Colossians "Paul" goes so far as to claim that by his sufferings he completes Christ's afflictions for the church. He strives on their behalf with God's energy (1:29–2:2). He states he is absent in body but present in spirit (2:5), thus vividly invoking the inter-personal communion central to the early Christ-movement (Esler 2005a: 148–70). The author of Colossians wants "Paul" to function as a personal presence for those to whom he writes.

In Ephesians the author establishes the exemplary nature of "Paul" by having his narrator include himself among those "who first hoped in Christ" (1:12); that the author is seeking to privilege this group is suggested by his using a word that appears here for the only time in the New Testament (*proēlpikotas* "who first hoped"). He assures his audience that he is suffering for their glory (3:13). He is in chains, an ambassador for the mystery of the gospel (6:20).

In 2 Timothy the author establishes explicit links between "Paul" and "Timothy" in relation to sharing in suffering and not being ashamed of the gospel (1:8 and 12). "Paul" endures everything for the sake of the elect (2:10). "Timothy" has observed everything about "Paul": his teaching, conduct, his aim in life, faith, patience, love, steadfastness, his persecutions and his sufferings, from all of which the Lord rescued him. Clearly, through his device of a letter to "Timothy" the author is proffering these aspects of Paul's experience as prototypical of the Christ-movement. "Paul" is on the point of death, but a crown of righteousness is laid up for him and, it is expressly stated, for all who (like Paul presumably) have loved the Lord's appearing (4:6–8).

Social Identity and Time
Early work by social identity theorists tended to focus upon a group at a particular moment, virtually frozen in time, usually in the present. Accordingly, their work so was not well suited to data such as this. More recently, however, the position has changed. In 1996 Susan Condor persuasively argued that we should not regard social groups as reified entities existing at a single point of micro-time, separate from the historical dimensions of life, but rather as ongoing processes, extending over macro-time. This emphasis is in line with how people experience themselves—not as radically decentred subjects limited to an ephemeral moment, but "as coherent beings-over-time" (1996: 302–3).

The relevance of this to Colossians, Ephesians and 2 Timothy is clear. The Christ-movement represented in these texts looks back—to the sinful condition of humanity before Jesus Christ (Col 1:12, 21; 3:7; Eph 2:11–12, 14), to his or God's saving acts (Col 1:12, 22, 27; 2:6, 10–15, 20; 3:1; Eph 1:3–8, 13, 19–23; 2:5–6, 13; 2 Tim 1:10; 2:8), to Paul's conversion (Col 1:25), the faith-producing effects of Paul's mission (Eph 3:2–3, 7–13; 2 Tim 1:8–14) and that of others (Col 1:5–8). It has a sense of the present—this current period when "Paul" is speaking to them. It also has a sense of the future—hope is an important characteristic of the Christ-movement (Col 1:5, 23, 24; Eph 1:18; 2:12; 4:4) and there is a recognition that there will be a time of wrath, divine judgment and vindication (Col 3:6, 25; Eph 2:7; 2 Tim 3:1). The followers of Christ plainly entertain a strong sense of temporal progression punctuated by significant conditions or events, for good or evil. There is a plan for the fullness of the ages (Eph 1:10).

In 1998 Marco Cinnirella developed this approach by introducing the notion of "possible selves," which refer to the beliefs held by an individual as to his or her self in the past and what it might become in the future, together with some estimate of the probability that different possible selves will be realized. He is particularly interested in expanding the boundaries of social identity theory so that it can address *past* social identities and assess how past, present and future are capable of being reworked to generate meaningful "stories" for both individuals and groups (1998: 243). On this approach, "Paul" who speaks, a figure from the past as far as the addressees of these works are concerned, offers a possible self for appropriation by members of the Christ-movement in the present. If, as seems quite likely, they are at risk of imprisonment, Paul "the prisoner" offers the exemplar of a possible self that reaches into the most difficult dimensions of their social identity. The audiences of the letters would have understood that they were part of an ongoing narrative that began with his evangelism in the past but continued with them in the here and now and also had a glorious future that beckoned.

2.4. *Integrating a Social Identity Approach to the Past and Collective Memory*

Outlining Collective Memory

In recent years I have found it useful to integrate such a social identity approach to the past with the notion of collective memory introduced between the First and Second World Wars by Maurice Halbwachs (1877–1945), a sociologist heavily influenced by Emile Durkheim (1858–1917).[8] The core of Halbwachs' position was that many of our memories are collective, that is, are derived from the groups to which we belong. "(I)t is in society," he wrote, "that people normally acquire their memories. It is also in society that they recall, recognize and localize their memories" (Halbwachs 1992: 38). His thesis was that memory was socially determined. Collective memory embraces a range of related phenomena, such as the situations in which memory is mobilized, how this happens and the contents of what is remembered (Billig 1990: 60). Collective remembering is central to the experience of any community or group. Halbwachs differed from Durkheim in

---

[8] I have considered Halbwachs' work at greater length in Esler 2005b. For recent work on collective memory, see Schwartz 1982 and 2000; Olick and Robbins 1998; Olick 2003. Kirk and Thatcher 2005 deals with collective memory and the early Christ-movement.

being interested in groups rather than society as a whole (so Coser 1980: 22). He also appreciated the role of individuals: "While the collective memory endures and draws strength from its base in a coherent body of people, it is individuals as group members who remember" (Halbwachs 1980: 48).

Halbwachs made a useful distinction between "autobiographical memory," by which he meant a memory of which the subject had had personal experience, and "historical memory," meaning a memory of events or persons known to the person not through personal experience but from the memory of others or through written records or commemorations, including of phenomena before a person was born. Halbwachs realistically insisted that one should not over-emphasise the distinction between autobiographical and historical memories, since they interpenetrated one another (Halbwachs 1980: 55–59). He regarded their interpenetration as "collective memory," meaning the zone of interaction between individual and personal remembrances and reference points from the memories of others or from historical records (1980: 59). Yet in spite of his recognition of this interpenetration, when Halbwachs claimed that such a "historical" memory "remains a borrowed memory, not my own" (1980: 51), he underestimated the extent to which a "historical memory" could impact on the sense of self, the identity, of the subject. I will return to this issue later.

Halbwachs was preoccupied with the activities of groups who were reconstructing their memories for present circumstances, typically by the invention of tradition.[9] Such a process is integrally linked with the maintenance or re-invention of the identities of such groups and hence with the social identities that the members derive from belonging to them. The integration of collective memory and social identity theory provides a fresh way to interpret the memorialisation of Paul and his imprisonment in Colossians, Ephesians and 2 Timothy. I will now briefly survey some of the possibilities.

Collective Memory and Social Identity
We have seen above how congenial the force and function of memory were to the authors of the three Pseudo-Pauline works and to their

---

[9] On this subject, see the useful collection of material and analysis in Hobsbawm and Ranger 1992. Also see Ben-Yehuda 1995 and Schwartz 2000. Fine 2001 covers the generation of tradition around villains and anti-heroes.

audiences. When we integrate social identity theory with the ideas on collective memory espoused by Halbwachs, we interpret the attribution of these works to Paul as an effort not only to mobilize memories of the great apostle current among the Christ-movement in the late first century, but also to augment, mould and re-direct those memories to serve the needs of the communities for which they were written in the present. Introducing social identity theory means recognizing the extent to which the primary need was to defend a particular view on the optimal identity of the Christ-movement entertained by the author of each of these works as he sought to win over those he envisaged being exposed to his viewpoint. It is probable that many, if not all, the addressees had no personal memory of Paul or of the people with whom he is described as interacting in these works; if any of them did, this would have been long ago. So the authors were not appealing to "autobiographical" memories in Halbwachs' sense. Instead, they were seeking to invent a body of tradition about Paul that would be taken over as "historical" memory by those who heard these letters read aloud, so that this material would fuse with their own personal memories to become part of the collective memory of those communities of the Christ-movement to which they belonged.

Problems with Halbwachs on Collective Memory
Yet there were certain lacunas in Halbwachs' position. Long ago F. C. Bartlett, in a perceptive and sympathetic interpretation of a sociologist by an experimental psychologist, astutely pointed to a revealing weakness in Halbwachs' approach. Whereas Halbwachs had been in the habit of speaking of the memory *of* a group, we could, in fact, only conceive of memories *in* a group. While Bartlett readily conceded that social direction and control of recall occurred *within* the group, it was speculation to suggest that a group itself possessed "a mental life over and above that of its individual members" (1932: 294–300, at 300).

As Paul Connerton has pointed out more recently (1989: 39), Halbwachs neglected the manner in which collective memories are passed on, communicated, from one generation to another. Connerton has correctly insisted that "to study the social formation of memory is to study those acts of transfer that make remembering in common possible." Halbwachs' failure to address the precise mechanisms by which memory is socially formed can be attributed to his Durkheimian legacy, where emphasis lay on the social rather than on the individual, that is, the cognitive dimensions to the processes of remembering.

This type of critique finds a responsive chord in Ilkka Pyysiäinen's critique of Durkheim and Geertz for proposing notions of society or a cultural system without attending to the manner in which religious ideas are actually acquired, represented and transmitted. For the latter avenue of enquiry, psychology, with its close attention to the cognitive processes of the individuals involved in such processes, is an indispensable aid (2001: ix–x). Pyysiäinen criticizes Geertz for the reason that he has no theory of learning or concept acquisition or therefore of cultural transmission (2001: 33). Geertz is guilty of "dogmatic anti-psychologism" (2001: 53). Similarly, Durkheim had been unable to account for the psychological origins of religion (2001: 74).

To meet the justifiable complaints of Bartlett and Connerton against Halbwachs and of Pyysiäinen against Durkheim and Geertz we need an explanation of how the memories are transmitted. Since this is a psychological issue, we are brought inevitably to cognitive science in the area of the psychology of memory. In taking this step, however, we should mention the view of Eviatar Zerubavel that much cognitive science has largely ignored the social dimension of cognition. He adds that a "truly comprehensive science of mind must also include a *sociology of thinking*," an intellectual enterprise he describes as "cognitive sociology" (1997: 5; emphasis original). Clearly we must not throw out the social when taking in the cognitive. Yet Zerubavel excepts from this tendency the recent work of "some developmental and social psychologists" and we will be concerned mainly with the findings of researchers such as these.

3. *Cognitive Science and Memory*

3.1. *Autobiographical Memory and Narrative*

In a now classic 1932 work the British psychologist F. C. Bartlett discussed experiments he had conducted on how information was passed from individual to individual using memory (1932: 118–85). An important result of his research was the rarity of literal recall of the stimulus meaning and the regularity with which it was not so much reproduced as constructed (1932: 205). Bartlett also found that his subjects transmitted folk tales with greater fidelity than any other material, such as descriptions of a scene or arguments (1932: 118–76, especially the summary at 171–76). He thought folk tales were transmitted more accurately because people possessed *schemas* (1932: 199–214). These constituted the underlying structures of masses of organised experience and around them those involved could reconstruct the specific details of a particular story. Each schema had its own "natural and essential time order" (1932: 205). Subsequent research by psychologists has elaborated the notion of the story schema to show that it consists of hierarchically organised frameworks beginning from the most general level, then branching out (in tree-like shape) into progressively more detailed possibilities. P. W. Thorndyke found in 1977 that stories with an underlying hierarchical structure were easier to understand and recall than stories without one. In addition, the higher up a detail was in a hierarchy, the more likely that it would be recalled. Recent work has discovered the operation of these hierarchically arranged narrative structures, now called "scripts" or "action scripts," in the *routine* events of everyday life, such as getting up, going out, going to a restaurant and so on.[10] These two areas of Bartlett's research—the extent to which memory is constructed and the mnemonic power of stories—are foundational for the discussion that follows.

During the last thirty years there has been considerable interest in the extent to which long-term memory can be broken up into subsystems. In 1972 E. Tulving distinguished semantic memory, referring to one's knowledge of the world and of language, from episodic memory, which referred to the recollection of personally experienced events. He further developed his understanding of episodic memory in 1983. Episodic memory consisted of the *focal elements* of an event, the salient happening, and the *setting*, meaning the time and place in which the event occurs, together with its significance for the rememberer (1983: 143).

Back in 1972 Tulving had also equated episodic memory with autobiographic memory and initially suggested that this reflected the operation of a psychologically and neurologically separable subsystem. The notion of autobiographical memory has attracted great attention, even if the idea that it was located in a separable neurological subsystem has been largely rejected. But what does autobiographical memory mean? At the most basic level "it refers to the recollection by subjects of their earlier lives" (Baddeley 1992: 13). One popular view is that it refers only to events or episodes in a person's past, where he or she directly

---

[10] See Schank and Abelson 1977; Bower, Black and Turner 1979; Zacks, Tversky, and Iyer 2001; and Mesoudi and Whiten 2004.

experienced their occurrence.[11] This is similar to Halbwachs' definition mentioned above. On this basis, to remember an encounter one had with a homeless person in London would constitute an autobiographical memory, whereas merely to remember that there were homeless people in London would not (Baddeley 1992: 20).

But a somewhat different approach entails defining autobiographical memory more widely as the memory for information that is related to the self. Craig Barclay and Thomas Smith have espoused this position.[12] The critical point here (although I do not consider this is sufficiently recognised among psychologists) is that our sense of self can be promoted not only by memories dependent on episodes and events in our own lives, but by what we have learned as we grow up of things which happened long before we were born or during our lifetimes but not directly experienced by us. As Eviatar Zerubavel has observed: "Being social presupposes the ability to experience things that happened to the groups to which we belong long before we joined them as if they were part of our personal past" (2003: 3).

Psychologist S. F. Larsen is alive to the importance of this type of recollection. He distinguishes these memories from autobiographical ones, but still finds an important place for them. He has developed Tulving's notion of the context of an event that constitutes an episodic memory by usefully distinguishing the external or environmental context of the event (= "setting") and the internal, cognitive environment of the person remembering, which is tied to the personal significance of the situation for him or her. Larsen has noted that episodic memory embraces autobiographical memories of this sort but also occasions on which we remember texts or other symbolic representations that describe something or tell some story in which we were not personally involved. Larsen calls these phenomena "narratives," understood in a very broad sense (1992: 60–61). Although the subject was not perceptually present at and involved in the core of such an event, the context of the event is very similar to directly experienced events, since he or she was present to receive the message at a particular place and time as a source relayed it to him or her. "It is thus a personal context and the memory conforms to the definition of episodic memories" (1992: 61).

---

[11] So William James in 1890; cited by Tulving 1983: 39, and Brewer 1986: 34.
[12] Barclay and Smith 1992: 80; although they cite Brewer (1986: 26) for this idea.

Yet of critical importance is an observation that Larsen makes but does not develop:

> The separation of autobiographical from narrative memories also seems to be everyday practice. Typically, what one has read, heard, or watched is not regarded as part of an individual's autobiography, *except if it has been the occasion of a significant personal experience... or has caused a change in the person's life so that the core of the event has become personal* (e.g. a religious conversion caused by reading). (Larsen 1992: 62.)

The exception, which I have italicised, is of critical importance, for here Larsen has recognised that sometimes a "narrative" type of memory may acquire as critical a significance for a person's sense of self as an autobiographical memory. To revert to an illustration above, sometimes a powerfully spoken or written description of someone else's meeting with one of London's homeless may have an impact on one similar to a personal encounter. On a broader scale, citizens of the United States tie their senses of self to memories of the War of Independence, as do Australians to the Gallipoli campaign of 1915.[13] In relation to the religious phenomena mentioned by Larsen, moreover, it is clear that learning something of this sort could take the form of a development or deepening of someone's religious life in addition to the more dramatic transformation represented by a conversion.

3.2. *Narrative and the Memorialisation of Paul's Imprisonment*

These cognitive science perspectives enable us to focus our interpretation of the motif of Paul's imprisonment in Colossians, Ephesians and 2 Timothy in new ways. Of critical importance is that the authors of these three works have all sought to evoke a *narrative* concerning Paul as a means to convey information and argument to their chosen audiences so that it would lodge in their memories. It is not a complete narrative, admittedly, but the outlines are clear. Simply attributing these works to Paul would have linked them to this great figure of the past, but the authors go further than this. Their narratives include occasional references to Paul's selection as an apostle, his missionary work and his sufferings but, above all, to his final imprisonment. The focus is on the last stage in the life of Paul on earth, the imprisonment that preceded

---

[13] See Kapferer 1988 for a discussion of the role of Anzac day (25th April) in Australian culture.

his death. All of this was a way of making the message that the authors wished to convey highly memorable.

The results from psychological research mentioned above indicate the capacity of story and narrative to be retained in the memory over other forms of information, even though our tendency to construct rather than just to recall when we remember is also a feature of remembering narrative. Underlying many narratives is a schema that has its own characteristic temporal progression. For the members of the early Christ-movement the time order for someone like Paul was imprisonment, trial, torture, death and then vindication. These three works contain the first two features, with the remaining three supplied by the memories and faith of their addressees.

Some of these addressees may have known Paul; most of them probably did not. This means that the elements of these narratives of Paul the prisoner were not part of their "autobiographical" memory in the narrow sense of events with which they were personally familiar. But by being promulgated to them through hearing these texts read aloud the narrative became an "autobiographical" memory in the broader sense of information related to one's self. The narrative also became an "episodic" memory in accordance with S. F. Larsen's suggestion of memories of stories (or other symbolic representations) of events in which we were not personally involved but which are tied to the personal context of the person remembering and have a particular significance for him or her. The narrative of Paul's imprisonment had the potential to become an occasion of significant personal experience and to cause a change in the life of the hearer/rememberer. The precise aspect of the context of the audience that makes this latter proposal highly likely is the incidence of harassment, persecution, imprisonment, trials and execution that members of the Christ-movement were experiencing. Paul was an exemplar of such suffering and this meant that the narrative of his imprisonment spoke directly to this aspect of their group identity.

So much for the effect of this narrative. Yet now we must probe more deeply into the social setting and processes in which narrative memories of this sort are constructed and transmitted.

3.3. *The Social Construction of Autobiographical Memory*

On the view preferred here that Colossians, Ephesians and 2 Timothy are pseudonymous, their authors have chosen to relate events and speak of figures—real or fictional—from the fairly recent past of the Christ-movement that relate to an imprisoned Paul. Cognitive psychology provides an interesting approach to answering why they have done this.

Basic Principles

To recount past experiences is an important part of social interaction: in spontaneous conversations among families, for example, past events can arise as often as five to seven times an hour (Fivush, Haden and Reese 1995: 341). Such conversations can relate either to experiences that some of those present did not share, or to those that were experienced by everyone present, with narrative being the form in which either type is likely to be expressed. In the former case, the element of information transfer might dominate, while in the latter—joint remembering or reminiscing—the focus is more upon creating interpersonal bonds that depend on a shared history:

> In the process of recounting, interpreting, and evaluating our experiences together, we are creating a shared understanding and representation of our world and the ways in which our lives are intertwined. (Fivush, Haden and Reese 1995: 341.)

This brings us to the helpful formulation of W. Hirst and D. Manier, who suggest that remembering is an act of communication in a particular context (1995: 288):

> Autobiographical memories are expressed in and shaped by conversations. Principles of communication, such as the importance of context and meaning, affect both how and what we remember, both to ourselves and others.

Application to Colossians, Ephesians and 2 Timothy

The production of the documents we know as Colossians, Ephesians and 2 Timothy by unknown authors in the late first century C.E. for other Christ-followers that recount/construct exemplary activities and outlook of an imprisoned Paul from the past represents a form of social interaction within the Christ-movement not dissimilar to that which occurs regularly within families. The occasion of the original oral publication of these texts was not, however, joint remembering or reminiscing—since we are proceeding on the basis that the authorship and many of the details are fictive—but rather an occasion on which the authors were seeking to transfer information to the their audiences, where it would become part of the abiding memories they retained as members of the movement. It is likely that the content of these writings was discussed at meetings of the Christ-movement. Clearly, the aim of the authors was to have those who encountered these documents come to share in their own understanding and representation of the realities of being members of a group characterised by faith in Christ. The material concerning Paul was of such moment that it is likely to have deeply affected how the Christ-followers exposed to it remembered the past and interpreted their experience and identity in the present. These memories became part of their own shared sense of self, or "autobiographical" in the wider sense discussed above.

3.4. *The Mechanism of Memory Transmission*

Basic Principles

Joint remembering assumes a number of individuals whose own memory systems are engaged during the period of the interaction. This brings us into the critical question of how autobiographical memories (in the broad sense of those that bear upon an individual's sense of self) are produced. It is necessary to explore the cognitive-psychological dimensions of this process, to assess the precise mechanisms involved in how a group installs its history, values and vision on the minds and emotions of individual members. To explore this area I will introduce insights concerning parent-child interactions derived from developmental psychology and then apply them to the three texts.

An important theorist here is L. S. Vygotsky (1896–1934), a psychologist in post-revolutionary Russia who, especially during his most productive years at the Institute of Psychology in Moscow (1924–1934), developed what has become an influential approach to cognitive development, particularly the relationship between language and thinking. Vygotsky stressed the roles of historical, social and cultural factors in cognition and maintained that language was the most important symbolic tool provided by society.[14] He argued that the higher cognitive functions developed through social interaction rather than solely as a product of internally generated cognitive change (Fivush and Reese 1992: 116). Note the emphasis here is on cognitive function. Unlike

---

[14] See his *Thought and Language* (1934), a classic text in psycholinguistics, and the important collection of his writings edited by Michael Cole et al. in 1978. For a discussion, see Wertsch 1985.

Halbwachs (1992), who came close to arguing that the totality of the content of children's autobiographical memories are constructed in linguistic interaction, Vygotsky proposed that the organizational and communicative functions of language are initially demonstrated to children and learned by them in social interaction. In time, these skills are internalized, thus becoming the intrapsychological competences of individuals (Fivush, Haden and Reese 1995: 344). For Vygotsky, "internalization begins in social speech acts between cultural novices and more knowledgeable others" (Barclay 1995: 101).

R. Fivush, E. Reese and C. Haden have persuasively argued that the key to the development of cognition in this way is the acquisition by children from their parents of a sense of narrative form which allows them to organise their autobiographical memories into a life story, a coherent personal history. In other words, young children learn "the culturally available narrative forms for recounting and for representing past experiences in early adult-child conversations" (Fivush and Reese 1992: 115; also see Fivush, Haden and Reese 1995). From when they first begin conversing with adults, at about twenty months, children gradually acquire from their parents (or carers) the ability to understand and then to create narrative structures conventional in their culture (and, inevitably, some narrative content). We are not speaking here of the ability simply to recall past experiences (which may be present as early as 16–18 months), but with "culturally canonical narratives." These encompass a chronological sequence of events, contextual information (how these events connect with other significant people and events) and evaluative information (how they convey personal meaning or significance; Fivush and Reese 1992: 116–17). The evidence suggests that different parenting narrative styles lead to differences in individuals' internally represented life stories (1992: 118–24).

Application to Colossians, Ephesians and 2 Timothy
While Vygotsky was concerned with how children acquired higher cognitive functions (and some but not all memory content) through interaction with adults, his position that "internalization begins in social speech acts between cultural novices and more knowledgeable others" plainly has a wider application. The authors of Colossians, Ephesians and 2 Timothy are "the more knowledgeable others" and their addressees the "cultural novices"—novices at least to the extent that they did not necessarily subscribe to the views expressed in the three works prior to hearing them. Although these Christ-followers had already developed

cognitive skills in childhood, the pseudonymous authors have composed the scripts to be embodied in the social speech acts of the movement that will hopefully lead to their audiences internalising the values and outlooks expressed in them.

The fact that the authors have chosen to adumbrate a narrative of Paul as prisoner reflects the sense of narrative form that they no doubt acquired from their parents and to which they now revert in the interests of pressing home their message. Just as human beings learn at an early age to organise their memories into a life story, a coherent personal history, so too do our three authors recall or construct an account of Paul's life that focuses on his final imprisonment and his endurance of suffering, most probably because these phenomena bear directly upon their lives and the difficulties their faith was capable of causing them. In a manner similar to that of parents with the children, the authors have created a "culturally canonical narrative" concerning the imprisoned Paul that encompasses a series of events (some express, others implied), contextual information (meaning how these events relate to the lives of others) and evaluative information (meaning how these events convey personal meaning or significance).

3.5. *Autobiographical Narratives and Groups*

Yet while this capacity to generate narrative is an important area of cognition, it is best to regard it as one form of causal thinking among many, not the only form. Storytelling is a pervasive mode of human thinking, and is central to the argument of this essay, but it is not the only mode, as Fitzgerald has urged (1992: 101–2). Even in Colossians, Ephesians and 2 Timothy meaning is conveyed by discursive argument as well as narrative form. Having lodged this caveat, however, we may move on, beyond the parent-child narrative, to autobiographical narratives shaped within specific groups. Here we will utilise research conducted by J. Bruner and C. F. Feldman into how the members of three theatre groups in New York related their personal experiences in each group.

Basic Principles

Bruner and Feldman have assimilated Bartlett's key insight that memory is constructed not simply "retrieved," and this applies to autobiography in narrative form (1995: 291). In the very act of writing our autobiographies we are actively transforming ourselves: "the self who constructs the past is changed by the outcome" of his or her own construction. Such a self is also working in relation to a self "schema," but one different from all others in that it possesses reflexivity. "For the self schema," they observe, "is, in a sense, the (interpretive) person as constituted by (prior, schematized) interpretations of life events" (1995: 292).

Yet someone composing an autobiographical narrative with the intention that it be made public must employ narrative properties such as genre and plot type that are widely shared in that setting, so that others may comprehend the meaning intended by the narrator (1995: 293). At times it will be necessary to share one's autobiography "with the groups one interacts with on a face-to-face basis. The story of a life, when all is said and done, must be shared with one's 'miniculture,' with the proximal group(s) on which one's cultural existence depends" (1995: 294). Bruner and Feldman discovered that close connections between accounts given by individual members of the three New York theatre groups and the identities of the groups. In other words: "A self account is used for interpreting shared events of its group members' lives, and contributes to constituting each of them as a social self *within the group*" (1995: 294; emphasis original). This conclusion reached by researchers within the field of cognitive psychology is clearly cognate with the approach to social identity developed in the social psychology of Henri Tajfel and others that we mentioned above.

Application to Colossians, Ephesians and 2 Timothy
We know nothing about the individuals who wrote these three works or what, if any, connection they had with Paul or the persons or events they mention. The research of Bruner and Feldman suggests, however, that whoever they were they must have transformed themselves in the process of constructing the past. Their accounts of Paul must have been or become autobiographical for them in the broad sense used above. Writing of Paul, the exemplary Christ-follower, they were also writing of themselves. Evoking the image of his identity linked to suffering and imprisonment, they were also evoking theirs. Plainly, moreover, they were not just writing for themselves but for communities of Christ-followers in the Mediterranean world of the late first century C.E. Their intention to publish their compositions led them to adopt a particular genre, that of the letter, to ensure that others got their point. This genre was not only widely practised and recognised in everyday human interactions but it had been the one which Paul himself had employed to reach out to communities of Christ-followers across the region, some of which he

had founded and some he had never even visited. These authors were interpreting significant events in the past of their movement relating to Paul as a way of interpreting and solidifying the present identity of group members. They were thus helping to constitute each individual Christ-followers as a social self within the group.

4. *Conclusion*

What have we learned from this exercise? Highlighting issues of identity and memory allows us to situate the texts in new frameworks of meaning that are quite different from the topics traditionally pursued by scholars. This approach also entails subjecting the major concepts employed in interpretation to a degree of theoretical explication which is unusual in existing literature, where critics tend to employ particular notions without subjecting them to critical scrutiny. In addition, the fact that the social-scientific concepts employed are drawn from modern research into issues of pressing social interest and importance necessarily means that the results of biblical interpretation using them are readily susceptible to application to contemporary issues and problems.

A central theme has been the way in which those wishing to propel a group in a particular direction re-construct group memories of one of its great figures from the past. The figure of an imprisoned Paul probably relates to a similar experience of suffering and imprisonment being experienced by some Christ-followers contemporary with the production of these documents.

Since I have considered three texts, I have been necessarily general in my coverage. The same approach could be applied more intensively to any one of these texts to bring out the distinctive messages for group identity they convey.

In the present essay, while I have gone beyond group-oriented social-scientific approaches to utilise cognitive-scientific ideas on cultural transmission through memory, I have only been able to scratch the surface of the psychological literature available. Nevertheless, it is clear that these three texts, jointly and severally, are ripe with promise as evidence for the processes by which memories are constructed and transmitted in the interests of creating and maintaining group identity. In remembering Paul's fetters, we are forced to move beyond the broad social function of this motif and to interrogate the manner in which three authors in the Christ-movement of the late first century

C.E. formulated recollections of the apostle and transmitted them to individual Christ-members of their period so that they might become the bearers of formative memory.

The view taken by most critics that Colossians, Ephesians and (almost universally) the Pastorals are non-Pauline, is often accompanied by diminished attention to these texts by interpreters, especially the Pastorals.[15] It is submitted that the broad approach chartered in this essay strengthens the case for bringing these works much more into the centre of scholarly consideration.

REFERENCES

Baddeley, Alan. 1992. "What is Autobiographical Memory?" In *Theoretical Perspectives on Autobiographical Memory*, edited by Martin A. Conway et al., 13–29. Nato Advanced Science Institute Series. Dordrecht: Kluwer Academic publishers.
Barclay, Craig R. 1995. "Autobiographical Remembering: Narrative Constraints on Objectified Selves." In *Remembering Our Past: Studies in Autobiographical Memory*, edited by David C. Rubin, 94–125. Cambridge: Cambridge University Press.
Barclay, Craig R., and Thomas S. Smith. 1992. "Autobiographical Remembering: Creating Personal Culture." In *Theoretical Perspectives on Autobiographical Memory*, edited by Martin A. Conway et al., 75–97. Nato Advanced Science Institute Series. Dordrecht: Kluwer Academic publishers.
Bartlett, Frederic C. 1932. *Remembering: A Study in Experimental and Social Psychology*. Cambridge: Cambridge University Press.
Bauckham, Richard. 1988. "The Pseudo-Apostolic Letters." *Journal of Biblical Literature* 107: 469–94.
———. 1992. "The Martyrdom of Peter in Early Christian Literature." *Aufstieg und Niedergang der römischen Welt: Geschichte und Kultur Roms im Spiegel der neueren Forschung* 2.26.1: 539–95.
Ben-Yehuda, Nachman. 1995. *The Masada Myth: Collective Memory and Mythmaking in Israel*. Madison, Wisc.: University of Wisconsin Press.
Billig, Michael. 1990. "Collective Memory, Ideology and the British Royal Family." In *Collective Remembering*, edited by David Middleton and Derek Edwards, 60–80. London: Sage Publications.
Boer, Martinus C. de. 1980. "Images of Paul in the Post-Apostolic Period." *Catholic Biblical Quarterly* 42: 359–80.
Bower, Gordon H., John B. Black, and Terrence J. Turner. 1979. "Scripts in Memory for Text." *Cognitive Psychology* 11: 177–220.
Boyer, Pascal. 2001. *Religion Explained: The Evolutionary Origins of Religious Thought*. New York: Basic Books.
Brewer, William F. 1986. "What is Autobiographical Memory?" In *Autobiographical Memory*, edited by David C. Rubin, 25–49. Cambridge: Cambridge University Press.
Bruner, Jerome, and Carol Fleisher Feldman. 1995. "Group Narrative as Cultural Context of Autobiography." In *Remembering Our Past: Studies in Autobiographical Memory*, edited by David C. Rubin, 291–317. Cambridge: Cambridge University Press.

---

[15] So, correctly, Johnson 1996: 4.

Cinnirella, Marco. 1998. "Exploring Temporal Aspects of Social Identity: The Concept of Possible Social Identities." *European Journal of Social Psychology* 28: 227–48.

Cole, Michael et al., eds. 1978. Lev Semenovich Vygotsgy, *Mind in Society: The Development of High Psychological Processes*. Cambridge, Mass.: Harvard University Press.

Condor, Susan. 1996. "Social Identity and Time." In *Social Groups and Identities: Developing the Legacy of Henri Tajfel*, edited by Peter Robinson, 285–315. Oxford: Butterworth Heinemann.

Connerton, Paul 1989. *How Societies Remember.* Themes in the Social Sciences. Cambridge: Cambridge University Press.

Coser, Lewis A. 1980. "Introduction." In Maurice Halbwachs, *On Collective Memory*, edited, translated with an introduction by Lewis A. Coser, 1–34. The Heritage of Sociology. Chicago, Ill.: The University of Chicago Press.

Dunn, James D. G. 1996. *The Epistles to the Colossians and to Philemon: A Commentary on the Greek Text.* Grand Rapids, Mich.: Eerdmans.

Esler, Philip F. 1998. *Galatians.* London: Routledge.

———. 2003. *Conflict and Identity in Romans: The Social Setting of Paul's letter.* Minneapolis, Minn.: Fortress.

———. 2005a. *New Testament Theology: Communion and Community.* Minneapolis, Minn.: Fortress.

———. 2005b. "Collective Memory and Hebrews 11: Outlining a New Investigative Framework." In *Memory, Tradition, and Text: Uses of the Past in Early Christianity*, edited by Alan Kirk and Tom Thatcher, 151–71. Semeia Studies, 52. Atlanta, Ga.: Society of Biblical Literature.

———. 2006. "Paul's Contestation of Israel's (Ethnic) Memory of Abraham in Galatians 3." *Biblical Theology Bulletin* 36: 23–34.

Fine, Gary Alan. 2001. *Difficult Reputations: Collective Memories of the Evil, the Inept, and Controversial.* Chicago, Ill.: University of Chicago Press.

Fitzgerald, Joseph M. 1992. "Autobiographical Memory and Conceptualizations of the Self." In *Theoretical Perspectives on Autobiographical Memory*, edited by Martin A. Conway et al., 99–114. Nato Advanced Science Institute Series. Dordrecht: Kluwer Academic Publishers.

Fivush, Robyn, and Elaine Reese. 1992. "The Social Construction of Autobiographical Memory." In *Theoretical Perspectives on Autobiographical Memory*, edited by Martin A. Conway et al., 115–32. Nato Advanced Science Institute Series. Dordrecht: Kluwer Academic Publishers.

Fivush, Robyn, Catherine Haden, and Elaine Reese. 1995. "Remembering, Recounting, and Reminiscing: The Development of Autobiographical Memory in Social Context." In *Remembering Our Past: Studies in Autobiographical Memory*, edited by David C. Rubin, 341–59. Cambridge: Cambridge University Press.

Goulder, Michael. 2004. "Did Peter Ever Go to Rome?" *Scottish Journal of Theology* 57: 377–96.

Guarducci, Margherita. 1984. *Pietro in Vaticano*. Rome: Istituto Poligrafico e Zecca dello Stato.

———. 1989. *La Tomba di San Pietro: Una Straordinaria Vicenda*. Milan: Rusoni.

Halbwachs, Maurice. 1980. *The Collective Memory.* ET of the 1950 French original *La Mémoire Collective* by Francis J. Ditter Jr. and Vida Yazdi Ditter, with an introduction by Mary Douglas. New York: Harper Colophon Books.

———. 1992. *On Collective Memory*. Edited, translated with an introduction by Lewis A. Coser. The Heritage of Sociology. Chicago: The University of Chicago Press. (This is a translation of large parts of *Les Cadres Sociaux de la Mémoire* [1925] and the concluding chapter of *La Topographie Légendaire des Évangiles en Terre Saint. Étude de Mémoire Collective* [1941]).

Hanson, Anthony Tyrrell. 1982. *The Pastoral Epistles.* The New Century Bible Commentary. Grand Rapids, Mich.: Eerdmans.

Haslam, S. Alexander. 2001 *Psychology in Organizations: The Social Identity Approach*. London: Sage Publications.
Hirst, William, and David Manier. 1995. "Remembering as Communication: A Family Recounts Its Past." In *Remembering Our Past: Studies in Autobiographical Memory*, edited by David C. Rubin, 271–90. Cambridge: Cambridge University Press.
Hobsbawm, Eric, and Terence Ranger, eds. 1992. *The Invention of Tradition*. Cambridge: Cambridge University Press.
Johnson, Luke Timothy. 1996. *Letters to Paul's Delegates: 1 Timothy, 2 Timothy, Titus*. Valley Forge, Pa.: Trinity Press International.
Kapferer, Bruce. 1988. *Legends of People, Myths of State: Violence, Intolerance, and Political Culture in Sri Lanka and Australia*. Washington, D.C.: Smithsonian Institute.
Kirk, Alan, and Tom Thatcher, eds. 2005. *Memory, Tradition, and Text: Uses of the Past in Early Christianity*. Semeia Studies, 52. Atlanta, Ga.: Society of Biblical Literature.
Larsen, Steen F. 1992. "Personal Context in Autobiographical and Narrative Memories." In *Theoretical Perspectives on Autobiographical Memory*, edited by Martin A. Conway et al., 53–71. Nato Advanced Science Institute Series. Dordrecht: Kluwer Academic publishers.
Lincoln, Andrew T. 1990. *Ephesians*. Word Biblical Commentary, 42. Dallas, Tex.: Word Books.
MacDonald, Margaret Y. 1988. *The Pauline Churches: A Socio-historical Study of Institutionalization in the Pauline and Deutero-Pauline Writings*. Society for New Testament Studies Monograph Series, 60. Cambridge: Cambridge University Press.
———. 2000. *Colossians and Ephesians*. Sacra Pagina, Volume 17. Collegeville, Minn.: The Liturgical Press.
Meade, David G. 1986. *Pseudonymity and Canon: An Investigation into the Relationship of Authorship and Authority in Jewish and Earliest Christian Tradition*. Wissenschaftliche Untersuchungen zum Neuen Testament, 39. Tübingen: J. C. B. Mohr (Paul Siebeck).
Mesoudi, Alex, and Andrew Whiten. 2004. "The Hierarchical Transformation of Event Knowledge in Human Cultural Transmission." *Journal of Cognition and Culture* 4: 1–24.
Olick, Jeffrey K., ed. 2003. *States of Memory: Continuities, Conflicts, and Transformations in National Retrospection*. Durham, N.C.: Duke University Press.
Olick, Jeffrey K., and Joyce Robbins. 1998. "Social Memory Studies: From 'Collective Memory' to the Historical Sociology of Mnemonic Practices." *Annual Review of Sociology* 24: 105–40 (cited here in the electronic version with different pagination).
Pyysiäinen, Ilkka. 2001. *How Religion Works: Towards a New Cognitive Science of Religion*. Leiden: Brill.
———. 2004. *Magic, Miracles and Religion: A Scientist's Perspective*. Walnut Creek, Calif.: AltaMira.
Schank, Roger C., and Robert P. Abelson. 1977. *Scripts, Plans, Goals and Understanding: An Inquiry into Human Knowledge Structures*. Oxford: Lawrence Erlbaum.
Schwartz, Barry. 1982. "The Social Context of Commemoration: A Study in Collective Memory." *Social Forces* 61: 374–402.
———. 2000. *Abraham Lincoln and the Forge of Memory*. Chicago, Ill.: University of Chicago Press.
Tajfel, Henri, ed. 1978. *Differentiation between Social Groups: Studies in the Social Psychology of Intergroup Relations*. London: Academic Press.
———. 1981. *Human Groups and Social Categories: Studies in Social Psychology*. Cambridge: Cambridge University Press.
Tajfel, Henri, and John C. Turner. 1979. "An Integrative Theory of Intergroup Conflict." In *The Social Psychology of Intergroup Relations*, edited by William G. Austin and Stephen Worchel, 33–47. Monterey, Calif.: Brooks-Cole.
Thorndyke, Perry W. 1977. "Cognitive Structures in Comprehension and Memory of Narrative Discourse." *Cognitive Psychology* 9: 77–110.

Toynbee, Jocelyn, and John Ward Perkins. 1956. *The Shrine of St. Peter and the Vatican Excavations*. London, New York and Toronto: Longmans, Green and Co.
Tulving, Endel. 1972. "Episodic and Semantic Memory." In *Organization of Memory*, edited by Endel Tulving and Wayne Donaldson, 381–403. New York: Academic Press.
——. 1983. *Elements of Episodic Memory*. Oxford: Oxford University Press.
Tulving, Endel, and Wayne Donaldson. 1972. *Organization of Memory*. New York: Academic Press.
Vygotsky, Lev Semenovich. 1978. *Mind in Society: The Development of High Psychological Processes*, edited by Michael Cole et al. Cambridge, Mass.: Harvard University Press.
Wertsch, James. 1985. *Vygotsky and the Social Formation of Mind*. Cambridge, Mass.: Harvard University Press.
Zacks, Jeffrey M., Barbara Tversky, and Gowri Iyer. 2001. "Perceiving, Remembering, and Communicating Structure in Events." *Psychological Bulletin* 127: 3–21.
Zerubavel, Eviatar. 1997. *Social Mindscapes: An Invitation to Cognitive Sociology*. Cambridge, Mass.: Harvard University Press.
——. 2003. *Time Maps: Collective Memory and the Social Shape of the Past*. Chicago: The University of Chicago Press.

SOCIAL IDENTITIES AND GROUP PHENOMENA IN SECOND TEMPLE JUDAISM

Raimo Hakola

One of the most dramatic changes in the 20th century studies of Second Temple Judaism and early Christianity started with the discovery of the Dead Sea Scrolls in 1947. The Scrolls contained many beliefs that had formerly been regarded as alien to Judaism and characteristic of Hellenistic or gnostic thinking. The gradual publication of the Scrolls has made evident that there was not just one way of being a Jew, but that Judaism was divided into many different groups having singular beliefs of their own. The Scrolls have challenged the traditional view, according to which the Pharisees were the most dominant Jewish group capable of defining the nature and limits of Judaism. This traditional portrayal of the Pharisees is not well in line with the picture derived from the Dead Sea Scrolls. However, there are certainly some Scrolls (4QMMT) or passages in the Scrolls where scholars have found allusions to Pharisaic legal agenda (see below). These alleged references to the Pharisees, however, are far too scattered to be used as evidence for the supreme position of the Pharisees in Second Temple Jewish society. The Pharisees in the Scrolls are not so much the leading force in society but a rival religious group representing legal positions that, at least at times, conflicted with the positions taken by the Qumran group.

The traditional portrayal of the Pharisees has been also challenged by the recent historical research on early rabbinic sources. Scholars formerly saw a very close connection between the pre-70 C.E. Pharisees and the post-70 rabbinic movement. It was claimed that the emergence of the rabbinic movement as the leading force in Judaism after the destruction of the Jerusalem temple was based on the authority and influence of the Pharisees in Second Temple Jewish society. In recent decades, however, many scholars have described the early rabbinic movement as a relatively powerless group (Hakola 2005: 55–65). This reappraisal of the early rabbinic movement has caused many scholars to also rethink the place of the Pharisees in pre-70 society. As James Charlesworth (1990: 37) says: "There was not one ruling, all-powerful group in Early Judaism; many groups claimed to possess the normative interpretation of the Torah....We should not think in terms of a monolithic first-century Palestinian Judaism."

1. *Common Judaism vs. Many Judaisms*

In current scholarship, there are two different ways of describing Second Temple Judaism where no particular group had dominion over other groups. E. P. Sanders (1992: 48) has used the term "common Judaism" to describe what the priests and the people in Palestine agreed on. This common Judaism was not defined by any particular group but "was based on internal assent and was 'normative' only to the degree that it was backed up by common opinion." Sanders allows many differences within common Judaism but claims that even such extreme groups as the Dead Sea Sect shared in "covenantal nomism," which Sanders describes as "the common-denominator theology" characterizing Judaism in the Graeco-Roman period (1992: iv, 377).

Jacob Neusner has much criticized Sanders' reconstruction of common Judaism.[1] According to Neusner (2000: 15), Sanders presupposes that "anything any Jew thought has to have been in the mind of all the other Jews." Neusner takes this as a harmonistic description of Judaism because, for Sanders, "all the Jews thought one and the same thing, and what they all thought was this religion, Judaism." Neusner claims that Sanders is unable to tell how Philo would have understood the Dead Sea Scrolls, the authors of apocalyptic writings, or Mishnah. Neusner (1981: 8) himself is quite specific that groups behind different types of Jewish literature "would not have understood one another, let alone accepted one another as part of the same social group and cultic community." Individuals like the Teacher of Righteousness, Aqiba, Josephus, or Bar Kokhba "would scarcely have understood one another, let alone have known they all evidenced the same *-ism*" (1981: 22). To avoid harmonistic tendencies, Neusner himself has proposed that, instead of speaking of Judaism in the singular, we should use the plural "Judaisms" to appreciate the diversity evident in different sources. Neusner (2001: 6) originally promulgated this proposition because it "underscored the autonomy of a coherent body of data and sidestepped

---

[1] For a perceptive response to Neusner, see Luomanen 2002: 114–19.

the problem of how to define a single 'Judaism' out of all the diverse data deemed to attest to that one Judaism."[2]

I want to deal with a part of the problem sketched above and ask how different Jewish groups perceived other Jews who did not share their convictions. In his emphasis on the diversity of ancient Judaism, Neusner maintains that various groups distinguished themselves from each other to the extent that they would not have seen much in common between themselves and other Jews. Sanders (1990: 327–28) has claimed that this is "evidently untrue" as various debates about the expected topics of common Judaism indicate. These debates are possible only because different groups, despite all the antagonism between them, shared a common background. Such groups as the Qumran community, the Sadducees or the Pharisees should be understood as Jewish sub-groups inside common Judaism; the concerns of these sub-groups could never be "completely different from the topics at issue in the larger group" (2000: 9–10). Sanders is here backed up by Albert Baumgarten who has defined different Jewish sects in the Second Temple period as "variations on the same theme;" despite differences among these sects, there is also a "fundamental similarity of different groups" in that they present "competing answers to the same sets of questions raised by the circumstances of their era" (Baumgarten 1997: 55–58).

In this essay, I propose that the research on the diverse Second Temple Judaism could greatly benefit if we take into account social-psychological theories connected to group and intergroup processes. I draw upon the so-called "social identity perspective" that comprises social identity theory and closely related self-categorization theory. This perspective helps to explain some cognitive and motivational processes that may lie in the background of our extant sources. I try to develop a valid theoretical framework which makes it possible to appreciate

---

[2] Neusner is not alone in urging that we should speak of each religion in plural to appreciate diverse manifestations of religious practice and experience. Jonathan Z. Smith (2004: 22–23) has opposed what he calls an "essentialist" definition of religion and argued that each religion in itself is a plurality which means that we should speak of Christianities, Judaisms and Hinduisms as plural entities. As Karel van der Toorn (2005: 584–87) has noted, the use of such plurals presupposes a common denominator which, if not found in the "essence" of different religions, must "consist in the genetic connections between divergent manifestations of Christianity, Judaism, and so on." Van der Toorn also perceptively adds that "the use of the singular does not prevent one from acknowledging the diversity within or the 'internal pluralism' of a particular religion."

both the diversity reflected in various sources and the suppressed sense of similarity that underlies, as I claim in agreement with Sanders and Baumgarten, even the most extreme claims for distinctiveness.

2. *The Social Identity Perspective on Group Formation*

Social identity theory was first developed by social psychologist Henri Tajfel and his colleagues in Great Britain in the late 1960s and early 1970s.[3] One of the key ideas behind the theory was formulated by Tajfel as the "minimal group paradigm" (Tajfel 1981: 233–38, 268–76; Tajfel and Turner 1979: 38–40). This paradigm seeks to discover necessary and sufficient reasons for the emergence of intergroup conflict. Realistic conflict theory had earlier maintained that intergroup conflicts arise if groups are in competition with each other for limited resources. In a series of experiments, Tajfel and his colleagues found out that, even in minimal groups where there is neither conflict of interest nor previously existing hostility, people tend to favor ingroup members over outgroup members. This means that it is not incompatible group interests that provoke intergroup discrimination but "the mere perception of belonging to two distinct groups—that is, social categorization *per se*—is sufficient to trigger intergroup discrimination favoring the ingroup" (Tajfel and Turner 1979: 38). The need for social differentiation between groups "is fulfilled through the creation of intergroup differences when such differences do not in fact exist, or the attribution of value to, and the enhancement of, whatever differences that do exist" (Tajfel 1981: 276).

The findings connected to minimal group studies resulted in the formulation of the concept of social identity which is understood as "that part of an individual's self-concept which derives from his knowledge of his membership of a social group (or groups) together with the value and emotional significance attached to that membership" (Tajfel 1978: 63). Tajfel (1978: 27–60, 1981: 228–53) also proposed that human social behavior varies along the "interpersonal and intergroup continuum." At the interpersonal extreme, social encounters are determined by personal relationships between human beings while at the intergroup extreme,

---

[3] For applications of the social identity approach to ancient Jewish and Christian writings, see Esler, 1998: 40–57, 2003: 19–39; Jokiranta 2005.

membership in different social groups determines human behavior. This continuum explains how, under certain conditions, social identity may become more salient than personal identity for the behavior of individuals. Two things suggest that this may well have been the case with different groups and their members in the Second Temple period. First, many cultural anthropologists have made a distinction between individualistic and collectivistic cultures; ancient Mediterranean culture is mostly described as a collectivistic culture where people were seen as deeply embedded in different groups that were essential for their identity (Esler 1998: 45–49). Individuals did not act or think of themselves as persons independent of these groups. Second, many studies on the Dead Sea Scrolls or early Christian writings, especially the gospels, have emphasized communal aspects in these writings; while written by different individuals, these writings give voice to different groups by expressing their collective convictions and shared view of the world. Given this collectivistic nature of the ancient culture in general and what can be gleaned from Jewish and Christian writings in particular, we have good reasons to think that human interaction in the Second Temple period was determined to a great extent by different groups that provided their members distinctive social identities.

Social identity theory is based on the observation that cognitive, emotional and motivational processes connected to intergroup relations cannot be seen as an extension of interpersonal relations and cannot be explained simply in terms of personal psychology. The distinction between personal and social identity is further clarified by self-categorization theory developed in particular by John Turner and his colleagues (Turner et al. 1987; Turner 1999: 10–14). Self-categorization theory is based on the observation that we experience ourselves as similar to one clearly-defined category of people and therefore, as different from those in other categories. When we see ourselves less as individual persons and more as indistinguishable representatives of some collective category, our shared social identity becomes salient and our "individual self-perception tends to become depersonalized" (Turner 1999: 12). This depersonalization lays the foundation for group behavior and results in the stereotyping, not only of the members of outgroups, but also the self itself. Therefore, the process of categorization concerns both the self-conception of an individual in relation to his or her ingroup and people who are perceived as different from the ingroup.

An important concept for self-categorization theory is the meta-contrast principle which is understood to direct the representation of groups. The meta-contrast principle "predicts that a given set of items is more likely to be categorized as a single entity *to the degree that differences within that set of items are less than the differences between that set and others within the comparative context*" (Oakes, Haslam and Turner 1994: 58). This means that social categorization tends to result in exaggeration and a polarization of perception whereby individuals belonging to different groups are viewed as being more different from each other than they really are while individuals belonging to the same group are perceived as more similar. Categorization is seen as a dynamic, context-bound process, which results in maximizing the clarity of intergroup boundaries in a given social context. This process helps individual group members to orientate themselves in variable social environments by making those environments more predictable and meaningful. Categorization can be described as "a cognitive grouping process that transforms differences into similarities, and vice versa" (Oakes, Haslam and Reynolds 1999: 62).

The above overview makes it possible to see how the social identity perspective helps to explain group phenomena in the Second Temple period. I think that this perspective increases our understanding of the period in three ways:

1) The social identity perspective suggests that groups tend to play down or suppress their common points with other groups in their comparative contexts and claim that they are distinctive.
2) The social identity perspective suggests that it is often the perceived similarity between groups that threatens the distinctiveness of the group and triggers intergroup conflict.
3) The social identity perspective suggests that social categorizations and social identities are not fixed but are always dependent on a given comparative context; if that context changes, people and groups can be categorized in a new way.

3. *Similarity Suppressed, Distinctiveness Claimed*

The tendency to suppress the similarity between different groups and claims of being distinctive are clearly seen in our extant sources where the relations among different Jewish groups are very often presented in polarized terms. Such writings as the Qumran Scrolls or early Christian sources are likely to have been written with insiders in mind and one of the most basic motives behind such writings is the enhancement of the social identity of ingroup members. It is quite obvious that this has resulted in maximizing the differences between the ingroup and outgroups. Self-categorization theory provides a reason for supposing that the people behind these documents shared a tendency to play down those qualities that connected their group to their contemporaries. They managed to do this by accentuating features characteristic of their own group alone, which means that, in the sources, these groups appear to be quite distinctive as compared to their contemporaries.

In light of the theories discussed, the tendency to portray the writer's own group as the only "true Israel" can be seen not only as a theological statement but also as a result of the categorization process underlying all intergroup relations. A group who claims to represent the true Israel understands itself as the sole heir of biblical Israel and regards other groups as unfaithful and more or less corrupt. Such a claim follows the logic of social categorization by placing one group in an elected position and ignoring features that this group shares with its neighboring groups. We meet this claim, for example, in such Qumran writings as the Damascus Document (CD I, 4–9; III, 13–14) or the Community Rule (1 QS VIII, 1–10) as well as in some early Christian writings (Rom 9:6; John 1:47). For Jacob Neusner, this claim is crucial in recognizing a Judaism, because "*a Judaic system derives from and focuses upon a social entity, a group of Jews who (in their minds at least) constitute not an Israel but Israel*" (2001: 11, italics original). According to this definition, each Judaic group has "a way of life characteristic of, perhaps *distinctive to*, that group of Jews; and a world-view that accounts for the group's forming a *distinctive* social entity and explains those indicative traits that define the entity" (2001: 9–10 my italics).

According to the social identity perspective, however, it is only natural that different groups tend to seek distinctiveness and define themselves as unique in relation to other groups in the same comparative social context. This tendency is clearly seen in group prototypes which

> maximize similarities within and differences between groups, and thus define groups as distinct entities and elevate their entitativity.... Because prototypes capture not only similarities within groups but also differences between groups, prototypes can often be extreme or polarized relative to the central tendency of a specific group. (Hogg 2001: 60.)

This means that the self-definitions we find in different sources do not prove that these groups are as unique in their view of the world or in their way of life as they claim to be.[4] For example, it is not clear whether claims to represent the true Israel totally exclude a different, wider understanding of Israel.

The Community Rule is often seen as one of the most exclusivistic writings among the Qumran Scrolls or even among the Second Temple sources in general. For example, George Nickelsburg (2003: 141) has said that the Community Rule "as a whole presents a coherent set of exclusivistic terms." The community is clearly presented as the ideal Israel, but this assertion does not necessarily imply that the group behind the document "saw themselves as Israel and the rest of the Jews as not-Israel," as Neusner claims (2001: 11). John J. Collins (2001: 32) has proposed that the Community Rule posits a two-fold separation within Israel (1QS VIII, 1–14): "The council of the community" is distinct from the larger entity of Israel, and a smaller group is set apart as holy within "the council of the community." Joining the community is understood as a "return" to the covenant of Moses (1QS V, 8), which clearly implies that the community is imagined in the context of biblical Israel. Those who participate in the covenant ceremony are referred to as "every man in Israel" (1QS II, 22) and those who have returned to the covenant as "the multitude of Israel" (1QS V, 22). Collins concludes that, "while the community is Israel as it ought to be, the existence of empirical, sinful Israel is not denied" (p. 33). This means that the Qumran people's definition of Israel "remains rooted firmly in the Torah, however sharply they might disagree with their contemporaries over its interpretation. If they separated themselves from the majority of the people it was only for a time" (p. 42).

The same kind of wavering between a more narrowly defined Israel and a larger body of Israel is seen in Paul's discussion in Romans 9–11. Paul first notes that "not all who are descended from Israel belong to Israel" (Rom 9:6). This seems to imply that Paul counts as "the true Israel" only those who have accepted the gospel. However, Paul later repeatedly refers to Israel as an ethnic entity that has failed to attain righteousness (9:30–33) and remained stubborn (10:19–21). Heikki Räisänen has proposed that Paul's ambiguous use of the concept of

---

[4] Cf. Luomanen (2002: 118) who notes that Neusner's concept of "Judaisms" places too much emphasis on the language of insiders. Instead of this concept, we need "terms and concepts that bridge the gap between our modern analytical point of view and the language of insiders."

Israel is a part of the difficulties caused by "the tension between a novel liberal practice and the pressure towards a more conservative ideology." Paul's abandonment of circumcision and food laws "amounts to a break with sacred tradition," while "his legitimating theory...stresses continuity" (Räisänen 1997: 27).

These tensions and ambiguities in how the concept of Israel is used in the sources show that processes connected to the formation of social identity were never based on simple either-or choices. Different groups made exclusive claims to represent the true Israel and these claims do not leave much room for acknowledging any parallels in beliefs and practices among various groups. Intergroup boundaries seem to be steady and unbridgeable, but, as the social identity perspective implies, claims for distinctiveness are quite natural in writings promoting social identities of various ingroups. These claims aim at maximizing the distinctiveness of intergroup boundaries, but this aim should not always be taken as evidence that such boundaries were firm or even closed in the real world. As a matter of fact, the social identity perspective suggests that sometimes the perceived similarity between different groups may be a central motivational factor in attempts to secure intergroup boundaries.

4. *Similarity As a Threat to Social Identity*

Marilynn Brewer has developed insights from the social identity perspective and suggested that there are two basic human needs in the background of all group identities: the need to be similar to others and a countervailing need for uniqueness. According to Brewer, "social identity can be viewed as a compromise between assimilation and differentiation from others, where the need for deindividuation is satisfied within in-groups, while the need for distinctiveness is met through intergroup comparisons." Brewer continues that the pursuit of the balance between these two opposing needs is a central factor in group processes. In an ideal case of optimal distinctiveness, a group identity "allows us to be the same and different at the same time" (Brewer 1991: 477).

The model of optimal distinctiveness implies that, in certain situations, similarity between different comparative groups may cause a threat to a social identity, which leads groups to "differentiate themselves from other groups that are too similar to the ingroup and which, accordingly, threaten group distinctiveness" (Branscombe et al. 1999: 45).[5] Therefore, conflicts between groups do not always result from their being totally different, but, on the contrary, similarity between groups may often cause intergroup conflicts. A good case in point is the polemic directed against the Pharisees in some Qumran writings.

It is probable that, in some Qumran texts, we find polemic against the Pharisees who are described as "those who seek after smooth things" (*dwršy hhlqwt*) The identification of this epithet with the Pharisees is most evident in the Pesher Nahum, which can be connected to Josephus' narratives about Alexander Jannaeus, Salome Alexandra and the Pharisees (Josephus *Jewish War* 1.88–98, 110–114 and *Jewish Antiquities* 13.372–383, 398–415; see VanderKam 2004: 299–311).[6] Specific legal positions are not ascribed to the ones who seek after smooth things, but the term itself suggests that it refers to a group which, from the viewpoint of the sectarians, are "looking for easy interpretations, not the full and perhaps harsh meaning of a law" (VanderKam 2004: 302). Such passages as CD I, 18–21 clearly imply that "those who seek for easy interpretations" have broken the law and violated the covenant.[7] From the emic position reflected in the text, the disparity between the Qumran group and disparaged "seekers" could not be more pointed, but this emic point of view may not tell the whole story.

In one of the Qumran Scrolls, 4QMMT, we may have an example of legal disagreements between the Qumran group and the Pharisees.

---

[5] The so-called theory of social differentiation emphasizes the same, see Lemaine, Kastersztein and Personnaz 1978: 269–300. They also show how many different social psychological theories, not only social identity theory, have concluded that "individuals or groups do not necessarily seek similar others, that being in a state of 'undistinctiveness' may provoke unpleasant feelings, and that a threat to what one considers important for one's 'identity' leads to a search for, or creation of, differences between self and others" (p. 291).

[6] Cf. also Stemberger, 1999: 210–14. Stemberger notes that we cannot automatically connect all the passages in the Scrolls where the term *dwršy hhlqwt* appears to the Pharisees. According to Stemberger, some texts (e.g., the Pesher Nahum) clearly refer to the Pharisees, while other texts may refer more loosely to groups which shared characteristics usually connected to the Pharisees (p. 215).

[7] CD 1:18–21: "They sought easy interpretations (*dwršw bhlqwt*), chose illusions, scrutinized loopholes, chose the handsome neck, acquitted the guilty and sentenced the just, violated the covenant, broke the precept, banded together against the life of the just man, their soul abominated all those who walk in perfection, they hunted them down with the sword and provoked the dispute of the people." The translation taken from García Martínez and Tigchelaar 1997–98: 551–53. For the possible connection between this polemic and the legal agenda of the Pharisees, see VanderKam 2003: 465–77.

This document contains a section dealing with the question of "flowing liquids;" the document presents the idea that, when one pours liquid from a ritually clean container to an unclean container, impurity "flows" against the current and defiles the pure container (4QMMT B 55–58). In the Mishnah, this position is attributed to the Sadducees while the Pharisees "declare clean an unbroken stream of liquid" (*m. Yad.* 4:7; cf. also *m. Toh.* 8:9). It is obvious that the position taken by the Pharisees in the Mishnah is an "easier" interpretation of the law than the position reflected in 4QMMT. It may be too daring to conclude that the members of the Qumran community always had a stricter attitude than the Pharisees in various legal debates, but the debate on flowing liquids illustrates what kinds of topics possibly distinguished these two groups from each other.[8] The debate hardly suggests that the Pharisees, while disagreeing with the Qumran community on a specific legal issue, had abandoned the covenant, as is suggested by some polemical passages in the Scrolls. Both Josephus (*J.W.* 1.110; 2.162; *Ant.* 14.41) and various passages in the New Testament gospels indicate that the Pharisees were known for their precise interpretation of the law. Therefore, the polemic against the Pharisees in the Scrolls does not describe in any adequate way how the Pharisees understood themselves or how they were understood by their contemporaries.

As a matter fact, from an analytical and etic point of view, there are striking similarities in the outlook of the Qumran community and the Pharisees: both groups were keenly devoted to the correct interpretation of the Torah and both groups valued highly cultic purity even though their detailed interpretations of how to achieve it may have varied. This suggests that the conflict between a part of the Qumran community and some Pharisees may have arisen more from the proximity of their positions than from their totally different interests.[9]

The discussion above has pointed out that intergroup conflicts and polemics in the Second Temple period should not be taken as evidence

---

[8] Stemberger (1999: 220–22) advises that we should be cautious in making comparisons between complete halakhic systems on the basis of individual legal positions. He also proposes that the equation of the legal agenda of the pre-70 Pharisees with the discussions in post-70 rabbinic sources may not be as simple as is often assumed.

[9] It was not only legal disagreements that separated different groups from each other. For example, the Pesher Nahum attacks "the seekers after smooth things" (i.e., the Pharisees) because of their political activity; the writer does not approve of the fact that the Pharisees turned to the Syrian king Demetrius III Eukeros in their struggle against Alexander Jannaeus.

for the distinctiveness of different groups and their world views. Rather, it is especially the fundamental similarity between different groups that lays the foundation for claims to be distinctive. While such claims are prominent in the sources to the extent that other Jews are presented as total outsiders in relation to the covenant, these self-understandings should not make us lose sight of the common ground between various groups. As Carol Newsom (2003: 165) has stated, even such exclusive groups as the Qumran community separate "from others over particular issues of belief and practice. What gives them the right to see themselves as the exclusive locus of salvation is what they claim to know about things that are matters of concern for the whole community." This deeply rooted but often suppressed similarity between different groups may well have resulted in a polarization of attitudes; from the social identity perspective, this is an example of how "the disagreement with similar others... triggers recategorization processes to highlight differences between oneself and those with whom one disagrees" (Mackie and Hunter 1999: 334).

The idea that it is fundamental to groups to secure their distinctiveness also helps to explain a problem articulated by Albert Baumgarten. Baumgarten (1997: 56) has concluded that "the law as observed by one group was not that different from the way it was fulfilled by others, similarities which contemporary scholars are hard pressed to explain: halachic positions turn out to be far from distinct to each of the sects." Baumgarten also notes that, "given the will, there is apparently no dispute on which compromise is impossible, and schism is avoided. Lacking the will, any issue can become the trigger for the emergence of groups" (p. 80). A reason why halachic differences which, at least in the eyes of outsiders, seem to be minute and trivial fermented intergroup conflict may lie in the need to establish the distinctiveness of one's own group in relation to other groups of the same era. While the concern for such things as the covenant, the Torah, temple, and purity created a common bond among different groups, this common interest in focal points of Jewish identity may not have provided the desired sense of distinctiveness for particular groups. Therefore, these groups tried to suppress their common points and sought more and more nuanced ways of expressing their unique characteristics; they thus proved right a social psychological prediction which states that "groups are likely actively to seek and propose additional comparative dimensions as a strategy for coping with a lack of positive group distinctiveness on the focal dimension" (Branscombe et al. 1999: 46).

These observations suggest that we should not understand even the most extreme groups in the Second Temple Period simply in terms of their distinctiveness from other Jews. Claims to be distinctive may be seen as a part of the interplay between an often suppressed sense of sameness and struggles for differentiation. This suggests that social categorization is always a dynamic process which is one of the basic claims of self-categorization theory.

5. *Varying Social Identities*

According to self-categorization theory, social categorization is always dependent on the specific social environment and those comparative relations that are present in that environment. Therefore, "people who are categorized and perceived as different in one context...can be recategorized and perceived as similar in another context" (Oakes, Haslam and Turner 1994: 98). This concept has proved helpful, especially in explaining how a majority group can sometimes be positively influenced even by a minority group which is otherwise held in contempt. John Turner has explained the relationship between majority and minority groups in a way that is worth citing at some length:

> It is hypothesized that ingroup minorities (radical subgroups who are "on our side" but more extreme than the moderate ingroup majority) will tend to be categorized as outgroup in the context of intragroup comparisons and as ingroup in the context of intergroup comparisons. In the context of disagreement within the sociological group, we shall tend to define who "we" are as the majority in contrast to the deviant minority. "We" will be defined as excluding the deviant minority, as "us" the majority as opposed to "them" the minority. However, in the context of a wider intergroup conflict with a more different "them", some more fundamentally discrepant outgroup, the deviant minority will tend to be recategorized as "us" in contrast to the even more opposed outgroup. (Turner 1999: 17–18)

This proposition makes quite plausible Baumgarten's conclusion that non-sectarian Jews "might have respected the devotion of sectarians, but also resented their exclusivist attitudes somewhat, regarding them with as least some disdain" (1997: 62). In terms of intergroup processes, it is quite conceivable that non-sectarians sometimes strongly opposed the claims of sectarian groups but still saw a common bond between themselves and these groups and counted even the most exclusive groups among their fellow Jews. This was possible because a Jewish identity was never formulated only in relation to other possible Jewish identities, but also in relation and in opposition to an ever present, more distant outgroup, the Gentile world.

Because social categories and social identities are not fixed but may vary from one comparative context to another, we should be cautious of interpreting all the differences in the sources as reflections of separate communities behind the documents. For example, Philip Davies (2000a: 219–32, 2000b: 27–43) has insisted that we should recognize many Judaisms behind the Qumran Scrolls or even behind a single document. From a social identity perspective, this conclusion may be too far-reaching, if we bear in mind the typical inclination of all groups to maximize similarities within the ingroup and tolerate internal disagreements and variation. Many disagreements may be tolerated in the context of intragroup discussions, while similar disagreements may become a bone of contention in the context of intergroup conflict. This general feature of group dynamics supports E. P. Sanders who has warned that we should not "find diverse groups where...we should allow for internal and individual variation" (2000: 38).[10]

While self-categorization theory calls attention to the flexibility of group identifications, some theorists have recently proposed that context-based determinants do not wholly define our social identities. Steven Sherman, David Hamilton and Amy Lewis (1999: 92–93) have made an important observation that, while "properties of the immediate context can be powerful determinants of the individual's momentary group identification,... certain chronic social identifications can exert a secondary influence on one's immediate experience." Thus, they propose that "there may be interesting joint influence of contextual and chronic self-categorizations that together can influence one's social identity value associated with those categorizations." This may have been the case also with the Second Temple Jewish groups, which quite often defined themselves as the only true Israel, but never saw Israel purely as a voluntary community void of any ethnic connotation. It is

---

[10] In a similar way, Sarianna Metso (2000a: 384) argues that various similarities between the Community Rule and the material found in Qumran Cave 4 show how "the Qumran community was aware of various, sometimes even contradictory, halakhic practices." Furthermore, similarities between the Community Rule and other material raise the question "How it is possible to identify the specific groups behind the manuscripts? If extensive sections of text from various manuscripts are borrowed and modified, what are the criteria that enable us to assign whole manuscripts to particular groups?" (2000b: 91).

possible to take the social identities of even the most radical groups as a mixture of contextual polemic against outgroups and more chronic and latent categorization of all Israel as the same. A good example is Paul's discussion in Romans 9:2–5, where Paul expresses his continuing identification with the people of Israel: "I have great sorrow and unceasing anguish in my heart. For I could wish that I myself were accursed and cut off from Christ for the sake of my own people, my kindred according to the flesh." Philip Esler (2003: 272) has proposed, from a social identity perspective, that Paul's "passionate outbursts are the product of his reconnecting with the often dormant but nevertheless deeply rooted Israelite dimension to his self-concept." In his career as "the apostle to the non-Jews," Paul mostly laid aside this aspect of his identity.

The view that the underlying sense of sameness is behind even the most extreme claims for distinctiveness may help to clarify reasons that led to the end of Jewish sectarianism after the destruction of the Jerusalem temple. In earlier studies, the end of Jewish sectarianism was often taken as an outcome of the new leadership of the rabbinic movement. This view, however, is not supported by recent rabbinic studies, according to which early rabbis were not representative of Judaism at the time, nor were they in any position to enforce their views on various deviant minorities. Instead of this traditional view, Shaye Cohen has proposed that the end of Jewish sectarianism is connected to a rabbinic "ideology of pluralism" that aimed at "the creation of the society which would tolerate, even foster, disputes and discussions but which could nonetheless maintain order" (1984: 48–50). It is possible, however, that the end of sectarianism may have more to do with the changed political and social realities than any kind of conscious policy of some specific group. Today, many scholars are ready to admit that "many of the Judaic worlds of Second Temple Judea and the Hellenistic Diaspora persisted for quite some time into the post-70 C.E. period and influenced rabbinic Judaism dramatically" (Jaffee 1997: 18). The disagreements among different groups perhaps never ceased, but they were now put into a new perspective because the threat of an even more distinct "other," the Gentile world, was all the more compelling. The loss of the temple and eventually the loss of all territorial independence dramatically changed the context in which Jews defined their social identities in relation to each other and the outside world. These kinds of "enduring changes in comparative context lead to enduring change in [group] prototypes" (Hogg 2001: 60). From a social identity perspective, it can be proposed that those aspects of Jewish identity that bound different groups together and that were earlier suppressed, gained more dominance at the cost of more narrowly oriented group categorizations after the catastrophe in 70 C.E. While detailed discussions around various halachic disagreements had earlier always a potential to trigger an intergroup conflict, henceforth these disagreements were tolerated and finally made the cornerstone of a new Jewish identity which was based to a great extent on a common, ethnically construed bond between different Jews.

REFERENCES

Baumgarten, Albert I. 1997. *The Flourishing of Jewish Sects in the Maccabean Era: An Interpretation*. Supplements to the Journal for the Study of Judaism 55. Leiden: Brill.

Branscombe, Nyla R. et al. 1999. "The Context and Content of Social Identity Threat." In *Social Identity: Context, Commitment, Content*, edited by Naomi Ellemers, Russell Spears and Bertjan Doosje, 35–58. Oxford: Blackwell.

Brewer, Marilynn B. 1991. "The Social Self: On Being the Same and Different at the Same Time." *Personality and Social Psychology Bulletin* 17: 475–82.

Charlesworth, James H. 1990. "Exploring Opportunities for Rethinking Relations among Jews and Christians." In *Jews and Christians: Exploring the Past, Present, and Future*, edited by James. H. Charlesworth, 35–59. New York: Crossroad.

Cohen, Shaye J. D. 1984. "The Significance of Yavneh: Pharisees, Rabbis, and the End of Jewish Sectarianism." *Hebrew Union College Annual* 55: 27–53.

Collins, John. J. 2001. "The Construction of Israel in the Sectarian Rule Books." In *Judaism in Late Antiquity*, Part Five: *The Judaism of Qumran: A Systematic Reading of the Dead Sea Scrolls*, Volume One: *Theory of Israel*, edited by Aalan. J. Avery-Peck, Jacob. Neusner and Bruce D. Chilton, 25–42. Handbook of Oriental Studies, Section One, Vol. 57. Leiden: Brill.

Davies, Philip R. 2000a. "Judaisms in the Dead Sea Scrolls: The case of the Messiah." In *The Dead Sea Scrolls in Their Historical Context*, edited by Timothy H. Lim, 219–32. Edinburgh: T & T Clark.

———. 2000b. "The Judaism(s) of the Damascus Document." In *The Damascus Document: A Centennial of Discovery*, edited by Joseph M. Baumgarten, Esther G. Chazon and Avital Pinnick, 27–43. Studies on the Texts of the Desert of Judah 34. Leiden: Brill.

Esler, Philip F. 1998. *Galatians*. New Testament Readings. Routledge: London and New York.

———. 2003. *Conflict and Identity in Romans: The Social Setting of Paul's Letter*. Minneapolis; Mich.: Fortress.

García Martínez, Florentino, and Eibert J.C. Tigchelaar. 1997–98. *The Dead Sea Scrolls: Study Edition*. Two volumes. Leiden: Brill.

Hakola, Raimo. 2005. *Identity Matters: John, the Jews and Jewishness*. Supplements to Novum Testamentum 118. Leiden: Brill.

Hogg, Michael A. 2001. "Social Categorization, Depersonalization and Group Behavior." In *Blackwell Handbook of Social Psychology: Group Processes*, edited by Michael A. Hogg and R. Scott Tindale, 56–85. Oxford: Blackwell.

Jaffee, Martin. 1997. *Early Judaism*. Upper Saddle River, N.J.: Pearson Education.

Jokiranta, Jutta M. 2005. "Identity on a Continuum: Constructing and Expressing Sectaria Social Identity in Qumran *Serakhim* and *Pesharim*." Ph. D. Diss., University of Helsinki.
Lemaine, Gérard, Joseph Kastersztein, and Bernard Personnaz. 1978. "Social Differentiation." In *Differentiation between Social Goups: Studies in the Social Psychology of Intergroup Relations*, edited by Henri Tajfel, 269–300. European Monographs in Social Psychology 14. London: Academic Press.
Luomanen, Petri. 2002. "The 'Sociology of Sectarianism' in Matthew: Modeling the Genesis of Early Jewish and Christian Communities." In *Fair Play: Diversity and Conflicts in Early Christianity. Essays in Honour of Heikki Räisänen*, edited by Ismo Dunderberg, Christopher Tuckett and Kari Syreeni. Supplements to Novum Testamentum 103. Leiden: Brill.
Mackie, Diane M., and Sarah B. Hunter. 1999. "Majority and Minority Influence: The Interactions of Social Identity and Social Cognition Mediators." In *Social Identity and Social Cognition*, edited by Dominic M. Abrams and Michael A. Hogg, 332–50. Oxford: Blackwell.
Metso, Sarianna. 2000a. "The Redaction of the Community Rule." In *The Dead Sea Scrolls: Fifty Years after Their Discovery*, edited by Lawrence W. Schiffmann, Emanuel Tov and James C. VanderKam, 377–84. Jerusalem: Israel Exploration Society.
———. 2000b. "The Relationship between the Damascus Document and the Community Rule." In *The Damascus Document: A Centennial of Discovery*, edited by Joseph M. Baumgarten, Esther G. Chazon and Avital Pinnick, 85–93. Studies on the Texts of the Desert of Judah 34. Leiden: Brill.
Neusner, Jacob. 1981. *Judaism: The Evidence of the Mishnah*. Chicago, Ill.: Chicago University Press.
———. 2000. "The Four Approaches to the Description of Ancient Judaism(s): Nominalist, Harmonistic, Theological, and Historical." In *Judaism in Late Antiquity, Part Four, Death, Life-After-Death, Resurrection and the World-To-Come in the Judaisms of Antiquity*, edited by Alan J. Avery-Peck and Jacob Neusner, 1–31. Handbook of Oriental Studies, Section One, Vol. 49. Leiden: Brill.
———. 2001. "What is 'a Judaism'?: Seeing the Dead Sea Library as the Statement of a Coherent Judaic Religious System." In *Judaism in Late Antiquity*, Part Five: *The Judaism of Qumran: A Systematic Reading of the Dead Sea Scrolls*, Volume One: *Theory of Israel*, edited by Alan J. Avery-Peck, Jacob Neusner and Bruce D. Chilton, 3–21. Handbook of Oriental Studies, Section One, vol. 56. Leiden: Brill.
Newsome, Carol A. 2003. "Response to 'Religious Exclusivism: A World View Governing Some Texts Found at Qumran.'" In *George W. Nickelsburg in Perspective: An Ongoing Dialogue of Learning, Vol. 1*, edited by Jacob Neusner and Alan J. Avery-Peck, 162–68. Supplements to the Journal for the Study of Judaism 80. Leiden: Brill.
Nickelsburg, George W. E. 2003. "Religious Exclusivism: A World View Governing Some Texts Found at Qumran." In *George W. Nickelsburg in Perspective: An Ongoing Dialogue of Learning*, Vol. 1, edited by Jacob Neusner and Alan J. Avery-Peck, 139–61. Supplements to the Journal for the Study of Judaism 80. Leiden: Brill.
Oakes, Penelope J., S. Alexander Haslam, and Katherine J. Reynolds. 1999. "Social Categorization and Social Context: Is Stereotype Change a Matter of Information or of Meaning?" In *Social Identity and Social Cognition*, edited by Dominic M. Abrams and Michael A. Hogg. 55–79. Oxford: Blackwell.
Oakes, Penelope J., S. Alexander Haslam and John C. Turner. 1994. *Stereotyping and Social Reality*. Oxford: Blackwell.
Räisänen, Heikki. 1997. *Marcion, Muhammad and the Mahatma: Exegetical Perspectives on the Encounter of Cultures and Faiths*. London: SCM Press.
Sanders, E. P. 1990. *Jewish Law from Jesus to the Mishnah: Five Studies*. London: SCM Press, 1990.

———. 1992. *Judaism: Practice and Belief 63 BCE – 66 CE*. London: SCM Press.

———. 2000. "The Dead Sea Sect and Other Jews: Commonalities, Overlaps and Differences." In *The Dead Sea Scrolls in Their Historical Context*, edited by Timothy H. Lim, 7–43. Edinburgh: T & T Clark.

Sherman, Steven J., David L. Hamilton, and Amy C. Lewis. 1999. "Perceived Entitativity and the Social Identity Value of Group Membership." In *Social Identity and Social Cognition*, edited by Dominic M. Abrams and Michael A. Hogg, 80–110. Oxford: Blackwell.

Smith, Jonathan Z. 2004. *Relating Religion: Essays in the Study of Religion*. Chicago, Ill.: University of Chicago Press.

Stemberger, Günther. 1999. "Qumran, die Pharisäer und das Rabbinat." In *Antikes Judentum und Frühes Christentum*, edited by Bernd Kollmann, Wolfgang Reinhold and Annette Steudel, 210–24. Beihefte zur Zeitschrift für die Neutestamentliche Wissenschaft und die Kunde der älteren Kirche 97. Berlin: Walter de Gruyter.

Tajfel, Henri. 1978. *Differentiation between Social Groups: Studies in the Social Psychology of Intergroup Relations*. European Monographs in Social Psychology 14. London: Academic Press.

———. 1981. *Human Groups and Social Categories: Studies in Social Psychology*. Cambridge: Cambridge University Press.

Tajfel, Henri and John C. Turner. 1979. "An Integrative Theory of Intergroup Conflict." In *The Social Psychology of Intergroup Relations*, edited by William G. Austin and Stephen Worchel, 33–47. Monterey, Calif.: Brooks/Cole.

Toorn, Karel van der. 2005. Review of Jonathan Z. Smith, *Relating Religion: Essays in the Study of Religion*, *Journal of Biblical Literature* 124: 484–87.

Turner, John. C. 1999. "Some Current Issues in Research on Social Identity and Self-Categorization Theories." In *Social Identity: Context, Commitment, Content*, edited by Naomi Ellemers, Russell Spears and Bertjan Doosje, 6–34. Oxford: Blackwell.

———. et al. 1987. *Rediscovering the Social Group: A Self-Categorization Theory*. Oxford: Blackwell.

VanderKam, James. 2003. "Those Who Look after Smooth Things, Pharisees, and Oral Law." In *Emanuel: Studies in Hebrew Bible, Septuagint and Dead Sea Scrolls in Honor of Emanuel Tov*, edited by Shalom M. Paul et al., 465–77. Supplements to Vetus Testamentum. Leiden: Brill.

———. 2004. "Pesher Nahum and Josephus." In *When Judaism and Christianity Began: Essays in Memory of Anthony J. Saldarini, Vol. 1*, edited by Alan J. Avery-Peck, Daniel J. Harrington and Jacob Neusner, 299–311. Supplements to the Journal for the Study of Judaism 85. Leiden: Brill.

SOCIAL IDENTITY IN THE QUMRAN MOVEMENT: THE CASE OF THE PENAL CODE

Jutta Jokiranta

1. *Introduction*

The Qumran movement existed between the second century B.C.E. and the first century C.E. The term "movement" is here used intentionally, instead of the more common "Qumran community," since this ancient social movement was probably not restricted to a single community or location (however, we know of this social movement through the texts found at Qumran, and thus the name "Qumran"), and since it fits in the social-scientific description of religious *movements*, groups seeking to cause or prevent social change, rather than religious *institutions*, which adapt to change, according to the definitions provided by Stark and Bainbridge (1987). Many aspects in the Qumran movement represent religious sectarianism—or fundamentalism, if this term is understood as demanding a *return* to previous religious values. As such, it provides an ancient counterpart to the modern fundamentalism which Pascal Boyer has analyzed from the cognitive point of view (2002: 327–40).[1] The Qumran movement demanded a return to the Law of Moses; it cherished scriptural ideals and scriptural language and opposed any relaxation of the correct praxis and legal interpretations as it understood them. Purity laws, the distribution of wealth, marriage laws, Sabbath practices and the legitimate calendar were their most prominent areas of concern.

Judaism of the Second Temple Period is a complex phenomenon which varied according to location and time, between political and domestic spheres (Esler 2001: 25–28), and among various subgroups.

---

[1] Boyer views fundamentalism as a phenomenon in which people focus on a return to religious values and are ready to accept violence to further this cause. The Qumran movement attacked outsiders and defended itself in words, but there is little, if any, evidence for actual violent acts towards other groups in the Dead Sea Scrolls. For Boyer's approach to social coalitions, see also footnotes 28 and 40, and Luomanen's essay in this volume.

The Qumran movement is often regarded as a special case within Judaism. The movement had a clear organization, and it was extreme in many aspects, however, it remained within the boundaries of the Israelite identity. Normally, it is taken for granted that, since the Qumranites were so strict in their interpretations of the Law (*halakhot*), they formed a strict and closed community, or, *vice versa*, since the community was exclusive, it had to have strict rules. In this essay, I would like to discuss the make-up and identity of the movement and, more specifically, the role of a specific rule collection in the Qumran texts, the penal code, in relation to this identity. Seemingly strict regulations cannot be taken as evidence of extreme fundamentalism or sectarianism without a more careful analysis of how these regulations relate to the overall ethos and identity within and around the movement. I shall utilize the social identity approach, and explain the penal code from that perspective.

The social identity approach provides a wider perspective on the issue at hand since it focuses on intergroup relations and the formation of social identities: what social psychological processes underlie the situation in which people act as group members rather than individuals? What are the effects of group membership on individuals, their behavior, perceptions and attitudes? The social identity approach also addresses questions of social change. How does a group achieve and maintain a positive social identity when it cannot perceive a (desired) change in its circumstances? These questions are relevant to the understanding of the Qumran movement, which criticized the society of its time but was not able to change it. Instead, it formed a subculture, which changed the lives of individuals who joined. Maintaining the desired social identity in such a subculture is a challenge throughout its existence.

2. *Rule Documents: the Damascus Document and the Community Rule*

The rule documents are texts which most explicitly describe and reflect the life and practices in the Qumran movement. The *Damascus Document* is unique among the Qumran corpus since it has been preserved in two medieval manuscripts, in addition to the ten fragmentary manuscripts from Qumran.[2] The expression "land of Damascus" stands for the loca-

---

[2] Medieval copies were found in a Cairo Genizah (CD A, B); Qimron 1992; Baumgarten and Schwartz 1995. Cave Four manuscripts are the most substantial of the Qumran

tion for the "new covenant." It is not clear whether "Damascus" should be understood as literally or symbolically—nevertheless, the designation the *Damascus Document* for the entire document is established among scholars. The document has two main sections: the Admonition and the Laws. The Law section includes both legal interpretations of the Torah (*halakhah*, e.g., on the observance of the Sabbath, on the proper taking of oaths, on purification from ritual impurity, etc.), and rules which apply in a particular community/communities in "camps:" the seating order in a community meeting, rules for various officials and the *penal code*.[3] By now it is clear that the *Damascus Document* also includes a penal code, but not a long ago, before the Cave Four material of the *Damascus Document* was published, this penal code was thought to be minimal or almost non-existent.[4] The *Damascus Document* was known only for its legal interpretations (*halakhah*), and for its rules in the "camps." In the following, I refer to the *Damascus Document* using the abbreviation "D" (and "CD" for the Cairo Genizah copy of D).

The *Community Rule*, on the other hand, is abbreviated with "S" for its Hebrew name, *Serekh ha-yahad*. The document has been preserved in twelve copies from Qumran.[5] It contains rules for admission into the community (*yahad*), an annual liturgy of renewal of the covenant, a dualistic discourse on two spirits, rules for the assembly (*rabbim*) as well as the wisdom teacher (*maskil*), a penal code, and a hymn of the wisdom teacher. However, it does not include any legal interpretations of the Torah (*halakhah*).

Both the *Damascus Document* (D) and the *Community Rule* (S) are composite works and have gone through extensive editing, some of which is visible in the manuscript evidence. The *Community Rule* is best taken as a collection of some rather diverse rules, not a definite handbook

---

manuscripts of the *Damascus Document* (4QD^{a-h}, 5QD, 6QD); Baumgarten 1996. The document was composed over a long period, being completed around 100 B.C.E.

[3] I follow the source-critical study by Hempel 1998, according to which the *halakhah* makes up an earlier layer, not necessarily restricted to the Qumran movement alone, and "community organization" is another major literary layer in the Law section.

[4] Only a few lines of the penal code have been preserved at the end of the medieval manuscript (CD XIV). In the Qumran fragments, the penal code is preserved in 4QD^a (4Q266) 10 I, 11–15; II, 1–15; 11 1–21; 4QD^b (4Q267) 9 VI, 1–5; and 4QD^e (4Q270) 7 I, 1–21; II, 11–15.

[5] The Cave One manuscript of S (1QS) is the best preserved, others are 4QS^{a-j} and 5QS; Qimron and Charlesworth 1994; Alexander and Vermes 1998. The *Community Rule* was also compiled around 100 B.C.E.: 1QS comes from 100–75 B.C.E. Both D and S—or some versions of them—continued to be used and copied within the Qumran movement throughout its history.

or "manual of discipline" for the community, as it has sometimes been designated. In all likelihood, D and S do not describe exactly the *same* groups in the same time and location, but I regard them as witnesses to the same movement.[6] The purpose of this essay is not to address the development and differences in specific groups but to understand the rough contours of the larger, long-term movement. Therefore, I concentrate on what D and S have in common.[7]

3. *Penal Code*

A special rule collection within both D and S is the penal code: a list of certain offences and their punishments. There is a literary dependence between the penal codes of D and S. Many of the cases are identical or very close to each other. The development of the codes, however, is complex and the direction of dependence cannot always be established with certainty.[8] For the purpose of this essay, I confine myself to the shared material, which probably preserves some of the earliest sets of principles.[9]

---

[6] Together with Cecilia Wassen, I have argued that both documents reflect groups that had a similar (sectarian) religious stance in their socio-cultural environment; Wassen and Jokiranta forthcoming.

[7] The changes that took place are of great interest but their study involves many more uncertainties. A balanced view demands that similarities are given their due place, even though we may not reach a specific historical group in detail in this way.

[8] Hempel (1997) thinks that the penal code, as a genre, is original in D. In her view, the S community drew upon D's penal code as well as revised D in the light of their new code. Metso (2004) assumes an earlier penal code which D and S reworked independently. Baumgarten (1992: 268–79; 2000: 455–60) also lists similarities and differences between the penal codes and presents some suggestions about their development. A related penal code is extant in yet another document, 4Q265, which is designated 4Q*Serekh Damascus* (= 4Q Miscellaneous Rules), since it contains material similar to both S and D.

[9] The kinds of differences between the penal codes show that the material was probably reworked in both documents. The punishments differ in formulation and in duration, and some offences that are included in the one are missing in the other. D includes five offences that are not found in S: despising the judgment of the Many; taking someone's food against the law; fornication with one's wife which is not according to the law; murmuring against the fathers; murmuring against the mothers. The absence of these offences in S indicates that the penal code of S was not just simply added in D, even though D would have been revised by S redactors. It is most probable that D preserves evidence of the existence of an earlier penal code. S includes several offences not found in D: disobeying a senior; using the divine name improperly; speaking against priests; lying knowingly (subject not specified); speaking deceptively; deceiving a neighbor; being careless with possessions; revenging oneself; spitting in the

These are the cases of the penal code that are shared in D and 1QS (Hempel 1997: 338–41):[10]

> lying knowingly about money/wealth
> insulting a neighbor
> bearing a grudge
> speaking folly
> interrupting a neighbor's speech
> falling asleep during a session of the Many (*rabbim*)
> leaving a session of the Many up to three times during a single meeting
> leaving while they are standing
> walking naked before another
> taking out a hand from underneath one's dress[11]
> guffawing foolishly
> gesticulating with the left hand
> slandering one's neighbor
> slandering the Many
> deviation of one's spirit

The following example reveals the way in which the offences and their punishments are formulated:[12]

> Whoever lies down and goes to sleep in the session of the Many, (he shall be punished) thirty days. And so, whoever leaves the session of the Many without permission or reason[13] up to three times during one session, he shall be punished ten days. (1QS VII, 10–11; par. 4QD^a 10 II, 5–8.)

> Whoever giggles inanely [causing his voice to be heard shall be excluded] for [th]irty and shall be punished for fif[teen] days. (4QD^a 10 II, 12–13; par. 1QS VII, 16–17.)

Rules are very explicit—scholars feel they can look right into the daily life of the members. The penal code has been regarded as highly

---

meeting of the Many; murmuring against the foundations of the community. Many of these are probably further developments of the penal code.

[10] For the penal code in D, see footnote 4. The penal code of S is best found in 1QS VI, 24–VII, 25 and VIII, 20–IX, 2. Parts of the penal code are also preserved in 4QS^e (4Q259) and 4QS^g (4Q261); these include minor variants to 1QS.

[11] Qimron and Charlesworth (1994) take this as a euphemism, translating: "whoever causes his penis to come out from under his garment..." Alexander and Vermes 1998: 138, oppose this view, since the passage continues: "...being dressed in rags, his nakedness is seen"—it would be tautological to mention "nakedness" if "hand" was a euphemism for penis.

[12] Translation is according to García Martínez and Tigchelaar 2000, modified.

[13] The reading *ḥnm* follows Qimron and Charlesworth 1994: 30.

important for understanding the ethos of the "Qumran community" (Baumgarten 1992: 268). In the words of Geza Vermes (1981: 92),

> the list of faults with their corresponding sentences tells us more about the mentality of the Dead Sea ascetics than any isolated exposition of their doctrine and principles can do.

Florentino García Martínez (1995: 39) describes the life of the community in the holistic survey *The People of the Dead Sea Scrolls*:

> Daily life is full of risks. Since the requirement of faithfulness is absolute, and the regulations established to safeguard the total observance of the precepts of the Law are many and various, any member runs the risk of breaking one or the other of them. The seriousness of the transgression in the eyes of the community determines how long the deprivation of sharing in the "purity" lasts, which is imposed on the one who is guilty.

The prominent role of the penal code in S easily creates an impression of an introverted group which was more concerned with monitoring the minor details of its members' behavior (e.g., falling asleep in a meeting, interrupting someone, laughing in a loud voice) than centering on the Torah—the detailed matters were punished by excluding the member for a certain period from the "purity," or by reducing his portion of food, or both (see below), and little discussion—if any—is devoted to deviations from the Law of Moses. The penal code of S has often been interpreted as functioning in a closed setting, as Lawrence Schiffman (1983: 157) has stated: "This collection of offences is clearly intended to facilitate life in a small, closed-in settlement such as that of Qumran."[14]

On the other hand, some scholars hold that the penal code reflects normal regulations that any voluntary association would have in Greco-Roman society (Weinfeld 1986; Klinghardt 1994: 251–70). The issue is related to the question about the origin of the rules. Schiffman (1983: 212; 1994: 273–87) takes the regulations as basically derived from Scripture through an exegetical exercise whereas Moshe Weinfeld (1986: 71–73) argues that they are not theologically motivated in any way.[15] Placing these positions in opposition to each other, however, is

---

[14] Similarly, García Martínez and Barrera 1995: 152: "This list of offences shows a withdrawn community, careful to avoid problems from its members living together."

[15] See also Forkman 1972 for the scriptural background of many offences, but also for the deviation from the scriptural system of expulsion, and Shemesh 2002: 44–74, for the scriptural paradigm behind the penalties.

not necessary. The penal code is not *merely* a collection of disciplinary regulations,[16] and not *merely* an application of written Scripture.[17]

Carol Newsom brings the discussion onto a more explanatory level. First of all, she rightly notes that the disparate parts of S serve as *samples* of the community's ethos (2004: 135). S is not a complete manual and source of information of the community procedures but "something that exemplifies that to which it refers." The penal code was in line with the common cultural ideas of such rules in voluntary groups (2004: 149). On the other hand, she sees the Qumran group as exercising "disciplinary power." In order to take hold of the hearts and minds of the members, the community has to take hold of their bodies (2004: 95–101). Disciplinary institutions aim at producing individuals who exercise self-control. To that end, even minor details of behavior, speech, body, and sexuality are controlled and disciplined. The system of penalties, which is created for offending the rules of control, operates to compare and to differentiate between members, to place them in a hierarchical order, to homogenize the group, and to exclude members who cross the ultimate limit of tolerance (2004: 98–99, quoting Foucault 1995: 182–83). The discipline produces behaviors and skills that become part of the individual's identity.

This explanation, however, does not fully answer the question of why it is that these particular rules are part of the penal code: what kind of individual do *these* rules aim at producing? And, secondly, the penal code may be educational and instructional, as Newsom's explanation assumes, but it is also something more. It is not only designed to maintain order in the meetings, or to create self-discipline. Newsom (2004: 148) herself notes the fact that, in S, the rules are not formulated as advisory warnings and exhortations to the readers but as exemplary cases of how the readers (the members) *should discipline others*:

> Rhetorically, the reader is not instructed about what he may or may not do but rather how he, as a member of the session, shall judge. He is addressed as one who is to exercise disciplinary power rather than as one who is subjected to it, although that fact is assumed.

---

[16] Walker-Ramisch 1996: 142 criticizes Weinfeld's comparison of the penal code and the Greco-Roman associations for not acknowledging the significantly Jewish "flavor" in the penal code and its use of culturally shared terminology. See also Newsom 2004: 149–50 for agreements and disagreements with Weinfeld.

[17] Metso (2000: 85–93, 2004: 315–35), stresses the possible oral decision-making in the groups. In 1QS, the written rules are not shown to be scripturally derived but are based on the authority of the *rabbim*.

The rhetorical formulation may not correspond to the functions of the code in its social settings. However, even in real-life situations, discipline of this kind functions to produce not only a certain kind of *individual* but also a certain kind of *group member*. I am interested in the *type* of order and social identity that the movement seeks to ensure through the penal code.

4. *Social Identity*

One additional perspective for interpreting the penal codes is offered by the social identity theory. *Social identity* was defined by Henri Tajfel (1978: 63) as

> that part of an individual's self concept which derives from his knowledge of his membership of a social group (or groups) together with the value and emotional significance attached to that membership.

It indicates one's *perception* of being similar to other members of the ingroup and different from the members of the outgroup, that is, one's self-categorization at a certain level. In consequence, one adopts the ingroup's beliefs, norms, rules and goals as he or she perceives them. Social identity is what makes group behavior possible. Social identity is often theoretically distinguished from *personal identity*, one's perception of oneself *as an individual*, made up of one's life history, personality, abilities, family relations, etc., i.e., those things that distinguish oneself from other individuals and that create a perception of oneself as a continuous and coherent personality.

In Tajfel's terms (1981: 246–47), *personal identity* is associated with *social mobility* beliefs, that is, assumptions that social systems are flexible and permeable and that one can freely move from one group to another. If a person finds his/her situation undesirable, s/he can pass into a high-status or more dominant group, in other words, improve his/her position *as an individual*. On the other hand, social (collective) identity is associated with *social change* beliefs, the assumption that one cannot escape one's group for self-enhancement, and group behavior is the only option for changing one's conditions.[18] A group may also

---

[18] See also Haslam 2004: 23–24. An "exit" from the group may be impossible for practical reasons, such as skin color, or due to the cost of investment in group membership. Tajfel (1981: 247–50) acknowledged that different cultures may promote either

create social change beliefs: in conditions where individual mobility from one group to another is *not* prevented, a group develops new ideologies and attitudes so that group members come to believe that group boundaries are strict and rigid (Tajfel 1981: 247–49). The Qumran movement certainly needed such beliefs in order to keep the group in existence for over a century. The penal code and the beliefs connected to it are shown below to serve social change beliefs and to hinder free, individual social mobility.

Furthermore, social identity is not fixed and stable but dependent on the situation where a person finds him/herself. "Different times, places, and circumstances render different self-identifications 'salient' self-images," as Hogg and Abrams (1988: 25) note. Social identity within a group needs to be constantly recreated. Because of the interplay between personal and social identities and because a person may have several contesting social identities, group members may have a different idea of what it means to belong to the ingroup. This also varies over the course of time, depending on the group development and the context. Achieving an agreement of the fundamental contents of ingroup identity is an ongoing process (Condor 1996: 285–315).

The concept of *group beliefs* helps to analyze the contents of social identity. All groups have group beliefs, "convictions that group members are aware that they share, and consider as defining their 'groupness,'" as defined by Daniel Bar-Tal (1998: 94). Acceptance of group beliefs is one indicator of group membership. The contents of group beliefs may be values, norms, goals, or a larger set of beliefs, ideology. Those patterns of behavior, desired future circumstances, or common experiences that a group believes distinguishes it as unique are group beliefs (Bar-Tal 1998: 93–101).[19] The belief that demonstrates the group's existence ("We are a group") is the *fundamental group belief*, but usually groups have additional group beliefs that contribute to the "we-ness" of

---

social mobility or social change beliefs; thus, it is not only a matter of free choice between different kinds of beliefs. Furthermore, later scholarship has emphasized that personal identity does not determine social mobility beliefs; a person may be fully aware of individual differences in the ingroup and yet have a strong social identity. It should also be noted that personal and social identities are theoretical poles on a continuum. A person hardly ever perceives him/herself purely in personal terms but usually social identities play some role.

[19] Not all beliefs that are shared by individuals are group beliefs. Group beliefs are those which serve to differentiate members from outgroups and provide information about the group, e.g., group history, group goals and group characteristics. They are salient in the group and have to have authority behind them; Bar-Tal 1998: 108–9.

the group (Bar-Tal 1998: 94). These additional group beliefs are often those which have impact on the emotional dimension of social identity, besides the mere cognitive awareness of belonging to a group.

Group beliefs are often held with great confidence since they express the basic "truth" about what the group is about; especially at the beginning of the group's formation, a group may demand greater confidence. However, group beliefs are not always equally central to all group members. The *centrality* reflects the importance of the group to a group member; an individual is always a member of several groups and puts different weight on different group memberships. The stronger the social identity, the more important are group beliefs for a person. Some group beliefs are also more central than others. Centrality is often promoted by having beliefs easily accessible, for example, by their repetition, vividness, or expression in visible, outward symbols/physical appearance (Bar-Tal 1998: 101–6).

5. *Social Identity in the Rule Documents: The Oath and the Penal Code*

From the social identity perspective, the process of identification with the group(s) reflected in D and S meant that a person categorized him/herself[20] as similar to other members of the group and dissimilar to the members of the outgroups. But what were the contents of such an identity? In other words, what was perceived as distinguishing group members from outsiders and making them similar to the insiders in the shared perception of the group? What was the member supposed to think, believe, learn, and how was s/he supposed to act after joining the group?

One answer to these questions may be found in the oath that a new member took. It can be argued that the oath upon admission contains central elements of what the group is about. This oath was a rite of passage that took place only once during a person's life and thus had permanent and remarkable effects on memory. From the cognitive

---

[20] The penal codes are silent about the presence of any women, except that D's penal code includes punishment for an offence against the "mothers;" however, the penalty is milder than concerning the "fathers." Other passages and documents show that at least some members had families (CD VII, 6–7), and that women were able to act as witnesses (1QSa I, 11). The evidence is unclear about whether women were full members or not. Wassen (2005) arrives at an affirmative result.

perspective (McCauley and Lawson 2002), not-repeated rituals can be understood as special agent rituals: they are performed by special agents (priests, experts) who, because of earlier rituals (such as their initiation or ordination), are connected to the gods, the superhuman agents. "When the gods act, either directly or through their intermediaries, the effects are super-permanent" (2002: 121–23). Although it is unclear whether Lawson and McCauley would interpret the oath as a special agent ritual,[21] it is interesting to note that an agent representing superhuman powers seemed indeed to be present in the oath: the Examiner or other full members in authority directed the event taking place and controlled the information and teaching that the initiate was about to receive.

The oath that the new members took, is referred to in D (CD XV, 5b–11a // 4QD^a 8 I, 1–2) in the following way:

> And those who enter the covenant for all of Israel as an eternal statute shall have their children, who have reached (the age) for passing among those who are mustered, take the oath of the covenant. Similar (is) the precept during the entire time of evil for everyone who repents from his corrupt way. On the day that he speaks with the Examiner for the Many, they shall muster him with the oath of the covenant which Moses made with Israel, the cove[na]nt to re[turn t]o the Torah of Moses with all (his) heart [and with all] (his) soul, to which is found to be done during the en[tire tim]e of [evi]l. Let no-one make the precepts known to him until he stands before the Examiner.[22]

According to S (1QS V, 7b–10a // 4QS^b 4 I, 6b–8a; 4QS^d 1 I, 5b–7a),[23]

---

[21] See reservations connected to the concept of "special agent rituals" below (footnote 28) and in Ketola's essay in this volume.

[22] The parallel in 4QD^a preserves only part of the passage. The translation of CD XV, 5b–11 is according to Baumgarten and Schwartz 1995: 39, except for minor changes (they translate "sons" but the gender-inclusive translation "children" is to be preferred). It is also possible to translate the beginning: "And those who have entered the covenant..."—this would refer to full members who will have their children initiated, see Wassen 2005: 132, n. 8.

[23] There are three sections in S which deal with the admission of new members: 1QS V, 7b–20a; V, 20b–VI, 1a; VI, 13b–23, see Metso 1997: 129–33. The last two differ from the first in that they describe the *examination* of the new member, refer to the *length* of the process, and do not include a reference to an oath or binding promise. Hempel (1999: 70–72) notes the close affinity between the admission processes of 1QS V and CD XV.

> *These are the regulations of their behavior concerning all these decrees when they are enrolled in the yahad.* Everyone who joins the council of the community shall enter into the covenant of God in the presence of those who willingly offer themselves. He shall undertake by a *binding* oath to return to the Torah of Moses with all his heart and soul, *following all that he has commanded*, and in accordance with all that has been revealed from *it to the sons of Zadok, the priests who keep the covenant and seek his will, and to the multitude of the men of their covenant who together willingly offer themselves for his truth and to walk according to his will.*[24]

The exact words of the oath that the initiate will utter are not mentioned. Instead, these passages explain the principles of the new life and accentuate the need to commit oneself to this promise in order to be counted in the covenant. Nevertheless, we have good reason to think that the admission to the community was a *public* event of some sort where the change in the status of a person was clearly marked by a solemn declaration, concession, or by other verbal means.[25] Although the oath is not systematically mentioned in the rule documents in connection to admission, I find it highly likely that such practice actually occurred, at least at some stage, given the presence of an oath in the biblical model of the covenant ceremony (Deut 29:10–12; Neh 10:29–30), the interest in oaths in general in various Qumran documents (e.g., CD XVI, 10–12; IX, 9–16), and the seriousness with which oaths were regarded. The oath was to be kept even at the price of death (CD XVI, 7b–9). It is, however, fairly easy to imagine that the oath might have been a short assertion at first,[26] and developed into a more elaborate pledge.[27]

---

[24] Apart from minor changes, the translation and italics (= parts missing from 4QS^{b,d}) are according to Metso 1997: 132. The passage continues in all manuscripts with another infinitive: "and to separate himself from all the men of injustice."

[25] The other sections of S that deal with the admission (V, 20b–VI, 1a; VI, 13b–23) have the emphasis on the *examination* of the new member, the *decision* reached by the ones in authority and the *teaching* of the novice. It is possible that new members were taken in at the annual renewal of the covenant liturgy (1QS I, 16–25), and this included confession of sins, blessings and curses recited by priests and Levites, and a confirmative response "amen, amen" by the entrants. For the initiation as part of the annual renewal of the covenant ceremony, see Wassen 2005: 26–27, 136–38.

[26] Perhaps admission first took place more informally, before the need arose to control admission and the procedure developed accordingly: cf. CD XIII, 7b–13 and the prohibition by other than the Examiner to accept a new member.

[27] Cf. the mention by Josephus of the "awesome oaths" the candidate had to take (*Jewish War* 2.139–142). However, we do not know what is the basis of Josephus' information. The list of oaths may also be a collection of various community ideals, principles, and practices that Josephus had observed or learned about. Nevertheless, oaths are seen as greatly significant: Josephus also informs us that,

That the oath truly meant transition from one state of existence to another is suggested by the statement in D in the same connection: "On the day when a man takes upon himself (an oath) to return to the Torah of Moses, the angel Mastema shall turn aside from following him, if he fulfills his words" (CD XVI, 4b–5). The person was transferred from one sphere (Evil) to another (God's), as long as he did what he said. Furthermore, the use of the divine name was banned, except for this oath, by the curses of the covenant (CD XV, 1–2). The initiation was, then, probably marked in the member's mind as significant and memorable.[28]

Moving on from the significance of the oath as a ritual, we turn to study its contents and its implications for the individual's social identity. We can see several beliefs underlying the oath (Jokiranta 2005: 80–101).

1. All people stand in need of returning to the Law of Moses.
2. The act of returning to the Torah of Moses is characterized by taking account of what is *revealed* of the Law.
3. This revelation is *collective*.

D emphasizes that knowledge of the Torah should not be distributed to outsiders, and, similarly, the quoted passage in S continues by instructing and describing the separation from outsiders, "the men of injustice,"

---

the one who is expelled is often brought to a most miserable fate. For since he is bound by their oaths and customs he is not able to partake of the food of others, but he feeds himself on wild herbs and his body wastes away from hunger until he dies. (Translation by Beall 1988: 19.)

[28] This also might have relevance concerning McCauley's and Lawson's theory which suggests that infrequent, special agent rituals usually contain high "sensory pageantry," which accentuate the significance of the event in the participant's mind. In the case of Qumran, however, we have little evidence what this kind of sensory stimulation as regards the oath might have been. The theory has also been criticized, see Ketola's essay in this book, and Boyer 2002: 287–300. On the other hand, Boyer (2002: 282) explains that

what is going on during these rites (of initiation) and produces real effects has little to do with changing the participants themselves and a lot to do with making possible the building of risky coalitions with other men.

In other words, rites of passage activate mental structures that are connected to *coalitional behavior*. In order to survive or succeed, people have had to rely on other people and trust that they behave in a certain way (e.g., in hunting or war). Rituals assure the participants that the others who have gone through a similar rite are trustworthy and loyal members.

who have not sought God in order to know the hidden. We may see how social change beliefs were upheld in the Qumran movement. It was believed that a person could not follow the Law individually and walk on the right path but was dependent on the group. An individual outside the group lacked the means to know and do what was right. The group as a collective changed the world.

The rule documents further reveal that the group that possessed this insider revelation was organized in a *hierarchical* manner:[29] a member submitted himself to his superiors and became a part of the community of counsel.[30] *A basic function of the community was to give counsel so that the Law could be fulfilled*. A member was a participant in this counseling according to a hierarchical system. The group ensured obedience to the Law by surveillance, counsel, reproof, teaching, and judgment. If the community meetings are considered the central means by which the community was realized (cf. Charlesworth 2000: 134; Newsom 2004: 145), then essentially *the community was this counseling*. It was thus not only the moral superiority but also *the necessary knowledge* and *the righteous order* that was believed to distinguish the group from outsiders. These can then be regarded as central group beliefs, reflected in some form in the oath as well as in the other sections of the rule documents. The meetings, in which the initiate progressively took part and which probably included a communal meal, repeatedly and concretely marked the status of every member. It is possible that the claims arising from each member's personal identity, or from other, competing social identities,[31] are successfully acknowledged by *emphasizing* one's own established position and role in the coherent system of counsel (cf. Jastram 1997: 368–72). In the Qumran movement, the process of identification with the group was presumably facilitated by many factors, such as a long admission procedure, testing of competence, frequent collective gatherings together with the demand to dis-

---

[29] The priests are the rank that has the highest authority in both documents. In S, it is the *rabbim* who have a pronounced position in the decision-making. Nevertheless, both documents also refer to the individual ranking of the members.

[30] I prefer to speak about "counsel" rather than "knowledge" as the prerequisite for obeying the Torah since "counsel" includes the aspect of transmitting knowledge to others. The use of property was obviously considered a major matter in which righteous counsel was needed (1QS I, 13).

[31] A member had, for example, social identities as a member of his family, ancestry, nation, place of origin, age-group, training, etc. (cf. Paul's description of himself in Phil. 3:5–6). Personal identity has more to do with one's special skills, opinions, characteristics and experiences that one thinks distinguishes oneself from others.

tinguish oneself from outsiders (e.g., concerning meals, wealth, work), the annual renewal of the covenant, and the new language a person learned to speak.[32]

Searching for central group beliefs in ancient texts, however, is not unproblematic. Cognitive scientists of religion have noted how people's "official" response to questions about their beliefs differ from their spontaneous, unconscious, and immediate responses (e.g., Boyer 2002: 101–3; Whitehouse 2004: 189; see also the Introduction to this volume). "Off-line theology" and "on-line intuitions" are not equal cognitive processes. Therefore, a person who had taken the oath and joined the community did not automatically have the above-mentioned group beliefs represented in his/her mind: in spontaneous situations, s/he might reproduce the central elements of what makes them a group quite differently from the "official" representation.[33] From the social identity point of view, this is related to the interplay between personal and social identities and the fluidity of social identity in various times and places. Social identity involves, after all, an individual's perception of him/herself in a given situation and the categorization of him/herself as similar to some people and dissimilar to others. Various identities can become salient, depending on the context (e.g., the level of abstraction: one is human, male, an inhabitant of X, a member of group Y, head of group Z), and the person's interpretation of the circumstances. In instant on-line situations, the centrality of the group beliefs may diminish due to his/her perception of the situation in terms of his/her personal identity. The person may give the central group beliefs his/her own interpretations, and s/he may act according to the group beliefs in some situations but not in others. The person's perception of him/herself will then affect his/her behavior.

---

[32] Newsom (2004: 6–21) studies the discourse in S from this perspective. Various common expressions (such as light and darkness, covenant, election) came to have a special meaning for the member when s/he acquired the ideology of the group. There were specific ways to speak about oneself, e.g., as humble and low, although the members were believed to be in union with the angels.

[33] However, it is to be noted that the rule documents are not "doctrinal" or "official" or systematic representations of the groups' beliefs. Instead, as noted above, they are more or less random collections of various principles and practices occurring in the movement over time. Despite the "treatise on the two spirits" (1QS III, 13–IV, 26) perhaps, which is sometimes understood as the "doctrine of the two spirits," the rule documents contain fewer ideas and theology than customs and practices. The authority in the movement may well lie in the group's constant work as the interpreter of the Torah rather than in specific philosophical and religious ideas.

Indirect evidence of acting against one's desired social identity and central group beliefs in the Qumran movement comes from the numerous references in the rule documents to traitors and to those expelled. These show that the process of identification with the group and the salience of that social identity were by no means self-evident. Many of the offences in the penal codes directly reflect a conflict between the personal and social identity of a member or a distorted understanding of the social identity in the eyes of the group. A member who objects to the basic principles of the community "takes the law into his/her own hands," and defies the authority of his/her fellow over him/her. We may imagine how a member (newly arrived, perhaps) presented his views, interrupting another member's speech, or insulted someone, or left the *rabbim* session. All this violated the central group beliefs about the need to return to the Torah and follow the collective interpretation of it. Furthermore, the member's actions may have been reported to the superiors, and, in consequence, he might have borne a grudge against other members. If he could not have his view taken seriously, he may have slandered his fellow members or the *rabbim*. Some of the violations of prohibitions may even happen quite unintentionally, thoughtlessly perhaps, and even happen to senior members—to live one's life without ever interrupting or insulting anyone is a rare achievement, even if these prohibitions applied to a formal community session. Many of the offences, as is often noted, are related to speech. The member could have his voice heard but this had to happen in an orderly manner in a community meeting (1QS VI, 10–11). It is not keeping to the right path as such that is vital but the one who "readily receives his judgment" is safe (4QD^a 11 1–8).

Nearly all the offences common to the penal codes of S and D can thus be seen as violations of those group beliefs that were expressed and reflected in the oath. They are either *direct violations of the community counsel* (deviation from the foundations of the community; lying about property),[34] or endangering the trust which is the prerequisite for the counseling (slandering the community or its leaders; insulting a neighbor; bearing a grudge; speaking folly; interrupting a neighbor's speech; falling asleep during the *rabbim* session; leaving the session without

---

[34] The place of this offence as the first in the penal codes (1QS VI, 24–25; CD XIV, 20) indicates the prominence of wealth in the community principles; see Murphy 2002: 447–50. Unity in property was an essential part of the agenda of the group as a righteous community.

permission; laughing noisily). Other offences (walking naked; exposing one's private parts; gesticulating with the left hand) are similarly threats to the credibility of the community meetings,[35] perhaps by threatening its concepts of purity.

Furthermore, the punishments in the penal codes are an integral part of the puzzle.[36] It is often noted that by excluding a member from the highest purposes of the group, holiness and purity, the offender was reduced to the stage of a novice who would defile the "holy of holies." The community had several levels of progressive purity, comparable to the Temple (García Martínez and Barrera 1995: 154). To this must be added that, whereas D includes a double punishment in most cases, a period of exclusion (*hwbdl*) and a period of penance (*n'nsh*), S refers in most cases only to a penance (*n'nsh*) of a certain period of time, and it is not clear if this penance means reduction of one's food ration (as it is defined in some cases),[37] or exclusion from the "purity" (and decision-making?), or both.[38] If the penal code in D represents an earlier formulation, it is likely that the inherent idea in the punishment was exclusion of some sort, and that this exclusion was related to the suspension of full rights as a member in the community of counsel.[39] If

---

[35] Weinfeld (1986: 26–27, 31) considers nudity, exposure, loud laughter, sleeping, and spitting (note that spitting is not found in the penal code of D) as "disturbances of the general order," but also as "rules of modesty." Note that, in D, walking naked happens "in a house" and "in the field." In S, this offence is placed among others that take place in the meeting of the *rabbim*.

[36] Hempel (1997: 337–38) thinks that punishments can change in one community over time, but perhaps not the punishable offences. "What constitutes a punishable offence, on the other hand, may well be distinct in one community from the next." However, adding offences, leaving something out, and even slight modifications according to situational factors must be allowed within the same community.

[37] 1QS VI, 25 refers to the reduction of one fourth, and 4Q*Serekh Damascus* (4Q265 1 I, 4–10) refers to the reduction of half of "his bread." Forkman (1972: 58) interprets this punishment as the reduction of the perfect fellowship in terms of economic unity.

[38] See Forkman 1972: 57–59; Schiffman 1983: 159–68; Baumgarten 1992: 272–73. When the penalty contains merely a "penance" in S, Schiffman regards it to mean only the reduction of the food ration—not exclusion from the "purity" (similarly, Newsom 2004: 151–52). When the penalty contains "exclusion" from the "purity" for a year, this meant, in Schiffman's opinion, exclusion from the pure *liquids*, not from the solid food. However, it is difficult to interpret "purity" in this way. Furthermore, Baumgarten is correct is noting that S does not always maintain a distinction between the terms for exclusion and penance. He considers the possibility that the "penance" in S could have meant exclusion (from "contact with purities"), but not reduction of food.

[39] Purity is not the only concern in the punishment. If the "purity" from which the member was excluded signifies the pure meal of the group and this is closely connected to the session for deliberations (cf. 1QS VI, 2–3), the punishment could include both reduction of food and some form of exclusion from the common meal (whether

this was the case, the *punishments were directly connected to the central group beliefs*: violation of the community as counsel resulted in exclusion from this community of counsel, and a lowering in the hierarchy. The penal code can then be read not merely as a warning against improper behavior, but almost as a "gospel": this system holds.[40] Even though a member might deviate, the group continued to be the bearer of correct revelation and the fulfiller of the Law.

From a theological point of view, this is understandable. There was a dilemma in the fact that even the righteous members of the community might sin. According to the basic group beliefs (as presented above), the community should be able to fulfill the righteous will of God. One relaxation of this problem is offered in S in the discourse of the two spirits (1QS III–IV): only in the end will it appear who is truly a son of light and who is a son of darkness. Secondly, the group naturally had a system for excluding members who intentionally broke the laws (permanent expulsion). However, some offences could take place unintentionally.[41] These could not go unnoticed or the group would lose its credibility. Furthermore, in addition to specific halakhic observance, the movement had a clear awareness of the need to actualize—perhaps the more abstract—values of love, truth, and righteousness, to show love especially towards their fellow members and the weak (e.g., 1QS I, 1–7; V, 3b–4a; V, 26b–VI, 1; CD VI, 20–21).[42] The solution

---

physical, or concerning the liquid, or some other form of distinction, cf. 1QS VII, 3), and also denial of full rights in participating in the sessions (see 1QS VI, 22–23; VII, 21; VIII, 16–19).

[40] Cf. Boyer 2002, who explains that fundamentalist violence is not directed at the victims but rather at possible defectors in order to show them that defection is costly. In the penal code, warning against defecting certainly involves the most severe punishment, expulsion, but the members did not only need warnings but also landmarks which made their social identity accessible, understandable, and feasible. These were provided by the system of surveillance and the minor punishments.

[41] Outside this penal code collection, S includes a section that seem to contradict this principle: 1QS VIII, 16b–19 merely states that intentional offenses had to be purified. On the other hand, 1QS VIII, 20–IX, 2 explicitly distinguishes intentional offenses, resulting in permanent expulsion, from unintentional ones. One unintentional sin was punished by exclusion from the purity and the council for two years, and if the member remained blameless during this time, s/he regained his/her previous standing.

[42] D more clearly preserves the concern with deuteronomic ideals: the community existed in order to provide for the poor and take care of the marginalized, and it criticized the wicked rich, and probably produced some kind of common property or welfare system. A member had to give two-days' wages per month to the Examiner of the community in order to provide for the needy (CD XIV, 12–16). The members were restricted in their business transactions with outsiders (4QD^a 9 III, 1–3). The same concern is probably behind the common property system in S: the community

to imperfectness in these areas lay in the hierarchy of the group. The one who had unintentionally offended had been shown to be lower than his standing indicated; thus, his standing was lowered for a time so that he was no longer in a position where he could give advice to others or be representative of the purity of the group. This interpretation is supported by the rule which defines ten years of membership to be the maximum for the temporary exclusion procedure; over that, permanent expulsion was the punishment (1QS VII, 22–24). According to the underlying thought, a senior member "should know better" but a junior member may still error. Therefore, the problem of sin *within* the group is not addressed by the punishments as such; the problem of sin will be left to God but the credibility of the group requires some measures be taken.

This analysis suggests that the penal code is one part of the construction of the community of counsel. It promotes the continuance of the *shared social identity: the awareness of being part of the righteous counseling, and emotional reliance on the trustworthiness of the group.* The existence of the penal codes in written form may well be one factor in making that identity more salient. Not every movement of an individual was regulated—after all, many matters are simply not controlled in the penal code, such as the manner of eating, seeing, sleeping, or the area where one could move freely. What was regulated was the cooperation in the community and the confidence in it.[43] If one member acted against it, the system rebalanced itself and continued working. The lack of specific halakhic issues, moral crimes, or clear matters of impurity among the penal code cases is striking.[44] Does this mean that every member was able to fulfill all of these high ideals and major commandments without

---

was one in "law and property" (1QS V, 2). The property was held in common, but members had some private rights of usage (VI, 18–23; VII, 6–8).

[43] By joining the community, many central areas of life (property, conduct, speech, sex, knowledge, emotions, even gestures) were subordinated, to a certain extent, to the community principles, but many of the rules in the penal code probably applied only to the community meetings.

[44] However, D includes regulations concerning crimes against the Torah in capital matters (CD IX, 16–22) and concerning the observance of the Sabbath/holy days (CD XII, 3–6), which can be regarded as "preliminary" penal code cases although these are not part of the penal code of D. The punishment for the capital matters includes some form of exclusion (from the "purity"), and for an infraction of the Sabbath observance, keeping guard for seven years before being readmitted to the congregation. In S, the misuse of the divine name (VI, 27–VII, 2) is a more serious case than others (but similar to unspecified crimes against the Law, cf. 1QS VIII, 21–24) and punished by expulsion.

any problems? My feeling is no. But that was not the crucial matter for the group. What the community needed was the judgment of who belongs in and who belongs out, and the counseling which ensured its members the right to be in.

In conclusion, the penal code alone may not be taken as an example of the strict mentality of the Qumran movement. It is essential to understand how central the Torah also was to the S group(s), not only to the D groups. The rules in S are perhaps more like a collection of "meta-rules" for the community and its leaders. The rules and the penal codes are not directly adopted from other similar groups of the time, but their resemblance shows that similar rules are felt to be necessary in groups which seek to have their group identity salient in all circumstances. With the help of the social identity approach, I have tried to show that the penal code is not a consequence of life in a closed community, nor of an ascetic and controlled mentality as such, but instead is the result of a promotion of the shared social identity, according to which an individual saw him/herself as a part of the community of counsel, called and mandated to follow the righteous Law of God.

REFERENCES

Alexander, Philip, and Geza Vermes. 1998. *Qumran Cave 4 XIX. 4QSerekh Ha-Yahad*. Discoveries in the Judean Desert 26. Oxford: Clarendon Press.
Bar-Tal, Daniel. 1998. "Group Beliefs as an Expression of Social Identity." In *Social Identity: International Perspectives*, edited by Steven Worchel et al., 93–113. London: SAGE Publications.
Baumgarten, Joseph M. 1992. The Cave 4 Versions of the Qumran Penal Code. *Journal of Jewish Studies* 43: 268–76.
——. 1996. *Qumran Cave 4 XIII. The Damascus Document (4Q266–4Q273)*. Discoveries in the Judean Desert 18. Oxford: Clarendon Press.
——. 2000. Judicial Procedures. In *Encyclopedia of the Dead Sea Scrolls*, edited by Lawrence H. Schiffman and James C. VanderKam, 455–601. Oxford: Oxford University Press.
Baumgarten, Joseph M., and Daniel R. Schwartz. 1995. "Damascus Document (CD)." In *The Dead Sea Scrolls: Hebrew, Aramaic, and Greek Texts with English Translations*, edited by James H. Charlesworth et al., 4–57. The Princeton Theological Seminary Dead Sea Scrolls Project 2. Tübingen: J. C. B. Mohr.
Beall, Todd S. 1998. *Josephus' Description of the Essenes Illustrated by the Dead Sea Scrolls*. Cambridge: Cambridge University Press.
Boyer, Pascal. 2002. *Religion Explained: The Human Instincts that Fashion Gods, Spirits and Ancestors*. London: Vintage.
Charlesworth, James H. 2000. "Community Organization in the Community Rule." In *Encyclopedia of the Dead Sea Scrolls*, edited by Lawrence H. Schiffman and James C. VanderKam, 133–361. Oxford: Oxford University Press.

Condor, Susan. 1996. "Social Identity and Time." In *Social Groups and Identities: Developing the Legacy of Henri Tajfel*, edited by W. Peter Robinson, 285–315. International Series in Social Psychology. Oxford: Butterworth-Heinemann.
Esler, Philip F. 2001. "Palestinian Judaism in the First Century." In *Religious Diversity in the Graeco-Roman World: A Survey of Recent Scholarship*, edited by Dan Cohn-Sherbok and John M. Court, 21–46. Sheffield: Sheffield Academic Press.
Forkman, Göran. 1972. *The Limits of the Religious Community: Expulsion from the Religious Community within the Qumran Sect, within Rabbinic Judaism, and within Primitive Christianity*. Coniectanea Biblica: New Testament Series 5. Lund, Sweden: CWK Gleerup.
Foucault, Michel. 1995. *Discipline and Punish: The Birth of the Prison*. Translated by Alan Sheridan. New York: Random House.
García Martínez, Florentino, and Eibert J. C. Tigchelaar. Eds. 2000. *The Dead Sea Scrolls Study Edition.* Vol. 1: 1Q1–4Q273. Leiden: Brill.
García Martínez, Florentino, and Julio Trebolle Barrera. 1995. *The People of the Dead Sea Scrolls: Their Writings, Beliefs and Practices*. Leiden: Brill.
Haslam, S. Alexander. 2004. *Psychology in Organizations: The Social Identity Approach*. London: SAGE Publications.
Hempel, Charlotte. 1997. "The Penal Code Reconsidered." In *Legal Texts and Legal Issues: Proceedings of the Second Meeting of the International Organization for Qumran Studies*, Cambridge 1995, edited by Moshe Bernstein, Florentino García Martínez and John Kampen, 337–48. Leiden: Brill.
———. 1998. *The Laws of the Damascus Document: Sources, Tradition and Redaction*. Studies on the Texts of the Desert of Judah 29. Leiden: Brill.
———. 1999. "Community Structures in the Dead Sea Scrolls: Admission, Organization, Disciplinary Procedures." In *The Dead Sea Scrolls after Fifty Years. A Comprehensive Assessment*. Vol. 2, edited by Peter W. Flint and James C. VanderKam, 67–92. Leiden: Brill.
Hogg, Michael A., and Dominic Abrams, 1988. *Social Identifications: A Social Psychology of Intergroup Relations and Group Processes*. London: Routledge.
Jastram, Nathan. 1997. "Hierarchy at Qumran." In *Legal Texts and Legal Issues: Proceedings of the Second Meeting of the International Organization for Qumran Studies*, Cambridge 1995, edited by Moshe Bernstein, Florentino García Martínez and John Kampen, 349–76. Studies on the Texts of the Desert of Judah 23. Leiden: Brill.
Jokiranta, Jutta. 2005. "Identity on a Continuum: Constructing and Expressing Sectarian Social Identity in Qumran Serakhim and Pesharim." Doctoral dissertation, University of Helsinki.
Klinghardt, Matthias. 1994. "The Manual of Discipline in the Light of Statutes of Hellenistic Associations." In *Methods of Investigation of the Dead Sea Scrolls and the Khirbet Qumran Site: Present Realities and Future Prospects*, edited by Michael O. Wise et al., 251–70. New York: The New York Academy of Sciences.
McCauley, Robert N., and E. Thomas Lawson. 2002. *Bringing Ritual to Mind: Psychological Foundations of Cultural Forms.* Cambridge: Cambridge University Press.
Metso, Sarianna. 1997. *The Textual Development of the Qumran Community Rule*. Studies on the Texts of the Desert of Judah 21. Leiden: Brill.
———. 2000. "The Relationship between the Damascus Document and the Community Rule." In *The Damascus Document: A Centennial of Discovery. Proceedings of the Third International Symposium of the Orion Center for the Study of the Dead Sea Scrolls and Associated Literature, 4–8 February, 1998*, edited by Joseph M. Baumgarten, Esther G. Chazon and Avital Pinnick, 85–93. Studies on the Texts of the Desert of Judah 34. Leiden: Brill.
———. 2004. "Methodological Problems in Reconstructing History from Rule Texts Found at Qumran." *Dead Sea Discoveries* 11: 315–35.
Murphy, Catherine M. 2002. *Wealth in the Dead Sea Scrolls and in the Qumran Community*. Studies on the Texts of the Desert of Judah 40. Leiden: Brill.

Newsom, Carol A. 2004. *The Self as Symbolic Space: Constructing Identity and Community at Qumran.* Studies on the Texts of the Desert of Judah 52. Leiden: Brill.
Qimron, Elisha. 1992. "The Text of CDC." In *The Damascus Document Reconsidred*, edited by Magen Broshi, 9–49. Jerusalem: The Israel Exploration Society.
Qimron, Elisha, and James H. Charlesworth. 1994. "Rule of the Community (1QS)." In *The Dead Sea Scrolls. Hebrew, Aramaic, and Greek Texts with English Translations.* Vol. 1: *Rule of the Community and Related Documents*, edited by James H. Charlesworth et al., 1–51. Tübingen: J. C. B. Mohr.
Schiffman, Lawrence H. 1983. *Sectarian Law in the Dead Sea Scrolls: Courts, Testimony and the Penal Code.* Brown Judaic Studies. Chico, Calif.: Scholars Press.
———. 1994. *Reclaiming the Dead Sea Scrolls: The History of Judaism, the Background of Christianity, the Lost Library of Qumran.* Philadelphia, Pa.: The Jewish Publication Society.
Shemesh, Aharon. 2002. "Expulsion and Exclusion in the Community Rule and the Damascus Document." *Dead Sea Discoveries* 9: 44–74.
Stark, Rodney, and William Sims Bainbridge. 1987. *A Theory of Religion.* Toronto Studies in Religion. New York: Peter Lang.
Tajfel, Henri. 1978. *Differentiation between Social Groups: Studies in the Social Psychology of Intergroup Relations.* London: Academic Press.
———. 1981. *Human Groups and Social Categories: Studies in Social Psychology.* Cambridge: Cambridge University Press.
Walker-Ramisch, Sandra. 1996. "Graeco-Roman Voluntary Associations and the Damascus Document: A Sociological Analysis." In *Voluntary Associations in the Graeco-Roman World*, edited by John S. Kloppenborg and Stephen G. Wilson, 128–45. London: Routledge.
Wassen, Cecilia. 2005. *Women in the Damascus Document.* Academica Biblica 21. Atlanta, Ga.: Society of Biblical Literature.
Wassen, Cecilia, and Jutta Jokiranta. Forthcoming. "Groups in Tension: Sectarianism in the Damascus Document and the Community Rule." In *Sectarianism in Early Judaism: Sociological Advances*, edited by David Chalcraft. Equinox Press.
Weinfeld, Moshe. 1986. *The Organizational Pattern and the Penal Code of the Qumran Sect: A Comparison with Guilds and Religious Associations of the Hellenistic-Roman Period.* Novum Testamentum et orbis antiquus 2. Fribourg: Éditions universitaires.
Vermes, Geza. 1981. *The Dead Sea Scrolls: Qumran in Perspective.* Philadelphia, Pa.: Fortress.
Whitehouse, Harvey. 2004. "Toward a Comparative Anthropology of Religion." In *Ritual and Memory: Toward a Comparative Anthropology of Religion*, edited by Harvey Whitehouse and James Laidlaw, 187–205. Walnut Creek, Calif.: Altamira Press.

EPILOGUE

Troels Engberg-Pedersen

1. *The Issue*

This volume is a bold attempt to switch the study of Christian origins and early Judaism into a new gear by explicitly and in detail connecting it with various sides of the new cognitive science of religion. For that purpose, it draws on certain specific approaches within the overall field of the current study of early Judaism and early Christianity, in particular those adopting modern social-scientific perspectives on the ancient data. The editors present the volume in exactly that way: "We hope...that [the volume]...will mark the beginning of a fruitful exchange of ideas between scholars interested in social-scientific, socio-rhetorical and cognitive study of religion." While social-scientific and socio-rhetorical types of study have been applied to early Judaism and early Christianity for quite some time, the general cognitive science of religion has not. Thus, the volume explicitly aims to further dialogue between, on the one hand, scholars of early Judaism and early Christianity with those specific, social-scientific and socio-rhetorical interests and, on the other, students of the cognitive science of religion in general.

This aim is carried out in intriguing and thought-provoking essays throughout the volume. But a question remains: what about the remaining group of scholars engaged in early Jewish and Christian studies, a group that probably constitutes by far the majority? What may they get out of a rapprochement between social-scientifically-oriented biblical scholars and students of the cognitive science of religion in general? Whatever they be mainly working on—be it textual, historical or ideological issues ("theology") in early Jewish and early Christian studies—is such a rapprochement a development that takes place on a different planet from their own? Or should it also be of interest to them? In the latter case, exactly how should one see the connections between their various endeavors and a rapprochement that they might well see from their individual perspectives as taking place somewhat on the fringe of their own endeavors? It is this broad question that I wish to take up here—tentatively and somewhat impressionistically—in order to consider whether the present volume should be of interest only to a relative minority of scholars in the field of early Jewish and early Christian studies, who may themselves feel—and in a way, rightly—that they are working at the forefront of current studies of these ancient religions, or whether it should also be of interest to the much larger group of scholars who are working in more traditional fields within the discipline.

2. *Some Strengths of the Rapprochement*

Before discussing this question, we should note some of the points where the essays in this volume both make claims for the strength of the proposed rapprochement and also attempt to make good those claims in concrete interpretive practice. The list might be extended, but it should certainly contain the following eight points, some of which are partially overlapping.

(1) The claim is repeatedly made that the rapprochement enables scholars to rely on testable hypotheses instead of mere "intuitions" concerning the ways human beings react psychologically to this or the other kind of input. One example is this (from Luomanen's essay; compare also those of Uro and Esler):

> The cognitive approach can contribute to the study of Christian origins especially by providing scientifically tested information and systematically formulated theories about the functions of the mind. Quite often scholars supplement their historical constructions with psychological assumptions about "reasonable" or "natural" human responses and strategies. Instead of doing these reconstructions instinctively, on the basis of gut feelings alone, it would be better if we could also use some systematically formulated and tested theories.

This claim presupposes, of course, that there are universal features of the way in which the human mind (and brain) functions, features that can be identified through modern psychological experiments and then brought into play with the ancient data. This claim can certainly be disputed, as it has been vociferously in the poststructuralist outlook of the last few decades. In the way it is introduced by the editors in the introduction to the present volume, however, the claim has a certain persuasiveness to it. The key term is that of certain "constraints" (e.g., in Martin's essay) in the way the human mind categorizes and operates on input whether from the outside or from its own internal operations.

If—together with what is probably the majority of philosophers working in the field—one operates with the notion of some form of mind-brain identity, the claim that there are such constraints on human cognition seems reasonably justified. In that case, the road should be open for trying to identify them in a more than merely "intuitive" way.

(2) Another point that is repeatedly made in the essays is that there is a need to combine a social perspective on the issues that are studied—e.g., the transmission of religious traditions—with a perspective that focuses on the individual mind and those "constraints" through which any kind of social knowledge is necessarily processed (again Luomanen, Pyysiäinen and Uro; Esler). This point is very well taken and it provides a valuable correction to the most extreme claims that have been made within social-scientific analysis of early Christianity, in particular, to the effect that there was no consciousness of the "self" or even of the "individual" in the ancient world—whereas the focus was throughout exclusively on the group. In contast, the approach adopted in the present volume emphasizes both the social and the individual character of knowledge acquisition in antiquity (as well as probably in the modern world, too). Then, as now, knowledge was basically socially engineered but through the medium of the individual cognitive mechanisms of the mind. By the same token, since one universal characteristic of the functioning of the human brain appears to be a fairly substantial degree of self-awareness, it seems reasonable to take the references one does find in ancient texts to a "self" and an "individual" to refer to just those notions—though evidently not necessarily with all the additional overtones of a modern "self" or "individual."

(3) A further point where many of the essays concur is an emphasis on social practice as opposed to mere ideas. Thus Luomanen, Pyysiäinen and Uro contrast "ideas" with "what was really going on in real-time religion." Uro also writes that "[s]cholars of early Christianity have generally approached their subject from theological or intellectualist perspectives preferring belief to action, thought-world to social world, or myth to ritual," whereas his own preference goes the other way round. Furthermore, this emphasis on social practice evidently lies behind those essays that consider the mechanisms of group behavior in terms of some version of social identity theory (Hakola; Jokiranta). This general orientation is a powerful one. It is certainly not new inasmuch as it is one of the root ideas in the social historical, sociological and social-scientific approach that has become a very significant thread in the web of early Jewish and early Christian studies during the last three

decades. Still, this approach has not lost its validity even when it has been supplemented with more text-orientated perspectives during the same period. Here the rapprochement with the cognitive science of religion helps to keep alive this focus on "what was really going on."

(4) One feature that is characteristic of many of the essays is a focus on the transmission of religious traditions (Luomanen, Pyysiäinen and Uro; Martin; Pyysiäinen; Ketola; Uro; Luomanen; Esler). The reason is fairly obvious. Transmission is necessarily a social phenomenon (compare the sociological dimension of traditional form history). At the same time, it opens up for an analysis in terms of those constraints of the individual human mind through which the social process of transmission will occur. Once more, the emphasis on transmission is not in itself new. But it does shift the focus in a healthy way from being exclusively on the intricacies of individual texts to the broader question of the social function of the ideas contained in those texts: how they work socially.

(5) A broader methodological feature of the approach adopted in the essays is the attempt to provide accounts of the data that will also genuinely explain the various historical developments reflected in them. This attempt is intrinsic to the method itself since it is precisely looking for universal features of human cognition that will explain the specific form taken by any given case of religious thinking and practice. Thus, the search for universal explanation is necessarily a comparative enterprise, and this is a strength since comparison is the only valid way to achieve real human understanding. The aim is, of course, not to neglect the unique features of the phenomena. Any historical phenomenon is unique in some respect or other. But it is only through comparison and an identification of potentially universal similarities that one will become able to identify any possibly unique differences.

(6) An even broader feature reflected in the essays is that, in many of them, the orientation towards the cognitive science of religion has the consequence of keeping in focus the question of what it is that makes the material that is being studied fall under the category of "religion." If—as the basic approach insists—the human cognitive machinery that is in operation in the material that is studied is the same as in any other cognitive field (Luomanen, Pyysiäinen and Uro; Martin; Lundhaug; Luomanen), then what is it that makes this particular field one of "religion"? Bearing this question constantly in mind is a strength since it at least holds out the hope that one may eventually come to understand more precisely what makes a set of ideas and practices a

"religious" one. This question is far too often left on one side as if it were already answered.

(7) An example of this acute awareness of the "religiosity" of religion is the focus on ritual that is pervasive throughout the volume (Luomanen, Pyysiäinen and Uro; Martin; Ketola; Uro), not least as reflecting the various approaches to ritual to be found in the frequently cited books by Lawson and McCauley and Harvey Whitehouse. It would be false to say that scholars of early Judaism and early Christianity have altogether neglected this important topic. Additionally, one should admit that for early Christianity, at least, the evidence for whatever rituals Christians may have adopted is somewhat meager. Still, there can be no doubt that this emphasis on ritual—in connection with some of the other themes I have highlighted, e.g., that of transmission—is a healthy one which brings a relatively neglected feature of early Judaism and early Christianity into sharper focus.

(8) Finally, there is another important field of both early Jewish and early Christian studies that may receive new focus from the approach presented in this volume. If Harvey Whitehouse's distinction between a doctrinal and an imagistic mode of religiosity is applied, for instance, to the New Testament writings, it immediately becomes clear that the kind of religiosity reflected in them belongs far more to the imagistic side than the doctrinal one. That is not new in itself, but it does open up the field for seeking out and emphasizing elements in the general rhetoric of those writings that speak to the imagination. In this area, too, one might point to an important field within the New Testament that might be further illuminated by the cognitive approach even though the connection is not explicitly drawn in the present volume, namely, the field of paraenesis ("moral exhortation"). It is noteworthy that the role of "exemplars" (see Luomanen's essay) is discussed by Seneca in the two letters (*Ep.* 94 and 95) in which he discusses the role of "rules" (a "doctrinal" element) and "exemplars" (an "imagistic" one) in paraenesis. Paul's self-presentation in his own letters has many features that fit an imagistic use of himself as an "exemplar."

3. *...and Some Weaknesses*

However, the rapprochement with the cognitive science of religion—at least as displayed in this volume—also reveals some weaknesses. Here I will mention only four, some of which are again partially overlapping.

(1) One noteworthy thing is how few essays take the additional step from social identity theory, social psychology or the like to neuroscience. (The essays by Czachesz and Luomanen are honorable exceptions here.) In itself this is not at all surprising since the attempt to locate in the brain specific features of human social functioning as identified under a psychological description is only at its very beginning. The fact remains that the neuroscientific identification and specification of the postulated "constraints" that is apparently possible at the present stage is a rather weak one.

(2) In connection with this, it appears that there is a certain risk of superficiality in the claims about the ancient data that this new approach invites. For instance, in spite of the use to which one may well put the distinction between "doctrine" and "image," it also seems from some of the essays that what can be said about the texts in those terms (e.g., about Paul) is very far from doing justice to everything that is going on in those texts and which one might hope to be able to connect with the new perspective. So far, the gap between the specificity allowed for by the theory and the specificity required by the texts appears to be rather great. And that, surely, is a weakness.

(3) There is a corresponding risk that the new approach will focus scholarly attention in a onesided manner on those features of the ancient data that do fit with what is at present allowed for by the theory. This is a potential weakness that does not touch the present volume in view of its fundamentally exploratory character. However, it is a general risk that should be recognized. If scholars of antiquity familiarize themselves with what can—at any given moment—be solidly said within the cognitive science of religion in its various forms and then consider the ancient material exclusively in terms of what data may fit the theory, then it is highly likely that there will be a huge amount of important material in the texts themselves that will not appear on the scholarly horizon. That would be not only a great pity but also a serious weakness of the approach itself.

(4) One overwhelming danger is that what I would call the normative content of the ancient texts disappears from view altogether. For instance, while the cognitive approach may well have something important to say about the "imagistic" function of the cross in early Christian discourse, it is unlikely to pay any serious attention to the meaning of this symbol that the early Christian texts are so keen on developing. To a large extent this is probably due to the emphasis in the cognitive approach as appropriated here on "what was really going

on in real-time religion" as opposed to the "ideas." Still, it remains a weakness, to which I shall come back below.

4. *Philosophy and Cognitive Science*

We may take as our starting point some remarks at the very end of Luomanen's essay in which he claims that philosophers are today "becoming more and more aware of the challenge of the cognitive science of religion to such philosophical (Platonic) traditions that ignore the embodied character of the mind." The point is well taken inasmuch as it contrasts the modern cognitive approach with much traditional philosophizing in a Platonic tradition that has in fact largely ignored the embodied character of the mind. If one goes back to antiquity, however, the situation looks somewhat different. Even in a "Platonist" like Aristotle, both the body and the social dimension of thought are recognized in ways that make it impossible to charge him with ignoring the embodied character of the mind. In any case, Platonism did not cover all of ancient philosophy. In antiquity, several types of philosophy were distinctly less disembodied than Platonism, e.g., Epicureanism and Stoicism.

The latter is interesting in this context for at least two reasons. First, it has been argued (by, among others, myself) that early Christian thinking about the Christ event, for instance in Paul, was to an important degree influenced by Stoic categories of thought, both ethical and cosmological ones, including the Stoic, "bodily" conception of the *pneuma* ("spirit"). Second, in many of those areas that are also in focus within modern cognitive science—both generally and as applied to religion—the Stoics articulated ideas springing from their "bodily" understanding of cognition and thought that are at least comparable in their general structure to what one finds among the new ideas. If these points can be maintained, then there is no necessary contrast between ancient philosophy and modern cognitive science; moreover, some early Christian thought may itself—through its contact with Stoic materialist philosophy—be far closer to the modern perspective than we are wont to think.

As regards the first claim, it should be emphasized that it at present constitutes a distinct minority position only. This is not the place to go into the whole issue, but it is worth pointing to the extent to which a more traditional theological reflection from the second century onwards has in fact been drawing on the philosophical outlook of Platonism (or Aristotelianism) rather than, e.g., Stoicism. How this came to be is a chapter of its own, which has to do with the way philosophy itself developed in the first two centuries after Christ—as it were, from Stoicism into (Middle-)Platonism and Aristotelianism—and also with the way Christian thinkers of the second century appropriated the Jewish philosopher Philo of Alexandria (a contemporary of Jesus and Paul), whose philosophy was basically shaped by Plato (even though he also incorporates large quantities of Stoicism). The issue is important since, with the appropriate definitions, one may well speak of Platonism as a "non-naturalistic" philosophy (of disembodied "ideas") and of Stoicism as a "naturalistic" one. In that case, the issue feeds immediately into the present topic. If early Christianity was itself in reasonably close contact with a type of philosophy that was "naturalistic," then the modern cognitive scientific approach need not be seen as coming completely from the outside as a purely modern alternative to ways of thinking that were embedded in early Christianity itself.

With regard to the second claim, I would like to give here a few examples of Stoic ideas that seem to belong to the same general way of thinking as that involved in modern cognitive science. This is intended purely by way of example and the claim is certainly not that these are identical theories. However, the general similarity—not least with the basic approach underlying the essays on conceptual blending by Lundhaug and Robbins—does seem worth noting.

One example concerns the way in which the Stoics thought that notions or concepts arise in the mind from perception. Here is one version of the Stoic idea as given by Sextus Empiricus (*Adversus Mathematicos* 3.40–42) in my own translation based on that of the Loeb edition:

> In general, everything conceived (*pan to nooumenon*) is conceived (*epinoeitai*) in two main ways, either by way of direct and clear contact (*kata periptōsin enargē*) or by way of transference (*kata...metabasin*) from things clear, and the latter way is threefold: by similarity (*homoiōtikōs*), by composition (*episynthetikōs*) or by analogy (*analogistikōs*). By the clarity of direct contact (*kata...periptōtikēn enargeian*) are conceived (*noeitai*) white, black, sweet and bitter. By transference, however, things are conceived either by similarity—such as Socrates himself from an image of Socrates—or by composition—such as the hippocentaur from horse and man (*for by mixing* [or "blending"] *the limbs of horse and man we have imagined the hippocentaur which is neither man nor horse but a compound* [*syntheton*] *of both*); by analogy, however, a thing is also conceived in two ways, sometimes by way of increase (*auxētikōs*), sometimes by decrease (*meiōtikōs*); for instance,

we have conceived the Cyclops...by way of increase from ordinary men..., and by way of decrease we conceive the Pygmy, whom we have not come across in direct contact.

This is fairly rudimentary, of course, but it seems clear that the Stoics were thinking about concept formation along the same general lines as in modern cognitive science.

Another example concerns the Stoic theory of how human beings have obtained the notion of God. This is the famous ancient, Stoic argument from design. Out of many possible texts, one might again quote the version given by Sextus Empiricus (*Adversus Mathematicos* 9.26–27). Here, however, I prefer to give a quotation from Philo that shows how, after having stated the Stoic view (97–99), he makes the Platonistic move (100) that brings him back (or forward) to his beloved Moses (101, *Allegorical Interpretation* 3.97–101, the Loeb translation with a few changes):

> (97) The first men sought to find how we came to conceive of the Deity. Next those whose philosophy was reputed the best [i.e. the Stoics] declared that it was from the world and its constituent parts and the forces subsisting in these that we gained our apprehension of the First Cause. (98) Should a man see a house carefully constructed with a gateway, and the other buildings, he will get the notion (*ennoia*) of the artificer (or "designer," *ho technitēs*), for he will be of the opinion that the house never reached that completeness without the skill (*technē*) of the craftsman (*dēmiourgos*); and in like manner in the case of a city and a ship and every smaller or greater construction. (99) Just so anyone entering this world, as it were some vast house or city, and beholding the sky circling round and embracing within it all things, and planets and fixed stars without any variation moving in rhythmical harmony and with advantage to the whole, and earth with the central space assigned to it, water and air flowing in set order as its boundary, and over and above these, living creatures, mortal and immortal beings, planets and fruits in great variety, he will surely argue (or "conclude," *logizesthai*) that these have not been crafted (*dēmiourgeisthai*) without consummate art (*technē*), but that the Maker (*dēmiourgos*) of this whole universe is God. Those who conclude (*epilogizesthai*) like this apprehend God by means of a shadow cast, discerning the Artificer (*technitēs*) by means of His works (*erga*). (100) There is, however, a mind more perfect and more thoroughly cleansed, which has undergone initiation into the great mysteries, a mind which gains its knowledge of the First Cause not from created things, as one may learn the substance from the shadow, but lifting its eyes above and beyond creation obtains a clear vision of the uncreated One, so as from Him to apprehend both Himself and His shadow. To apprehend that was, as we saw, to apprehend both the Word (or "reason," *ho logos*) and this world (*hode ho kosmos*). (101) The mind of which I speak is Moses who says...

This text shows both that the Stoics provided an analysis of the genesis of the human conception of God that can easily be connected with modern cognitive science—and also that this naturalistic way of thinking was, in the end, contested by Philo, the Platonist, who thereby laid the ground for the adoption of the kind of philosophy, namely non-naturalistic Platonism, that one finds in the later Christian tradition (from the second century onwards).

5. *A Challenge*

Suppose that philosophy as such is not to be contrasted with modern cognitive science—witness the example of ancient Stoicism. In that case, the road may be open for trying to account, from a cognitive perspective, for far more of the data for Christian origins and early Judaism than might immediately appear. In particular, one might then try to close the gap between "what was really going on in real-time religion" and "ideas" and attempt to bring the ideas, too, within the horizon of the cognitive approach. Philosophy is about ideas. However, if philosophy itself—and hence the ideas as well—is a bodily and social phenomenon, then it might be possible to apply a cognitive perspective to basic early Jewish and early Christian ideas that seem—to judge from the texts themselves—to have played a very important role in explaining the successful functioning of these religions. This is the challenge to the cognitive approach that I think should be made on behalf of more traditional work with early Judaism and early Christianity. If one believes that the cognitive approach is on the right track, then one simply must try to find room within that perspective for some of what superficially appears to be most important in the ancient texts—and what has in fact also had an enormous influence on shaping later culture: the ideas.

How may one proceed to fulfil this task? I can only suggest a few possibilities. Will the Pauline idea in 1 Corinthians of the group of Christ followers as the "body of Christ"—an idea that in itself draws on Stoic terminology—not be open to cognitive analysis? Or what about the closely connected Pauline idea of "love" (*agapē*): God's love for human beings and the love of human beings for one another? Is it possible to see in this idea an evolutionary breakthrough that lifts to a higher level of awareness a universal fact about human beings that constitutes some kind of—not formal, but—substantive constraint on the way human beings may think about themselves and the world?

The line behind this idea of substantive constraints might be this. Because human beings individually have a brain (of the kind that is the human one), each human being will necessarily have some more or less rudimentary conception of "self" and the "individual," namely, him- or herself. This is a function of the self-reflexivity that is characteristic of the human brain, and the notion of "self" or "individual" that is involved is not a very substantial one. However, the moment this notion is discovered or articulated in a self-reflexive process in the brain, one (i.e. a "person" as we may probably now call the self-reflecting individual) also discovers "others like oneself," that is, entities different from oneself who appear to be functioning in the same way as oneself. (One also, of course, discovers other entities that do not appear to be functioning like oneself, that is, other "things.") It goes without saying that this whole process is not just an "individualistic" one, but on the contrary, highly social, and this accounts for the fact that the notions of "selves" that develop in different cultures differ so much from one another.

However, is it not then possible to think that the development may take one additional step? The effect might be that the initial distinction between "oneself" and "others" is now—once more through the self-reflexivity of the human brain—overcome in such a way that the essential sense of one's own identity is now placed by the operating brain, not in that brain itself or in the notion of an individual self to which it has given rise, but in the social "self" that is made up of all those human beings who function in the same way. This is the basic claim of Stoic ethics as developed in their theory of *oikeiōsis* ("appropriation" or "accommodation"), but it might also be what underlies Paul's maxim in Philippians 2:4 when he enjoins his readers as follows: "Let *each* of you look not to your own interests, *but rather* to the interests of the others."

Exactly how should we think that this additional step is taken? Here it is at least noteworthy that both in Paul and in the naturalistic philosophy of Stoicism, the step involves a third entity: God. This holds in a general way. In Paul, there is a kind of triad consisting of what God has done in love for human beings, how human beings will (or should) receive that with love for God and how they will then extend this love to love for other human beings. The same kind of story may be found in Stoicism, for instance, in Seneca's splendid work *De Beneficiis*. If one does not, however, go for "stories," Stoicism also contains the idea that the level of awareness of other brains like one's own to which one may eventually rise is, in a way, itself ... God. (I take this to be the import of the Stoic talk of God "within.") In addition to this general similarity, there also is a difference between Stoicism and Paul in the account given of how love will come about—a difference that directly opens the way for a cognitive analysis of Paul's account. In Stoicism, the love of human beings for one another is derived from both the leap in awareness of oneself and others that we spoke of and also from the fact that children will have a very distinct experience of a love that is genuinely altruistic (though this love is also to be explained naturalistically), namely, that of their parents for the children themselves. Is it not, then, noteworthy that, according to Paul, when Christ followers rise from the baptismal water, they will precisely greet God with the cry of "Father!" (Gal 4:6, Rom 8:15)? Does this whole configuration not open itself up to the kind of social psychological—and presumably also neuroscientific—analysis that is part of the cognitive approach? Is it not likely that there is some kind of universal—and probably evolutionary—substantive constraint on the human attitude to oneself and others that was raised to consciousness at more or less the same time in antiquity in those two bodies of thought we have considered (and some others in addition)?

The aim here has been to suggest that it may turn out to be possible to include within the cognitive perspective far more of the important data about early Judaism and early Christianity than has previously been supposed, in such a way that more traditionally-working scholars may not end up feeling that what they themselves consider crucial to these data has been left completely out of consideration. That, at least, is the challenge I think one should issue to cognitive scientists of religion on behalf of traditional thinking about those data.

6. *Summary*

There is a range of topics on which I have not touched here, e.g., those of determinism and reductionism. These are so important that they cannot be satisfactorily addressed within a short space. Suffice it to say that the issue of determinism is so complex and contested in modern philosophy that one certainly cannot employ any given position within that field as a lever for rejecting the cognitive approach altogether. Similarly, reduction comes in many forms and is, in any case, endemic to any kind of scientific endeavor.

Here I have wanted to suggest that the cognitive approach to Christian origins and early Judaism constitutes a strong scientific proposal that must be reckoned with by anyone who wishes to understand better this formative period of two major world religions. It has several strengths of its own. It immediately fits the social-scientific and socio-rhetorical types of investigation that are already part of scholarship in this field (as so strongly represented here by Esler and Robbins). As noted in some of the essays (e.g., those of Martin, Uro and Luomanen), it also presupposes traditional historical queries for providing the "ethnographic data" (Uro) for its own further queries. And finally, I have ventured to suggest, it should be seen as having the potential for addressing in new and illuminating ways some of the most important parts of the ancient material, including some its most cherished "ideas." Since some of us are undertaking the scientific investigation of Christian origins and early Judaism not just as "critics," but also, in a way, as "caretakers" and in particular by rejecting any idea of a necessary contrast between the two, this holds out hopes for a fairly drastic extension of the relevance of the new approach.

INDEX OF ANCIENT SOURCES

English names and abbreviations follow *The SBL Handbook of Style: for Ancient Near Eastern, Biblical, and early Christian studies*, edited by Patrick H. Alexander et al. Peabody, Mass.: Hendrickson Publishers, 1999.

1. Hebrew Bible

Genesis		Deuteronomy	
3:16	147	29:10–12	288
17:9–14	102		
17:12	99	2 Kings	
		2:11	62
Exodus		Nehemiah	
28	182	10:29–30	288
Leviticus			
12:3	99		

2. Old Testament Apocrypha and Pseudepigrapha

2 Enoch		Sirach	
20:1	179	43:26	177
61:10	179		
		Testament of Levi	
		3:8	179

3. Dead Sea Scrolls and Related Texts

Damascus Document

CD		XVI, 7b–9	288
I, 4–9	265	XVI, 10–12	288
I, 18–21	268		
III, 13–14	265	4QDª (4Q266)	
VI, 27–VII, 2	295	8 I, 1–2	287
VII, 3–6	295	9 III, 1–3	294
VII, 6–7	286	10 I, 11–15	279
IX, 9–16	288	10 II, 1–15	279
IX, 16–22	295	10 II, 5–8	281
XIII, 7b–13	288	10 II, 13–14	281
XIV	279	11 1–8	292
XIV, 12–16	294	11 1–21	279
XIV, 20	292		
XV, 1–2	279	4QDᵇ (4Q267)	
XV, 5b–11a	287	9 VI, 1–5	279
XVI, 4b–5	289		
		4QDᵉ (4Q270)	
		7 I, 1–21	279
		7 II, 11–15	279

314 INDEX OF ANCIENT SOURCES

Miscellaneous Rules (or 4Q*Serekh Damascus*; 4Q265)
1 I, 4–10   293

Rule of the Community

1 QS			
I, 1–7	294	VI, 22–23	294
I, 13	290	VI, 24–25	292
I, 16–25	288	VI, 24–VII, 25	281
II, 22	266	VI, 25	293
III–IV	294	VII, 3	294
III, 13–IV, 26	291	VII, 10–11	281, 292
V, 2	294–95	VII, 16–17	281
V, 3b–4a	294	VII, 21	294
V, 7b–10a	287–88	VII, 22–24	295
V, 7b–20a	287	VIII, 1–10	265
V, 20b–VI, 1a	287–88	VIII, 1–14	266
VI, 13b–23	287–88	VIII, 16–19	294
V, 8	266	VIII, 20–IX, 2	281, 294
V, 22	266	VIII, 21–24	295
V, 26b–VI, 1	294	4QS^b (4Q256)	
VI, 2–3	293	4 I, 6b–8a	287–88
VI, 18–23	294	4QS^d (4Q258)	
VI, 20–21	294	1 I, 5b–7a	287–88

Rule of the Congregation

1 QSa (1Q28a)
I, 11   286

Some of the Torah Observations / 4QMMT

the entire document   259, 268
55–58   269

4. Mishnah

m. Yad. 4:7	269	m. Toh. 8:9	269
m. Sanh. 6:5–6	58		

5. New Testament

Matthew		Mark	
3:1–17	48	1:2–11	48
3:7–10	48	1:30	186
26:61	111	4:17	236
27:40	111	13:9	236
27:64	62	14:58	111
28:9–10, 20	62	15:29	111
		16:8	62
		16:9–20	62

Luke			12:1–31	181
2:1–7	43		12:13	48–49
3:1–22	48		13:13	173
3:7–9	48		14:5	49
3:8	239		14:13–15	49
6:18	187		14:37	49
6:19	185, 187		14:38	49
6:20	188		15:3	60
6:20–49	188		15:3–8	59–60
6:21	188		15:3–11	59
6:27–30	188		15:20	178
24:13–27	62		15:23	178
24:34	60		15:24	178
24:36–37	62		15:25–26	178
			15:27–28	178

John		
1:15–34	48	
1:47	265	
3:7	154	
2:19	111	
20:11–29	62	

2 Corinthians	
7:1	149

Galatians	
1:6–9	49–50
1:11–12	49
1:12	60
4:6	311

Acts	
1:15	60
2:38–41	48
3:15	178
9:3–9	61
15:20	149
15:29	149
21:25	149
22:6–16	61
26:12–18	61
26:33	178

Romans	
1:9	234
1:16	49
1:17	49
3:26	49
3:28	49
3:30	49
5:1–5	173
8:15	310
9:2–5	273
9:6	265–66
9:30–33	266
10:19–21	266
12:6–12	173

1 Corinthians	
1:10–17	50
1:14–17	49
5:9–10	150
6:18	149
8:5	183
11:3	147
12	49

Ephesians	
1:2	236
1:3–8	240
1:7–8	236
1:11–14	236
1:9	237
1:10	240
1:12	239
1:13	240
1:15–18	173
1:16	234
1:18	240
1:19–23	240
2:1–2	236
2:2	236
2:5–6	240
2:7	240
2:10	190–91
2:11	234
2:11–12	240
2:12	234, 240
2:13	240
2:14	240
3:1	233
3:3	237
3:3–4	238
3:4	237
3:9	237
3:13	239
4:1	233
4:2–5	173
4:4	240

4:6–14	236	4:10–11	232–33
5:32	147, 237	4:18	231, 234, 238
6:12	150		
6:19	237	**1 Thessalonians**	
6:19–20	233	1:2	234
6:20	239	1:3	173
		2:14	236
Philippians		4:3	149
2:4	309	5:8	173
3:5–6	290		
3:17	238	**2 Thessalonians**	
		1:4	173
Colossians		3:9	238
1:1	232		
1:1–2	176	**1 Timothy**	
1:2	232, 236	1:16	238
1:3	176	2:15	155
1:4	176		
1:4–5	173	**2 Timothy**	
1:5–8	240	1:3	235
1:5	240	1:3–6	235
1:12	240	1:4	235
1:13	176	1:5	235
1:15	176, 180	1:6	235
1:15–17	176	1:8	233, 237, 240
1:15–18	179	1:10	240
1:15–20	176–84	1:12	240
1:16	178, 179	1:13	233, 238
1:16–17	183	1:16	233
1:17	177, 179	1:17	233
1:18	177–79, 181	2:3	233, 237
1:18a	183	2:8	235, 240
1:18–20	180–81, 184	2:10	240
1:20	182–83	2:11–13	235
1:21	240	2:14	235
1:22	240	3:1	237, 240
1:23	240	3:2–9	237
1:24	240	3:3	237
1:26	183	3:11	233
1:27	183, 240	3:12	234, 237
1:29–2:2	239	4:6	234
2:1	232	4:6–8	240
2:2	183	4:17	234
2:5	239		
2:6	240	**Titus**	
2:10–15	240	3:5	155
2:14f.	181		
2:20	240	**1 Peter**	
3:1	240	1:3–5	178
3:4	183		
3:6	240	**2 Peter**	
3:7	240	1:5	153
3:25	240	1:5–8	172–76
4:3	183, 232	1:5–11	173
4:4	183	1:9–10	174
4:5	236	1:11	174–75
		Revelation	
		1:5	176

INDEX OF ANCIENT SOURCES

6. Nag Hammadi Codices

Exegesis on the Soul
127.19–22	141, 145
127.21–22	154
127.22–25	147
127.25–128.4	147
128.7–17	147
128.21–26	154
130.28–131.2	149
131.2–13	150
131.16–22	142
131.23–27	148
131.27–132.2	150–51
132.2	156
132.15	147
133.9–10	147
133.34–134.6	154
134.4–5	154
134.6–8	155
134.28–29	154
137.6–7	147, 157

Gospel of Philip
55–56 [§ 18]	120
57 [§ 25]	121
58 [§26b]	119
59 [§ 31]	121
60 [§ 39]	119
64 [§ 59]	122
64 [§ 57]	120
64 [§ 59]	121–22, 132
67 [§ 66]	121, 124
67 [§ 67]	121, 124
67 [§ 68]	118, 120, 124
68 [§ 71]	119
69–70 [§ 74–79]	124
69 [§ 75]	121, 122
69 [§ 76]	118, 120
70 [§ 78–79]	119
71 [§ 82]	124
72 [§ 87]	124
74 [§ 95]	120–22, 124
74 [§ 97]	120
75 [§ 100]	121
75 [§ 101]	121
76 [§ 102]	124
84 [§ 125]	120, 124
84–86 [125–127]	124
86 [§ 127]	124

Gospel of Thomas
1	48
46	48

7. Other Ancient Literature

Ambrose
Epistulae variae
40–41	118

Aristotle
Poetica (Poetics)
7.3	39

Rhetorica (Rhetoric)
2.23.1–29	168

Athanasius
De synodis (On the Councils of Ariminum and Seleucia)
15	177

Cicero
De legibus
1.7.22	173

Epiphanius
Panarion
29	221–22
30.13.7–8	48
30.17.1	221–22

Gospel of the Ebionites
Epiphanius,
Panarion 30.13.7–8	48

Hippolytus
Traditio apostolica (The Apostolic Tradition)
21.3	48
20.3	48

Refutatio omnium haeresium (Refutation of All Heresies)
6.39.1–42.2	130
6.41.4–5	123

Ignatius
To the Romans
4.2–3	231

Irenaeus
Adversus haereses (Against Heresies)
1, preface	117
1.6.3	124
1.6.4	122–23
1.11.1	123
1.13.2	130

1.13.3	118, 130
1.21.1	123
1.21.1–5	118
1.21.3	118, 123
1.13.1	121
5.13	121

Josephus
Antiquitates judaicae (Jewish Antiquites)

13.372–383	268
13.398–415	268
14.41	

Bellum judaicum (Jewish War)

1.88–98	268
1.110	269
1.110–114	268
2.139–142	288
2.162	269

Justin Martyr
1 Apology

61	48
65	121

Philo
Legum allegoriae (Allegorical Interpretation)

3.97–101	307–8
3.180	148

De specialibus legibus (On the Special Laws)

1.96	182
1.97	182
2.192	182

Pliny
Naturalis Historia (Natural History)

28.11	45

Seneca
Epistulae morales

85:2	173
94	303
95	303

Sextus Empiricus
Adversus mathematicos
  (Against Mathematicians)

3.40–42	306–7
9.26–27	307

Tacitus
Annales

15.44	237

Tertullian
De baptismo (Baptism)

5	48
20	48

De corona militis (The Crown)

3	48

De praescriptione haereticorum
  (Prescriptions against Heretics)

40	48
41	131

Adversus Valentinianos (Against the Valentinians)

1.1–4	129
1.16–18	129

Valerius Maximus

Val. Max. 1.1.1a–b	45

INDEX OF MODERN AUTHORS

Abelson, Robert P. 245
Abrams, Dominic 2, 21–23, 26, 208, 214–15, 285
Adam, Andrew Keith Malcolm 1
Adams, Edward 205
Aftanas, L. I. 83
Aguilar, Mario I. 127
Ahn, Woo-Kyong et al. 24
Aittola, Tapio 202–3
Alcorta, Candace 96
Alexander, Philip 279, 281
Alt, Albrecht 42
Andresen, Jensine 126
Anttonen, Veikko 1, 95, 126
Arditi, Jorge 202
Arnal, William E. 48, 206
Atran, Scott 1, 4–5, 12, 17, 43, 61, 95–96, 100, 131
Ayres, Lewis 177
Azari, Nina P. et al. 77

Baddeley, Alan 245–46
Bainbridge, William Sims 277
Bar-Tal, Daniel 285–86
Barabási, Albert-László 83, 87
Barclay, Craig R. 246, 251
Baron-Cohen, Simon 50
Barrera, Julio Trebolle 282, 293
Barrett, Charles K. 60
Barrett, Justin L. 4, 6–7, 9–10, 50, 59, 61, 66, 103, 209
Barsalou, Lawrence W. 213, 226
Barth, Fredrik 40, 42
Bartlett, Frederic C. 243–44
Bateson, Gregory 40
Bauckham, Richard 231
Bauer, Walter 47
Baumgarten, Albert I. 261–62, 270
Baumgarten, Joseph M. 278–80, 282, 287, 293
Beall, Todd S. 289
Beard, Mary et al. 45
Becker, Carl L. 38–39
Bekkering, Harold 89
Bell, Catherine 116, 126
Ben-Yehuda, Nachman 242
Berger, Peter L. 16, 200–209, 224–25

Bering, Jesse M. 7, 57, 62–63, 65, 68, 79
Berlitz, Charles 66
Billig, Michael 241
Bivar, A. D. H. 51
Black, John B. 245
Blasi, Anthony J. 16
Bless, Herber 209
Boer, Martinus C. 231
Boer, Roland 164
Boroditsky, Lera 42
Bower, Gordon H. 245
Boyd, Robert 89
Boyer, Pascal 1, 3–10, 12–13, 15, 17–18, 26, 37, 46–47, 49, 57, 61, 66–67, 79–80, 88, 102, 119, 199–200, 209, 215–16, 232, 277, 289, 291, 294
Bradshaw, Paul F. 115–16, 122
Branscombe, Nyla R. et al. 268, 270
Brass, Marcel 85
Brewer, Marilynn B. 213, 267
Brewer, William F. 246
Brock, Sebastian P. 151
Brogan, David C. 75
Brower, Aaron M. 26
Bruckstein, Alfred M. 76
Bruner, Jerome 253
Brunvand, Jan Harold 64
Buchanan, Mark 73, 87
Buckley, Jorunn Jacobsen 119, 121
Bultmann, Rudolf 6, 59
Byrne, Richard W. 85

Cameron, Ron 47
Camp, Claudia V. 164
Carlyle, Thomas 43
Carney, Thomas F. 18–19, 164
Carrier, Richard C. 59–60, 66
Casti, John L. 73
Chadwick, Henry 42
Chaiken, Shelly 9
Charlesworth, James H. 259, 279, 281, 290
Chomsky, Noam 3, 11, 13–14, 80, 199
Chwe, Michael Suk-Young 10
Cinnirella, Marco 26, 214, 222, 240
Clark, Andy 74, 82–83

Cohen, Emma 22
Cohen, Shaye J. D. 273
Cole, Michael et al. 250
Collingwood, Robin G. 37, 39
Collins, John J. 266
Condor, Susan 240, 285
Connerton, Paul 243–44
Coser, Lewis A. 242
Cosmides, Leda 24–25, 43, 215
Costall, Alan 85
Coulson, Seana 142, 144, 158, 162, 164
Crossan, John Dominic 58–59, 110
Csermely, Péter 88
Cumont, Franz 58, 62
Czachesz, István 10, 67, 69, 80–81, 87, 161–62, 199, 304

D'Andrade, Roy 47
Daisuke, Nakanishi 90
Davies, Philip R. 272
Day, Matthew 84
DeConick, April D. 121
Dennett, Daniel C. 64
Denton, Trevor 83
Desjardins, Michel R. 119, 121, 134
Dewey, Joanna 6
Dillon, John J. 123
Dodd, C. H. 48
Donald, Merlin 39, 41, 44
Dorrien, Gary 205
Dozeman, Thomas B. 164
Draper, Jonathan A. 115
Droysen, Johan G. 43
Duhaime, Jean 16
Dunbar, Kevin 145
Dunbar, Robin I. M. 47
Dunbar, Robin I. M. et al. 40
Dunderberg, Ismo 118, 125, 134
Dunn, James D. G. 6, 177, 179, 231, 233

Edelman, Gerald M. 41
Eichenbaum, Howard 79
Elliott, John H. 16, 18–19, 127, 178
Esler, Philip F. 2, 6, 16, 18–19, 21, 26, 69, 127, 201–2, 205, 208, 210, 214, 220, 224, 234–35, 239, 241, 262–63, 273, 277, 300–302, 311
Eubanks, Philip 142

Farkas, Illés J. 75, 88, 90
Fauconnier, Gilles 14–15, 40, 142–44, 151, 162–64, 175, 184–89, 191

Feldman, Carol Fleisher 252–53
Fessler, Daniel M. T. 17
Fiedler, Klaus 209
Fine, Gary Alan 242
Fish, Stanley 158
Fiske, Susan T. 26
Fitch, W. Tecumseh 80
Fitzgerald, Joseph M. 252
Fivush, Robyn 249–51
Flanagan, James W. 164
Forkman, Göran 282, 293
Foucault, Michel 164, 192
Fox, Robin 47
Francis, Dave 85
Franzmann, Majella 156
Frazier, S. L. 213
Frith, Chris 85
Frith, Uta 85
Fuglseth, Kåre Sigvald 205
Funk, Robert W. 48
Fustel de Coulanges, Numa Denis 58, 62

Gaddis, John Lewis 44
Gaffron, Hans-Georg 121
Gager, John G. 16, 204
Gallese, Vittorio et al. 89
García Martínez, Florentino 268, 282, 293
Garrett, Susan R. 15, 18–19
Gavins, Joanna 142
Gazzaniga, Michael S. 199, 217–19
Geertz, Clifford 7, 244
Gelder, Timothy van 83
Gellner, Ernest 109
Gentner, Dedre et al. 41
Gerhardsson, Birger 6
Gibbs, Raymond W., Jr. 145–46
Gil-White, Francisco J. 209, 213–14, 217
Godelier, Maurice 37
Golocheikine, S. A. 83
Gonce, Lauren O. et al. 5
Good, Deirdre 157
Goodwin, Stephanie A. 26
Gordon, Richard 42
Gottschall, Jonathan 40
Goulder, Michael 231
Gragg, Douglas L. 48, 132
Green, Henry A. 118, 123
Green, William Scott 110
Griffin, David Ray 66
Guarducci, Margherita 231
Gunn, David M. 164, 192

Haden, Catherine   249, 251
Hakola, Raimo   21, 25–26, 201, 259, 301
Halbwachs, Maurice   26, 241–44, 246, 251
Hamilton, David L.   214, 272
Hanson, Anthony Tyrrell   231
Harris, Paul L.   62
Haslam, S. Alexander   211–14, 216, 239, 264, 271, 284
Hauser, Marc D.   79–80
Hay, David M.   182–83
Heath, Chip et al.   64
Hegel, G. W. F.   38
Helbing, Dirk   75, 88, 90
Helbing, Dirk et al.   75
Hempel, Charlotte   279, 280–81, 287, 293
Heyes, Cecilia   85
Hinde, Robert A.   88
Hirst, William   249
Hobsbawm, Eric   242
Hodgins, Jessica K.   75
Hoff, Eva V.   63, 85
Hogan, Patrick Colm   145, 156
Hogg, Michael A.   2, 21–23, 26, 208, 265, 273, 285
Holmberg, Bengt   16, 18
Honko, Lauri   10, 62, 64
Hood, Ralph W.   77
Hooper, David S.   75
Hopkins, Keith   58, 62
Horrell, David G.   16–20, 127, 205–7
Horsley, Richard A.   206
Hunt, Lynn   10
Hunter, Sarah B.   270

Isenberg, Wesley W.   120
Ivry, Richard B.   199, 217–19
Iyer, Gowri   245

Jackendoff, Ray   14
Jaffee, Martin   273
Jastram, Nathan   290
Jeremias, Joachim   48
Johnson, Carl N.   62
Johnson, Craig   212
Johnson, Luke Timothy   231, 255
Johnson, Mark   14–15, 143, 162, 183, 210, 226
Johnston, Sarah Iles   62
Jokiranta, Jutta M.   12, 21, 26, 113, 201, 262, 280, 289, 301

Kameda, Tatsuya   90
Kandel, Eric R.   79
Kapferer, Bruce   247
Kastersztein, Joseph   268
Kee, Howard C.   205
Keil, Frank C.   9, 50, 59
Kelber, Werner H.   6
Ketola, Kimmo   12, 14, 131, 302–3
King, Karen L.   116
Kirby, Peter   59
Kirk, Alan   2, 6, 26, 241
Klinghardt, Matthias   282
Klintberg, Bengt   64
Knoblich, Günther   89
Kövecses, Zoltán   143, 146
Kurzban, Robert   24–25, 215
Kurzban, Robert et al.   24
Kuschel, Karl-Josef   176–77, 180–81

Labib, Pahor   117
Laidlaw, James   103, 133
Lakoff, George   14–15, 143, 145, 162, 183, 210, 226
Lampe, Peter   125
Lapinkivi, Pirjo   124
Larsen, Steen F.   246–47
Lawrence, Louise J.   127, 192, 282
Lawson, E. Thomas   1, 3, 10–13, 43–44, 60–61, 81, 88, 95, 99–106, 112, 126–27, 131, 199, 287
Layton, Bentley   118, 120–21, 141, 150–51
Lease, Gary   37
Leeuwen, Marco van   74, 83
Lefèbvre, Henri   163–164
Lemaine, Gérard   268
Lemche, Niels Peter   41
Leopold, Anita Maria   132
Leudar, Ivan   85
Lévi-Strauss, Claude   10, 41
Lewis, Amy C.   272
Lewis, James R.   66
Leyens, Jaques-Philippe   25
Liénard, Pierre   10, 12
Lincoln, Andrew T.   31, 233
Livingston, Kenneth R.   61, 77
Lloyd, Dan   39
Lohse, Eduard   177–79, 181–83
Lord, R. G.   213
Luckmann, Thomas   201–7, 209, 224–25
Lüdemann, Gerd   59–60
Lundhaug, Hugo   15, 302, 306

Luomanen, Petri 18, 21, 113, 205–6, 222, 224, 260, 266, 301–4, 311
Luttikhuizen, Gerard P. 88

MacDonald, Margaret Y. 205, 231, 238
Mack, Burton L. 48, 59, 69
Mackie, Diane M. 270
Mainzer, Klaus 74, 76
Malbon, Elizabeth Struthers 41
Malina, Bruce J. 16–18
Malley, Brian 49, 103
Mangun, George R. 199, 217–19
Manier, David 249
Marjanen, Antti 116, 134
Markschies, Christoph 117–18
Marques, José M. 215
Marshall, Gordon 18, 202–3, 208
Martin, Dale B. 16–19
Martin, Luther H. 40, 43, 46–47, 57, 67–69, 103, 113, 302–3, 311
Matthews, Victor H. 164
McCauley, Robert N. 1, 3, 10–13, 43, 60, 81, 88, 95, 99–102, 104–6, 126–27, 131–32, 199, 287, 303
McClymond, Michael J. 106–7, 109, 110
McGarty, Craig 21
McKeever, Michael C. 164
McNutt, Paula M. 164
McVann, Mark 115
Meade, David 50, 237–38
Medin, Douglas L. 213
Meeks, Wayne A. 15–16, 204
Ménard, Jacques E. 120
Mesoudi, Alex 245
Metso, Sarianna 272, 280, 283, 287–88
Meyer, Marvin W. 156
Miller, George A. 42
Miller, Merrill 47
Mitchell, W. J. Thomas 179
Moore, William 66
Mullen, Brian 212
Munz, Peter 14
Murphy, Catherine M. 292
Murray, R. P. R. 224
Myllykoski, Matti 58–60, 69, 224

Nabarz, Payam 51
Navarrete, Carlos David 17
Nemeroff, Caro 17
Nettle, Daniel 40
Neusner, Jacob 260–61, 265–66

Newsom, Carol A. 270, 283, 290–91, 293
Neyrey, Jerome H. 16–17, 164, 173–74
Nickelsburg, George W. E. 266
Nicolis, Grégoire 76
Norenzayan, Ara 1, 4–5
Nye, Judith L. 26
Nyhof, Melanie A. 4

Oakes, Penelope J. 211–14, 216, 264, 271
Oakley, Todd V. 142–43
Olick, Jeffrey K. 241
Oltvai, Zoltán N. 83
Osiek, Carolyn 16
Overman, J. Andrew 110, 205

Páez, Dario 214–15
Pagels, Elaine 121, 123, 131
Parsons, Keith 59, 63
Penn, Michael 121
Pentikäinen, Juha 62, 64
Percha, Bethany et al. 83
Perkins, John Ward 231
Persinger, Michael 77
Personnaz, Bernard 268
Pickett, Raymond 205
Pilch, John J. 16
Pinker, Steven 14, 83
Popper, Karl 43
Port, Robert F. 83
Price, Robert M. 60, 61
Prigogine, Ilya 76
Proudfoot, Wayne 61
Pyysiäinen, Ilkka 1, 4, 6–7, 9–10, 12–13, 61, 63–67, 69, 77, 81, 95–96, 103, 109, 113, 119, 126, 131–33, 161, 217, 226, 232, 244, 301–3

Qimron, Elisha 278–79, 281

Radden, Günter 151
Räisänen, Heikki 63, 67, 69, 209, 266–67
Raiskila, Vesa 202–3
Ramble, Charles 4
Ranger, Terence 242
Rappaport, Roy A. 96
Reese, Elaine 249–51
Reitzenstein, Richard 49, 115
Resnick, Mitchel 74, 76
Revel, Jacques 10
Reynolds, Craig W. 74–75
Reynolds, Katherine J. 264

INDEX OF MODERN AUTHORS

Richerson, Peter J. 89
Rizzolatti, Giacomo et al. 85
Robbins, Vernon K. 15, 69, 162–64, 166, 180
Robbins, Joyce 241
Robinson, William C. Jr. 142–43, 148–49
Rosch, Eleanor 211, 212
Rosengren, Karl S. 62
Rothbart, Myron 214
Rozell, Drew 212
Rozin, Paul 17
Rubin, David 81

Sack, Jeremy D. 214
Sack, Robert D. 64
Saler, Benson 66, 67
Samellas, Antigone 18
Sanders, E. P. 96–99, 103, 106, 108, 110, 260–62, 272
Sawicki, Marianne 58
Schacter, Daniel L. 145
Schadron, Georges 25
Schank, Roger C. 245
Scheid, John 45
Schenke, Hans-Martin 117, 119–22
Schiffman, Lawrence H. 282, 293
Schmidt, Brian B. 62
Schunn, Christian D. 145
Schwartz, Barry 241–42
Schwartz, Daniel R. 278, 287
Scopello, Madeleine 157
Scroggs, Robin 16
Sebanz, Natalie 89
Segal, Robert A. 126
Segelberg, Eric 120, 156
Sellew, Philip H. 18
Semin, Gün R. 80
Sevrin, Jean-Marie 146
Sharf, Robert H. 61
Shemesh, Aharon 282
Sherman, Steven I. 214, 272
Sides, Hampton 47
Simmel, Georg 37, 39, 51
Smith, Eliot R. 80, 212, 219
Smith, Jonathan Z. 42, 46, 116, 261
Smith, Richard 149
Smith, Thomas S. 246
Snyder, Bob 145
Snyder, Graydon F. 41, 48
Soden, Wolfram von 42
Soja, Edward W. 164
Sørensen, Jesper 15
Sosis, Richard 96

Sperber, Dan 3, 5, 7–8, 17, 26, 42–43, 50, 66, 79, 86, 126, 199, 215
Squire, Larry R. 79
Srull, Thomas K. 9
Stark, Rodney 67, 69, 95, 277
Steen, Gerard 142
Stegemann, Wolfgang 16
Stemberger, Günther 268–69
Stiller, James et al. 40
Stockwell, Peter 142
Stowers, Stanley K. 19
Strack, Fritz 209
Strecker, Christian 115
Strogatz, Steven 83, 88–89
Sun, Ron 9
Sutton, David E. 39
Sweetser, Eve 143
Swindler, Ann 202
Syreeni, Kari 205

Tajfel, Henri 2, 21–24, 208–11, 235–36, 253, 262, 284–85
Taylor, Marjorie 85
Thaden, Robert von 162
Thatcher, Tom 2, 6, 26, 241
Theissen, Gerd 16, 205–6
Thomassen, Einar 46, 48, 117, 119, 121, 129
Thorndyke, Perry W. 245
Tiemann, Brian 75
Tigchelaar, Eibert J. C. 268, 281
Tiger, Lionel 47
Till, Walter C. 117
Tocqueville, Alexis de 46
Tooby, John 24–25, 43, 215
Toorn, Karel van der 261
Toulmin, Stephen 164
Toynbee, Jocelyn 231
Tremlin, Todd 1, 9, 126
Tripp, D. H. 120
Trope, Yacoov 9
Tulving, Endel 127, 145, 245–46
Turcotte, Paul-André 16
Turner, John C. 211, 212–14, 216, 235–36, 262–64, 271
Turner, John C. et al. 263
Turner, John D. 117, 126
Turner, Mark 14–15, 40, 142–44, 151, 163–64, 175, 185–89, 191
Turner, Martha Lee 119–20
Turner, Terrence J. 245
Turner, Victor 115
Tversky, Barbara 245
Tweney, Ryan D. et al. 5

Unger, Dominic J.   123
Upal, Afzal et al.   5
Uro, Risto   14, 109, 113, 124, 134, 199, 300–303, 311

VanderKam, James   268
Vermes, Geza   106, 108–9, 279, 281–82
Vicsek, Tamás   75, 88, 90
Vogt, Kari   156
Vygotsky, Lev Semenovic   250–51

Wagner, Israel A.   76
Walker, P. W. L.   58
Walker, Susan   62
Walker-Ramisch, Sandra   283
Wansbrough, Henry   6
Ward, Andrew R.   81
Wassen, Cecilia   280, 286–88
Watson, Francis   205
Weinfeld, Moshe   282–83, 293
Wertsch, James   250
Whitehouse, Harvey   6, 12–13, 41, 43–47, 81, 86, 88, 95, 100–104, 116, 126–29, 132–33, 199, 291, 303

Whiten, Andrew   245
Wiebe, Donald   133
Wiebe, Phillip   60
Wilder, Amos   161
Wilensky, Uri   86
Wilkes, A. L.   23, 209
Willhoite, Jr., Fred H.   47
Williams, Michael A.   116, 121, 157
Wilson, David Slone   40
Wilson, Deidre   3, 7–8
Wilson, Robert McL.   120
Wineburg, Sam   39
Wisse, Frederik   141, 156–57
Wulff, David M.   77
Wyer, Robert S.   9

Yarnold, Edward   156
Yzerbyt, Vincent   25

Zacks, Jeffrey M.   245
Zárate, Michael A.   212
Zerubavel, Eviatar   202, 244, 246
Ziegler, Charles A.   66
Zimmermann, Ruben   124

INDEX OF SUBJECTS

Achamoth/Echmoth 118
Agent(s) and agency 10–12, 37, 50, 57–58, 60–62, 68, 74–75, 80–82, 85–86, 102–4, 109, 112, 131–2, 287
Algorithmic models 73, 90
Allegory 156
Ancestors 24, 86, 162
Anthropology 1, 3, 8, 16–17, 40, 43, 115–16, 199
Anthropomorphism 50
Apostolic Tradition 116, 121, 127, 131
Apotheosis 50
Apparitions (of Christ) 59–63
Automatic and controlled processes 9

Baptism 11, 48–49, 109, 112, 120–23, 125, 127, 130, 132, 150–52, 155–56, 174
Behavioral ecology 40
Beliefs 6–9, 61–63, 65, 67–68, 78–85, 115, 130, 240–41, 259, 285–86, 291–94
Biographies 50–51
Blending (theory of) see Conceptual blending
Brain 37, 47, 61, 77–78, 82–83, 162, 200, 217–19, 300–301, 304, 309
"Bridal chamber" (*nymphōn*) 118, 120–21, 124–26, 130

Categorization 2, 4, 17, 19–20, 23–26, 41, 146, 208, 210–12, 216, 218, 263, 271–72; prototypes and exemplars 26, 210–22
Charisma(tic) 16, 49, 109, 112, 127, 238
Circumcision 99, 102 n.5, 110–12, 267
Cognition 2–3, 6–7, 14, 17–18, 21, 23–25, 37–40, 44, 47, 52, 67, 85, 127, 162, 207, 209, 213, 244, 301–2
Cognitive optimum 4–7, 47
Cognitive science 1–2, 6–10, 17–20, 37–38, 40, 57, 69, 76, 95–96, 104, 116, 126–27, 133–34, 161–62, 199–200, 208, 232, 247, 254, 291, 299, 302–5, 311
"Common Judaism" 260–61

Conceptual blend(ing) 2, 14–15, 40, 141–58, 161–92
Context group 16–17, 19
Corinth 49, 59, 61, 150
Counterintuitiveness 4–6, 11, 14, 80
Culture 7, 16–20, 41, 42–43, 46–47, 66, 69, 73, 79, 84, 263; cross-cultural regularities 1
cultural (social) construction 1–2, 7, 43, 200–204; material culture 41, 47, 50, 80–82

Dead Sea Scrolls 259–60, 263–69, 272, 277–79
Death 57–58, 62–63, 65, 68, 119
Didache 48, 116, 121
Didascalia Apostolorum 116
Dual-process theories see Automatic and controlled processes
Dynamical (distributed) systems 73–76, 80, 82–84, 86, 88–90

Emotions/affects 12–13, 44–45, 47–48, 57, 64–65, 97–102, 219, 238, 286
Epidemiology of beliefs 2–3, 6–8, 43, 66, 69
Epilepsy 78
Essence/essentialism 24, 213, 215–17, 220
Essenes 106 n.9, 107
Eucharist 41, 111, 120–22, 128, 130
Evolution 1, 3, 18, 46–47, 81, 199; evolutionary psychology 40
Experience (religious) 61, 64, 68, 77–79, 81

Faith 49–50, 96, 173 fig.
"Flocking rules/paradigm" 73–76, 82, 86
Form-criticism 6–7, 47
Fundamentalism 26, 277–78

Gentiles 272–73
Ghosts 62, 79
Glossolalia 49
Gnosticism 59, 115–37, 259

God   5–6, 9–11, 50, 60, 67, 77–80, 102, 109, 111–12, 166, 169, 177, 184, 189–92, 287, 290
Gospel of Philip   117–25
Gospel of Thomas   42, 48, 120

Healing   109, 186–88, 191
Heilsgeschichte   37
Heresy/heretics   116–18, 123, 220–22
History of ideas   15–16
History-of-religion (school)   115
Holy Spirit   121–23

Ideology   52, 206, 224, 267, 273, 285, 301
Imitation   85, 90
Impurity and pollution   17–18, 153–54, 269
Inference(s)   3, 8–9, 41, 43–44, 66–68
Initiation see ritual(s)
Intuition(s)   2–10, 67–68, 79–80, 215, 291, 299

Jesus movement   96, 107, 109–112; Christ-movement   231, 235–37, 239–40, 241 n.8, 243, 250, 254

"*Listenwissenschaft*"   42
Literacy   6–8, 42, 69, 81

Magic   15
Memory/memories   2–8, 12, 14, 22, 38–39, 42, 44, 46–47, 50, 67–68, 77, 88, 100, 101 n.4, 127–28, 132, 145–46, 165, 218, 232–35, 246–54; collective memory   26, 232, 235, 238, 241–43, 254; Bartlett on 243–45; Tulving on   245–46
Mental space   14–15, 143–45
Mentalities (history of)   9, 43
Metaphors   14, 124, 130, 141–50, 153, 156–57, 162, 199, 210
Mind/mental   1, 6–8, 10, 38, 63, 66, 79, 81, 83, 146, 162, 165, 207, 226, 300–301
Miracles   51, 162–63, 170, 185–87
Mirror neurons   85
Mithraism   39, 45, 48, 50–51, 88
Models   6, 8, 16, 18–20, 64, 73, 75–76, 86–90, 95, 115, 223
Modes theory (of religiosity)   12–14, 43–49, 81, 95, 101, 127–33, 303
Modules   83, 199, 217, 221
Mystery cults   45–47, 115, 129, 131

Myth   39, 115–16, 126, 176

Nag Hammadi (literature)   15, 117, 141, 156
Narrative(s)   39–42, 47, 50–51, 68, 143, 156, 161–62, 245–7, 251–53
Natural selection   7; cultural   43–44, 61, 64, 66
Networks   84–88, 96
Neuroscience   1, 41, 199–200, 220, 304, 310

Oath (as ritual)   279, 286–91
Omniscience   80
Ontology   2, 4, 80, 201, 210
Orthodoxy   12, 50, 96, 123, 128, 133–34, 237–38
Orthopraxis/orthopraxy   96, 123, 237–38

Parables of Jesus   48, 50
Passover (*Pesah*)   58, 97–98
Pattern recognition   41
Pharisees   62, 100, 106–7, 110, 259–60, 261, 268–69
Platonism   305–8
Prayer   98, 103, 112, 182
Pseudo-Pauline letters   231ff.
Psychology   1, 3, 6, 9, 26, 37, 66, 68, 101, 127, 244, 248–50, 300; social psychology   9, 21–26, 200–226, 235 n.6, 261, 270, 304
Purity regulations   98, 107–110, 277, 293

Q (sayings of Jesus)   42, 48
Qumran community   96, 106–112, 264–70, 272 n.10, 277–96

Recursion   80
Redaction criticism   47
"Redemption" (Gnostic)   118, 120, 123–24
Reductionism   310
Reflective thinking   9, 79
Relevance (theory of)   3, 8, 162
Religion (concept)   84, 302–3
Representations (mental)   4, 37–40, 43–44, 52, 66, 79–80; public   81–82
Resurrection   59–60, 67, 107
Revelations   48–49, 60–61
Rhetoric   141–42, 146, 153–54, 199, 284, 299; socio-rhetorical analysis 162–65, 170, 186, 189, 299, 311

INDEX OF SUBJECTS

Rhetórolects 15, 162–67, 170–71, 184–89, 191–92
Ritual(s) 10–14, 45–46, 49, 57, 60–61, 65, 78–79, 81–84, 88–89, 96–111, 115–35; form theory of 10–12, 60–61, 81, 95 100–107, 109–12, 131–32, 269, 287, 303; modes theory of 12–14, 81, 101–3, 115–35; of initiation 45–6, 48–9, 51, 118, 120–24, 130–32, 286–87
Roman Empire 47, 58; religion of 45, 50, 118

Sacred/holy 15, 81, 98, 120, 293
Sacrifice 45, 97–8, 170, 182
Sadducees 100, 106–7, 261, 269
Script(s)/schema(s) 44–45, 161–62, 245, 253
Self-organization 74, 82–83
"Sensory pageantry" 12, 44, 99–106, 112
Sitz im Leben 6, 146
Social behavior 73, 90, 96, 238, 301
Social groups 25, 85, 110, 210, 216, 240–42, 261–70, 277, 295
Social identity (approach/theory) 2, 16, 20–26, 200–226, 232, 235, 238ff., 278, 284–86, 291, 301
Social memory see Memory
Social science 1–2, 15–22, 69, 95, 205, 254, 299
Sociology 115, 201, 203, 206, 208, 224–25, 238, 244, 301
Sociology of knowledge 16, 199–226

Socio-political organization 95, 103–4, 107, 110, 115, 127, 130
Sol Invictus 50
Spatiality theory 162–4, 170
Splinter groups 105–7, 111, 118, 124–26, 128, 133
Standard Model (of cognitive science of religion) 15
Stoicism 306–10
Strategic information 80
Symbolism 3, 59, 100, 117, 121, 126, 157, 202–6, 208, 224–25, 246, 248, 250, 279, 286, 304; symbolic universe 203–6, 208, 224–25
Synoptic Gospels 48, 62, 109, 205

"Tedium effect" 104–105, 133
Theology 8–9, 16, 67, 69, 111, 115–16, 129, 206, 225, 294, 299, 301, 305; theological correctness 9, 59, 291
Theory of mind 50, 80, 85, 89
Tradition 2, 6, 8, 61, 64, 66, 242, 267; transmission of 2, 5–8, 10, 12, 26, 43–44, 49–50, 69, 79, 81, 127, 244–45, 301–2; tradition criticism 47
Trullan Synod 118

Urban legends 63–66, 68

Valentinian movement 117–33

Zealots 106

www.ingramcontent.com/pod-product-compliance
Lightning Source LLC
Chambersburg PA
CBHW021118300426
44113CB00006B/190